John Kneeland

Masterpieces of American Literature

John Kneeland

Masterpieces of American Literature

ISBN/EAN: 9783744651936

Printed in Europe, USA, Canada, Australia, Japan

Cover: Foto ©Thomas Meinert / pixelio.de

More available books at **www.hansebooks.com**

MASTERPIECES OF AMERICAN LITERATURE

FRANKLIN: IRVING: BRYANT: WEBSTER: EVERETT
LONGFELLOW: HAWTHORNE: WHITTIER
EMERSON: HOLMES: LOWELL
THOREAU: O'REILLY

*WITH BIOGRAPHICAL SKETCHES
AND PORTRAITS*

BOSTON, NEW YORK, AND CHICAGO
HOUGHTON, MIFFLIN AND COMPANY
The Riverside Press, Cambridge

PREFACE.

THIS volume owes its existence to the desire of the Boston school authorities for a collection of productions from American authors of distinction, especially suitable for use in the most advanced class of the grammar schools. Its contents are taken mostly from the *Riverside Literature Series.*

At the request of the committee on text-books, the board of supervisors, after conferring with the publishers, planned the book and approved every selection. Their action was reported to the committee on text-books, and upon the recommendation of this committee the school board, by a unanimous vote, adopted the proposed book, *Masterpieces of American Literature*, as a text-book for reading in the first class of the grammar schools.

The considerations that guided in the make-up of the book were that the various authors should be represented by characteristic and noted productions; that these productions, though generally above the present range of the thought and experience of the students, should yet be within their reach; that they should be inspiring and uplifting in their influence upon life and character, and fitted to serve the great purpose of developing a sense of what real literature is, both in form and in spirit.

While holding to these considerations, it was also kept in mind that the book must be a reading-book, in the school sense. It is to be used for improvement in the art of oral reading as well as for studies in literature. Therefore, a variety of styles in both prose and poetry is needed. This will explain why, in some instances, a particular selection is made from an author rather than some other selection. The more mechanical part of oral reading — the development and management of the voice, the rendering flexible the organs of speech and securing precision in their action — may receive due attention without much regard to the meaning of the exercises used in practice. But to gain the ability to read well orally — to convey exact thought and quicken feeling by the utterance, in appropriate tones, of what another has written — requires extended practice upon pieces rich in thought and various in style and sentiment.

The brief biographical sketches of the thirteen authors represented here, while helpful for the information which they contain, will, it is hoped, inspire the reader to a further study of the authors and their works.

As this book has been especially prepared for the advanced class in the grammar schools of Boston to meet an acknowledged want, there can be no doubt that it will render the same good service in classes of similar grade elsewhere.

The selections from the following named authors are used by permission of, and by arrangement with, the authorized publishers of their works : —

WASHINGTON IRVING, . .	Messrs. G. P. Putnam's Sons.
W. C. BRYANT, ...	Messrs. D. Appleton & Co.
J. B. O'REILLY, ...	The Cassell Publishing Company.
DANIEL WEBSTER and	
EDWARD EVERETT, . . .	Messrs. Little, Brown & Co.

CONTENTS.

viii CONTENTS.

WASHINGTON IRVING.

BIOGRAPHICAL SKETCH.

IRVING may be named as the first author in the United States whose writings made a place for themselves in general literature. Franklin, indeed, had preceded him with his autobiography, but Franklin belongs rather to the colonial period. It was under the influences of that time that his mind and taste were formed, and there was a marked difference between the Boston and Philadelphia of Franklin's youth and the New York of Irving's time. Politics, commerce, and the rise of industries were rapidly changing social relations and manners, while the country was still dependent on England for its higher literature. It had hardly begun to find materials for literature in its own past or in its aspects of nature, yet there was a very positive element in life which resented foreign interference. There were thus two currents crossing each other : the common life which was narrowly American, and the cultivated taste which was English, or imitative of England. Irving's first ventures, in company with his brothers and Paulding, were in the attempt to represent New York in literature upon the model of contemporary or recent presentations of London. "The town" in the minds of these young writers was that portion of New York society which might be construed into a miniature reflection of London wit and amusement. His associates never advanced beyond this stage, but with Washington Irving the sketches which he wrote under the signature of *Jonathan Old Style* and in the medley of *Salmagundi* were only the first experiments of a mind capable of larger things. After five or six years of trifling with his pen, he wrote and published, in 1809, *A History of New York, by Diedrich Knickerbocker*, which he began in company with his brother Peter as a mere *jeu d'esprit*, but turned into a more determined work of humor, as the capabilities of the subject disclosed themselves. Grave historians had paid little attention to the record of New York under the Dutch; Irving, who saw the humorous contrast between the traditional Dutch society of his day and the pushing new democracy, seized upon the early history and made it the occasion for a good-natured burlesque. He shocked the old families about him, but he amused everybody else, and the book, going to England, made his name at once known to those who had the making there of literary reputations.

Irving himself was born of a Scottish father and English mother, who had come to this country only twenty years before. He was but little removed, therefore, from the traditions of Great Britain, and his brothers and he carried on a trading business with the old country. His own tastes were not mercantile, and he was only silent partner in the house; he wrote occasionally and was for a time the editor of a magazine, but his pleasure was chiefly in travel, good literature, and good society. It was while he was in England, in 1818, that the house in which he was a partner failed, and he was thrown on his own resources. Necessity gave the slight spur which was wanting to his inclination, and he began with deliberation the career of an author. He had found himself at home in England. His family origin and his taste for the best literature had made him English in his sympathies and tastes, and his residence and travels there. the society which he entered and the friends he made, confirmed him in English habits. Nevertheless he was sturdily American in his principles; he was strongly attached to New York and his American friends, and was always a looker-on in England. His foreign birth and education gave him significant advantages as an observer of English life, and he at once began the writing of those papers, stories, and sketches which appeared in the separate numbers of *The Sketch Book*, in *Bracebridge Hall*, and in *Tales of a Traveller*. They were chiefly drawn from material accumulated abroad, but an occasional American subject was taken. Irving instinctively felt that by the circumstances of the time and the bent of his genius he could pursue his calling more safely abroad than at home. He remained in Europe seventeen years, sending home his books for publication, and securing also the profitable results of publication in London. During that time, besides the books above named, he wrote the *History of the Life and Voyages of Christopher Columbus;* the *Voyages and Discoveries of the Companions of Columbus; A Chronicle of the Conquest of Granada;* and *The Alhambra.* The Spanish material was obtained while residing in Spain, whither he went at the suggestion of the American minister to make translations of documents relating to the voyages of Columbus which had recently been collected. Irving's training and tastes led him rather into the construction of popular narrative than into the work of a scientific historian, and, with his strong American affections, he was quick to see the interest and value which lay in the history of Spain as connected with America. He was eminently a *raconteur*, very skilful and graceful in the shaping of old material; his humor played freely over the surface of his writing, and, with little power to create characters or plots, he had an unfailing perception of the literary capabilities of scenes and persons which came under his observation.

He came back to America in 1832 with an established reputation, and was welcomed enthusiastically by his friends and countrymen. He travelled into the new parts of America, and spent ten years at home, industriously working at the material which had accumulated in his hands when abroad, and had been increased during his travels in the West. In this period he published *Legends of the Conquest of Spain; The Crayon Miscellany,* including his *Tour on the Prairies, Abbotsford and Newstead Abbey; Astoria;* a number of papers in the *Knickerbocker Magazine,* afterwards published under the title of *Wolfert's Roost;* and edited the *Adventures of Captain Bonneville, U. S. A., in the Rocky Mountains and the Far West.*

In 1842 he went back to Spain as American minister, holding the office for four years, when he returned to America, established himself at his home, Sunnyside on the banks of the Hudson, and remained there until his death in 1859. The fruits of this final period were *Mahomet and his Successors,* which, with a volume of posthumous publication, *Spanish Papers and other Miscellanies,* completed the series of Spanish and Moorish subjects which form a distinct part of his writings; *Oliver Goldsmith, a Biography;* and finally a *Life of Washington,* which occupied the closing years of his life, — years which were not free from physical suffering. In this book Irving embodied his strong admiration for the subject, whose name he bore and whose blessing he had received as a child; he employed, too, a pen which had been trained by its labors on the Spanish material, and, like that series, the work is marked by good taste, artistic sense of proportion, faithfulness, and candor, rather than by the severer work of the historian. It is a popular and a fair life of Washington and account of the war for independence.

Irving's personal and literary history is recorded in *The Life and Letters of Washington Irving,* by his nephew, Pierre M. Irving. His death was the occasion of many affectionate and graceful eulogies and addresses, a number of which were gathered into *Irvingiana: a Memorial of Washington Irving.*

Rip Van Winkle is from *The Sketch Book.*

THE story of Rip Van Winkle purported to have been written by Diedrich Knickerbocker, who was a humorous invention of Irving's, and whose name was familiar to the public as the author of *A History of New York.* The *History* was published in 1809, but it was ten years more before the first number of *The Sketch Book of Geoffrey Crayon, Gent.*, was published. This number, which contained *Rip Van Winkle*, was, like succeeding numbers, written by Irving in England and sent home to America for publication. He laid the scene of the story in the Kaatskills, but he drew upon his imagination and the reports of others for the scenery, not visiting the spot until 1833. The story is not absolutely new ; the fairy tale of *The Sleeping Beauty in the Wood* has the same theme ; so has the story of Epimenides of Crete, who lived in the sixth or seventh century before Christ. He was said to have fallen asleep in a cave when a boy, and to have awaked at the end of fifty-seven years, his soul, meanwhile, having been growing in stature. There is the legend also of the Seven Sleepers of Ephesus, Christian martyrs who were walled into a cave to which they had fled for refuge, and there were miraculously preserved for two centuries. Among the stories in which the Harz Mountains of Germany are so prolific is one of Peter Klaus, a goatherd who was accosted one day by a young man who silently beckoned him to follow, and led him to a secluded spot, where he found twelve knights playing, voiceless, at skittles. He saw a can of wine which was very fragrant, and, drinking of it, was thrown into a deep sleep, from which he did not wake for twenty years. The story gives incidents of his awaking and of the changes which he found in the village to which he returned. This story, which was published with others in 1800, may very likely have been the immediate suggestion to Irving, who has taken nearly the same framework. The humorous additions which he has made, and the grace with which he has invested the. tale, have caused his story to supplant earlier ones in the popular mind, so that Rip Van Winkle has passed into familiar speech, and allusions to him are clearly understood by thousands who have never read Irving's story. The recent dramatizing of the story, though following the outline only, has done much to fix the conception of the character. The story appeals very directly to a common sentiment of curiosity as to the future, which is not far removed from what some have regarded as an instinct of the human mind pointing to personal immortality. The name Van Winkle was happily chosen by Irving, but not invented by him. The printer of the *Sketch Book*, for one, bore the name. The name Knickerbocker, also, is among the Dutch names, but Irving's use of it has made it representative. In *The Author's Apology*, which he prefixed to a new edition of the *History of New York*, he says: "I find its very name become a 'household word,' and used to give the home stamp to everything recommended for popular acceptation, such as Knickerbocker societies; Knickerbocker insurance companies; Knickerbocker steamboats; Knickerbocker omnibuses, Knickerbocker bread, and Knickerbocker ice; and . . . New Yorkers of Dutch descent priding themselves upon being 'genuine Knickerbockers.'"

RIP VAN WINKLE.

A POSTHUMOUS WRITING OF DIEDRICH KNICKERBOCKER.

> By Woden, God of Saxons,
> From whence comes Wensday, that is Wodensday.
> Truth is a thing that ever I will keep
> Unto thylke day in which I creep into
> My sepulchre.   CARTWRIGHT.[1]

THE following tale was found among the papers of the late Diedrich Knickerbocker, an old gentleman of New York, who was very curious in the Dutch history of the province, and the manners of the descendants from its primitive settlers. His historical researches, however, did not lie so much among books as among men; for the former are lamentably scanty on his favorite topics; whereas he found the old burghers, and still more their wives, rich in that legendary lore so invaluable to true history. Whenever, therefore, he happened upon a genuine Dutch family, snugly shut up in its low-roofed farmhouse under a spreading sycamore, he looked upon it as a little clasped volume of black-letter, and studied it with the zeal of a book-worm.

The result of all these researches was a history of the province during the reign of the Dutch governors, which he published some years since. There have been various opinions as to the literary character of his work, and, to tell the truth, it is not a whit better than it should be. Its chief merit is its scrupulous accuracy, which indeed was a little questioned on its first appearance, but has since been completely established; and it is now admitted into all historical collections, as a book of unquestionable authority.

The old gentleman died shortly after the publication of his work, and now that he is dead and gone, it cannot do much harm

---

[1] William Cartwright, 1611–1643, was a friend and disciple of Ben Jonson.

to his memory [1] to say that his time might have been much better employed in weightier labors.   He, however, was apt to ride his hobby his own way ; and though it did now and then kick up the dust a little in the eyes of his neighbors, and grieve the spirit of some friends, for whom he felt the truest deference and affection ; yet his errors and follies are remembered "more in sorrow than in anger," and it begins to be suspected that he never intended to injure or offend.   But however his memory may be appreciated by critics, it is still held dear by many folk, whose good opinion is worth having ; particularly by certain biscuit-bakers, who have gone so far as to imprint his likeness on their new-year cakes ; [2] and have thus given him a chance for immortality, almost equal to the being stamped on a Waterloo Medal, or a Queen Anne's Farthing. [3]

---

[1] *The History of New York* had given offence to many old New Yorkers because of its saucy treatment of names which were held in veneration as those of founders of families, and its general burlesque of Dutch character.   Among the critics was a warm friend of Irving, Gulian C. Verplanck, who in a discourse before the New York Historical Society plainly said : "It is painful to see a mind, as admirable for its exquisite perception of the beautiful as it is for its quick sense of the ridiculous, wasting the richness of its fancy on an ungrateful theme, and its exuberant humor in a coarse caricature."   Irving took the censure good-naturedly, and as he read Verplanck's words just as he was finishing the story of *Rip Van Winkle,* he gave them this playful notice in the introduction.

[2] An oblong seed-cake, still made in New York at New Year's time, and of Dutch origin.

[3] There was a popular story that only three farthings were struck in Queen Anne's reign ; that two were in public keeping, and that the third was no one knew where, but that its lucky finder would be able to hold it at an enormous price.   As a matter of fact there were eight coinings of farthings in the reign of Queen Anne, and numismatists do not set a high value on the piece.

WHOEVER has made a voyage up the Hudson must remember the Kaatskill Mountains. They are a dismembered branch of the great Appalachian family, and are seen away to the west of the river, swelling up to a noble height, and lording it over the surrounding country. Every change of season, every change of weather, indeed, every hour of the day, produces some change in the magical hues and shapes of these mountains, and they are regarded by all the good wives, far and near, as perfect barometers. When the weather is fair and settled, they are clothed in blue and purple, and print their bold outlines on the clear evening sky; but sometimes when the rest of the landscape is cloudless they will gather a hood of gray vapors about their summits, which, in the last rays of the setting sun, will glow and light up like a crown of glory.

At the foot of these fairy[1] mountains, the voyager may have descried the light smoke curling up from a village, whose shingle-roofs gleam among the trees, just where the blue tints of the upland melt away into the fresh green of the nearer landscape. It is a little village of great antiquity, having been founded by some of the Dutch colonists in the early time of the province, just about the beginning of the government of the good Peter Stuyvesant,[2] (may he rest in peace!) and there were some of the houses of the original settlers standing within a few years, built of small yellow

---

[1] A light touch to help the reader into a proper spirit for receiving the tale.

[2] Stuyvesant was governor of New Netherlands from 1647 to 1664. He plays an important part in *Knickerbocker's History of New York,* as he did in actual life. Until quite recently a pear tree was shown on the Bowery, said to have been planted by him.

bricks brought from Holland, having latticed windows
and gable fronts, surmounted with weathercocks.

In that same village, and in one of these very houses
(which, to tell the precise truth, was sadly time-worn
and weather-beaten), there lived many years since,
while the country was yet a province of Great Britain,
a simple, good-natured fellow, of the name of Rip Van
Winkle.   He was a descendant of the Van Winkles
who figured so gallantly in the chivalrous days of
Peter Stuyvesant, and accompanied him to the siege
of Fort Christina.[1]   He inherited, however, but little
of the martial character of his ancestors.   I have
observed that he was a simple, good-natured man; he
was, moreover, a kind neighbor, and an obedient hen-
pecked husband.   Indeed, to the latter circumstance
might be owing that meekness of spirit which gained
him such universal popularity; for those men are
most apt to be obsequious and conciliating abroad,
who are under the discipline of shrews at home.
Their tempers, doubtless, are rendered pliant and mal-
leable in the fiery furnace of domestic tribulation; and
a curtain lecture is worth all the sermons in the world
for teaching the virtues of patience and long-suffering.
A termagant wife may, therefore, in some respects be
considered a tolerable blessing, and if so, Rip Van
Winkle was thrice blessed.

Certain it is, that he was a great favorite among all
the good wives of the village, who, as usual with the
amiable sex, took his part in all family squabbles;
and never failed, whenever they talked those matters

---

[1] The Van Winkles appear in the illustrious catalogue of
heroes who accompanied Stuyvesant to Fort Christina, and were
                    " Brimful of wrath and cabbage."
See *History of New York*, book VI. chap. viii.

over in their evening gossipings, to lay all the blame
on Dame Van Winkle. The children of the village,
too, would shout with joy whenever he approached.
He assisted at their sports, made their playthings,
taught them to fly kites and shoot marbles, and told
them long stories of ghosts, witches, and Indians.
Whenever he went dodging about the village, he was
surrounded by a troop of them, hanging on his skirts,
clambering on his back, and playing a thousand tricks
on him with impunity; and not a dog would bark at
him throughout the neighborhood.

The great error in Rip's composition was an insu-
perable aversion to all kinds of profitable labor. It
could not be from the want of assiduity or persever-
ance; for he would sit on a wet rock, with a rod as
long and heavy as a Tartar's lance, and fish all day
without a murmur, even though he should not be en-
couraged by a single nibble. He would carry a fowl-
ing-piece on his shoulder for hours together, trudging
through woods and swamps, and up hill and down
dale, to shoot a few squirrels or wild pigeons. He
would never refuse to assist a neighbor, even in the
roughest toil, and was a foremost man at all country
frolics for husking Indian corn, or building stone-
fences; the women of the village, too, used to employ
him to run their errands, and to do such little odd
jobs as their less obliging husbands would not do for
them. In a word, Rip was ready to attend to any-
body's business but his own; but as to doing family
duty, and keeping his farm in order, he found it im-
possible.

In fact, he declared it was of no use to work on his
farm; it was the most pestilent little piece of ground
in the whole country; everything about it went wrong,

and would go wrong, in spite of him. His fences were continually falling to pieces; his cow would either go astray or get among the cabbages; weeds were sure to grow quicker in his fields than anywhere else; the rain always made a point of setting in just as he had some out-door work to do; so that though his patrimonial estate had dwindled away under his management, acre by acre, until there was little more left than a mere patch of Indian corn and potatoes, yet it was the worst-conditioned farm in the neighborhood.

His children, too, were as ragged and wild as if they belonged to nobody. His son Rip, an urchin begotten in his own likeness, promised to inherit the habits, with the old clothes of his father. He was generally seen trooping like a colt at his mother's heels, equipped in a pair of his father's cast-off galligaskins, which he had much ado to hold up with one hand, as a fine lady does her train in bad weather.

Rip Van Winkle, however, was one of those happy mortals, of foolish, well-oiled dispositions, who take the world easy, eat white bread or brown, whichever can be got with least thought or trouble, and would rather starve on a penny than work for a pound. If left to himself, he would have whistled life away in perfect contentment; but his wife kept continually dinning in his ears about his idleness, his carelessness, and the ruin he was bringing on his family. Morning, noon, and night her tongue was incessantly going, and everything he said or did was sure to produce a torrent of household eloquence. Rip had but one way of replying to all lectures of the kind, and that, by frequent use, had grown into a habit. He shrugged his shoulders, shook his head, cast up his eyes, but said nothing. This, however, always provoked a fresh volley from his wife; so that he was fain to draw off his forces, and take to the outside of the house — the only side which, in truth, belongs to a henpecked husband.

Rip's sole domestic adherent was his dog Wolf, who was as much henpecked as his master; for Dame Van Winkle regarded them as companions in idleness, and even looked upon Wolf with an evil eye, as the cause of his master's going so often astray. True it is, in all points of spirit befitting an honorable dog, he was as courageous an animal as ever scoured the woods — but what courage can withstand the ever-during and all-besetting terrors of a woman's tongue? The moment Wolf entered the house his crest fell, his tail drooped to the ground, or curled between his legs, he sneaked about with a gallows air, casting many a side-long glance at Dame Van Winkle, and at the least flourish of a broomstick or ladle he would fly to the door with yelping precipitation.

Times grew worse and worse with Rip Van Winkle as years of matrimony rolled on; a tart temper never mellows with age, and a sharp tongue is the only edged tool that grows keener with constant use. For a long while he used to console himself, when driven from home, by frequenting a kind of perpetual club of the sages, philosophers, and other idle personages of the village; which held its sessions on a bench before a small inn, designated by a rubicund portrait of His Majesty George the Third. Here they used to sit in the shade through a long lazy summer's day, talking listlessly over village gossip, or telling endless sleepy stories about nothing. But it would have been worth any statesman's money to have heard the profound discussions that sometimes took place, when by chance an old newspaper fell into their hands from some passing traveller. How solemnly they would listen to the contents, as drawled out by Derrick Van Bummel, the school-master, a dapper learned little man, who was not to be daunted by the most gigantic word in the dictionary; and how sagely they would deliberate upon public events some months after they had taken place.

The opinions of this junto were completely controlled by Nicholas Vedder, a patriarch of the village, and landlord of the inn, at the door of which he took his seat from morning till night, just moving sufficiently to avoid the sun and keep in the shade of a large tree; so that the neighbors could tell the hour by his movements as accurately as by a sun-dial. It is true he was rarely heard to speak, but smoked his pipe incessantly. His adherents, however (for every great man has his adherents), perfectly understood him, and knew how to gather his opinions. When anything that was read or related displeased him, he was observed to smoke his pipe vehemently, and to send forth short, frequent and angry puffs; but when pleased, he would inhale the smoke slowly and tranquilly, and emit it in light and placid clouds; and sometimes, taking the pipe from his mouth, and letting the fragrant vapor curl about his nose, would gravely nod his head in token of perfect approbation.

From even this stronghold the unlucky Rip was at length routed by his termagant wife, who would suddenly break in upon the tranquillity of the assemblage and call the members all to naught; nor was that august personage, Nicholas Vedder himself, sacred from the daring tongue of this terrible virago, who charged him outright with encouraging her husband in habits of idleness.

Poor Rip was at last reduced almost to despair;

and his only alternative, to escape from the labor of the farm and clamor of his wife, was to take gun in hand and stroll away into the woods. Here he would sometimes seat himself at the foot of a tree, and share the contents of his wallet with Wolf, with whom he sympathized as a fellow-sufferer in persecution. "Poor Wolf," he would say, "thy mistress leads thee a dog's life of it; but never mind, my lad, whilst I live thou shalt never want a friend to stand by thee!" Wolf would wag his tail, look wistfully in his master's face, and if dogs can feel pity I verily believe he reciprocated the sentiment with all his heart.

In a long ramble of the kind on a fine autumnal day, Rip had unconsciously scrambled to one of the highest parts of the Kaatskill Mountains. He was after his favorite sport of squirrel shooting, and the still solitudes had echoed and reëchoed with the reports of his gun. Panting and fatigued, he threw himself, late in the afternoon, on a green knoll, covered with mountain herbage, that crowned the brow of a precipice. From an opening between the trees he could overlook all the lower country for many a mile of rich woodland. He saw at a distance the lordly Hudson, far, far below him, moving on its silent but majestic course, with the reflection of a purple cloud, or the sail of a lagging bark, here and there sleeping on its glassy bosom, and at last losing itself in the blue highlands.

On the other side he looked down into a deep mountain glen, wild, lonely, and shagged, the bottom filled with fragments from the impending cliffs, and scarcely lighted by the reflected rays of the setting sun. For some time Rip lay musing on this scene; evening was gradually advancing; the mountains began to throw

their long blue shadows over the valleys; he saw that
it would be dark long before he could reach the village,
and he heaved a heavy sigh when he thought of en-
countering the terrors of Dame Van Winkle.

As he was about to descend, he heard a voice from
a distance, hallooing, "Rip Van Winkle! Rip Van
Winkle!" He looked round, but could see nothing
but a crow winging its solitary flight across the moun-
tain.   He thought his fancy must have deceived him,
and turned again to descend, when he heard the same
cry ring through the still evening air: "Rip Van
Winkle! Rip Van Winkle!" — at the same time Wolf
bristled up his back, and giving a low growl, skulked
to his master's side, looking fearfully down into the
glen.   Rip now felt a vague apprehension stealing
over him; he looked anxiously in the same direction,
and perceived a strange figure slowly toiling up the
rocks, and bending under the weight of something he
carried on his back.   He was surprised to see any
human being in this lonely and unfrequented place;
but supposing it to be some one of the neighborhood
in need of his assistance, he hastened down to yield it.

On nearer approach he was still more surprised at
the singularity of the stranger's appearance.   He was
a short, square-built old fellow, with thick bushy hair,
and a grizzled beard.   His dress was of the antique
Dutch fashion: a cloth jerkin strapped round the
waist, several pair of breeches, the outer one of ample
volume, decorated with rows of buttons down the
sides, and bunches at the knees.   He bore on his
shoulder a stout keg, that seemed full of liquor, and
made signs for Rip to approach and assist him with
the load.   Though rather shy and distrustful of this
new acquaintance, Rip complied with his usual alac-

rity; and mutually relieving one another, they clambered up a narrow gully, apparently the dry bed of a mountain torrent. As they ascended, Rip every now and then heard long rolling peals like distant thunder, that seemed to issue out of a deep ravine, or rather cleft, between lofty rocks, toward which their rugged path conducted. He paused for a moment, but supposing it to be the muttering of one of those transient thunder-showers which often take place in mountain heights, he proceeded. Passing through the ravine, they came to a hollow, like a small amphitheatre, surrounded by perpendicular precipices, over the brinks of which impending trees shot their branches, so that you only caught glimpses of the azure sky and the bright evening cloud. During the whole time Rip and his companion had labored on in silence; for though the former marvelled greatly what could be the object of carrying a keg of liquor up this wild mountain, yet there was something strange and incomprehensible about the unknown, that inspired awe and checked familiarity.

On entering the amphitheatre, new objects of wonder presented themselves. On a level spot in the centre was a company of odd-looking personages playing at ninepins. They were dressed in a quaint outlandish fashion; some wore short doublets, others jerkins, with long knives in their belts, and most of them had enormous breeches of similar style with that of the guide's. Their visages, too, were peculiar; one had a large beard, broad face, and small piggish eyes; the face of another seemed to consist entirely of nose, and was surmounted by a white sugar-loaf hat, set off with a little red cock's tail. They all had beards, of various shapes and colors. There was one who seemed to be the commander. He was a stout old gentleman, with a weather-beaten countenance; he wore a laced doublet, broad belt and hanger, high-crowned hat and feather, red stockings, and high-heeled shoes, with roses in them. The whole group reminded Rip of the figures in an old Flemish painting in the parlor of Dominie Van Shaick, the village parson, which had been brought over from Holland at the time of the settlement.

What seemed particularly odd to Rip was, that though these folks were evidently amusing themselves, yet they maintained the gravest faces, the most mysterious silence, and were, withal, the most melancholy party of pleasure he had ever witnessed. Nothing interrupted the stillness of the scene but the noise of the balls, which, whenever they were rolled, echoed along the mountains like rumbling peals of thunder.

As Rip and his companion approached them, they suddenly desisted from their play, and stared at him with such fixed, statue-like gaze, and such strange, uncouth, lack-lustre countenances, that his heart turned within him, and his knees smote together. His companion now emptied the contents of the keg into large flagons, and made signs to him to wait upon the company. He obeyed with fear and trembling; they quaffed the liquor in profound silence, and then returned to their game.

By degrees Rip's awe and apprehension subsided. He even ventured, when no eye was fixed upon him, to taste the beverage, which he found had much of the flavor of excellent Hollands. He was naturally a thirsty soul, and was soon tempted to repeat the draught. One taste provoked another; and he reiterated his visits to the flagon so often that at length his senses were overpowered, his eyes swam in his head, his head gradually declined, and he fell into a deep sleep.

On waking, he found himself on the green knoll whence he had first seen the old man of the glen. He rubbed his eyes — it was a bright, sunny morning. The birds were hopping and twittering among the bushes, and the eagle was wheeling aloft, and breasting the pure mountain breeze. " Surely," thought Rip, " I have not slept here all night." He recalled the occurrences before he fell asleep. The strange man with a keg of liquor — the mountain ravine — the wild retreat among the rocks — the woe-begone party at nine-pins — the flagon — " Oh ! that flagon ! that wicked flagon ! " thought Rip — " what excuse shall I make to Dame Van Winkle ? "

He looked round for his gun, but in place of the clean, well-oiled fowling-piece, he found an old firelock lying by him, the barrel incrusted with rust, the lock falling off, and the stock worm-eaten. He now suspected that the grave roisters of the mountain had put a trick upon him, and, having dosed him with liquor, had robbed him of his gun. Wolf, too, had disappeared, but he might have strayed away after a squirrel or partridge. He whistled after him, and shouted his name, but all in vain ; the echoes repeated his whistle and shout, but no dog was to be seen.

He determined to revisit the scene of the last evening's gambol, and if he met with any of the party, to demand his dog and gun. As he rose to walk, he found himself stiff in the joints, and wanting in his usual activity. " These mountain beds do not agree with me," thought Rip, " and if this frolic should lay me up with a fit of the rheumatism, I shall have a blessed time with Dame Van Winkle." With some difficulty he got down into the glen; he found the gully up which he and his companion had ascended the preceding evening; but to his astonishment a mountain stream was now foaming down it, leaping from rock to rock, and filling the glen with babbling murmurs. He, however, made shift to scramble up its sides, working his toilsome way through thickets of birch, sassafras, and witch-hazel, and sometimes tripped up or entangled by the wild grapevines that twisted their coils or tendrils from tree to tree, and spread a kind of network in his path.

At length he reached to where the ravine had opened through the cliffs to the amphitheatre; but no traces of such opening remained. The rocks presented a high, impenetrable wall, over which the torrent came tumbling in a sheet of feathery foam, and fell into a broad, deep basin, black from the shadows of the surrounding forest. Here, then, poor Rip was brought to a stand. He again called and whistled after his dog; he was only answered by the cawing of a flock of idle crows, sporting high in air about a dry tree that overhung a sunny precipice; and who, secure in their elevation, seemed to look down and scoff at the poor man's perplexities. What was to be done? the morning was passing away, and Rip felt famished for want of his breakfast. He grieved to give up his dog and gun; he dreaded to meet his wife; but it would not do to starve among the mountains. He shook his head, shouldered the rusty firelock, and, with a heart full of trouble and anxiety, turned his steps homeward.

As he approached the village he met a number of people, but none whom he knew, which somewhat sur-

prised him, for he had thought himself acquainted
with every one in the country round. Their dress,
too, was of a different fashion from that to which he
was accustomed. They all stared at him with equal
marks of surprise, and whenever they cast their eyes
upon him, invariably stroked their chins. The con-
stant recurrence of this gesture induced Rip, involun-
tarily, to do the same, when, to his astonishment, he
found his beard had grown a foot long !

He had now entered the skirts of the village. A
troop of strange children ran at his heels, hooting
after him, and pointing at his gray beard. The dogs,
too, not one of which he recognized for an old ac-
quaintance, barked at him as he passed. The very
village was altered ; it was larger and more populous.
There were rows of houses which he had never seen
before, and those which had been his familiar haunts
had disappeared. Strange names were over the doors
— strange faces at the windows, — everything was
strange. His mind now misgave him ; he began to
doubt whether both he and the world around him
were not bewitched. Surely this was his native vil-
lage, which he had left but the day before. There
stood the Kaatskill Mountains — there ran the silver
Hudson at a distance — there was every hill and dale
precisely as it had always been — Rip was sorely per-
plexed — "That flagon last night," thought he, " has
addled my poor head sadly ! "

It was with some difficulty that he found the way
to his own house, which he approached with silent
awe, expecting every moment to hear the shrill voice
of Dame Van Winkle. He found the house gone to
decay — the roof fallen in, the windows shattered,
and the doors off the hinges. A half-starved dog that

looked like Wolf was skulking about it. Rip called him by name, but the cur snarled, showed his teeth, and passed on. This was an unkind cut indeed — "My very dog," sighed poor Rip, "has forgotten me!"

He entered the house, which, to tell the truth, Dame Van Winkle had always kept in neat order. It was empty, forlorn, and apparently abandoned. This desolateness overcame all his connubial fears — he called loudly for his wife and children — the lonely chambers rang for a moment with his voice, and then again all was silence.

He now hurried forth, and hastened to his old resort, the village inn — but it, too, was gone. A large, rickety wooden building stood in its place, with great gaping windows, some of them broken and mended with old hats and petticoats, and over the door was painted, "The Union Hotel, by Jonathan Doolittle." Instead of the great tree that used to shelter the quiet little Dutch inn of yore, there now was reared a tall naked pole, with something on the top that looked like a red night-cap, and from it was fluttering a flag, on which was a singular assemblage of stars and stripes — all this was strange and incomprehensible. He recognized on the sign, however, the ruby face of King George, under which he had smoked so many a peaceful pipe; but even this was singularly metamorphosed. The red coat was changed for one of blue and buff, a sword was held in the hand instead of a sceptre, the head was decorated with a cocked hat, and underneath was painted in large characters, GENERAL WASHINGTON.

There was, as usual, a crowd of folk about the door, but none that Rip recollected. The very character of

the people seemed changed. There was a busy, bus-
tling, disputatious tcne about it, instead of the accus-
tomed phlegm and drowsy tranquillity. He looked in
vain for the sage Nicholas Vedder, with his broad
face, double chin, and fair long pipe, uttering clouds
of tobacco-smoke instead of idle speeches ; or Van
Bummel, the school-master, doling forth the contents
of an ancient newspaper. In place of these, a lean,
bilious-looking fellow, with his pockets full of hand-
bills, was haranguing vehemently about rights of citi-
zens — elections — members of congress — liberty —
Bunker's Hill — heroes of seventy-six — and other
words, which were a perfect Babylonish jargon to the
bewildered Van Winkle.

The appearance of Rip, with his long grizzled beard,
his rusty fowling-piece, his uncouth dress, and an army
of women and children at his heels, soon attracted
the attention of the tavern-politicians. They crowded
round him, eying him from head to foot with great
curiosity. The orator bustled up to him, and, draw-
ing him partly aside, inquired " on which side he
voted ? " Rip started in vacant stupidity. Another
short but busy little fellow pulled him by the arm,
and, rising on tiptoe, inquired in his ear, " Whether
he was Federal or Democrat ? " Rip was equally at
a loss to comprehend the question; when a knowing,
self-important old gentleman, in a sharp cocked hat,
made his way through the crowd, putting them to the
right and left with his elbows as he passed, and plant-
ing himself before Van Winkle, with one arm akimbo,
the other resting on his cane, his keen eyes and sharp
hat penetrating, as it were, into his very soul, de-
manded in an austere tone, " what brought him to the
election with a gun on his shoulder, and a mob at his

heels, and whether he meant to breed a riot in the village?" — "Alas! gentlemen," cried Rip, somewhat dismayed, "I am a poor quiet man, a native of the place, and a loyal subject of the king, God bless him!"

Here a general shout burst from the bystanders — "A tory! a tory! a spy! a refugee! hustle him! away with him!" It was with great difficulty that the self-important man in the cocked hat restored order; and, having assumed a tenfold austerity of brow, demanded again of the unknown culprit what he came there for, and whom he was seeking? The poor man humbly assured him that he meant no harm, but merely came there in search of some of his neighbors, who used to keep about the tavern.

"Well — who are they? — name them."

Rip bethought himself a moment, and inquired, "Where's Nicholas Vedder?"

There was a silence for a little while, when an old man replied, in a thin, piping voice: "Nicholas Vedder! why, he is dead and gone these eighteen years! There was a wooden tombstone in the churchyard that used to tell all about him, but that's rotten and gone too."

"Where's Brom Dutcher?"

"Oh, he went off to the army in the beginning of the war; some say he was killed at the storming of Stony Point [1] — others say he was drowned in a squall at the foot of Antony's Nose.[2] I don't know — he never came back again."

---

[1] On the Hudson. The place is famous for the daring assault made by Mad Anthony Wayne, July 15, 1779.

[2] A few miles above Stony Point is the promontory of Antony's Nose. If we are to believe Diedrich Knickerbocker, it

" Where 's Van Bummel, the school-master ? "

" He went off to the wars too, was a great militia general, and is now in Congress."

Rip's heart died away at hearing of these sad changes in his home and friends, and finding himself thus alone in the world. Every answer puzzled him too, by treating of such enormous lapses of time, and of matters which he could not understand: war — Congress — Stony Point; he had no courage to ask after any more friends, but cried out in despair, " Does nobody here know Rip Van Winkle ? "

" Oh, Rip Van Winkle ! " exclaimed two or three, " Oh, to be sure ! that 's Rip Van Winkle yonder, leaning against the tree."

Rip looked, and beheld a precise counterpart of himself, as he went up the mountain: apparently as lazy, and certainly as ragged. The poor fellow was now completely confounded. He doubted his own identity, and whether he was himself or another man.

---

was named after Antony Van Corlear, Stuyvesant's trumpeter. " It must be known, then, that the nose of Antony the trumpeter was of a very lusty size, strutting boldly from his countenance like a mountain of Golconda. . . . Now thus it happened, that bright and early in the morning the good Antony, having washed his burly visage, was leaning over the quarter railing of the galley, contemplating it in the glassy wave below. Just at this moment the illustrious sun, breaking in all his splendor from behind a high bluff of the highlands, did dart one of his most potent beams full upon the refulgent nose of the sounder of brass — the reflection of which shot straightway down, hissing hot, into the water and killed a mighty sturgeon that was sporting beside the vessel ! . . . When this astonishing miracle came to be made known to Peter Stuyvesant he . . . marvelled exceedingly ; and as a monument thereof, he gave the name of *Antony's Nose* to a stout promontory in the neighborhood, and it has continued to be called Antony's Nose ever since that time." *History of New York*, book VI. chap. iv.

In the midst of his bewilderment, the man in the cocked hat demanded who he was, and what was his name?

"God knows," exclaimed he, at his wit's end; "I'm not myself — I'm somebody else — that's me yonder — no — that's somebody else got into my shoes — I was myself last night, but I fell asleep on the mountain, and they've changed my gun, and everything's changed, and I'm changed, and I can't tell what's my name, or who I am!"

The bystanders began now to look at each other. nod, wink significantly, and tap their fingers against their foreheads. There was a whisper, also, about securing the gun, and keeping the old fellow from doing mischief, at the very suggestion of which the self-important man in the cocked hat retired with some precipitation. At this critical moment a fresh, comely woman pressed through the throng to get a peep at the gray-bearded man. She had a chubby child in her arms, which, frightened at his looks, began to cry. "Hush, Rip," cried she, "hush, you little fool; the old man won't hurt you." The name of the child, the air of the mother, the tone of her voice, all awakened a train of recollections in his mind. "What is your name, my good woman?" asked he.

"Judith Gardenier."

"And your father's name?"

"Ah, poor man, Rip Van Winkle was his name, but it's twenty years since he went away from home with his gun, and never has been heard of since, — his dog came home without him; but whether he shot himself, or was carried away by the Indians, nobody can tell. I was then but a little girl."

Rip had but one question more to ask; and he put it with a faltering voice: —

" Where 's your mother ? "

" Oh, she too had died but a short time since ; she broke a blood-vessel in a fit of passion at a New England peddler."

There was a drop of comfort at least, in this intelligence. The honest man could contain himself no longer. He caught his daughter and her child in his arms. " I am your father ! " cried he — " Young Rip Van Winkle once — old Rip Van Winkle now ! Does nobody know poor Rip Van Winkle ? "

All stood amazed, until an old woman tottering out from among the crowd, put her hand to her brow, and peering under it in his face for a moment, exclaimed, " Sure enough it is Rip Van Winkle — it is himself ! Welcome home again, old neighbor — Why, where have you been these twenty long years ? "

Rip's story was soon told, for the whole twenty years had been to him but as one night. The neighbors stared when they heard it ; some were seen to wink at each other, and put their tongues in their cheeks ; and the self-important man in the cocked hat, who when the alarm was over, had returned to the field, screwed down the corners of his mouth, and shook his head — upon which there was a general shaking of the head throughout the assemblage.

It was determined, however, to take the opinion of old Peter Vanderdonk, who was seen slowly advancing up the road. He was a descendant of the historian of that name,[1] who wrote one of the earliest accounts of the province. Peter was the most ancient inhabitant of the village, and well versed in all the wonderful events and traditions of the neighborhood. He recollected Rip at once, and corroborated his story

[1] Adrian Vanderdonk.

in the most satisfactory manner. He assured the company that it was a fact, handed down from his ancestor the historian, that the Kaatskill Mountains had always been haunted by strange beings. That it was affirmed that the great Hendrick Hudson, the first discoverer of the river and country, kept a kind of vigil there every twenty years, with his crew of the Half-moon; being permitted in this way to revisit the scenes of his enterprise, and keep a guardian eye upon the river and the great city called by his name. That his father had once seen them in their old Dutch dresses playing at ninepins in a hollow of the mountain; and that he himself had heard, one summer afternoon, the sound of their balls like distant peals of thunder.

To make a long story short, the company broke up, and returned to the more important concerns of the election. Rip's daughter took him home to live with her; she had a snug well-furnished house, and a stout cheery farmer for a husband, whom Rip recollected for one of the urchins that used to climb upon his back. As to Rip's son and heir, who was the ditto of himself, seen leaning against the tree, he was employed to work on the farm; but evinced an hereditary disposition to attend to anything else but his business.

Rip now resumed his old walks and habits; he soon found many of his former cronies, though all rather the worse for the wear and tear of time ; and preferred making friends among the rising generation, with whom he soon grew into great favor.

Having nothing to do at home, and being arrived at that happy age when a man can be idle with impunity, he took his place once more on the bench at the inn door, and was reverenced as one of the patriarchs

of the village, and a chronicle of the old times " before
the war." It was some time before he could get into
the regular track of gossip, or could be made to com-
prehend the strange events that had taken place dur-
ing his torpor. How that there had been a revolu-
tionary war — that the country had thrown off the
yoke of old England — and that, instead of being a
subject of his Majesty George the Third, he was now
a free citizen of the United States. Rip, in fact, was
no politician ; the changes of states and empires made
but little impression on him ; but there was one spe-
cies of despotism under which he had long groaned,
and that was — petticoat government. Happily that
was at an end ; he had got his neck out of the yoke of
matrimony, and could go in and out whenever he
pleased, without dreading the tyranny of Dame Van
Winkle. Whenever her name was mentioned, how-
ever, he shook his head, shrugged his shoulders, and
cast up his eyes, which might pass either for an ex-
pression of resignation to his fate, or joy at his deliv-
erance.

He used to tell his story to every stranger that ar-
rived at Mr. Doolittle's hotel. He was observed, at
first, to vary on some points every time he told it,
which was, doubtless, owing to his having so recently
awaked. It at last settled down precisely to the tale
I have related, and not a man, woman, or child in the
neighborhood but knew it by heart. Some always
pretended to doubt the reality of it, and insisted that
Rip had been out of his head, and that this was one
point on which he always remained flighty. The old
Dutch inhabitants, however, almost universally gave
it full credit. Even to this day they never hear a
thunder-storm of a summer afternoon about the Kaats-

kill, but they say Hendrick Hudson and his crew are at their game of ninepins; and it is a common wish of all henpecked husbands in the neighborhood, when life hangs heavy on their hands, that they might have a quieting draught out of Rip Van Winkle's flagon.

NOTE.

The foregoing Tale, one would suspect, had been suggested to Mr. Knickerbocker by a little German superstition about the Emperor Frederick *der Rothbart*,[1] and the Kypphaüser mountain; the subjoined note, however, which he had appended to the tale, shows that it is an absolute fact, narrated with his usual fidelity.

"The story of Rip Van Winkle may seem incredible to many, but nevertheless I give it my full belief, for I know the vicinity of our old Dutch settlements to have been very subject to marvellous events and appearances. Indeed, I have heard many stranger stories than this, in the villages along the Hudson; all of which were too well authenticated to admit of a doubt. I have even talked with Rip Van Winkle myself, who, when last I saw him, was a very old venerable man, and so perfectly rational and consistent on every other point, that I think no conscientious person could refuse to take this into the bargain; nay, I have seen a certificate on the subject taken before a country justice and signed with a cross, in the justice's own handwriting. The story therefore, is beyond the possibility of doubt.

"D. K."

POSTSCRIPT.

The following are travelling notes from a memorandum-book of Mr. Knickerbocker:—

The Kaatsberg, or Catskill Mountains, have always been a region full of fable. The Indians considered them the abode of spirits, who influenced the weather, spreading sunshine or clouds

---

[1] Frederick I. of Germany, 1121–1190, called Barbarossa, *der Rothbart* (Redbeard or Rufus), was fabled not to have died but to have gone into a long sleep, from which he would awake when Germany should need him. The same legend was told by the Danes of their Holger.

over the landscape, and sending good or bad hunting seasons. They were ruled by an old squaw spirit, said to be their mother. She dwelt on the highest peak of the Catskills, and had charge of the doors of day and night to open and shut them at the proper hour. She hung up the new moons in the skies, and cut up the old ones into stars. In times of drought, if properly propitiated, she would spin light summer clouds out of cobwebs and morning dew, and send them off from the crest of the mountain, flake after flake, like flakes of carded cotton, to float in the air ; until, dissolved by the heat of the sun, they would fall in gentle showers, causing the grass to spring, the fruits to ripen, and the corn to grow an inch an hour. If displeased, however, she would brew up clouds black as ink, sitting in the midst of them like a bottle-bellied spider in the midst of its web ; and when these clouds broke, woe betide the valleys !

In old times, say the Indian traditions, there was a kind of Manitou or Spirit, who kept about the wildest recesses of the Catskill Mountains, and took a mischievous pleasure in wreaking all kinds of evils and vexations upon the red men. Sometimes he would assume the form of a bear, a panther, or a deer, lead the bewildered hunter a weary chase through tangled forest and among ragged rocks ; and then spring off with a loud ho ! ho ! leaving him aghast on the brink of a beetling precipice or raging torrent.

The favorite abode of this Manitou is still shown. It is a great rock or cliff on the loneliest part of the mountains, and from the flowering vines which clamber about it, and the wild flowers which abound in its neighborhood, is known by the name of the Garden Rock. Near the foot of it is a small lake, the haunt of the solitary bittern, with water-snakes basking in the sun on the leaves of the pond-lilies which lie on the surface. This place was held in great awe by the Indians, insomuch that the boldest hunter would not pursue his game within its precincts. Once upon a time, however, a hunter, who had lost his way, penetrated to the Garden Rock, where he beheld a number of gourds placed in the crotches of trees. One of these he seized and made off with it, but in the hurry of his retreat he let it fall among the rocks, when a great stream gushed forth, which washed him away and swept him down precipices, where he was dashed to pieces, and the stream made its way to the Hudson, and continues to flow to the present day ; being the identical stream known by the name of the Kaaters-kill.

WILLIAM CULLEN BRYANT.

BIOGRAPHICAL SKETCH.

WILLIAM CULLEN BRYANT was born at Cummington, Massachusetts, November 3, 1794; he died in New York, June 12, 1878. His first poem, *The Embargo*, was published in Boston in 1809, and was written when he was but thirteen years old; his last poem, *Our Fellow Worshippers*, was published in 1878. His long life thus was a long career as a writer, and his first published poem prefigured the twofold character of his literary life, for while it was in poetic form it was more distinctly a political article. He showed very early a taste for poetry, and was encouraged to read and write verse by his father, Dr. Peter Bryant, a country physician of strong character and cultivated tastes. He was sent to Williams College in the fall of 1810, where he remained two terms, when he decided to leave and enter Yale College; but pecuniary troubles interfered with his plans, and he never completed his college course. He pursued his literary studies at home, then began the study of law and was admitted to the bar in 1815. Meantime he had been continuing to write, and during this period wrote with many corrections and changes the poem by which he is still perhaps best known, *Thanatopsis*. It was published in the *North American Review* for September, 1817, and the same periodical published a few months afterward his lines *To a Waterfowl*, one of the most characteristic and lovely of Bryant's poems. Literature divided his attention with law, but evidently had his heart. In 1821 he was invited to read a poem before the Phi Beta Kappa Society of Harvard College, and he read *The Ages*, a stately grave poem which shows his own poetic power, his familiarity with the great masters of literature, and his lofty, philosophic nature.　Shortly after this he issued a small volume of poems, and his name began to be known as that of the first American who had written poetry that could take its place in universal literature.　His own decided preference for literature, and the encouragement of friends, led to his abandonment of the law in 1825, and his removal to New York, where he undertook the associate editorship of *The New York Review and Athenæum Magazine.*　Poetic genius is not caused or controlled by circumstance, but a purely literary life in a country not yet educated in literature was impossible to a man of no other means of support, and in a few months, after the *Review* had vainly tried to maintain life by a frequent change of name, Bryant accepted an appointment as assistant editor of the *Evening Post.*　From 1826, then, until his death, Bryant was a journalist by profession.　One effect of this change in his life was to eliminate from his poetry that political character which was displayed in his first published poem and had several times since shown itself.　Thenceafter he threw into his journalistic occupation all those thoughts and experiences which made him by nature a patriot and political thinker; he reserved for poetry the calm reflection, love of nature, and purity of aspiration which made him a poet.　His editorial writing was made strong and pure by his cultivated taste and lofty ideals, but he presented the rare combination of a poet who never sacrificed his love of high literature and his devotion to art, and of a publicist who retained a sound judgment and pursued the most practical ends.

His life outwardly was uneventful.　He made four journeys to Europe, in 1834, 1845, 1852, 1857, and he made frequent tours in his own country.　His observations on his travels were published in *Letters from a Traveller, Letters*

William Cullen Bryant

from the East, and *Letters from Spain and other Countries.* He never held public office, except that in 1860 he was a presidential elector, but he was connected intimately with important movements in society, literature, and politics, and was repeatedly called upon to deliver addresses commemorative of eminent citizens, as of Washington Irving, and James Fenimore Cooper, and at the unveiling of the bust of Mazzini in the Central Park. His *Orations and Addresses* have been gathered into a volume.

The bulk of his poetry apart from his poetic translations is not considerable, and is made up almost wholly of short poems which are chiefly inspired by his love of nature. R. H. Dana in his preface to *The Idle Man* says: "I shall never forget with what feeling my friend Bryant some years ago [1] described to me the effect produced upon him by his meeting for the first time with Wordsworth's *Ballads.* He lived, when quite young, where but few works of poetry were to be had; at a period, too, when Pope was still the great idol of the Temple of Art. He said that upon opening Wordsworth a thousand springs seemed to gush up at once in his heart, and the face of nature of a sudden to change into a strange freshness and life."

This was the interpreting power of Wordsworth suddenly disclosing to Bryant, not the secrets of nature, but his own powers of perception and interpretation. Bryant is in no sense an imitator of Wordsworth, but a comparison of the two poets would be of great interest as showing how individually each pursued the same general poetic end. Wordsworth's *Three Years She Grew in Sun and Shower* and Bryant's *O Fairest of the Rural Maids* offer an admirable opportunity for disclosing the separate treatment of similar subjects. In Bryant's lines, musical and full of a gentle revery, the poet seems to go deeper and deeper into the forest, almost forgetful of the "fairest of the rural maids;" in Wordsworth's lines, with what simple yet profound feeling

---

[1] This was written in 1833.

the poet, after delicately disclosing the interchange of nature and human life, returns into those depths of human sympathy where nature must forever remain as a remote shadow.

Bryant translated many short poems from the Spanish, but his largest literary undertaking was the translation of the *Iliad* and *Odyssey* of Homer. He brought to this task great requisite powers, and if there is any failure it is in the absence of Homer's lightness and rapidity, qualities which the elasticity of the Greek language especially favored.

A pleasant touch of a simple humor appeared in some of his social addresses, and occasionally is found in his poems, as in *Robert of Lincoln*. Suggestions of personal experience will be read in such poems as *The Cloud on the Way*, *The Life that Is*, and in the half-autobiographic poem, *A Lifetime*.

THANATOPSIS.

To him who in the love of Nature holds
Communion with her visible forms, she speaks
A various language; for his gayer hours
She has a voice of gladness, and a smile
And eloquence of beauty, and she glides   5
Into his darker musings, with a mild
And healing sympathy, that steals away
Their sharpness, ere he is aware.   When thoughts
Of the last bitter hour come like a blight
Over the spirit, and sad images   10
Of the stern agony, and shroud, and pall,
And breathless darkness, and the narrow house,
Make thee to shudder, and grow sick at heart; —
Go forth, under the open sky, and list
To Nature's teachings, while from all around —   15
Earth and her waters, and the depths of air —
Comes a still voice — Yet a few days, and thee
The all-beholding sun shall see no more
In all his course; nor yet in the cold ground,
Where thy pale form was laid, with many tears,   20
Nor in the embrace of ocean, shall exist
Thy image.   Earth, that nourished thee, shall claim
Thy growth, to be resolved to earth again,
And, lost each human trace, surrendering up
Thine individual being, shalt thou go   25
To mix for ever with the elements,
To be a brother to the insensible rock

And to the sluggish clod, which the rude swain
Turns with his share, and treads upon. The oak
Shall send his roots abroad, and pierce thy mould.   80

    Yet not to thine eternal resting-place
Shalt thou retire alone, nor couldst thou wish
Couch more magnificent. Thou shalt lie down
With patriarchs of the infant world — with kings,
The powerful of the earth — the wise, the good,   85
Fair forms, and hoary seers of ages past,
All in one mighty sepulchre. The hills
Rock-ribbed and ancient as the sun, — the vales
Stretching in pensive quietness between;
The venerable woods — rivers that move   40
In majesty, and the complaining brooks
That make the meadows green; and, poured round
      all,
Old Ocean's gray and melancholy waste, —
Are but the solemn decorations all
Of the great tomb of man. The golden sun,   45
The planets, all the infinite host of heaven,
Are shining on the sad abodes of death,
Through the still lapse of ages. All that tread
The globe are but a handful to the tribes
That slumber in its bosom. — Take the wings   50
Of morning, pierce the Barcan wilderness,
Or lose thyself in the continuous woods
Where rolls the Oregon, and hears no sound,
Save his own dashings — yet the dead are there:
And millions in those solitudes, since first   55
The flight of years began, have laid them down
In their last sleep — the dead reign there alone.
So shalt thou rest, and what if thou withdraw
In silence from the living, and no friend

Take note of thy departure?   All that breathe   60
Will share thy destiny.   The gay will laugh
When thou art gone, the solemn brood of care
Plod on, and each one as before will chase
His favorite phantom ; yet all these shall leave
Their mirth and their employments, and shall come 65
And make their bed with thee.   As the long train
Of ages glide away, the sons of men,
The youth in life's green spring, and he who goes
In the full strength of years, matron and maid,
The speechless babe, and the gray-headed man —   70
Shall one by one be gathered to thy side,
By those, who in their turn shall follow them.

So live, that when thy summons comes to join
The innumerable caravan, which moves
To that mysterious realm, where each shall take   75
His chamber in the silent halls of death,
Thou go not, like the quarry-slave at night,
Scourged to his dungeon, but, sustained and soothed
By an unfaltering trust, approach thy grave,
Like one who wraps the drapery of his couch   80
About him, and lies down to pleasant dreams.

TO A WATERFOWL.

WHITHER, midst falling dew,
While glow the heavens with the last steps of day,
Far, through their rosy depths, dost thou pursue
    Thy solitary way?

    Vainly the fowler's eye   5
Might mark thy distant flight to do thee wrong,

As, darkly painted on the crimson sky,
    Thy figure floats along.

    Seek'st thou the plashy brink
Of weedy lake, or marge of river wide,
Or where the rocking billows rise and sink
    On the chafed ocean-side?

    There is a Power whose care
Teaches thy way along that pathless coast—
The desert and illimitable air—
    Lone wandering, but not lost.

    All day thy wings have fanned,
At that far height, the cold, thin atmosphere,
Yet stoop not, weary, to the welcome land,
    Though the dark night is near.

    And soon that toil shall end;
Soon shalt thou find a summer home, and rest,
And scream among thy fellows; reeds shall bend,
    Soon, o'er thy sheltered nest.

    Thou 'rt gone, the abyss of heaven
Hath swallowed up thy form; yet, on my heart
Deeply hath sunk the lesson thou hast given,
    And shall not soon depart.

    He who, from zone to zone,
Guides through the boundless sky thy certain flight,
In the long way that I must tread alone,
    Will lead my steps aright.

BENJAMIN FRANKLIN.

BIOGRAPHICAL SKETCH.

In reading the life of Franklin we are constantly surprised at the versatility of his powers. He achieved an undying reputation as a man of business, as a scientist, as a writer, as a statesman, and as a diplomatist. It is impossible to give here an adequate idea of his greatness or of the debt of gratitude which we all owe him for the help he rendered our nation in times of sore need. For the events of his life the reader is referred to his Autobiography [1] — a classic masterpiece with which every American should be familiar. What follows is a review of Franklin's character by John T. Morse, Jr., at the end of his admirable biography of Franklin, in the *American Statesmen Series* : —

"Among illustrious Americans Franklin stands preëminent in the interest which is aroused by a study of his character, his mind and his career. One becomes attached to him, bids him farewell with regret, and feels that for such as he the longest span of life is all too short. Even though dead, he attracts a personal regard which renders easily intelligible the profound affection which so many men felt for him while living. It may be doubted whether any one man ever had so many, such constant, and such firm friends as in three different nations formed about him a veritable host. In the States and in France he was loved, and as he grew into old age he was revered, not by those who heard

[1] See Riverside Literature Series, Nos. 19 and 20.

of him only, but most warmly by those who best knew him. Even in England, where for years he was the arch rebel of all America, he was generally held in respect and esteem, and had many constant friends whose confidence no events could shake. . . . Moral, intellectual, and material boons he conferred in such abundance that few such benefactors of the race can be named, though one should survey all the ages. A man of a greater humanity never lived: and the quality which stood Abou Ben Adhem in good stead should suffice to save Franklin from human criticism. He not only loved his kind, but he also trusted them with an implicit confidence, reassuring if not extraordinary in an observer of his shrewdness and experience. . . .

"Franklin's inborn ambition was the noblest of all ambitions: to be of practical use to the multitude of men. The chief motive of his life was to promote the welfare of mankind. Every moment which he could snatch from enforced occupations was devoted to doing, devising, or suggesting something advantageous more or less generally to men. . . . His desire was to see the community prosperous, comfortable, happy, advancing in the accumulation of money and of all physical goods, but not to the point of luxury; it was by no means the pile of dollars which was his end, and he did not care to see many men rich, but rather to see all men well to do. He was perfectly right in thinking that virtuous living has the best prospects in a well-to-do society. He gave liberally of his own means and induced others to give, and promoted in proportion to the ability of the community a surprising number of public and *quasi*-public enterprises; and always the fireside of the poor man was as much in his thought as the benefit of the richer circle. Fair dealing and kindliness, prudence and economy in order to procure the comforts and simpler luxuries of life, reading and knowledge for those uses which wisdom subserves, constituted the real essence of his teaching. His inventive genius was ever at work devising methods of making daily life more agreeable,

comfortable, and wholesome for all who have to live. In a word, the service of his fellow-men was his constant aim; and he so served them that those public official functions which are euphemistically called 'public services' seemed in his case almost an interruption of the more direct and far-reaching services which he was intent upon rendering to all civilized peoples. . . .

"As a patriot none surpassed him. Again it was the love of the people that induced this feeling, which grew from no theory as to forms of government, no abstractions and doctrines about 'the rights of man.' . . . During the struggle of the States no man was more hearty in the cause than Franklin; and the depth of feeling shown in his letters, simple and unrhetorical as they are, is impressive. All that he had he gave. What also strikes the reader of his writings is the broad national spirit which he manifested. He had an immense respect for the dignity of America; he was perhaps fortunately saved from disillusionment by his distance from home. But be this as it may, the way in which he felt and therefore genuinely talked about his nation and his country was not without its moral effect in Europe.

"Intellectually there are few men who are Franklin's peers in all the ages and nations. He covered, and covered well, vast ground. The reputation of doing and knowing various unrelated things is wont to bring suspicion of perfunctoriness; but the ideal of the human intellect is an understanding to which all knowledge and all activity are germane. There have been a few, very few minds which have approximated toward this ideal, and among them Franklin's is prominent. He was one of the most distinguished scientists who have ever lived. Bancroft calls him 'the greatest diplomatist of his century.'[1] His ingenious and useful devices and inventions were very numerous. He possessed a masterly shrewdness in business and practical affairs. He was a profound thinker and preacher in morals and on the

---

[1] Bancroft, *History of the United States*, ix. 134.

conduct of life ; so that with the exception of the founders
of great religions it would be difficult to name any persons
who have more extensively influenced the ideas, motives,
and habits of life of men. He was one of the most, perhaps
the most agreeable conversationist of his age. He was a
rare wit and humorist, and in an age when 'American
humor' was still unborn, amid contemporaries who have
left no trace of a jest, still less of the faintest appreciation
of humor, all which he said and wrote was brilliant with
both the most charming qualities of the human mind. . . .
He was a man who impressed his ability upon all who met
him ; so that the abler the man and the more experienced
in judging men, the higher did he rate Franklin when
brought into direct contact with him ; politicians and states-
men of Europe, distrustful and sagacious, trained readers
and valuers of men, gave him the rare honor of placing con-
fidence not only in his personal sincerity, but in his broad
fairmindedness, a mental quite as much as a moral trait.

"It is hard indeed to give full expression to a man of such
scope in morals, in mind, and in affairs. He illustrates
humanity in an astonishing multiplicity of ways at an infi-
nite number of points. He, more than any other, seems to
show us how many-sided our human nature is. No individ-
ual, of course, fills the entire circle ; but if we can imagine
a circumference which shall express humanity, we can place
within it no one man who will reach out to approach it and
to touch it at so many points as will Franklin. A man of
active as well as universal good will, of perfect trustfulness
towards all dwellers on the earth, of supreme wisdom
expanding over all the interests of the race, none has earned
a more kindly loyalty. By the instruction which he gave,
by his discoveries, by his inventions, and by his achieve-
ments in public life he earns the distinction of having ren-
dered to men varied and useful services excelled by no other
one man ; and thus he has established a claim upon the
gratitude of mankind so broad that history holds few who
can be his rivals."

CHRONOLOGICAL LIST OF THE PRINCIPAL EVENTS IN THE LIFE OF FRANKLIN.

Born in Boston, Massachusetts . . . . January 17, 1706
Is apprenticed to his brother, a printer 1718
Begins to write for the "New England Courant" 1719
Runs away to New York, and finally to Philadelphia . . 1723
Goes to England and works at his trade as a journeyman
    printer in London 1725
Returns to Philadelphia 1726
Marries 1730
Establishes the "Philadelphia Gazette" 1730
First publishes "Poor Richard's Almanac" 1732
Is appointed Postmaster of Philadelphia 1737
Establishes the Philadelphia Public Library 1742
Establishes the American Philosophical Society and the Uni-
    versity of Philadelphia 1744
Carries on the investigations by which he proves the identity
    of lightning with electricity 1746–52
Assists in founding a hospital 1751
Is appointed Postmaster-General for the Colonies . . . 1753
Is sent by the Assembly of the Province of Pennsylvania as an
    emissary to England in behalf of the colonists . . 1757
Receives the degree of LL. D. from St. Andrews, Oxford, and
    Edinburgh 1764
Procures a repeal of the Stamp Act 1766
Is elected F. R. S., and receives the Copley Gold Medal for his
    papers on the nature of lightning 1775
Is elected to the Continental Congress 1775
Signs the Declaration of Independence (having been one of the
    committee to draft it) 1776
Is employed in the diplomatic service of the United States,
    chiefly at Paris 1776–85
Is President of the Pennsylvania Supreme Council . . 1785–88
Is a delegate to the convention to draw up the United States
    Constitution 1787
Dies at Philadelphia . . . . April 17, 1790

POOR RICHARD'S ALMANAC.

[IN Franklin's lifetime the almanac was the most popular form of literature in America. A few people read newspapers, but every farmer who could read at all had an almanac hanging by the fireplace. Besides the monthly calendar and movements of the heavenly bodies, the almanac contained anecdotes, scraps of useful information, and odds and ends of literature. Franklin began the publication of such an almanac in 1732, pretending that it was written by one Richard Saunders. It was published annually for twenty-five years. "I endeavored," says Franklin, "to make it both entertaining and useful; and it accordingly came to be in such demand, that I reaped considerable profit from it, vending annually near ten thousand. And observing that it was generally read, scarce any neighborhood in the province being without it, I considered it as a proper vehicle for conveying instruction among the common people, who bought scarcely any other books; I therefore filled all the little spaces that occurred between the remarkable days in the calendar with proverbial sentences, chiefly such as inculcated industry and frugality as the means of procuring wealth, and thereby securing virtue; it being more difficult for a man in want to act always honestly, as, to use here one of those proverbs, '*it is hard for an empty sack to stand upright.*'" In the almanac Franklin introduced his proverbs by the phrase *Poor Richard says*, as if he were quoting from Richard Saunders, and so the almanac came to be called *Poor Richard's Almanac*.

"These proverbs," he continues, "which contain the wisdom of many ages and nations, I assembled and formed into a connected discourse, prefixed to the almanac of 1757, as the harangue of a wise old man to the people attending an auction. The bringing all these scattered counsels thus into a focus enabled them to make greater impression. The piece, being universally approved, was copied in all the newspapers of the continent [that is, the American continent]; reprinted in Britain on a broadside, to be stuck up in houses ; two translations were made of it in French, and great numbers bought by the clergy and gentry, to distribute *gratis* among their poor parishioners and tenants. In Pennsylvania, as it discouraged useless expense in foreign superfluities, some thought it had its share of influence in producing that growing plenty of money which was observable for several years after its publication."

Franklin's example was followed by other writers, — Noah Webster, the maker of dictionaries, among them ; and one can see in the popular almanacs of to-day, such as *The Old Farmer's Almanac*, the effect of Franklin's style. When the king of France gave Captain John Paul Jones a ship with which to make attacks upon British merchantmen in the war for independence, it was named, out of compliment to Franklin, the *Bon Homme Richard*, which might be translated Clever Richard. The pages which follow are the connected discourse prefixed to the almanac of 1757.]

COURTEOUS READER : —

I have heard that nothing gives an author so great pleasure as to find his works respectfully quoted by other learned authors. This pleasure I have seldom enjoyed. For though I have been, if I may say it without vanity, an *eminent* author of *Almanacs* annually, now for a full quarter of a century, my brother authors in the same way, for what reason I know not, have ever been very sparing in their applauses; and no other author has taken the least notice of me ; so that did not my writings produce me some solid pudding, the great deficiency of praise would have quite discouraged me.

I concluded at length, that the people were the best judges of my merit; for they buy my works ; and besides, in my rambles, where I am not personally known, I have frequently heard one or other of my adages repeated, with *as Poor Richard says* at the end of it. This gave me some satisfaction, as it showed, not only that my instructions were regarded, but discovered likewise some respect for my authority; and I own, that to encourage the practice of remembering and repeating those sentences, I have sometimes quoted myself with great gravity.

Judge, then, how much I must have been gratified by an incident I am going to relate to you. I stopped my horse lately where a great number of people were collected at a vendue of merchant's goods. The hour of sale not being come, they were conversing on the badness of the times; and one of the company called to a plain, clean old man with white locks, " Pray, Father Abraham, what think you of the times? Won't these heavy taxes quite ruin the country? How shall we ever be able to pay them? What would you advise us to?" Father Abraham stood up and replied: " If you would have my advice, I will give it you in short; for *A word to the wise is enough*, and *Many words won't fill a bushel*, as Poor Richard says." They all joined, desiring him to speak his mind, and gathering round him, he proceeded as follows: —

Friends, says he, and neighbors, the taxes are indeed very heavy, and if those laid on by the government were the only ones we had to pay, we might the more easily discharge them; but we have many others, and much more grievous to some of us. We are taxed twice as much by our IDLENESS, three times as much by our PRIDE, and four times as much by our FOLLY; and from these taxes the commissioners cannot ease or deliver us, by allowing an abatement. However, let us hearken to good advice, and something may be done for us; *God helps them that helps themselves*, as Poor Richard says in his *Almanac* of 1733.

It would be thought a hard government that should

tax its people one tenth part of their TIME, to be em-
ployed in its service, but idleness taxes many of us
much more, if we reckon all that is spent in absolute
sloth, or doing of nothing ; with that which is spent
in idle employments or amusements that amount to
nothing. Sloth, by bringing on diseases, absolutely
shortens life. *Sloth, like rust, consumes faster than
labor wears ; while the used key is always bright,* as
Poor Richard says. *But dost thou love life? then do
not squander time, for that's the stuff life is made of,*
as Poor Richard says.

How much more that is necessary do we spend in
sleep ? forgetting, that *the sleeping fox catches no
poultry,* and that *there will be sleeping enough in the
grave,* as Poor Richard says. If time be of all things
the most precious, *wasting of time must be,* as Poor
Richard says, *the greatest prodigality ;* since, as he
elsewhere tells us, *lost time is never found again ;* and
what we call *time enough ! always proves little enough.*
Let us then up and be doing, and doing to the purpose;
so, by diligence, shall we do more with less perplexity.
*Sloth makes all things difficult, but industry all
things easy,* as Poor Richard says ; and *He that riseth
late must trot all day, and shall scarce overtake his
business at night ; while laziness travels so slowly
that Poverty soon overtakes him,* as we read in Poor
Richard ; who adds, *Drive thy business ! let not that
drive thee ! and* —

> *Early to bed and early to rise*
> *Makes a man healthy, wealthy and wise.*

So what signifies *wishing* and *hoping* for better
times? We may make these times better, if we bestir
ourselves. *Industry need not wish,* as Poor Richard
says, and *He that lives on hope will die fasting.*

There are no gains without pains ; then help, hands! for I have no lands ; or, if I have, they are smartly taxed. And, as Poor Richard likewise observes, *He that hath a trade hath an estate, and he that hath a calling hath an office of profit and honor ;* but then the trade must be worked at, and the calling well followed, or neither the estate nor the office will enable us to pay our taxes. If we are industrious we shall never starve ; for, as Poor Richard says, *At the working-man's house hunger looks in, but dares not enter.* Nor will the bailiff or the constable enter, for *Industry pays debts, while despair increaseth them.*

What though you have found no treasure, nor has any rich relation left you a legacy, *Diligence is the mother of good luck,* as Poor Richard says, *and God gives all things to industry.*

> *Then plough deep while sluggards sleep,*
> *And you shall have corn to sell and to keep,*

says Poor Dick. Work while it is called to-day, for you know not how much you may be hindered tomorrow ; which makes Poor Richard say, *One to-day is worth two to-morrows ;* and farther, *Have you somewhat to do to-morrow? Do it to-day!* If you were a servant, would you not be ashamed that a good master should catch you idle? Are you then your own master? *Be ashamed to catch yourself idle,* as Poor Dick says. When there is so much to be done for yourself, your family, your country, and your gracious king, be up by peep of day! *Let not the sun look down and say, "Inglorious here he lies!"* Handle your tools without mittens! remember that *The cat in gloves catches no mice!* as Poor Richard says.

'T is true there is much to be done, and perhaps you are weak-handed; but stick to it steadily, and you will see great effects; for *Constant dropping wears away stones;* and *By diligence and patience the mouse ate in two the cable;* and *Little strokes fell great oaks;* as Poor Richard says in his *Almanac,* the year I cannot just now remember.

Methinks I hear some of you say, "Must a man afford himself no leisure?" I will tell thee, my friend, what Poor Richard says, *Employ thy time well, if thou meanest to gain leisure;* and *Since thou art not sure of a minute, throw not away an hour!* Leisure is time for doing something useful; this leisure the diligent man will obtain, but the lazy man never; so that, as Poor Richard says, *A life of leisure and a life of laziness are two things.* Do you imagine that sloth will afford you more comfort than labor? No! for, as Poor Richard says, *Trouble springs from idleness, and grievous toil from needless ease. Many, without labor, would live by their wits only, but they'll break for want of stock* [i. e. capital]; whereas industry gives comfort, and plenty, and respect. *Fly pleasures, and they'll follow you. The diligent spinner has a large shift;* and —

> *Now I have a sheep and a cow,*
> *Everybody bids me good morrow.*

All which is well said by Poor Richard. But with our industry we must likewise be steady, settled, and careful, and oversee our own affairs *with our own eyes,* and not trust too much to others; for, as Poor Richard says, —

> *I never saw an oft-removed tree*
> *Nor yet an oft-removed family*
> *That throve so well as those that settled be.*

And again, *Three removes are as bad as a fire;* and again, *Keep thy shop, and thy shop will keep thee;* and again, *If you would have your business done, go; if not, send.* And again,—

> He that by the plough would thrive,
> Himself must either hold or drive.

And again, *The eye of the master will do more work than both his hands;* and again, *Want of care does us more damage than want of knowledge;* and again, *Not to oversee workmen is to leave them your purse open.*

Trusting too much to others' care is the ruin of many; for, as the Almanac says, *In the affairs of this world men are saved, not by faith, but by the want of it;* but a man's own care is profitable; for saith Poor Dick, *Learning is to the studious, and Riches to the careful;* as well as, *Power to the bold,* and *Heaven to the virtuous.* And further, *If you would have a faithful servant, and one that you like, serve yourself.*

And again, he adviseth to circumspection and care, even in the smallest matters; because sometimes, *A little neglect may breed great mischief;* adding, *for want of a nail the shoe was lost; for want of a shoe the horse was lost; and for want of a horse the rider was lost;* being overtaken and slain by the enemy; all for want of a little care about a horse-shoe nail!

So much for industry, my friends, and attention to one's own business; but to these we must add frugality, if we would make our industry more certainly successful. *A man may,* if he knows not how to save as he gets, *keep his nose all his life to the grindstone, and die not worth a groat at last. A fat kitchen makes a lean will,* as Poor Richard says; and —

Many estates are spent in the getting,
Since women for tea [1] *forsook spinning and knitting,*
And men for punch forsook hewing and splitting.

If you would be wealthy, says he in another Almanac, *Think of saving as well as of getting.* *The Indies have not made Spain rich; because her outgoes are greater than her incomes.*

Away, then, with your expensive follies, and you will not have so much cause to complain of hard times, heavy taxes, and chargeable families; for, as Poor Dick says, —

Women and wine, game and deceit,
Make the wealth small and the wants great.

And farther, *What maintains one vice would bring up two children.* You may think, perhaps, that a *little* tea, or a *little* punch now and then; a diet a *little* more costly; clothes a *little* more finer; and a *little* more entertainment now and then, can be no great matter; but remember what Poor Richard says, *Many a little makes a mickle;* and further, *Beware of little expenses; A small leak will sink a great ship;* and again, —

Who dainties love, shall beggars prove;

and moreover, *Fools make feasts, and wise men eat them.*

Here are you all got together at this vendue of fineries and knick-knacks. You call them *goods;* but if you do not take care, they will prove evils to some of you. You expect they will be sold cheap, and perhaps they may for less than they cost; but, if you have no occasion for them, they must be *dear* to

[1] Tea at this time was a costly drink, and was regarded as a luxury.

you. Remember what Poor Richard says : *Buy what thou hast no need of, and ere long thou shalt sell thy necessaries.* And again, *At a great pennyworth pause a while.* He means, that perhaps the cheapness is apparent only, and not real ; or the bargain by straitening thee in thy business, may do thee more harm than good. For in another place he says, *Many have been ruined by buying good pennyworths.*

Again, Poor Richard says, '*T is foolish to lay out money in a purchase of repentance ;* and yet this folly is practised every day at vendues for want of minding the *Almanac.*

Wise men, as Poor Richard says, *learn by others' harms ; Fools scarcely by their own ;* but *Felix quem faciunt aliena pericula cautum.*[1] Many a one, for the sake of finery on the back, has gone with a hungry belly, and half-starved their families. *Silks and satins, scarlets and velvets,* as Poor Richard says, *put out the kitchen fire.* These are not the necessaries of life; they can scarcely be called the conveniences ; and yet, only because they look pretty, how many *want* to have them! The artificial wants of mankind thus become more numerous than the natural ; and, as Poor Dick says, *For one* poor *person there are a hundred* indigent.

By these, and other extravagances, the genteel are reduced to poverty, and forced to borrow of those whom they formerly despised, but who, through industry and frugality, have maintained their standing ; in which case it appears plainly, that *A ploughman on his legs is higher than a gentleman on his knees,* as Poor Richard says. Perhaps they have had a

[1] He 's a lucky fellow who is made prudent by other men's perils.

small estate left them, which they knew not the getting of; they think, *'T is day, and will never be night ;* that *a little to be spent out of so much is not worth minding ;* (*A child and a fool*, as Poor Richard says, *imagine* twenty shillings and twenty years can never be spent,) but *Always taking out of the meal-tub, and never putting in, soon comes to the bottom.* Then, as Poor Dick says, *When the well's dry, they know the worth of water.* But this they might have known before, if they had taken his advice. *If you would know the value of money, go and try to borrow some ;* for *He that goes a borrowing, goes a sorrowing,* and indeed so does he that lends to such people, *when he goes to get it in again.*

Poor Dick further advises, and says —

> *Fond pride of dress is, sure a very curse ;*
> *Ere fancy you consult, consult your purse.*

And again, *Pride is as loud a beggar as Want, and a great deal more saucy.* When you have bought one fine thing, you must buy ten more, that your appearance may be all of a piece ; but Poor Dick says, *'T is easier to suppress the first desire, than to satisfy all that follow it.* And 't is as truly folly for the poor to ape the rich, as for the frog to swell in order to equal the ox.

> *Great estates may venture more,*
> *But little boats should keep near shore.*

'T is, however, a folly soon punished ; for, *Pride that dines on vanity sups on contempt,* as Poor Richard says. And in another place, *Pride breakfasted with Plenty, dined with Poverty, and supped with Infamy.*

And after all, of what use is this pride of appearance, for which so much is risked, so much is suffered? It cannot promote health or ease pain; it makes no increase of merit in the person; it creates envy; it hastens misfortune.

> *What is a butterfly?   At best*
> *He's but a caterpillar drest,*
> *The gaudy fop's his picture just,*

as Poor Richard says.

But what madness must it be to *run into debt* for these superfluities!   We are offered, by the terms of this vendue, six months' credit; and that, perhaps, has induced some of us to attend it, because we cannot spare the ready money, and hope now to be fine without it.   But, ah! think what you do when you run in debt: *You give to another power over your liberty.* If you cannot pay at the time, you will be ashamed to see your creditor; you will be in fear when you speak to him; you will make poor, pitiful, sneaking excuses, and by degrees come to lose your veracity, and sink into base, downright lying; for, as Poor Richard says, *The second vice is lying, the first is running into debt;* and again, to the same purpose, *lying rides upon debt's back;* whereas a free-born Englishman ought not to be ashamed or afraid to see or speak to any man living.   But poverty often deprives a man of all spirit and virtue.   *'Tis hard for an empty bag to stand upright!* as Poor Richard truly says.   What would you think of that prince, or the government, who should issue an edict forbidding you to dress like a gentleman or gentlewoman, on pain of imprisonment or servitude?   Would you not say that you are free, have a right to dress as you please, and that such an edict would be a breach of your privileges, and such a government tyrannical?   And yet you are about to put yourself under such tyranny, when you run in debt for such dress! Your creditor has authority, at his pleasure, to deprive you of your liberty, by confining you in jail for life, or to sell you for a servant, if you should not be able to pay him.[1] When you have got your bargain, you may, perhaps, think little of payment; but *Creditors* (Poor Richard tells us) *have better memories than debtors;* and in another place says, *Creditors are a superstitious set, great observers of set days and times.* The day comes round before you are aware, and the demand is made before you are prepared to satisfy it; or, if you bear your debt in mind, the term which at first seemed so long, will, as it lessens, appear extremely short. Time will seem to have added wings to his heels as well as his shoulders. *Those have a short Lent,* saith Poor Richard, *who owe money to be paid at Easter.* Then since, as he says, *The borrower is a slave to the lender, and the debtor to the creditor,* disdain the chain, preserve your freedom, and maintain your independency. Be *industrious* and *free;* be *frugal* and *free.* At present, perhaps, you may think yourself in thriving circumstances, and that you can bear a little extravagance without injury; but —

> *For age and want, save while you may,*
> *No morning sun lasts a whole day.*

As Poor Richard says, gain may be temporary and uncertain; but ever, while you live, expense is constant and certain; and *'Tis easier to build two chimneys than to keep one in fuel,* as Poor Richard says; so, *Rather go to bed supperless than rise in debt.*

---

[1] At the time when this was written, and for many years afterward, the laws against bankrupts and poor debtors were extremely severe.

Get what you can and what you get hold ;
  'T is the stone that will turn all your lead into gold,[1]

as Poor Richard says; and, when you have got the Philosopher's stone, sure, you will no longer complain of bad times or the difficulty of paying taxes.

This doctrine, my friends, is reason and wisdom; but, after all, do not depend too much upon your own industry and frugality and prudence, though excellent things; for they may all be blasted without the blessing of Heaven; and therefore, ask that blessing humbly, and be not uncharitable to those that at present seem to want it, but comfort and help them. Remember Job suffered, and was afterwards prosperous.

And now, to conclude, *Experience keeps a dear school, but fools will learn in no other, and scarce in that ;* for it is true, *We may give advice, but we cannot give conduct*, as poor Richard says. However, remember this, *They that won't be counselled, can't be helped*, as Poor Richard says; and further, that, *If you will not hear reason, she 'll surely rap your knuckles.*

Thus the old gentleman ended his harangue. The people heard it, and approved the doctrine; and immediately practised the contrary, just as if it had been a common sermon. For the vendue opened, and they began to buy extravagantly, notwithstanding all his cautions, and their own fear of taxes. I found the good man had thoroughly studied my *Almanacs*, and digested all I had dropped on those topics during the course of five-and-twenty years. The frequent men-

---

[1] In the Middle Ages there was a great search made for the philosopher's stone, as it was called, a mineral which should have the power of turning base metals into gold.

tion he made of me must have tired any one else ; but my vanity was wonderfully delighted with it, though I was conscious that not a tenth part of the wisdom was my own which he ascribed to me, but rather the gleanings that I had made of the sense of all ages and nations. However, I resolved to be the better for the echo of it ; and, though I had at first determined to buy stuff for a new coat, I went away resolved to wear my old one a little longer. Reader, if thou wilt do the same, *thy* profit will be as great as mine. I am, as ever, thine to serve thee,

RICHARD SAUNDERS.

July 7, 1757.

FROM "POOR RICHARD'S ALMANAC," 1756.

PLAN FOR SAVING ONE HUNDRED THOUSAND POUNDS.

As I spent some weeks last winter in visiting my old acquaintance in the Jerseys, great complaints I heard for want of money, and that leave to make more paper bills could not be obtained. Friends and countrymen, my advice on this head shall cost you nothing ; and, if you will not be angry with me for giving it, I promise you not to be offended if you do not take it.

You spend yearly at least *two hundred thousand pounds*, it is said, in European, East-Indian, and West-Indian commodities. Suppose one half of this expense to be in *things absolutely necessary*, the other half may be called *superfluities*, or, at best, conveniencies, which, however, you might live without for one little year, and not suffer exceedingly. Now, to save this half, observe these few directions : —

1. When you incline to have new clothes, look first well over the old ones, and see if you cannot shift with them another year, either by scouring, mending, or even patching if necessary. Remember, a patch on your coat, and money in your pocket, is better and more creditable than a writ on your back, and no money to take it off.

2. When you are inclined to buy China ware, chintzes, India silks, or any other of their flimsy, slight manufactures, I would not be so bad with you as to insist on your absolutely *resolving against it;* all I advise is, to *put it off* (as you do your repentance) *till another year;* and this, in some respects, may prevent an occasion of repentance.

TO SAMUEL MATHER.

PASSY, *May* 12, 1784.

I received your kind letter, with your excellent advice to the people of the United States, which I read with great pleasure, and hope it will be duly regarded. Such writings, though they may be lightly passed over by many readers, yet, if they make a deep impression on one active mind in a hundred, the effects may be considerable. Permit me to mention one little instance, which, though it relates to myself, will not be quite uninteresting to you. When I was a boy, I met with a book entitled, "Essays to do Good," which I think was written by your father.[1] It had been so little regarded by a former possessor, that several leaves of it were torn out; but the remainder gave me such a turn of thinking, as to have an influence on my conduct through life, for I have always set a greater

[1] Cotton Mather. — ED.

value on the character of a *doer of good* than on any other kind of reputation; and if I have been, as you seem to think, a useful citizen, the public owes the advantage of it to that book.

You mention your being in your seventy-eighth year. I am in my seventy-ninth year; we are growing old together. It is now more than sixty years since I left Boston, but I remember well both your father and grandfather, having heard them both in the pulpit and seen them in their houses. The last time I saw your father was in the beginning of 1724, when I visited him after my first trip to Pennsylvania. He received me in his library, and on my taking leave showed me a shorter way out of the house through a narrow passage, which was crossed by a beam overhead. We were still talking as I withdrew, he accompanying me behind, and I turning partly towards him, when he said hastily, " Stoop, stoop!" I did not understand him till I felt my head hit against the beam. He was a man that never missed any occasion of giving instruction, and upon this he said to me, " *You are young, and have the world before you;* STOOP *as you go through it, and you will miss many hard thumps.*" This advice, thus beat into my head, has frequently been of use to me; and I often think of it when I see pride mortified, and misfortunes brought upon people by their carrying their heads too high.

TO THE REV. DR. LATHROP, BOSTON.

PHILADELPHIA, 31 *May*, 1788.

REVEREND SIR: I received your obliging favor of the 6th instant by Mr. Hillard, with whose conversation I was much pleased, and would have been glad to have had more of it if he would have spared it to me; but the short time of his stay has prevented. You need make no apology for introducing any of your friends to me. I consider it as doing me honor, as well as giving me pleasure. I thank you for the pamphlet of the Humane Society. In return, please to accept one of the same kind, which was published while I resided in France. If your Society have not hitherto seen it, it may possibly afford them useful hints.

It would certainly, as you observe, be a very great pleasure to me if I could once again visit my native town, and walk over the grounds I used to frequent when a boy, and where I enjoyed many of the innocent pleasures of youth, which would be so brought to my remembrance, and where I might find some of my old acquaintance to converse with. But when I consider how well I am situated here, with everything about me that I can call either necessary or convenient; the fatigues and bad accommodations to be met with and suffered in a land journey, and the unpleasantness of sea voyages to one who, although he has crossed the Atlantic eight times and made many smaller trips, does not recollect his having ever been at sea without taking a firm resolution never to go to sea again; and that, if I were arrived in Boston, I should see but little of it, as I could neither bear walking nor riding in a carriage over its pebbled streets; and, above all, that I should find very few indeed of my old friends living, it being now sixty-five years since I left it to settle here, — all this considered, I say, it seems probable, though not certain, that I shall hardly again visit that beloved place. But I enjoy the company and conversation of its inhabitants, when any of them are so good as to visit me; for, besides their general good sense, which I value, the Boston manner, turn of phrase, and even tone of voice and accent in pronunciation, all please, and seem to refresh and revive me.

I have been long impressed with the same sentiments you so well express of the growing felicity of mankind, from the improvements in philosophy, morals, politics, and even the conveniences of common living, and the invention and acquisition of new and useful utensils and instruments, so that I have sometimes almost wished it had been my destiny to be born two or three centuries hence; for invention and improvement are prolific, and beget more of their kind. The present progress is rapid. Many of great importance, now unthought of, will before that period be produced; and then I might not only enjoy their advantages, but have my curiosity gratified in knowing what they are to be. I see a little absurdity in what I have just written; but it is to a friend, who will wink and let it pass, while I mention one reason more for such a wish, which is, that, if the art of physic shall be improved in proportion to other arts, we may then be able to avoid diseases, and live as long as the patriarchs in Genesis, to which I suppose we should have little objection.

I am glad my dear sister has so good and kind a neighbor. I sometimes suspect she may be backward in acquainting me with circumstances in which I might be more useful to her. If any such should occur to your observation, your mentioning them to me will be a favor I shall be thankful for.

With great esteem, I have the honor to be, reverend sir, your most obedient and most humble servant,

B. FRANKLIN.

TO BENJAMIN WEBB.

PASSY, 22 *April*, 1784.

I received yours of the 15th instant, and the memorial it enclosed. The account they give of your situation grieves me. I send you herewith a bill for ten louis d'ors. I do not pretend to *give* such a sum; I only *lend* it to you. When you shall return to your country with a good character, you cannot fail of getting into some business that will in time enable you to pay all your debts. In that case, when you meet with another honest man in similar distress, you must pay me by lending this sum to him ; enjoining him to discharge the debt by a like operation when he shall be able, and shall meet with such another opportunity. I hope it may thus go through many hands before it meets with a knave that will stop its progress. This is a trick of mine for doing a deal of good with a little money. I am not rich enough to afford *much* in good works, and so am obliged to be *cunning*, and make the most of a *little*. With best wishes for the success of your memorial and your future prosperity, I am, dear sir, your most obedient servant,

B. FRANKLIN.

OLIVER WENDELL HOLMES.

BIOGRAPHICAL SKETCH.

OLIVER WENDELL HOLMES was born at Cambridge, Massachusetts, August 29, 1809. The house in which he was born stood between the sites now occupied by the Hemenway Gymnasium and the Law School of Harvard University, and was of historic interest as having been the headquarters of General Artemas Ward, and of the Committee of Safety in the days just before the Revolution. Upon the steps of the house stood President Langdon, of Harvard College, tradition says, and prayed for the men who, halting there a few moments, marched forward under Colonel Prescott's lead to throw up intrenchments on Bunker Hill on the night of June 16, 1775. Dr. Holmes's father carried forward the traditions of the old house, for he was Rev. Dr. Abiel Holmes, whose *American Annals* was the first careful record of American history written after the Revolution.

Born and bred in the midst of historic associations, Holmes had from the first a lively interest in American history and politics, and though possessed of strong humorous gifts, has often turned his song into patriotic channels, while the current of his literary life has been distinctly American.

He began to write poetry when in college at Cambridge, and some of his best-known early pieces, like *Evening, by a Tailor, The Meeting of the Dryads, The Spectre Pig*, were contributed to the *Collegian*, an undergraduate journal, while he was studying law the year after his graduation. At the same time he wrote the well-known poem *Old Ironsides*, a protest against the proposed breaking up of the frigate Constitution; the poem was printed in the *Boston Daily Advertiser*, and its indignation and fervor carried it through the country, and raised such a popular feeling that the ship was saved from an ignominious destruction. Holmes shortly gave up the study of law, went abroad to study medicine, and returned to take his degree at Harvard in 1836. At the same time he delivered a poem, *Poetry: a Metrical Essay*, before the Phi Beta Kappa Society of Harvard, and ever since his profession of medicine and his love of literature have received his united care and thought. In 1838 he was appointed Professor of Anatomy and Physiology at Dartmouth College, but remained there only a year or two, when he returned to Boston, married, and practised medicine. In 1847 he was made Parkman Professor of Anatomy and Physiology in the Medical School of Harvard College, a position which he retained until the close of 1882, when he retired, to devote himself more exclusively to literature.

In 1857, when the *Atlantic Monthly* was established, Professor Lowell, who was asked to be editor, consented on condition that Dr. Holmes should be a regular contributor. Dr. Holmes at that time was known as the author of a number of poems of grace, life, and wit, and he had published several professional papers and books, but his brilliancy as a talker gave him a strong local reputation, and Lowell shrewdly guessed that he would bring to the new magazine a singularly fresh and unusual power. He was right, for *The Autocrat of the Breakfast-Table*, beginning in the first number, unquestionably insured the *Atlantic* its early success. The readers of the day had forgotten that Holmes, twenty-five years before, had begun a series with the same title in Buckingham's *New England Magazine*, a periodical of short life, so they did not at first understand why he should begin his first article, " I was just going to say when

I was interrupted." From that time Dr. Holmes was a frequent contributor to the magazine, and in it appeared successively, *The Autocrat of the Breakfast-Table*, *The Professor at the Breakfast-Table*, *The Professor's Story* (afterward called *Elsie Venner*), *The Guardian Angel*, *The Poet at the Breakfast-Table*, *The New Portfolio* (afterward called *A Mortal Antipathy*), *Our Hundred Days in Europe*, and *Over the Teacups*, — prose papers and stories with occasional insertion of verse; here also have been printed the many poems which he has so freely and happily written for festivals and public occasions, including the frequent poems at the yearly meetings of his college class. The wit and humor which have made his poetry so well known would never have given him his high rank had they not been associated with an admirable art which makes every word necessary and felicitous, and a generous nature which is quick to seize upon what touches a common life.

GRANDMOTHER'S STORY OF BUNKER HILL BATTLE.

AS SHE SAW IT FROM THE BELFRY.

[This poem was first published in 1875, in connection with the centenary of the battle of Bunker Hill. The belfry could hardly have been that of Christ Church, since tradition says that General Gage was stationed there watching the battle, and we may make it to be what was known as the New Brick Church, built in 1721, on Hanover, corner of Richmond Street, Boston, rebuilt of stone in 1845, and pulled down at the widening of Hanover Street in 1871. There are many narratives of the battle of Bunker Hill. Frothingham's *History of the Siege of Boston* is one of the most comprehensive accounts, and has furnished material for many popular narratives. The centennial celebration of the battle called out magazine and newspaper articles, which give the story with little variation. There are not many disputed points in connection with the event, the principal one being the discussion as to who was the chief officer.]

'T IS like stirring living embers when, at eighty, one
    remembers
All the achings and the quakings of "the times that
    tried men's souls;"

2. In December, 1776, Thomas Paine, whose *Common Sense* had so remarkable a popularity as the first homely expression of public opinion on Independence, began issuing a series of tracts called *The Crisis*, eighteen numbers of which appeared. The familiar words quoted by the grandmother must often have been

Oliver Wendell Holmes.

When I talk of *Whig* and *Tory*, when I tell the *Rebel* story,
To you the words are ashes, but to me they 're burning coals.

I had heard the muskets' rattle of the April running battle ;   5
Lord Percy's hunted soldiers, I can see their red coats still ;
But a deadly chill comes o'er me, as the day looms up before me,
When a thousand men lay bleeding on the slopes of Bunker's Hill.

heard and used by her. They begin the first number of *The Crisis :* "These are the times that try men's souls : the summer soldier and the sunshine patriot will, in this crisis, shrink from the service of his country ; but he that stands it now deserves the love and thanks of man and woman."

3. The terms *Whig* and *Tory* were applied to the two parties in England who represented, respectively, the Whigs political and religious liberty, the Tories royal prerogative and ecclesiastical authority. The names first came into use in 1679 in the struggles at the close of Charles II.'s reign, and continued in use until a generation or so ago, when they gave place to somewhat corresponding terms of Liberal and Conservative. At the breaking out of the war for Independence, the Whigs in England opposed the measures taken by the crown in the management of the American colonies, while the Tories supported the crown. The names were naturally applied in America to the patriotic party, who were termed Whigs, and the loyalist party, termed Tories. The Tories in turn called the patriots rebels.

5. The Lexington and Concord affair of April 19, 1775, when Lord Percy's soldiers retreated in a disorderly manner to Charlestown, annoyed on the way by the Americans who followed and accompanied them.

'T was a peaceful summer's morning, when the first
    thing gave us warning
Was the booming of the cannon from the river and
    the shore: 10
"Child," says grandma, "what's the matter, what is
    all this noise and clatter?
Have those scalping Indian devils come to murder us
    once more?"

Poor old soul! my sides were shaking in the midst of
    all my quaking,
To hear her talk of Indians when the guns began to
    roar:
She had seen the burning village, and the slaughter
    and the pillage,   15
When the Mohawks killed her father with their bul-
    lets through his door.

Then I said, "Now, dear old granny, don't you fret
    and worry any,
For I 'll soon come back and tell you whether this is
    work or play;
There can't be mischief in it, so I won't be gone a
    minute " —
For a minute then I started.   I was gone the livelong
    day.   20

No time for bodice-lacing or for looking-glass grima-
    cing;

16. The Mohawks, a formidable part of the Six Nations, were
held in great dread, as they were the most cruel and warlike of
all the tribes. In connection with the French they fell upon the
frontier settlements during Queen Anne's war, early in the
eighteenth century, and committed terrible deeds, long remem-
bered in New England households.

Down my hair went as I hurried, tumbling half-way
　　to my heels;
God forbid your ever knowing, when there 's blood
　　around her flowing,
How the lonely, helpless daughter of a quiet house-
　　hold feels!

In the street I heard a thumping; and I knew it was
　　the stumping　　　　　　　　　　　　　　　25
Of the Corporal, our old neighbor, on the wooden leg
　　he wore,
With a knot of women round him, — it was lucky I
　　had found him,
So I followed with the others, and the Corporal
　　marched before.

They were making for the steeple, — the old soldier
　　and his people;
The pigeons circled round us as we climbed the creak-
　　ing stair,　　　　　　　　　　　　　　　30
Just across the narrow river — Oh, so close it made
　　me shiver! —
Stood a fortress on the hill-top that but yesterday was
　　bare.

Not slow our eyes to find it; well we knew who stood
　　behind it,
Though the earthwork hid them from us, and the stub-
　　born walls were dumb:
Here were sister, wife, and mother, looking wild upon
　　each other,　　　　　　　　　　　　　　35
And their lips were white with terror as they said,
　　THE HOUR HAS COME!

The morning slowly wasted, not a morsel had we
    tasted,
And our heads were almost splitting witb the cannons'
    deafening thrill,
When a figure tall and stately round the rampart
    strode sedately;
It was PRESCOTT, one since told me; he commanded
    on the hill.   40

Every woman's heart grew bigger when we saw his
    manly figure,
With the banyan buckled round it, standing up so
    straight and tall;
Like a gentleman of leisure who is strolling out for
    pleasure,
Through the storm of shells and cannon-shot he
    walked around the wall.

At eleven the streets were swarming, for the red-coats'
    ranks were forming;   45
At noon in marching order they were moving to the
    piers;
How the bayonets gleamed and glistened, as we looked
    far down, and listened
To the trampling and the drum-beat of the belted
    grenadiers!

40. Colonel William Prescott, who commanded the detach-
ment which marched from Cambridge, June 16, 1775, to fortify
Breed's Hill, was the grandfather of William Hickling Prescott,
the historian. He was in the field during the entire battle of
the 17th, in command of the redoubt.

42. *Banyan* — a flowered morning gown which Prescott is said
to have worn during the hot day, a good illustration of the un-
military appearance of the soldiers engaged. His nonchalant
walk upon the parapets is also a historic fact, and was for the
encouragement of the troops within the redoubt.

At length the men have started, with a cheer (it
    seemed faint-hearted),
In their scarlet regimentals, with their knapsacks on
    their backs,   50
And the reddening, rippling water, as after a sea-
    fight's slaughter,
Round the barges gliding onward blushed like blood
    along their tracks.

So they crossed to the other border, and again they
    formed in order ;
And the boats came back for soldiers, came for sol-
    diers, soldiers still :
The time seemed everlasting to us women faint and
    fasting, —   55
At last they 're moving, marching, marching proudly
    up the hill.

We can see the bright steel glancing all along the
    lines advancing —
Now the front rank fires a volley — they have thrown
    away their shot ;
For behind their earthwork lying, all the balls above
    them flying,
Our people need not hurry ; so they wait and answer
    not.   60

Then the Corporal, our old cripple (he would swear
    sometimes and tipple), —
He had heard the bullets whistle (in the old French
    war) before, —

62. Many of the officers as well as men on the American side
had become familiarized with service through the old French
war, which came to an end in 1763.

Calls out in words of jeering, just as if they all were
    hearing, —
And his wooden leg thumps fiercely on the dusty bel-
    fry floor : —

" Oh ! fire away, ye villains, and earn King George's
    shillin's,   65
But ye 'll waste a ton of powder afore a ' rebel ' falls ;
You may bang the dirt and welcome, they 're as safe
    as Dan'l Malcolm
Ten foot beneath the gravestone that you 've splin-
    tered with your balls ! "

In the hush of expectation, in the awe and trepidation
Of the dread approaching moment, we are well-nigh
    breathless all ;   70
Though the rotten bars are failing on the rickety bel-
    fry railing,
We are crowding up against them like the waves
    against a wall.

67. Dr. Holmes makes the following note to this line : " The
following epitaph is still to be read on a tall gravestone, stand-
ing as yet undisturbed among the transplanted monuments of the
dead in Copp's Hill Burial Ground, one of the three city [Boston]
cemeteries which have been desecrated and ruined within my
own remembrance : —

    " Here lies buried in a
    Stone Grave 10 feet deep
  Capt. DANIEL MALCOLM Mercht
    Who departed this Life
      October 23, 1769,
      Aged 44 years,
    A true son of Liberty,
    A Friend to the Publick,
    An Enemy to oppression,
    And one of the foremost
  In opposing the Revenue Acts
      On America."

Just a glimpse (the air is clearer), they are nearer,
   — nearer, — nearer,
When a flash — a curling smoke-wreath — then a
   crash — the steeple shakes —
The deadly truce is ended; the tempest's shroud is
   rended;   75
Like a morning mist it gathered, like a thunder-cloud
   it breaks!

O the sight our eyes discover as the blue-black smoke
   blows over!
The red-coats stretched in windrows as a mower rakes
   his hay;
Here a scarlet heap is lying, there a headlong crowd
   is flying
Like a billow that has broken and is shivered into
   spray.   80

Then we cried, " The troops are routed! they are
   beat — it can't be doubted!
God be thanked, the fight is over!" — Ah! the grim
   old soldier's smile!
" Tell us, tell us why you look so?" (we could hardly
   speak we shook so), —
" Are they beaten? *Are* they beaten? ARE they
   beaten?" — " Wait a while."

O the trembling and the terror! for too soon we saw
   our error: 85
They are baffled, not defeated; we have driven them
   back in vain;
And the columns that were scattered, round the colors
   that were tattered,
Toward the sullen silent fortress turn their belted
   breasts again.

All at once, as we were gazing, lo ! the roofs of Charles-
    town blazing !
They have fired the harmless village ; in an hour it
    will be down !   90
The Lord in Heaven confound them, rain his fire and
    brimstone round them, —
The robbing, murdering red-coats, that would burn a
    peaceful town !

They are marching, stern and solemn ; we can see
    each massive column
As they near the naked earth-mound with the slanting
    walls so steep.
Have our soldiers got faint-hearted, and in noiseless
    haste departed ?   95
Are they panic-struck and helpless ?   Are they palsied
    or asleep ?

Now ! the walls they 're almost under ! scarce a rod
    the foes asunder !
Not a firelock flashed against them ! up the earthwork
    they will swarm !
But the words have scarce been spoken when the
    ominous calm is broken,
And a bellowing crash has emptied all the vengeance
    of the storm !   100

So again, with murderous slaughter, pelted backwards
    to the water,
Fly Pigot's running heroes and the frightened braves
    of Howe;

102. The generals on the British side were Howe, Clinton,
and Pigot.

And we shout, " At last they 're done for, it 's their
    barges they have run for :
They are beaten, beaten, beaten ; and the battle 's over
    now ! "

And we looked, poor timid creatures, on the rough
    old soldier's features,   105
Our lips afraid to question, but he knew what we
    would ask :
" Not sure," he said ; " keep quiet, — once more, I
    guess, they 'll try it —
Here 's damnation to the cut-throats ! " —— then he
    handed me his flask,

Saying, " Gal, you 're looking shaky ; have a drop of
    Old Jamaiky ;
I 'm afeard there 'll be more trouble afore the job is
    done ; "   110
So I took one scorching swallow ; dreadful faint I felt
    and hollow,
Standing there from early morning when the firing
    was begun.

All through those hours of trial I had watched a calm
    clock dial,
As the hands kept creeping, creeping, — they were
    creeping round to four,
When the old man said, " They 're forming with their
    bagonets fixed for storming :   115
It 's the death-grip that 's a coming, — they will try
    the works once more."

With brazen trumpets blaring, the flames behind them
    glaring,

The deadly wall before them, in close array they
    come ;
Still onward, upward toiling, like a dragon's fold un-
    coiling, —
Like the rattlesnake's shrill warning the reverberating
    drum !   120

Over heaps all torn and gory — shall I tell the fearful
    story,
How they surged above the breastwork, as a sea
    breaks over a deck ;
How, driven, yet scarce defeated, our worn-out men
    retreated,
With their powder-horns all emptied, like the swim-
    mers from a wreck ?

It has all been told and painted ; as for me, they say
    I fainted,   125
And the wooden-legged old Corporal stumped with
    me down the stair :
When I woke from dreams affrighted the evening
    lamps were lighted, —
On the floor a youth was lying ; his bleeding breast
    was bare.

And I heard through all the flurry, " Send for WAR-
    REN ! hurry ! hurry !
Tell him here 's a soldier bleeding, and he 'll come
    and dress his wound ! "   130
Ah, we knew not till the morrow told its tale of death
    and sorrow,

129. Dr. Joseph Warren, of equal note at the time as a medi-
cal man and a patriot. He was a volunteer in the battle, and
fell there, the most serious loss on the American side.

How the starlight found him stiffened on the dark
    and bloody ground.

Who the youth was, what his name was, where the
    place from which he came was,
Who had brought him from the battle, and had left
    him at our door,
He could not speak to tell us; but 't was one of our
    brave fellows,   135
As the homespun plainly showed us which the dying
    soldier wore.

For they all thought he was dying, as they gathered
    round him crying, —
And they said, " Oh, how they 'll miss him ! " and,
    " What *will* his mother do ? "
Then, his eyelids just unclosing like a child's that has
    been dozing,
He faintly murmured, " Mother ! " —— and — I saw
    his eyes were blue.   140

— " Why grandma, how you 're winking ! " — Ah, my
    child, it sets me thinking
Of a story not like this one.   Well, he somehow lived
    along ;
So we came to know each other, and I nursed him like
    a — mother,
Till at last he stood before me, tall, and rosy-cheeked,
    and strong.

And we sometimes walked together in the pleasant
    summer weather ;   145
— " Please to tell us what his name was ? " — Just
    your own, my little dear,

There 's his picture Copley painted: we became so
    well acquainted,
That, — in short, that 's why I 'm grandma, and you
    children are all here!

•

THE PLOUGHMAN.

ANNIVERSARY OF THE BERKSHIRE AGRICULTURAL
SOCIETY, OCTOBER 4, 1849.

CLEAR the brown path, to meet his coulter's gleam!
Lo! on he comes, behind his smoking team,
With toil's bright dew-drops on his sunburnt brow,
The lord of earth, the hero of the plough!

First in the field before the reddening sun,   5
Last in the shadows when the day is done,
Line after line, along the bursting sod,
Marks the broad acres where his feet have trod;
Still where he treads, the stubborn clods divide,
The smooth, fresh furrow opens deep and wide;   10
Matted and dense the tangled turf upheaves,
Mellow and dark the ridgy cornfield cleaves;
Up the steep hillside, where the laboring train
Slants the long track that scores the level plain;
Through the moist valley, clogged with oozing clay,   15
The patient convoy breaks its destined way;
At every turn the loosening chains resound,

147. John Singleton Copley was a portrait painter of cele-
brity, who was born in America in 1737, and painted many
famous portraits, which hang in private and public galleries in
Boston and vicinity chiefly. He lived in England the latter half
of his life, dying there in 1815.

The swinging ploughshare circles glistening round,
Till the wide field one billowy waste appears,
And wearied hands unbind the panting steers.   20

These are the hands whose sturdy labor brings
The peasant's food, the golden pomp of kings;
This is the page whose letters shall be seen
Changed by the sun to words of living green;
This is the scholar whose immortal pen   25
Spells the first lesson hunger taught to men;
These are the lines which heaven-commanded Toil
Shows on his deed, — the charter of the soil!

O gracious Mother, whose benignant breast
Wakes us to life, and lulls us all to rest,   30
How thy sweet features, kind to every clime,
Mock with their smile the wrinkled front of time!
We stain thy flowers,—they blossom o'er the dead;
We rend thy bosom, and it gives us bread;
O'er the red field that trampling strife has torn,   35
Waves the green plumage of thy tasselled corn;
Our maddening conflicts scar thy fairest plain,
Still thy soft answer is the growing grain.
Yet, O our Mother, while uncounted charms
Steal round our hearts in thine embracing arms   40
Let not our virtues in thy love decay,
And thy fond sweetness waste our strength away.

No! by these hills, whose banners now displayed
In blazing cohorts Autumn has arrayed;
By yon twin summits, on whose splintery crests   45
The tossing hemlocks hold the eagles' nests;
By these fair plains the mountain circle screens,
`And feeds with streamlets from its dark ravines, —

True to their home, these faithful arms shall toil
To crown with peace their own untainted soil;   50
And, true to God, to freedom, to mankind,
If her chained bandogs Faction shall unbind,
These stately forms, that bending even now
Bowed their strong manhood to the humble plough,
Shall rise erect, the guardians of the land,   55
The same stern iron in the same right hand,
Till o'er the hills the shouts of triumph run,
The sword has rescued what the ploughshare won!

THE CHAMBERED NAUTILUS.

THIS is the ship of pearl, which, poets feign,
    Sails the unshadowed main, —
    The venturous bark that flings
On the sweet summer wind its purpled wings
In gulfs enchanted, where the Siren sings,   5
    And coral reefs lie bare,
Where the cold sea-maids rise to sun their streaming
    hair.

Its webs of living gauze no more unfurl;
    Wrecked is the ship of pearl!
    And every chambered cell,   10
Where its dim dreaming life was wont to dwell,
As the frail tenant shaped his growing shell,
    Before thee lies revealed, —
Its irised ceiling rent, its sunless crypt unsealed!

Year after year beheld the silent toil   15
    That spread his lustrous coil;
    Still, as the spiral grew,

He left the past year's dwelling for the new,
Stole with soft step its shining archway through,
    Built up its idle door,   20
Stretched in his last-found home, and knew the old no
    more.

Thanks for the heavenly message brought by thee,
    Child of the wandering sea,
    Cast from her lap, forlorn !
From thy dead lips a clearer note is born   25
Than ever Triton blew from wreathèd horn !
    While on my ear it rings,
Through the deep caves of thought I hear a voice that
    sings : —

Build thee more stately mansions, O my soul,
    As the swift seasons roll !   30
    Leave thy low-vaulted past !
Let each new temple, nobler than the last,
Shut thee from heaven with a dome more vast,
    Till thou at length art free,
Leaving thine outgrown shell by life's unresting
    sea !   35

THE IRON GATE.

READ AT THE BREAKFAST GIVEN IN HONOR OF DR. HOLMES'S
SEVENTIETH BIRTHDAY BY THE PUBLISHERS OF THE ATLAN-
TIC MONTHLY, BOSTON, DECEMBER 3, 1879.

WHERE is this patriarch you are kindly greeting ?
    Not unfamiliar to my ear his name,
Nor yet unknown to many a joyous meeting
    In days long vanished,—is he still the same,

Or changed by years, forgotten, and forgetting,   5
  Dull-eared, dim-sighted, slow of speech and thought,
Still o'er the sad, degenerate present fretting,
  Where all goes wrong, and nothing as it ought?

Old age, the graybeard!   Well, indeed, I know him,
  Shrunk, tottering, bent, of aches and ills the prey;   10
In sermon, story, fable, picture, poem,
  Oft have I met him from my earliest day :

In my old Æsop, toiling with his bundle, —
  His load of sticks, — politely asking Death
Who comes when called for, — would he lug or trun-
    dle   15
  His fagot for him? — he was scant of breath.

And sad " Ecclesiastes, or the Preacher," —
  Has he not stamped the image on my soul,
In that last chapter, where the worn-out Teacher
  Sighs o'er the loosened cord, the broken bowl?   20

Yes, long, indeed, I 've known him at a distance,
  And now my lifted door-latch shows him here;
I take his shrivelled hand without resistance,
  And find him smiling as his step draws near.

What though of gilded baubles he bereaves us,   25
  Dear to the heart of youth, to manhood's prime;
Think of the calm he brings, the wealth he leaves us,
  The hoarded spoils, the legacies of time!

Altars once flaming, still with incense fragrant,
  Passion's uneasy nurslings rocked asleep,   30
Hope's anchor faster, wild desire less vagrant,
  Life's flow less noisy, but the stream how deep!

Still as the silver cord gets worn and slender,
  Its lightened task-work tugs with lessening strain,
Hands yet more helpful, voices grown more tender, 35
  Soothe with their softened tones the slumberous
    brain.

Youth longs and manhood strives, but age remembers,
  Sits by the raked-up ashes of the past,
Spreads its thin hands above the whitening embers
  That warm its creeping life-blood till the last. 40

Dear to its heart is every loving token
  That comes unbidden ere its pulse grows cold,
Ere the last lingering ties of life are broken,
  Its labors ended and its story told.

Ah, while around us rosy youth rejoices, 45
  For us the sorrow-laden breezes sigh,
And through the chorus of its jocund voices
  Throbs the sharp note of misery's hopeless cry.

As on the gauzy wings of fancy flying
  From some far orb I track our watery sphere, 50
Home of the struggling, suffering, doubting, dying,
  The silvered globule seems a glistening tear.

But Nature lends her mirror of illusion
  To win from saddening scenes our age-dimmed eyes,
And misty day-dreams blend in sweet confusion 55
  The wintry landscape and the summer skies.

So when the iron portal shuts behind us,
  And life forgets us in its noise and whirl,
Visions that shunned the glaring noon-day find us,
  And glimmering starlight shows the gates of pearl. 60

— I come not here your morning hour to sadden,
  A limping pilgrim, leaning on his staff, —
I, who have never deemed it sin to gladden
  This vale of sorrow with a wholesome laugh.

If word of mine another's gloom has brightened,   65
  Through my dumb lips the heaven-sent message
      came ;
If hand of mine another's task has lightened,
  It felt the guidance that it dares not claim.

But, O my gentle sisters, O my brothers,
  These thick-sown snow-flakes hint of toil's release ; 70
These feebler pulses bid me leave to others
  The tasks once welcome ; evening asks for peace.

Time claims his tribute ; silence now is golden ;
  Let me not vex the too long suffering lyre ;
Though to your love untiring still beholden,   75
  The curfew tells me — cover up the fire.

And now with grateful smile and accents cheerful,
  And warmer heart than look or word can tell,
In simplest phrase — these traitorous eyes are tear-
      ful —
  Thanks, Brothers, Sisters — Children — and fare-
      well !   80

NATHANIEL HAWTHORNE.

BIOGRAPHICAL SKETCH.

IT was Hawthorne's wont to keep note-books, in which he recorded his observations and reflections; sometimes he spoke in them of himself, his plans, and his prospects. He began the practice early, and continued it through life; and after his death selections from these note-books were published in six volumes, under the titles: *Passages from the American Note-Books of Nathaniel Hawthorne, Passages from the English Note-Books of Nathaniel Hawthorne,* and *Passages from the French and Italian Note-Books of Nathaniel Hawthorne.* In these books, and in prefaces which appear in the front of the volumes containing his collected stories, one finds many frank expressions of the interest which Hawthorne took in his work, and the author appeals very ingenuously to the reader, speaking with an almost confidential closeness of his stories and sketches. Then the *Note-Books* contain the unwrought material of the books which the writer put out in his lifetime. One finds there the suggestions of stories, and frequently pages of observation and reflection, which were afterward transferred, almost as they stood, into the author's works. It is very interesting labor to trace Hawthorne's stories and sketches back to these records in his note-books, and to compare the finished work with the rough material. It seems, also, as if each reader was admitted into the privacy of the author's mind. That is the first impression, but a closer study reveals two facts very clearly.   One is stated by Hawthorne himself in his preface to *The Snow-Image and other Twice-Told Tales:* "I have been especially careful [in my Introductions] to make no disclosures respecting myself which the most indifferent observer might not have been acquainted with, and which I was not perfectly willing that my worst enemy should know. . . . I have taken facts which relate to myself [when telling stories] because they chance to be nearest at hand, and likewise are my own property.   And, as for egotism, a person who has been burrowing, to his utmost ability, into the depths of our common nature for the purposes of psychological romance — and who pursues his researches in that dusky region, as he needs must, as well by the tact of sympathy as by the light of observation — will smile at incurring such an imputation in virtue of a little preliminary talk about his external habits, his abode, his casual associates, and other matters entirely upon the surface.   These things hide the man instead of displaying him. You must make quite another kind of inquest, and look through the whole range of his fictitious characters, good and evil, in order to detect any of his essential traits."

There has rarely been a writer of fiction, then, whose personality has been so absolutely separate from that of each character created by him, and at the same time has so intimately penetrated the whole body of his writing.   Of no one of his characters, male or female, is one ever tempted to say, This is Hawthorne, except in the case of Miles Coverdale in *The Blithedale Romance,* where the circumstances of the story tempt one into an identification; yet all Hawthorne's work is stamped emphatically with his mark. Hawthorne wrote it, is very simple and easy to say of all but the merest trifle in his collected works; but the world has yet to learn who Hawthorne was, and even if he had not forbidden a biography of himself, it is scarcely likely that any Life could have disclosed more than he has chosen himself to reveal.

The advantage of this is that it leaves the student free to concentrate his attention upon the writings rather than on the man. Hawthorne, in the passage quoted above, speaks of himself as one " who has been burrowing, to his utmost ability, into the depths of our common nature for the purposes of psychological romance ; " and this states, as closely as so short a sentence can, the controlling purpose and end of the author. The vitality of Hawthorne's characters is derived but little from any external description ; it resides in the truthfulness with which they respond to some permanent and controlling operation of the human soul. Looking into his own heart, and always, when studying others, in search of fundamental rather than occasional motives, he proceeded to develop these motives in conduct and life. Hence he had a leaning toward the allegory, where human figures are merely masks for spiritual activities, and sometimes he employed the simple allegory, as in *The Celestial Railroad*. More often in his short stories he has a spiritual truth to illustrate, and uses the simplest, most direct means, taking no pains to conceal his purpose, yet touching his characters quietly or playfully with human sensibilities, and investing them with just so much real life as answers the purpose of the story. This is exquisitely done in *The Snow-Image*. The consequence of this "burrowing into the depths of our common nature " has been to bring much of the darker and concealed life into the movement of his stories. The fact of evil is the terrible fact of life, and its workings in the human soul had more interest for Hawthorne than the obvious physical manifestations. Since his observations are less of the men and women whom everybody sees and recognizes than of the. souls which are hidden from most eyes, it is not strange that his stories should often lay bare secrets of sin, and that a somewhat dusky light should seem to be the atmosphere of much of his work. Now and then, especially when dealing with childhood, a warm, sunny glow spreads over the pages of his books ; but the reader must be prepared for the most part to read stories which lie in the shadow of life.

There was one class of subjects which had a peculiar interest for Hawthorne, and in a measure affected his work. He had a strong taste for New England history, and he found in the scenes and characters of that history favorable material for the representation of spiritual conflict. He was himself the most New English of New Englanders, and held an extraordinary sympathy with the very soil of his section of the country. By this sympathy, rather than by any painful research, he was singularly acquainted with the historic life of New England. His stories, based directly on historic facts, are true to the spirit of the times in something more than an archæological way. One is astonished at the ease with which he seized upon characteristic features, and reproduced them in a word or phrase. Merely careful and diligent research would never be adequate to give the life-likeness of the images in *Howe's Masquerade.*

There is, then, a second fact discovered by a study of Hawthorne, that while one finds in the *Note-Books*, for example, the material out of which stories and sketches seem to have been constructed, and while the facts of New England history have been used without exaggeration or distortion, the result in stories and romances is something far beyond a mere report of what has been seen and read. The charm of a vivifying imagination is the crowning charm of Hawthorne's stories, and its medium is a graceful and often exquisitely apt diction. Hawthorne's sense of touch as a writer is very fine. He knows when to be light, and when to press heavily; a very conspicuous quality is what one is likely to term quaintness, — a gentle pleasantry which seems to spring from the author's attitude toward his own work, as if he looked upon that, too, as a part of the spiritual universe which he was surveying.

Hawthorne spent much of his life silently, and there are touching passages in his note-books regarding his sense of loneliness and his wish for recognition from the world. His early writings were short stories, sketches, and biographies, scattered in magazines and brought together into *Twice-Told Tales*, in two volumes, published, the first in 1837, the second in 1842 ; *Mosses from an Old Manse*, in 1846 ; *The Snow-Image and other Twice-Told Tales*, in 1851. They had a limited circle of readers. Some recognized his genius, but it was not until the publication of *The Scarlet Letter*, in 1850, that Hawthorne's name was fairly before the world as a great and original writer of romance. *The House of the Seven Gables* followed in 1851 ; *The Blithedale Romance* in 1852. He spent the years 1853–1860 in Europe, and the immediate result of his life there is in *Our Old Home : A Series of English Sketches*, published in 1863 and *The Marble Faun, or the Romance of Monte Beni*, in 1860. For young people he wrote *Grandfather's Chair*, a collection of stories from New England history, *The Wonder-Book* and *Tanglewood Tales*, containing stories out of classic mythology. There are a few other scattered writings which have been collected into volumes and published in the complete series of his works.

Hawthorne was born July 4, 1804, and died May 19, 1864.

The student of Hawthorne will find in G. P. Lathrop's *A Study of Hawthorne*, and Henry James, Jr.'s *Hawthorne*, in the series *English Men of Letters*, material which will assist him. Dr. Holmes published, shortly after Hawthorne's death, a paper of reminiscences which is included in *Soundings from the Atlantic ;* and Longfellow welcomed *Twice-Told Tales* with a glowing article in the *North American Review*, xlviii. 59, which is reproduced in his prose works. The reader will find it an agreeable task to discover what the poets, Longfellow, Lowell, Stedman, and others, have said of this man of genius.

ONE afternoon, when the sun was going down, a mother and her little boy sat at the door of their cottage, talking about the Great Stone Face. They had but to lift their eyes, and there it was plainly to be seen, though miles away, with the sunshine brightening all its features.

And what was the Great Stone Face?

Embosomed amongst a family of lofty mountains there was a valley so spacious that it contained many thousand inhabitants. Some of these good people dwelt in log huts, with the black forest all around them, on the steep and difficult hillsides. Others had their homes in comfortable farm-houses, and cultivated the rich soil on the gentle slopes or level surfaces of the valley. Others, again, were congregated into populous villages, where some wild, highland rivulet, tumbling down from its birthplace in the upper mountain region, had been caught and tamed by human cunning and compelled to turn the machinery of cotton-factories. The inhabitants of this valley, in short, were numerous, and of many modes of life. But all of them, grown people and children, had a kind of familiarity with the Great Stone Face, although some possessed the gift of distinguishing this grand natural phenomenon more perfectly than many of their neighbors.

The Great Stone Face, then, was a work of Nature

in her mood of majestic playfulness, formed on the perpendicular side of a mountain by some immense rocks, which had been thrown together in such a position as, when viewed at a proper distance, precisely to resemble the features of the human countenance. It seemed as if an enormous giant, or a Titan, had sculptured his own likeness on the precipice. There was the broad arch of the forehead, a hundred feet in height; the nose, with its long bridge; and the vast lips, which, if they could have spoken, would have rolled their thunder accents from one end of the valley to the other. True it is, that if the spectator approached too near he lost the outline of the gigantic visage, and could discern only a heap of ponderous and gigantic rocks, piled in chaotic ruin one upon another. Retracing his steps, however, the wondrous features would again be seen; and the farther he withdrew from them, the more like a human face, with all its original divinity intact, did they appear; until, as it grew dim in the distance, with the clouds and glorified vapor of the mountains clustering about it, the Great Stone Face seemed positively to be alive.

It was a happy lot for children to grow up to manhood or womanhood with the Great Stone Face before their eyes, for all the features were noble, and the expression was at once grand and sweet, as if it were the glow of a vast, warm heart, that embraced all mankind in its affections, and had room for more. It was an education only to look at it. According to the belief of many people, the valley owed much of its fertility to this benign aspect that was continually beaming over it, illuminating the clouds, and infusing its tenderness into the sunshine.

As we began with saying, a mother and her little

boy sat at their cottage-door, gazing at the Great Stone Face, and talking about it. The child's name was Ernest.

"Mother," said he, while the Titanic visage smiled on him, "I wish that it could speak, for it looks so very kindly that its voice must needs be pleasant. If I were to see a man with such a face, I should love him dearly."

"If an old prophecy should come to pass," answered his mother, "we may see a man, some time or other, with exactly such a face as that."

"What prophecy do you mean, dear mother?" eagerly inquired Ernest. "Pray tell me all about it!"

So his mother told him a story that her own mother had told to her, when she herself was younger than little Ernest; a story, not of things that were past, but of what was yet to come; a story, nevertheless, so very old, that even the Indians, who formerly inhabited this valley, had heard it from their forefathers, to whom, as they affirmed, it had been murmured by the mountain streams, and whispered by the wind among the tree-tops. The purport was, that, at some future day, a child should be born hereabouts, who was destined to become the greatest and noblest personage of his time, and whose countenance, in manhood, should bear an exact resemblance to the Great Stone Face. Not a few old-fashioned people, and young ones likewise, in the ardor of their hopes, still cherished an enduring faith in this old prophecy. But others, who had seen more of the world, had watched and waited till they were weary, and had beheld no man with such a face, nor any man that proved to be much greater or nobler than his neighbors, concluded it to be nothing but an idle tale. At all events, the great man of the prophecy had not yet appeared.

" O mother, dear mother!" cried Ernest, clapping his hands above his head, " I do hope that I shall live to see him!"

His mother was an affectionate and thoughtful woman, and felt that it was wisest not to discourage the generous hopes of her little boy. So she only said to him, " Perhaps you may."

And Ernest never forgot the story that his mother told him. It was always in his mind, whenever he looked upon the Great Stone Face. He spent his childhood in the log cottage where he was born, and was dutiful to his mother, and helpful to her in many things, assisting her much with his little hands, and more with his loving heart. In this manner, from a happy yet often pensive child, he grew up to be a mild, quiet, unobtrusive boy, and sun-browned with labor in the fields, but with more intelligence brightening his aspect than is seen in many lads who have been taught at famous schools. Yet Ernest had had no teacher, save only that the Great Stone Face became one to him. When the toil of the day was over, he would gaze at it for hours, until he began to imagine that those vast features recognized him, and gave him a smile of kindness and encouragement, responsive to his own look of veneration. We must not take upon us to affirm that this was a mistake, although the face may have looked no more kindly at Ernest than at all the world besides. But the secret was, that the boy's tender and confiding simplicity discerned what other people could not see ; and thus the love, which was meant for all, became his peculiar portion.

About this time there went a rumor throughout the valley, that the great man, foretold from ages long ago, who was to bear a resemblance to the Great Stone Face, had appeared at last. It seems that, many years before, a young man had migrated from the valley and settled at a distant seaport, where, after getting together a little money, he had set up as a shopkeeper. His name — but I could never learn whether it was his real one, or a nickname that had grown out of his habits and success in life — was Gathergold. Being shrewd and active, and endowed by Providence with that inscrutable faculty which develops itself in what the world calls luck, he became an exceedingly rich merchant, and owner of a whole fleet of bulky-bottomed ships. All the countries of the globe appeared to join hands for the mere purpose of adding heap after heap to the mountainous accumulation of this one man's wealth. The cold regions of the north, almost within the gloom and shadow of the Arctic Circle, sent him their tribute in the shape of furs; hot Africa sifted for him the golden sands of her rivers, and gathered up the ivory tusks of her great elephants out of the forests; the East came bringing him the rich shawls, and spices, and teas, and the effulgence of diamonds, and the gleaming purity of large pearls. The ocean, not to be behind-hand with the earth, yielded up her mighty whales, that Mr. Gathergold might sell their oil, and make a profit on it. Be the original commodity what it might, it was gold within his grasp. It might be said of him, as of Midas in the fable, that whatever he touched with his finger immediately glistened, and grew yellow, and was changed at once into sterling metal, or, which suited him still better, into piles of coin. And, when Mr. Gathergold had become so very rich that it would have taken him a hundred years only to count his wealth, he bethought himself of his native valley, and resolved to go back thither, and end his days where he was born. With this purpose in view, he sent a skilful architect to build him such a palace as should be fit for a man of his vast wealth to live in.

As I have said above, it had already been rumored in the valley that Mr. Gathergold had turned out to be the prophetic personage so long and vainly looked for, and that his visage was the perfect and undeniable similitude of the Great Stone Face. People were the more ready to believe that this must needs be the fact, when they beheld the splendid edifice that rose, as if by enchantment, on the site of his father's old weather-beaten farmhouse. The exterior was of marble, so dazzlingly white that it seemed as though the whole structure might melt away in the sunshine, like those humbler ones which Mr. Gathergold, in his young play-days, before his fingers were gifted with the touch of transmutation, had been accustomed to build of snow. It had a richly ornamented portico, supported by tall pillars, beneath which was a lofty door, studded with silver knobs, and made of a kind of variegated wood that had been brought from beyond the sea. The windows, from the floor to the ceiling of each stately apartment, were composed, respectively, of but one enormous pane of glass, so transparently pure that it was said to be a finer medium than even the vacant atmosphere. Hardly anybody had been permitted to see the interior of this palace ; but it was reported, and with good semblance of truth, to be far more gorgeous than the outside, insomuch that whatever was iron or brass in other houses was silver or gold in this; and Mr. Gathergold's bedchamber, especially, made such a glittering appearance that no ordinary man would have been able to close his eyes there. But, on the other hand, Mr. Gathergold was now so inured to wealth, that perhaps he could not have closed his eyes unless where the gleam of it was certain to find its way beneath his eyelids.

In due time, the mansion was finished; next came the upholsterers, with magnificent furniture; then a whole troop of black and white servants, the harbingers of Mr. Gathergold, who, in his own majestic person, was expected to arrive at sunset. Our friend Ernest, meanwhile, had been deeply stirred by the idea that the great man, the noble man, the man of prophecy, after so many ages of delay, was at length to be made manifest to his native valley. He knew, boy as he was, that there were a thousand ways in which Mr. Gathergold, with his vast wealth, might transform himself into an angel of beneficence, and assume a control over human affairs as wide and benignant as the smile of the Great Stone Face. Full of faith and hope, Ernest doubted not that what the people said was true, and that now he was to behold the living likeness of those wondrous features on the mountain-side. While the boy was still gazing up the valley, and fancying, as he always did, that the Great Stone Face returned his gaze and looked kindly at him, the rumbling of wheels was heard, approaching swiftly along the winding road.

"Here he comes!" cried a group of people who were assembled to witness the arrival. "Here comes the great Mr. Gathergold!"

A carriage drawn by four horses dashed round the

turn of the road. Within it, thrust partly out of the window, appeared the physiognomy of a little old man, with a skin as yellow as if his own Midas-hand had transmuted it. He had a low forehead, small, sharp eyes, puckered about with innumerable wrinkles, and very thin lips, which he made still thinner by pressing them forcibly together.

"The very image of the Great Stone Face!" shouted the people. "Sure enough, the old prophecy is true; and here we have the great man come, at last!"

And, what greatly perplexed Ernest, they seemed actually to believe that here was the likeness which they spoke of. By the roadside there chanced to be an old beggar-woman and two little beggar-children, stragglers from some far-off region, who, as the carriage rolled onward, held out their hands and lifted up their doleful voices, most piteously beseeching charity. A yellow claw — the very same that had clawed together so much wealth — poked itself out of the coach-window, and dropped some copper coins upon the ground; so that, though the great man's name seems to have been Gathergold, he might just as suitably have been nicknamed Scattercopper. Still, nevertheless, with an earnest shout, and evidently with as much good faith as ever, the people bellowed, —

"He is the very image of the Great Stone Face!"

But Ernest turned sadly from the wrinkled shrewdness of that sordid visage, and gazed up the valley, where, amid a gathering mist, gilded by the last sunbeams, he could still distinguish those glorious features which had impressed themselves into his soul. Their aspect cheered him. What did the benign lips seem to say?

" He will come ! Fear not, Ernest ; the man will come ! "

The years went on, and Ernest ceased to be a boy. He had grown to be a young man now. He attracted little notice from the other inhabitants of the valley ; for they saw nothing remarkable in his way of life, save that, when the labor of the day was over, he still loved to go apart and gaze and meditate upon the Great Stone Face. According to their idea of the matter, it was a folly, indeed, but pardonable, inasmuch as Ernest was industrious, kind, and neighborly, and neglected no duty for the sake of indulging this idle habit. They knew not that the Great Stone Face had become a teacher to him, and that the sentiment which was expressed in it would enlarge the young man's heart, and fill it with wider and deeper sympathies than other hearts. They knew not that thence would come a better wisdom than could be learned from books, and a better life than could be moulded on the defaced example of other human lives. Neither did Ernest know that the thoughts and affections which came to him so naturally, in the fields and at the fireside, and wherever he communed with himself, were of a higher tone than those which all men shared with him. A simple soul, — simple as when his mother first taught him the old prophecy, — he beheld the marvellous features beaming adown the valley, and still wondered that their human counterpart was so long in making his appearance.

By this time poor Mr. Gathergold was dead and buried ; and the oddest part of the matter was, that his wealth, which was the body and spirit of his existence, had disappeared before his death, leaving nothing of him but a living skeleton, covered over

with a wrinkled, yellow skin. Since the melting away
of his gold, it had been very generally conceded that
there was no such striking resemblance, after all, be-
twixt the ignoble features of the ruined merchant and
that majestic face upon the mountain-side. So the
people ceased to honor him during his lifetime, and
quietly consigned him to forgetfulness after his de-
cease. Once in a while, it is true, his memory was
brought up in connection with the magnificent palace
which he had built, and which had long ago been
turned into a hotel for the accommodation of stran-
gers, multitudes of whom came every summer to visit
that famous natural curiosity, the Great Stone Face.
Thus, Mr. Gathergold being discredited and thrown
into the shade, the man of prophecy was yet to come.

It so happened that a native-born son of the val-
ley, many years before, had enlisted as a soldier, and,
after a great deal of hard fighting, had now become an
illustrious commander. Whatever he may be called
in history, he was known in camps and on the battle-
field under the nickname of Old Blood-and-Thunder.
This war-worn veteran, being now infirm with age and
wounds, and weary of the turmoil of a military life,
and of the roll of the drum and the clangor of the
trumpet, that had so long been ringing in his ears,
had lately signified a purpose of returning to his
native valley, hoping to find repose where he remem-
bered to have left it. The inhabitants, his old neigh-
bors and their grown-up children, were resolved to
welcome the renowned warrior with a salute of can-
non and a public dinner ; and all the more enthusias-
tically, it being affirmed that now, at last, the likeness
of the Great Stone Face had actually appeared. An
aide-de-camp of Old Blood-and-Thunder, travelling

through the valley, was said to have been struck with
the resemblance. Moreover the schoolmates and
early acquaintances of the general were ready to testify,
on oath, that to the best of their recollection, the
aforesaid general had been exceedingly like the majes-
tic image, even when a boy, only that the idea had
never occurred to them at that period. Great, there-
fore, was the excitement throughout the valley ; and
many people, who had never once thought of glancing
at the Great Stone Face for years before, now spent
their time in gazing at it, for the sake of knowing
exactly how General Blood-and-Thunder looked.

On the day of the great festival, Ernest, with all
the other people of the valley, left their work, and
proceeded to the spot where the sylvan banquet was
prepared. As he approached, the loud voice of the
Rev. Dr. Battleblast was heard, beseeching a blessing
on the good things set before them, and on the dis-
tinguished friend of peace in whose honor they were
assembled. The tables were arranged in a cleared
space of the woods, shut in by the surrounding trees,
except where a vista opened eastward, and afforded
a distant view of the Great Stone Face. Over the
general's chair, which was a relic from the home of
Washington, there was an arch of verdant boughs,
with the laurel profusely intermixed, and surmounted
by his country's banner, beneath which he had won
his victories. Our friend Ernest raised himself on
his tip-toes, in hopes to get a glimpse of the celebrated
guest ; but there was a mighty crowd about the tables
anxious to hear the toasts and speeches, and to catch
any word that might fall from the general in reply ;
and a volunteer company, doing duty as a guard,
pricked ruthlessly with their bayonets at any particu-

larly quiet person among the throng. So Ernest, being of an unobtrusive character, was thrust quite into the background, where he could see no more of Old Blood-and-Thunder's physiognomy than if it had been still blazing on the battle-field. To console himself, he turned towards the Great Stone Face, which, like a faithful and long-remembered friend, looked back and smiled upon him through the vista of the forest. Meantime, however, he could overhear the remarks of various individuals, who were comparing the features of the hero with the face on the distant mountain-side.

" 'T is the same face, to a hair!" cried one man, cutting a caper for joy.

" Wonderfully like, that's a fact!" responded another.

" Like! why, I call it Old Blood-and-Thunder himself in a monstrous looking-glass!" cried a third. " And why not? He's the greatest man of this or any other age, beyond a doubt."

And then all three of the speakers gave a great shout, which communicated electricity to the crowd, and called forth a roar from a thousand voices, that went reverberating for miles among the mountains, until you might have supposed that the Great Stone Face had poured its thunder-breath into the cry. All these comments, and this vast enthusiasm, served the more to interest our friend; nor did he think of questioning that now, at length, the mountain-visage had found its human counterpart. It is true, Ernest had imagined that this long-looked-for personage would appear in the character of a man of peace, uttering wisdom, and doing good, and making people happy. But, taking an habitual breadth of view, with all his

simplicity, he contended that Providence should choose
its own method of blessing mankind, and could con-
ceive that this great end might be effected even by a
warrior and a bloody sword, should inscrutable wis-
dom see fit to order matters so.

"The general! the general!" was now the cry.
"Hush! silence! Old Blood-and-Thunder's going
to make a speech."

Even so; for, the cloth being removed, the general's
health had been drunk amid shouts of applause, and
he now stood upon his feet to thank the company.
Ernest saw him. There he was, over the shoulders
of the crowd, from the two glittering epaulets and
embroidered collar upward, beneath the arch of green
boughs with intertwined laurel, and the banner droop-
ing as if to shade his brow! And there, too, visible
in the same glance, through the vista of the forest,
appeared the Great Stone Face! And was there, in-
deed, such a resemblance as the crowd had testified?
Alas, Ernest could not recognize it. He beheld a
war-worn and weather-beaten countenance, full of en-
ergy, and expressive of an iron will; but the gentle
wisdom, the deep, broad, tender sympathies, were al-
together wanting in Old Blood-and-Thunder's visage;
and even if the Great Stone Face had assumed his
look of stern command, the milder traits would still
have tempered it.

"This is not the man of prophecy," sighed Ernest
to himself, as he made his way out of the throng.
"And must the world wait longer yet?"

The mists had congregated about the distant moun-
tain-side, and there were seen the grand and awful
features of the Great Stone Face, awful but benignant,
as if a mighty angel were sitting among the hills and

enrobing himself in a cloud-vesture of gold and pur-
ple. As he looked, Ernest could hardly believe but
that a smile beamed over the whole visage, with a
radiance still brightening, although without motion of
the lips. It was probably the effect of the western
sunshine, melting through the thinly diffused vapors
that had swept between him and the object that he
gazed at. But — as it always did — the aspect of his
marvellous friend made Ernest as hopeful as if he
had never hoped in vain.

" Fear not, Ernest," said his heart, even as if the
Great Face were whispering him, — " fear not, Ernest;
he will come."

More years sped swiftly and tranquilly away.
Ernest still dwelt in his native valley, and was now
a man of middle age. By imperceptible degrees, he
had become known among the people. Now, as here-
tofore, he labored for his bread, and was the same
simple-hearted man that he had always been. But he
had thought and felt so much, he had given so many
of the best hours of his life to unworldly hopes for
some great good to mankind, that it seemed as though
he had been talking with the angels, and had imbibed
a portion of their wisdom unawares. It was visible
in the calm and well-considered beneficence of his
daily life, the quiet stream of which had made a wide
green margin all along its course. Not a day passed
by that the world was not the better because this man,
humble as he was, had lived. He never stepped aside
from his own path, yet would always reach a blessing
to his neighbor. Almost involuntarily, too, he had
become a preacher. The pure and high simplicity of
his thought, which, as one of its manifestations, took
shape in the good deeds that dropped silently from his

hand, flowed also forth in speech. He uttered truths that wrought upon and moulded the lives of those who heard him. His auditors, it may be, never suspected that Ernest, their own neighbor and familiar friend, was more than an ordinary man; least of all did Ernest himself suspect it; but, inevitably as the murmur of a rivulet, came thoughts out of his mouth that no other human lips had spoken.

When the people's minds had had a little time to cool, they were ready enough to acknowledge their mistake in imagining a similarity between General Blood-and-Thunder's truculent physiognomy and the benign visage on the mountain-side. But now, again, there were reports and many paragraphs in the newspapers, affirming that the likeness of the Great Stone Face had appeared upon the broad shoulders of a certain eminent statesman. He, like Mr. Gathergold and Old Blood-and-Thunder, was a native of the valley, but had left it in his early days, and taken up the trades of law and politics. Instead of the rich man's wealth and the warrior's sword, he had but a tongue, and it was mightier than both together. So wonderfully eloquent was he, that whatever he might choose to say, his auditors had no choice but to believe him; wrong looked like right, and right like wrong; for when it pleased him he could make a kind of illuminated fog with his mere breath, and obscure the natural daylight with it. His tongue, indeed, was a magic instrument; sometimes it rumbled like the thunder; sometimes it warbled like the sweetest music. It was the blast of war, — the song of peace; and it seemed to have a heart in it, when there was no such matter. In good truth, he was a wondrous man; and when his tongue had acquired him all other im-

aginable success, — when it had been heard in halls
of state, and in the courts of princes and potentates, —
after it had made him known all over the world, even
as a voice crying from shore to shore, — it finally per-
suaded his countrymen to select him for the Presi-
dency. Before this time, — indeed, as soon as he be-
gan to grow celebrated, — his admirers had found out
the resemblance between him and the Great Stone
Face; and so much were they struck by it that through-
out the country this distinguished gentleman was
known by the name of Old Stony Phiz. The phrase
was considered as giving a highly favorable aspect to
his political prospects ; for, as is likewise the case with
the Popedom, nobody ever becomes President without
taking a name other than his own.

While his friends were doing their best to make
him President, Old Stony Phiz, as he was called, set
out on a visit to the valley where he was born. Of
course, he had no other object than to shake hands
with his fellow-citizens, and neither thought nor cared
about any effect which his progress through the country
might have upon the election. Magnificent prepara-
tions were made to receive the illustrious statesman ;
a cavalcade of horsemen set forth to meet him at the
boundary line of the State, and all the people left their
business and gathered along the wayside to see him
pass. Among these was Ernest. Though more than
once disappointed, as we have seen, he had such a
hopeful and confiding nature, that he was always
ready to believe in whatever seemed beautiful and
good. He kept his heart continually open, and thus
was sure to catch the blessing from on high, when it
should come. So now again, as buoyantly as ever, he
went forth to behold the likeness of the Great Stone
Face.

The cavalcade came prancing along the road, with a great clattering of hoofs and a mighty cloud of dust, which rose up so dense and high that the visage of the mountain-side was completely hidden from Ernest's eyes. All the great men of the neighborhood were there on horseback; militia officers, in uniform; the member of Congress; the sheriff of the county; the editors of newspapers; and many a farmer, too, had mounted his patient steed, with his Sunday coat upon his back. It really was a very brilliant spectacle, especially as there were numerous banners flaunting over the cavalcade, on some of which were gorgeous portraits of the illustrious statesman and the Great Stone Face, smiling familiarly at one another, like two brothers. If the pictures were to be trusted, the mutual resemblance, it must be confessed, was marvellous. We must not forget to mention that there was a band of music, which made the echoes of the mountains ring and reverberate with the loud triumph of its strains; so that airy and soul-thrilling melodies broke out among all the heights and hollows, as if every nook of his native valley had found a voice to welcome the distinguished guest. But the grandest effect was when the far-off mountain precipice flung back the music; for then the Great Stone Face itself seemed to be swelling the triumphant chorus, in acknowledgment that, at length, the man of prophecy was come.

All this while the people were throwing up their hats and shouting, with enthusiasm so contagious that the heart of Ernest kindled up, and he likewise threw up his hat, and shouted, as loudly as the loudest, "Huzza for the great man! Huzza for Old Stony Phiz!" But as yet he had not seen him.

"Here he is now! " cried those who stood near Ernest. "There! There! Look at Old Stony Phiz and then at the Old Man of the Mountain, and see if they are not as like as two twin-brothers! "

In the midst of all this gallant array, came an open barouche, drawn by four white horses; and in the barouche, with his massive head uncovered, sat the illustrious statesman, Old Stony Phiz himself.

"Confess it," said one of Ernest's neighbors to him, "the Great Stone Face has met its match at last! "

Now, it must be owned that, at his first glimpse of the countenance which was bowing and smiling from the barouche, Ernest did fancy that there was a resemblance between it and the old familiar face upon the mountain-side. The brow, with its massive depth and loftiness, and all the other features, indeed, were boldly and strongly hewn, as if in emulation of a more than heroic, of a Titanic model. But the sublimity and stateliness, the grand expression of a divine sympathy, that illuminated the mountain visage, and etherealized its ponderous granite substance into spirit, might here be sought in vain. Something had been originally left out, or had departed. And therefore the marvellously gifted statesman had always a weary gloom in the deep caverns of his eyes, as of a child that has outgrown its playthings, or a man of mighty faculties and little aims, whose life, with all its high performances, was vague and empty, because no high purpose had endowed it with reality.

Still Ernest's neighbor was thrusting his elbow into his side, and pressing him for an answer.

"Confess! confess! Is not he the very picture of your Old Man of the Mountain? "

"No!" said Ernest, bluntly, "I see little or no likeness."

"Then so much the worse for the Great Stone Face!" answered his neighbor; and again he set up a shout for Old Stony Phiz.

But Ernest turned away, melancholy, and almost despondent; for this was the saddest of his disappointments, to behold a man who might have fulfilled the prophecy, and had not willed to do so. Meantime, the cavalcade, the banners, the music, the barouches swept past him, with the vociferous crowd in the rear, leaving the dust to settle down, and the Great Stone Face to be revealed again, with the grandeur that it had worn for untold centuries.

"Lo, here I am, Ernest!" the benign lips seemed to say. "I have waited longer than thou, and am not yet weary. Fear not; the man will come."

The years hurried onward, treading in their haste on one another's heels. And now they began to bring white hairs, and scatter them over the head of Ernest; they made reverend wrinkles across his forehead, and furrows in his cheeks. He was an aged man. But not in vain had he grown old: more than the white hairs on his head were the sage thoughts in his mind; his wrinkles and furrows were inscriptions that Time had graved, and in which he had written legends of wisdom that had been tested by the tenor of a life. And Ernest had ceased to be obscure. Unsought for, undesired, had come the fame which so many seek, and made him known in the great world, beyond the limits of the valley in which he had dwelt so quietly. College professors, and even the active men of cities, came from far to see and converse with Ernest; for the report had gone abroad that this simple husbandman had ideas unlike those of other men, not gained from books, but of a higher tone, — a tranquil and familiar majesty, as if he had been talking with the angels as his daily friends. Whether it were sage, statesman, or philanthropist, Ernest received these visitors with the gentle sincerity that had character-ized him from boyhood, and spoke freely with them of whatever came uppermost, or lay deepest in his heart or their own. While they talked together his face would kindle, unawares, and shine upon them, as with a mild evening light. Pensive with the fulness of such discourse, his guests took leave and went their way; and passing up the valley, paused to look at the Great Stone Face, imagining that they had seen its likeness in a human countenance, but could not remember where.

While Ernest had been growing up and growing old, a bountiful Providence had granted a new poet to this earth. He, likewise, was a native of the valley, but had spent the greater part of his life at a distance from that romantic region, pouring out his sweet music amid the bustle and din of cities. Often, how-ever, did the mountains which had been familiar to him in his childhood lift their snowy peaks into the clear atmosphere of his poetry. Neither was the Great Stone Face forgotten, for the poet had cele-brated it in an ode which was grand enough to have been uttered by its own majestic lips. The man of genius, we may say, had come down from heaven with wonderful endowments. If he sang of a mountain, the eyes of all mankind beheld a mightier grandeur reposing on its breast, or soaring to its summit, than had before been seen there. If his theme were a lovely lake, a celestial smile had now been thrown over

it, to gleam forever on its surface. If it were the vast
old sea, even the deep immensity of its dread bosom
seemed to swell the higher, as if moved by the emo-
tions of the song. Thus the world assumed another
and a better aspect from the hour that the poet blessed
it with his happy eyes. The Creator had bestowed
him, as the last best touch to his own handiwork.
Creation was not finished till the poet came to inter-
pret, and so complete it.

The effect was no less high and beautiful when his
human brethren were the subject of his verse. The
man or woman, sordid with the common dust of life,
who crossed his daily path, and the little child who
played in it, were glorified if he beheld them in his
mood of poetic faith. He showed the golden links of
the great chain that intertwined them with an angelic
kindred; he brought out the hidden traits of a celes-
tial birth that made them worthy of such kin. Some,
indeed, there were, who thought to show the soundness
of their judgment by affirming that all the beauty and
dignity of the natural world existed only in the poet's
fancy. Let such men speak for themselves, who un-
doubtedly appear to have been spawned forth by Nature
with a contemptuous bitterness; she having plastered
them up out of her refuse stuff, after all the swine were
made. As respects all things else, the poet's ideal was
the truest truth.

The songs of this poet found their way to Ernest.
He read them after his customary toil, seated on the
bench before his cottage door, where for such a length
of time he had filled his repose with thought, by gazing
at the Great Stone Face. And now as he read stanzas
that caused the soul to thrill within him, he lifted his
eyes to the vast countenance beaming on him so benig-
nantly.

"O majestic friend," he murmured, addressing the Great Stone Face, "is not this man worthy to resemble thee?"

The Face seemed to smile, but answered not a word.

Now it happened that the poet, though he dwelt so far away, had not only heard of Ernest, but had meditated much upon his character, until he deemed nothing so desirable as to meet this man, whose untaught wisdom walked hand in hand with the noble simplicity of his life. One summer morning, therefore, he took passage by the railroad, and, in the decline of the afternoon, alighted from the cars at no great distance from Ernest's cottage. The great hotel, which had formerly been the palace of Mr. Gathergold, was close at hand, but the poet, with his carpet-bag on his arm, inquired at once where Ernest dwelt, and was resolved to be accepted as his guest.

Approaching the door, he there found the good old man, holding a volume in his hand, which alternately he read, and then, with a finger between the leaves, looked lovingly at the Great Stone Face.

"Good evening," said the poet. "Can you give a traveller a night's lodging?"

"Willingly," answered Ernest; and then he added, smiling, "methinks I never saw the Great Stone Face look so hospitably at a stranger."

The poet sat down on the bench beside him, and he and Ernest talked together. Often had the poet held intercourse with the wittiest and the wisest, but never before with a man like Ernest, whose thoughts and feelings gushed up with such a natural freedom, and who made great truths so familiar by his simple utterance of them. Angels, as had been so often said, seemed to have wrought with him at his labor in the fields; angels seemed to have sat with him by the fire-side; and, dwelling with angels as friend with friends, he had imbibed the sublimity of their ideas, and imbued it with the sweet and lowly charm of household words. So thought the poet. And Ernest, on the other hand, was moved and agitated by the living images which the poet flung out of his mind, and which peopled all the air about the cottage door with shapes of beauty, both gay and pensive. The sympathies of these two men instructed them with a profounder sense than either could have attained alone. Their minds accorded into one strain, and made delightful music which neither of them could have claimed as all his own, nor distinguished his own share from the other's. They led one another, as it were, into a high pavilion of their thoughts, so remote, and hitherto so dim, that they had never entered it before, and so beautiful that they desired to be there always.

As Ernest listened to the poet, he imagined that the Great Stone Face was bending forward to listen too. He gazed earnestly into the poet's glowing eyes.

" Who are you, my strangely gifted guest ? " he said.

The poet laid his finger on the volume that Ernest had been reading.

" You have read these poems," said he. " You know me, then, — for I wrote them."

Again, and still more earnestly than before, Ernest examined the poet's features; then turned towards the Great Stone Face; then back, with an uncertain aspect, to his guest. But his countenance fell; he shook his head, and sighed.

" Wherefore are you sad ? " inquired the poet.

" Because," replied Ernest, " all through life I have awaited the fulfilment of a prophecy; and, when

I read these poems, I hoped that it might be fulfilled in you."

" You hoped," answered the poet, faintly smiling, "to find in me the likeness of the Great Stone Face. And you are disappointed, as formerly with Mr. Gathergold, and Old Blood-and-Thunder, and Old Stony Phiz. Yes, Ernest, it is my doom. You must add my name to the illustrious three, and record another failure of your hopes. For — in shame and sadness do I speak it, Ernest — I am not worthy to be typified by yonder benign and majestic image."

" And why?" asked Ernest. He pointed to the volume. " Are not those thoughts divine?"

" They have a strain of the Divinity," replied the poet. "You can hear in them the far-off echo of a heavenly song. But my life, dear Ernest, has not corresponded with my thought. I have had grand dreams, but they have been only dreams, because I have lived — and that, too, by my own choice — among poor and mean realities. Sometimes even — shall I dare to say it? — I lack faith in the grandeur, the beauty, and the goodness, which my own works are said to have made more evident in nature and in human life. Why, then, pure seeker of the good and true, shouldst thou hope to find me in yonder image of the divine?"

The poet spoke sadly, and his eyes were dim with tears. So, likewise, were those of Ernest.

At the hour of sunset, as had long been his frequent custom, Ernest was to discourse to an assemblage of the neighboring inhabitants in the open air. He and the poet, arm in arm, still talking together as they went along, proceeded to the spot. It was a small nook among the hills, with a gray precipice behind,

the stern front of which was relieved by the pleasant
foliage of many creeping plants, that made a tapestry
for the naked rock, by hanging their festoons from
all its rugged angles. At a small elevation above the
ground, set in a rich framework of verdure, there
appeared a niche, spacious enough to admit a hu-
man figure, with freedom for such gestures as sponta-
neously accompany earnest thought and genuine emo-
tion. Into this natural pulpit Ernest ascended, and
threw a look of familiar kindness around upon his
audience. They stood, or sat, or reclined upon the
grass, as seemed good to each, with the departing
sunshine falling obliquely over them, and mingling
its subdued cheerfulness with the solemnity of a grove
of ancient trees, beneath and amid the boughs of
which the golden rays were constrained to pass. In
another direction was seen the Great Stone Face, with
the same cheer, combined with the same solemnity, in
its benignant aspect.

Ernest began to speak, giving to the people of what
was in his heart and mind. His words had power,
because they accorded with his thoughts; and his
thoughts had reality and depth, because they harmo-
nized with the life which he had always lived. It was
not mere breath that this preacher uttered; they were
the words of life, because a life of good deeds and
holy love was melted into them. Pearls, pure and rich,
had been dissolved into this precious draught. The
poet, as he listened, felt that the being and character
of Ernest were a nobler strain of poetry than he had
ever written. His eyes glistening with tears, he gazed
reverentially at the venerable man, and said within
himself that never was there an aspect so worthy of a
prophet and a sage as that mild, sweet, thoughtful

countenance, with the glory of white hair diffused about it. At a distance, but distinctly to be seen, high up in the golden light of the setting sun, appeared the Great Stone Face, with hoary mists around it, like the white hairs around the brow of Ernest. Its look of grand beneficence seemed to embrace the world.

At that moment, in sympathy with a thought which he was about to utter, the face of Ernest assumed a grandeur of expression, so imbued with benevolence, that the poet,[1] by an irresistible impulse, threw his arms aloft, and shouted, —

" Behold! Behold! Ernest is himself the likeness of the Great Stone Face ! "

Then all the people looked and saw that what the deep-sighted poet said was true. The prophecy was fulfilled. But Ernest, having finished what he had to say, took the poet's arm, and walked slowly homeward, still hoping that some wiser and better man than himself would by and by appear, bearing a resemblance to the GREAT STONE FACE.

MY VISIT TO NIAGARA.

NEVER did a pilgrim approach Niagara with deeper enthusiasm than mine. I had lingered away from it, and wandered to other scenes, because my treasury of anticipated enjoyments, comprising all the wonders of

---

[1] That the poet should have been the one to discover the resemblance accords with the conception of the poet himself in this little apologue. Poetic insight is still separable from integrity of character, and it was quite possible for this poet to see the ideal beauty in another, while conscious of his own defect. The humility of Ernest, as the last word of the story, completes the certainty of the likeness.

the world, had nothing else so magnificent, and I was loath to exchange the pleasures of hope for those of memory so soon. At length the day came. The stage-coach, with a Frenchman and myself on the back seat, had already left Lewiston, and in less than an hour would set us down in Manchester. I began to listen for the roar of the cataract, and trembled with a sensation like dread, as the moment drew nigh, when its voice of ages must roll, for the first time, on my ear. The French gentleman stretched himself from the window, and expressed loud admiration, while, by a sudden impulse, I threw myself back and closed my eyes. When the scene shut in, I was glad to think, that for me the whole burst of Niagara was yet in futurity. We rolled on, and entered the village of Manchester, bordering on the falls.

I am quite ashamed of myself here. Not that I ran like a madman to the falls, and plunged into the thickest of the spray, — never stopping to breathe, till breathing was impossible ; not that I committed this, or any other suitable extravagance. On the contrary, I alighted with perfect decency and composure, gave my cloak to the black waiter, pointed out my baggage, and inquired, not the nearest way to the cataract, but about the dinner-hour. The interval was spent in arranging my dress. Within the last fifteen minutes, my mind had grown strangely benumbed, and my spirits apathetic, with a slight depression, not decided enough to be termed sadness. My enthusiasm was in a deathlike slumber. Without aspiring to immortality, as he did, I could have imitated that English traveller, who turned back from the point where he first heard the thunder of Niagara, after crossing the ocean to behold it. Many a Western trader, by the by, has performed a similar act of heroism with more heroic simplicity, deeming it no such wonderful feat to dine at the hotel and resume his route to Buffalo or Lewiston, while the cataract was roaring unseen.

Such has often been my apathy, when objects, long sought, and earnestly desired, were placed within my reach. After dinner — at which an unwonted and perverse epicurism detained me longer than usual — I lighted a cigar and paced the piazza, minutely attentive to the aspect and business of a very ordinary village. Finally, with reluctant step, and the feeling of an intruder, I walked towards Goat Island. At the toll-house, there were farther excuses for delaying the inevitable moment. My signature was required in a huge ledger, containing similar records innumerable, many of which I read. The skin of a great sturgeon, and other fishes, beasts, and reptiles; a collection of minerals, such as lie in heaps near the falls; some Indian moccasons, and other trifles, made of deer-skin and embroidered with beads; several newspapers, from Montreal, New York, and Boston, — all attracted me in turn. Out of a number of twisted sticks, the manufacture of a Tuscarora Indian, I selected one of curled maple, curiously convoluted, and adorned with the carved images of a snake and a fish. Using this as my pilgrim's staff, I crossed the bridge. Above and below me were the rapids, a river of impetuous snow, with here and there a dark rock amid its whiteness, resisting all the physical fury, as any cold spirit did the moral influences of the scene. On reaching Goat Island, which separates the two great segments of the falls, I chose the right-hand path, and followed it to the edge of the American cascade. There, while the falling sheet was yet invisible,

I saw the vapor that never vanishes, and the Eternal Rainbow of Niagara.

It was an afternoon of glorious sunshine, without a cloud, save those of the cataracts. I gained an insulated rock, and beheld a broad sheet of brilliant and unbroken foam, not shooting in a curved line from the top of the precipice, but falling headlong down from height to depth. A narrow stream diverged from the main branch, and hurried over the crag by a channel of its own, leaving a little pine-clad island and a streak of precipice between itself and the larger sheet. Below arose the mist, on which was painted a dazzling sunbow with two concentric shadows, — one, almost as perfect as the original brightness; and the other, drawn faintly round the broken edge of the cloud.

Still I had not half seen Niagara. Following the verge of the island, the path led me to the Horseshoe, where the real, broad St. Lawrence, rushing along on a level with its banks, pours its whole breadth over a concave line of precipice, and thence pursues its course between lofty crags towards Ontario. A sort of bridge, two or three feet wide, stretches out along the edge of the descending sheet, and hangs upon the rising mist, as if that were the foundation of the frail structure. Here I stationed myself in the blast of wind, which the rushing river bore along with it. The bridge was tremulous beneath me, and marked the tremor of the solid earth. I looked along the whitening rapids, and endeavored to distinguish a mass of water far above the falls, to follow it to their verge, and go down with it, in fancy, to the abyss of clouds and storm. Casting my eyes across the river, and every side, I took in the whole scene at a glance, and tried to comprehend it in one vast idea. After an hour thus spent, I left the bridge, and by a staircase, winding almost interminably round a post, descended to the base of the precipice. From that point, my path lay over slippery stones, and among great fragments of the cliff, to the edge of the cataract, where the wind at once enveloped me in spray, and perhaps dashed the rainbow round me. Were my long desires fulfilled? And had I seen Niagara?

Oh that I had never heard of Niagara till I beheld it! Blessed were the wanderers of old, who heard its deep roar, sounding through the woods, as the summons to an unknown wonder, and approached its awful brink, in all the freshness of native feeling. Had its own mysterious voice been the first to warn me of its existence, then, indeed, I might have knelt down and worshipped. But I had come thither, haunted with a vision of foam and fury, and dizzy cliffs, and an ocean tumbling down out of the sky, — a scene, in short, which nature had too much good taste and calm simplicity to realize. My mind had struggled to adapt these false conceptions to the reality, and finding the effort vain, a wretched sense of disappointment weighed me down. I climbed the precipice, and threw myself on the earth, feeling that I was unworthy to look at the Great Falls, and careless about beholding them again. . . .

All that night, as there has been and will be for ages past and to come, a rushing sound was heard, as if a great tempest were sweeping through the air. It mingled with my dreams, and made them full of storm and whirlwind. Whenever I awoke, and heard this dread sound in the air, and the windows rattling as with a mighty blast, I could not rest again, till looking forth, I saw how bright the stars were, and that every leaf in the garden was motionless. Never was a summer night more calm to the eye, nor a gale of autumn louder to the ear. The rushing sound proceeds from the rapids, and the rattling of the casements is but an effect of the vibration of the whole house, shaken by the jar of the cataract. The noise of the rapids draws the attention from the true voice of Niagara, which is a dull, muffled thunder, resounding between the cliffs. I spent a wakeful hour at midnight, in distinguishing its reverberations, and rejoiced to find that my former awe and enthusiasm were reviving.

Gradually, and after much contemplation, I came to know, by my own feelings, that Niagara is indeed a wonder of the world, and not the less wonderful, because time and thought must be employed in comprehending it. Casting aside all preconceived notions, and preparation to be dire-struck or delighted, the beholder must stand beside it in the simplicity of his heart, suffering the mighty scene to work its own impression. Night after night, I dreamed of it, and was gladdened every morning by the consciousness of a growing capacity to enjoy it. Yet I will not pretend to the all-absorbing enthusiasm of some more fortunate spectators, nor deny that very trifling causes would draw my eyes and thoughts from the cataract.

The last day that I was to spend at Niagara, before my departure for the Far West, I sat upon the Table Rock. This celebrated station did not now, as of old, project fifty feet beyond the line of the precipice, but was shattered by the fall of an immense fragment, which lay distant on the shore below. Still, on the utmost verge of the rock, with my feet hanging over it, I felt as if suspended in the open air. Never before had my mind been in such perfect unison with the scene. There were intervals, when I was conscious of nothing but the great river, rolling calmly into the abyss, rather descending than precipitating itself, and acquiring tenfold majesty from its unhurried motion. It came like the march of Destiny. It was not taken by surprise, but seemed to have anticipated, in all its course through the broad lakes, that it must pour their collected waters down this height. The perfect foam of the river, after its descent, and the ever-varying shapes of mist, rising up, to become clouds in the sky, would be the very picture of confusion, were it merely transient, like the rage of a tempest. But when the beholder has stood awhile, and perceives no lull in the storm, and considers that the vapor and the foam are as everlasting as the rocks which produce them, all this turmoil assumes a sort of calmness. It soothes, while it awes the mind.

Leaning over the cliff, I saw the guide conducting two adventurers behind the falls. It was pleasant, from that high seat in the sunshine, to observe them struggling against the eternal storm of the lower regions, with heads bent down, now faltering, now pressing forward, and finally swallowed up in their victory. After their disappearance, a blast rushed out with an old hat, which it had swept from one of their heads. The rock, to which they were directing their unseen course, is marked, at a fearful distance on the exterior of the sheet, by a jet of foam. The attempt to reach it appears both poetical and perilous to a looker-on, but may be accomplished without much more difficulty or hazard than in stemming a violent northeaster. In a few moments, forth came the children of the mist. Dripping and breathless, they crept along the base of the cliff, ascended to the guide's cottage, and received, I presume, a certificate of their achievement, with three verses of sublime poetry on the back.

My contemplations were often interrupted by strangers who came down from Forsyth's to take their first view of the falls. A short, ruddy, middle-aged gentleman, fresh from Old England, peeped over the rock, and evinced his approbation by a broad grin. His spouse, a very robust lady, afforded a sweet example of maternal solicitude, being so intent on the safety of her little boy that she did not even glance at Niagara. As for the child, he gave himself wholly to the enjoyment of a stick of candy. Another traveller, a native American, and no rare character among us, produced a volume of Captain Hall's tour, and labored earnestly to adjust Niagara to the captain's description, departing, at last, without one new idea or sensation of his own. The next comer was provided, not with a printed book, but with a blank sheet of foolscap, from top to bottom of which, by means of an ever-pointed pencil, the cataract was made to thunder. In a little talk which we had together, he awarded his approbation to the general view, but censured the position of Goat Island, observing that it should have been thrown farther to the right, so as to widen the American falls, and contract those of the Horseshoe. Next appeared two traders of Michigan, who declared, that, upon the whole, the sight was worth looking at; there certainly was an immense water-power here; but that, after all, they would go twice as far to see the noble stone-works of Lockport, where the Grand Canal is locked down a descent of sixty feet. They were succeeded by a young fellow, in a homespun cotton dress, with a staff in his hand, and a pack over his shoulders. He advanced close to the edge of the rock, where his attention, at first wavering among the different components of the scene, finally became fixed in the angle of the Horse-shoe falls, which is, indeed, the central point of inter-est. His whole soul seemed to go forth and be trans-ported thither, till the staff slipped from his relaxed grasp, and falling down — down — down — struck upon the fragment of the Table Rock.

In this manner I spent some hours, watching the varied impression, made by the cataract, on those who disturbed me, and returning to unwearied contempla-tion, when left alone. At length my time came to de-part. There is a grassy footpath through the woods, along the summit of the bank, to a point whence a causeway, hewn in the side of the precipice, goes wind-ing down to the Ferry, about half a mile below the Table Rock. The sun was near setting, when I emerged from the shadow of the trees, and began the descent. The indirectness of my downward road con-tinually changed the point of view, and showed me, in rich and repeated succession, now, the whitening rap-ids and majestic leap of the main river, which ap-peared more deeply massive as the light departed; now, the lovelier picture, yet still sublime, of Goat Island, with its rocks and grove, and the lesser falls, tumbling over the right bank of the St. Lawrence, like a tributary stream; now, the long vista of the river, as it eddied and whirled between the cliffs, to pass through Ontario toward the sea, and everywhere to be wondered at, for this one unrivalled scene. The golden sunshine tinged the sheet of the American cas-cade, and painted on its heaving spray the broken semicircle of a rainbow, heaven's own beauty crown-

ing earth's sublimity. My steps were slow, and I
paused long at every turn of the descent, as one lin-
gers and pauses who discerns a brighter and brighten-
ing excellence in what he must soon behold no more.
The solitude of the old wilderness now reigned over
the whole vicinity of the falls. My enjoyment be-
came the more rapturous, because no poet shared it,
nor wretch devoid of poetry profaned it ; but the spot
so famous through the world was all my own!

JOHN GREENLEAF WHITTIER.

BIOGRAPHICAL SKETCH.

JOHN GREENLEAF WHITTIER, of Quaker birth in Puritan surroundings, was born at the homestead near Haverhill, Massachusetts, December 17, 1807. Until his eighteenth year he lived at home, working upon the farm and in the little shoemaker's shop which nearly every farm then had as a resource in the otherwise idle hours of winter. The manual, homely labor upon which he was employed was in part the foundation of that deep interest which the poet never has ceased to take in the toil and plain fortunes of the people. Throughout his poetry runs this golden thread of sympathy with honorable labor and enforced poverty, and many poems are directly inspired by it. While at work with his father he sent poems to the *Haverhill Gazette*, and that he was not in subjection to his work is very evident by the fact that he translated it and similar occupations into *Songs of Labor.* He had two years' academic training, and in 1829 became editor in Boston of the *American Manufacturer*, a paper published in the interest of the tariff. In 1831 he published his *Legends of New England*, prose sketches in a department of literature which has always had strong claims upon his interest. No American writer, unless Irving be excepted, has done so much to throw a graceful veil of poetry and legend over the country of his daily life. Essex County, in Massachusetts, and the beaches lying between Newburyport and Portsmouth blossom with flowers of Whittier's planting. He has made rare use of the homely stories which he had heard in his childhood, and learned afterward from familiar intercourse with country people, and he has himself used invention delicately and in harmony with the spirit of the New England coast. Although of a body of men who in earlier days had been persecuted by the Puritans of New England, his generous mind has not failed to detect all the good that was in the stern creed and life of the persecutors, and to bring it forward into the light of his poetry.

In 1836 he published *Mogg Megone*, a poem which stood first in the collected edition of his poems issued in 1857, and was admitted there with some reluctance, apparently, by the author. In that and the *Bridal of Pennacook* he draws his material from the relation held between the Indians and the settlers. His sympathy was always with the persecuted and oppressed, and while historically he found an object of pity and self-reproach in the Indian, his profoundest compassion and most stirring indignation were called out by African slavery. From the earliest he was upon the side of the abolition party. Year after year poems fell from his pen in which with all the eloquence of his nature he sought to enlist his countrymen upon the side of emancipation and freedom. It is not too much to say that in the slow development of public sentiment Whittier's steady song was one of the most powerful advocates that the slave had, all the more powerful that it was free from malignity or unjust accusation.

Whittier's poems have been issued in a number of small volumes, and collected into single larger volumes. Besides those already indicated, there are a number which owe their origin to his tender regard for domestic life and the simple experience of the men and women about him. Of these *Snow-Bound* is the most memorable. Then his fondness for a story has led him to use the ballad form in many cases, and *Mabel Martin* is one of a number, in which the narrative is blended with a fine and strong charity. The catholic mind of this writer and his instinct for discovering the pure moral in human action are disclosed by a number of poems, drawn from a wide range of historical fact, dealing with a great variety of religious faiths and circumstances of life, but always pointing to some sweet and strong truth of the divine life. Of such are *The Brother of Mercy, The Gift of Tritemius, The Two Rabbis,* and others. Whittier's *Prose Works* are comprised in three volumes, and consist mainly of his contributions to journals and of *Leaves from Margaret Smith's Journal,* a fictitious diary of a visitor to New England in 1678.

SNOW–BOUND.

A WINTER IDYL.

"As the Spirits of Darkness be stronger in the dark, so good Spirits which be Angels of Light are augmented not only by the Divine light of the Sun, but also by our common VVood fire : and as the Celestial Fire drives away dark spirits, so also this our Fire of VVood doth the same." — COR. AGRIPPA, *Occult Philosophy*, Book I. ch. v.

"Announced by all the trumpets of the sky,
Arrives the snow ; and, driving o'er the fields,
Seems nowhere to alight ; the whited air
Hides hills and woods, the river and the heaven,
And veils the farm-house at the garden's end.
The sled and traveller stopped, the courier's feet
Delayed, all friends shut out, the housemates sit
Around the radiant fireplace, inclosed
In a tumultuous privacy of storm."
EMERSON, *The Snow-Storm.*

THE sun that brief December day
Rose cheerless over hills of gray,
And, darkly circled, gave at noon
A sadder light than waning moon.
Slow tracing down the thickening sky   5
Its mute and ominous prophecy,
A portent seeming less than threat,
It sank from sight before it set.
A chill no coat, however stout,
Of homespun stuff could quite shut out,   10

John G. Whittier

A hard, dull bitterness of cold,
  That checked, mid-vein, the circling race
  Of life-blood in the sharpened face,
The coming of the snow-storm told.
The wind blew east; we heard the roar   15
Of Ocean on his wintry shore,
And felt the strong pulse throbbing there
Beat with low rhythm our inland air.

Meanwhile we did our nightly chores, —
Brought in the wood from out of doors,   20
Littered the stalls, and from the mows
Raked down the herd's-grass for the cows:
Heard the horse whinnying for his corn;
And, sharply clashing horn on horn,
Impatient down the stanchion rows   25
The cattle shake their walnut bows;
While, peering from his early perch
Upon the scaffold's pole of birch,
The cock his crested helmet bent
And down his querulous challenge sent.   30
Unwarmed by any sunset light
The gray day darkened into night,
A night made hoary with the swarm
And whirl-dance of the blinding storm,
As zigzag wavering to and fro   35
Crossed and recrossed the wingéd snow:
And ere the early bedtime came
The white drift piled the window-frame,
And through the glass the clothes-line posts
Looked in like tall and sheeted ghosts.   40

So all night long the storm roared on:
The morning broke without a sun;

In tiny spherule traced with lines
Of Nature's geometric signs,
In starry flake and pellicle   45
All day the hoary meteor fell;
And, when the second morning shone,
We looked upon a world unknown,
On nothing we could call our own.
Around the glistening wonder bent   50
The blue walls of the firmament,
No cloud above, no earth below, —
A universe of sky and snow!
The old familiar sights of ours
Took marvellous shapes; strange domes and towers
Rose up where sty or corn-crib stood,   55
Or garden-wall, or belt of wood;
A smooth white mound the brush-pile showed,
A fenceless drift what once was road;
The bridle-post an old man sat   60
With loose-flung coat and high cocked hat;
The well-curb had a Chinese roof;
And even the long sweep, high aloof,
In its slant splendor, seemed to tell
Of Pisa's leaning miracle.   65

A prompt, decisive man, no breath
Our father wasted : " Boys, a path ! "

65. The Leaning Tower of Pisa, in Italy, which inclines from
the perpendicular a little more than six feet in eighty, is a cam-
panile, or bell-tower, built of white marble, very beautiful, but
so famous for its singular deflection from perpendicularity as to
be known almost wholly as a curiosity. Opinions differ as to
the leaning being the result of accident or design, but the better
judgment makes it an effect of the character of the soil on
which it is built. The Cathedral to which it belongs has suf-
fered so much from a similar cause that there is not a vertical
line in it.

Well pleased, (for when did farmer boy
Count such a summons less than joy ?)
Our buskins on our feet we drew ; 70
   With mittened hands, and caps drawn low
   To guard our necks and ears from snow,
We cut the solid whiteness through.
And, where the drift was deepest, made
A tunnel walled and overlaid 75
With dazzling crystal : we had read
Of rare Aladdin's wondrous cave,
And to our own his name we gave,
With many a wish the luck were ours
To test his lamp's supernal powers. 80
We reached the barn with merry din,
And roused the prisoned brutes within.
The old horse thrust his long head out,
And grave with wonder gazed about ;
The cock his lusty greeting said, 85
And forth his speckled harem led ;
The oxen lashed their tails, and hooked,
And mild reproach of hunger looked ;
The hornéd patriarch of the sheep,
Like Egypt's Amun roused from sleep, 90
Shook his sage head with gesture mute,
And emphasized with stamp of foot.

All day the gusty north-wind bore
The loosening drift its breath before ;
Low circling round its southern zone, 95
The sun through dazzling snow-mist shone,
No church-bell lent its Christian tone

90. *Amun*, or Ammon, was an Egyptian being, representing
an attribute of Deity under the form of a ram.

To the savage air, no social smoke
Curled over woods of snow-hung oak.
A solitude made more intense   100
By dreary-voicéd elements,
The shrieking of the mindless wind,
The moaning tree-boughs swaying blind,
And on the glass the unmeaning beat
Of ghostly finger-tips of sleet.   105
Beyond the circle of our hearth
No welcome sound of toil or mirth
Unbound the spell, and testified
Of human life and thought outside.
We minded that the sharpest ear   110
The buried brooklet could not hear,
The music of whose liquid lip
Had been to us companionship,
And, in our lonely life, had grown
To have an almost human tone.   115

As night drew on, and, from the crest
Of wooded knolls that ridged the west,
The sun, a snow-blown traveller, sank
From sight beneath the smothering bank,
We piled with care our nightly stack   120
Of wood against the chimney-back, —
The oaken log, green, huge, and thick,
And on its top the stout back-stick;
The knotty forestick laid apart,
And filled between with curious art   125
The ragged brush; then, hovering near,
We watched the first red blaze appear,
Heard the sharp crackle, caught the gleam
On whitewashed wall and sagging beam,
Until the old, rude-furnished room   130

Burst, flower-like, into rosy bloom ;
While radiant with a mimic flame
Outside the sparkling drift became,
And through the bare-boughed lilac-tree
Our own warm hearth seemed blazing free. 135
The crane and pendent trammels showed,
The Turk's heads on the andirons glowed ;
While childish fancy, prompt to tell
The meaning of the miracle,
Whispered the old rhyme : " *Under the tree* 140
When fire outdoors burns merrily,
There the witches are making tea."

The moon above the eastern wood
Shone at its full ; the hill-range stood
Transfigured in the silver flood, 145
Its blown snows flashing cold and keen,
Dead white, save where some sharp ravine
Took shadow, or the sombre green
Of hemlocks turned to pitchy black
Against the whiteness of their back. 150
For such a world and such a night
Most fitting that unwarming light,
Which only seemed where'er it fell
To make the coldness visible.

Shut in from all the world without, 155
We sat the clean-winged hearth about,
Content to let the north-wind roar
In baffled rage at pane and door,
While the red logs before us beat
The frost-line back with tropic heat ; 160
And ever, when a louder blast
Shook beam and rafter as it passed,

The merrier up its roaring draught
The great throat of the chimney laughed,
The house-dog on his paws outspread
Laid to the fire his drowsy head,
The cat's dark silhouette on the wall
A couchant tiger's seemed to fall ;
And, for the winter fireside meet,
Between the andirons' straddling feet,
The mug of cider simmered slow,
The apples sputtered in a row,
And, close at hand, the basket stood
With nuts from brown October's wood.

What matter how the night behaved ?
What matter how the north-wind raved ?
Blow high, blow low, not all its snow
Could quench our hearth-fire's ruddy glow.
O Time and Change ! — with hair as gray
As was my sire's that winter day,
How strange it seems, with so much gone
Of life and love, to still live on !
Ah, brother ! only I and thou
Are left of all that circle now, —
The dear home faces whereupon
That fitful firelight paled and shone.
Henceforward, listen as we will,
The voices of that hearth are still ;
Look where we may, the wide earth o'er,
Those lighted faces smile no more.
We tread the paths their feet have worn,
    We sit beneath their orchard trees,
    We hear, like them, the hum of bees
And rustle of the bladed corn ;
We turn the pages that they read,

Their written words we linger o'er,
But in the sun they cast no shade,
No voice is heard, no sign is made,
    No step is on the conscious floor!
Yet Love will dream and Faith will trust   200
(Since He who knows our need is just)
That somehow, somewhere, meet we must.
Alas for him who never sees
The stars shine through his cypress-trees!
Who, hopeless, lays his dead away,   205
Nor looks to see the. breaking day
Across the mournful marbles play!
Who hath not learned, in hours of faith,
    The truth to flesh and sense unknown,
That Life is ever lord of Death,   210
    And Love can never lose its own!

We sped the time with stories old,
Wrought puzzles out, and riddles told,
Or stammered from our school-book lore
" The chief of Gambia's golden shore."   215
How often since, when all the land
Was clay in Slavery's shaping hand,
As if a trumpet called, I 've heard
Dame Mercy Warren's rousing word:
" Does not the voice of reason cry,   220
    Claim the first right which Nature gave,
From the red scourge of bondage fly,
    Nor deign to live a burdened slave!"
Our father rode again his ride

219. Mrs. Mercy Warren was the wife of James Warren, a
prominent patriot at the beginning of the Revolution. Her poe-
try was read in an age that had in America little to read under
that name ; her society was sought by the best men.

On Memphremagog's wooded side ;
Sat down again to moose and samp
In trapper's hut and Indian camp ;
Lived o'er the old idyllic ease
Beneath St. François' hemlock-trees ;
Again for him the moonlight shone
On Norman cap and bodiced zone ;
Again he heard the violin play
Which led the village dance away,
And mingled in its merry whirl
The grandam and the laughing girl.
Or, nearer home, our steps he led
Where Salisbury's level marshes spread
Mile-wide as flies the laden bee ;
   Where merry mowers, hale and strong,
    Swept, scythe on scythe, their swaths along
The low green prairies of the sea.
We shared the fishing off Boar's Head,
   And round the rocky Isles of Shoals
    The hake-broil on the driftwood coals ;
The chowder on the sand-beach made,
Dipped by the hungry, steaming hot,
With spoons of clam-shell from the pot.
We heard the tales of witchcraft old,
And dream and sign and marvel told
To sleepy listeners as they lay
Stretched idly on the salted hay,
Adrift along the winding shores,
   When favoring breezes deigned to blow
    The square sail of the gundelow,
And idle lay the useless oars.

Our mother, while she turned her wheel
Or run the new-knit stocking heel,

Told how the Indian hordes came down
At midnight on Cochecho town,
And how her own great-uncle bore   260
His cruel scalp-mark to fourscore.
Recalling, in her fitting phrase,
   So rich and picturesque and free
   (The common unrhymed poetry
Of simple life and country ways),   265
The story of her early days, —
She made us welcome to her home;
Old hearths grew wide to give us room;
We stole with her a frightened look
At the gray wizard's conjuring-book,   270
The fame whereof went far and wide
Through all the simple country-side;
We heard the hawks at twilight play,
The boat-horn on Piscataqua,
The loon's weird laughter far away;   275
We fished her little trout-brook, knew
What flowers in wood and meadow grew,
What sunny hillsides autumn-brown
She climbed to shake the ripe nuts down,
Saw where in sheltered cove and bay   280
The duck's black squadron anchored lay,
And heard the wild geese calling loud
Beneath the gray November cloud.
Then, haply, with a look more grave,
And soberer tone, some tale she gave   285
From painful Sewel's ancient tome,

259. Dover in New Hampshire.
286. William Sewel was the historian of the Quakers. Charles
Lamb seemed to have as good an opinion of the book as Whit-
tier. In his essay *A Quakers' Meeting*, in *Essays of Elia*, he says:
" Reader, if you are not acquainted with it, I would recommend

Beloved in every Quaker home,
Of faith fire-winged by martyrdom,
Or Chalkley's Journal, old and quaint, —
Gentlest of skippers, rare sea-saint! —   290
Who, when the dreary calms prevailed,
And water-butt and bread-cask failed,
And cruel, hungry eyes pursued
His portly presence, mad for food,
With dark hints muttered under breath   295
Of casting lots for life or death,

to you, above all church-narratives, to read Sewel's *History of the Quakers.* . . . It is far more edifying and affecting than anything you will read of Wesley or his colleagues."

289. Thomas Chalkley was an Englishman of Quaker parentage, born in 1675, who travelled extensively as a preacher, and finally made his home in Philadelphia. He died in 1749; his *Journal* was first published in 1747. His own narrative of the incident which the poet relates is as follows: "To stop their murmuring, I told them they should not need to cast lots, which was usual in such cases, which of us should die first, for I would freely offer up my life to do them good. One said, 'God bless you! I will not eat any of you.' Another said, 'He would rather die before he would eat any of me;' and so said several. I can truly say, on that occasion, at that time, my life was not dear to me, and that I was serious and ingenuous in my proposition: and as I was leaning over the side of the vessel, thoughtfully considering my proposal to the company, and looking in my mind to Him that made me, a very large dolphin came up towards the top or surface of the water, and looked me in the face; and I called the people to put a hook into the sea, and take him, for here is one come to redeem me (I said to them). And they put a hook into the sea, and the fish readily took it, and they caught him. He was longer than myself. I think he was about six feet long, and the largest that ever I saw. This plainly showed us that we ought not to distrust the providence of the Almighty. The people were quieted by this act of Providence, and murmured no more. We caught enough to eat plentifully of, till we got into the capes of Delaware."

Offered, if Heaven withheld supplies,
To be himself the sacrifice.
Then, suddenly, as if to save
The good man from his living grave,   300
A ripple on the water grew,
A school of porpoise flashed in view.
"Take, eat," he said, "and be content;
These fishes in my stead are sent
By Him who gave the tangled ram   305
To spare the child of Abraham."

Our uncle, innocent of books,
Was rich in lore of fields and brooks,
The ancient teachers never dumb
Of Nature's unhoused lyceum.   310
In moons and tides and weather wise,
He read the clouds as prophecies,
And foul or fair could well divine,
By many an occult hint and sign,
Holding the cunning-warded keys   315
To all the woodcraft mysteries;
Himself to Nature's heart so near
That all her voices in his ear
Of beast or bird had meanings clear,
Like Apollonius of old,   320
Who knew the tales the sparrows told,
Or Hermes, who interpreted

310. The measure requires the accent ly′ceum, but in stricter use the accent is lyce′um.

320. A philosopher born in the first century of the Christian era, of whom many strange stories were told, especially regarding his converse with birds and animals.

322. Hermes Trismegistus, a celebrated Egyptian priest and philosopher, to whom was attributed the revival of geometry, arithmetic, and art among the Egyptians. He was little later than Apollonius.

What the sage cranes of Nilus said;
A simple, guileless, childlike man,
Content to live where life began;   325
Strong only on his native grounds,
The little world of sights and sounds
Whose girdle was the parish bounds,
Whereof his fondly partial pride
The common features magnified,   330
As Surrey hills to mountains grew
In White of Selborne's loving view, —
He told how teal and loon he shot,
And how the eagle's eggs he got,
The feats on pond and river done,   335
The prodigies of rod and gun;
Till, warming with the tales he told,
Forgotten was the outside cold,
The bitter wind unheeded blew,
From ripening corn the pigeons flew,   340
The partridge drummed i' the wood, the mink
Went fishing down the river-brink.
In fields with bean or clover gay,
The woodchuck, like a hermit gray,
    Peered from the doorway of his cell;   345
The muskrat plied the mason's trade,
And tier by tier his mud-walls laid;
And from the shagbark overhead
    The grizzled squirrel dropped his shell.

Next, the dear aunt, whose smile of cheer   350
And voice in dreams I see and hear, —

332. Gilbert White, of Selborne, England, was a clergyman
who wrote the *Natural History of Selborne*, a minute, affection-
ate, and charming description of what could be seen, as it were,
from his own doorstep. The accuracy of his observation and the
delightfulness of his manner have kept the book a classic.

The sweetest woman ever Fate
Perverse denied a household mate,
Who, lonely, homeless, not the less
Found peace in love's unselfishness,   355
And welcome whereso'er she went,
A calm and gracious element,
Whose presence seemed the sweet income
And womanly atmosphere of home, —
Called up her girlhood memories,   360
The huskings and the apple-bees,
The sleigh-rides and the summer sails,
Weaving through all the poor details
And homespun warp of circumstance
A golden woof-thread of romance.   365
For well she kept her genial mood
And simple faith of maidenhood;
Before her still a cloud-land lay,
The mirage loomed across her way;
The morning dew, that dried so soon   370
With others, glistened at her noon;
Through years of toil and soil and care,
From glossy tress to thin gray hair,
All unprofaned she held apart
The virgin fancies of the heart.   375
Be shame to him of woman born
Who hath for such but thought of scorn.

There, too, our elder sister plied
Her evening task the stand beside;
A full, rich nature, free to trust,   380
Truthful and almost sternly just,
Impulsive, earnest, prompt to act,
And make her generous thought a fact,
Keeping with many a light disguise

The secret of self-sacrifice.   385
O heart sore-tried! thou hast the best
That Heaven itself could give thee, — rest,
Rest from all bitter thoughts and things!
   How many a poor one's blessing went
   With thee beneath the low green tent   390
Whose curtain never outward swings!

As one who held herself a part
Of all she saw, and let her heart
   Against the household bosom lean,
Upon the motley-braided mat   395
Our youngest and our dearest sat,
Lifting her large, sweet, asking eyes,
   Now bathed within the fadeless green
And holy peace of Paradise.
Oh, looking from some heavenly hill,   400
   Or from the shade of saintly palms,
   Or silver reach of river calms,
Do those large eyes behold me still?
With me one little year ago : —
The chill weight of the winter snow   405
   For months upon her grave has lain;
And now, when summer south-winds blow
   And brier and harebell bloom again,
I tread the pleasant paths we trod,
I see the violet-sprinkled sod,   410
Whereon she leaned, too frail and weak
The hillside flowers she loved to seek,
Yet following me where'er I went
With dark eyes full of love's content.
The birds are glad; the brier-rose fills   415

398. *Th' unfading green* would be harsher, but more correct,
since the termination *less* is added to nouns and not to verbs.

The air with sweetness ; all the hills
Stretch green to June's unclouded sky ;
But still I wait with ear and eye
For something gone which should be nigh,
A loss in all familiar things, 420
In flower that blooms, and bird that sings.
And yet, dear heart ! remembering thee,
    Am I not richer than of old ?
Safe in thy immortality,
    What change can reach the wealth I hold ? 425
    What chance can mar the pearl and gold
Thy love hath left in trust with me ?
And while in life's late afternoon,
    Where cool and long the shadows grow,
I walk to meet the night that soon 430
    Shall shape and shadow overflow,
I cannot feel that thou art far,
Since near at need the angels are ;
And when the sunset gates unbar,
    Shall I not see thee waiting stand, 435
And, white against the evening star,
    The welcome of thy beckoning hand ?

Brisk wielder of the birch and rule,
The master of the district school
Held at the fire his favored place ; 440
Its warm glow lit a laughing face
Fresh-hued and fair, where scarce appeared
The uncertain prophecy of beard.
He teased the mitten-blinded cat,
Played cross-pins on my uncle's hat, 445
Sang songs, and told us what befalls
In classic Dartmouth's college halls.
Born the wild Northern hills among,

From whence his yeoman father wrung
By patient toil subsistence scant,   450
Not competence and yet not want,
He early gained the power to pay
His cheerful, self-reliant way;
Could doff at ease his scholar's gown
To peddle wares from town to town;   455
Or through the long vacation's reach
In lonely lowland districts teach,
Where all the droll experience found
At stranger hearths in boarding round,
The moonlit skater's keen delight,   460
The sleigh-drive through the frosty night,
The rustic party, with its rough
Accompaniment of blind-man's-buff,
And whirling plate, and forfeits paid,
His winter task a pastime made.   465
Happy the snow-locked homes wherein
He tuned his merry violin,
Or played the athlete in the barn,
Or held the good dame's winding yarn,
Or mirth-provoking versions told   470
Of classic legends rare and old,
Wherein the scenes of Greece and Rome
Had all the commonplace of home,
And little seemed at best the odds
'Twixt Yankee pedlers and old gods;   475
Where Pindus-born Arachthus took
The guise of any grist-mill brook,
And dread Olympus at his will

476. Pindus is the mountain chain which, running from north
to south, nearly bisects Greece. Five rivers take their rise from
the central peak, the Aöus, the Arachthus, the Haliacmon, the
Penëus, and the Achelöus.

Became a huckleberry hill.
A careless boy that night he seemed ;   480
  But at his desk he had the look
And air of one who wisely schemed,
  And hostage from the future took
  In trainéd thought and lore of book.
Large-brained, clear-eyed, — of such as he   485
Shall Freedom's young apostles be,
Who, following in War's bloody trail,
Shall every lingering wrong assail ;
All chains from limb and spirit strike,
Uplift the black and white alike ;   490
Scatter before their swift advance
The darkness and the ignorance,
The pride, the lust, the squalid sloth,
Which nurtured Treason's monstrous growth,
Made murder pastime, and the hell   495
Of prison-torture possible ;
The cruel lie of caste refute,
Old forms remould, and substitute
For Slavery's lash the freeman's will,
For blind routine, wise-handed skill ;   500
A school-house plant on every hill,
Stretching in radiate nerve-lines thence
The quick wires of intelligence ;
Till North and South together brought
Shall own the same electric thought,   505
In peace a common flag salute,
  And, side by side in labor's free
  And unresentful rivalry,
Harvest the fields wherein they fought.

Another guest that winter night   510
Flashed back from lustrous eyes the light.

Unmarked by time, and yet not young,
The honeyed music of her tongue
And words of meekness scarcely told
A nature passionate and bold,   515
Strong, self-concentred, spurning guide,
Its milder features dwarfed beside
Her unbent will's majestic pride.
She sat among us, at the best,
A not unfeared, half-welcome guest,   520
Rebuking with her cultured phrase
Our homeliness of words and ways.
A certain pard-like, treacherous grace
   Swayed the lithe limbs and dropped the lash,
   Lent the white teeth their dazzling flash;   525
   And under low brows, black with night,
   Rayed out at times a dangerous light;
The sharp heat-lightnings of her face
Presaging ill to him whom Fate
Condemned to share her love or hate.   530
   A woman tropical, intense
   In thought and act, in soul and sense,
   She blended in a like degree
   The vixen and the devotee,
   Revealing with each freak or feint   535
The temper of Petruchio's Kate,
   The raptures of Siena's saint.
Her tapering hand and rounded wrist
Had facile power to form a fist;
The warm, dark languish of her eyes   540
Was never safe from wrath's surprise.
Brows saintly calm and lips devout

536. See Shakespeare's comedy of the *Taming of the Shrew.*
537. St. Catherine of Siena, who is represented as having wonderful visions. She made a vow of silence for three years.

Knew every change of scowl and pout;
And the sweet voice had notes more high
And shrill for social battle-cry.   545
Since then what old cathedral town
Has missed her pilgrim staff and gown,
What convent-gate has held its lock
Against the challenge of her knock!
Through Smyrna's plague-hushed thoroughfares,   550
Up sea-set Malta's rocky stairs,
Gray olive slopes of hills that hem
Thy tombs and shrines, Jerusalem,
Or startling on her desert throne
The crazy Queen of Lebanon   555
With claims fantastic as her own,
Her tireless feet have held their way;
And still, unrestful, bowed, and gray,
She watches under Eastern skies,
  With hope each day renewed and fresh,   560
  The Lord's quick coming in the flesh,
Whereof she dreams and prophesies!

555. An interesting account of Lady Hester Stanhope, an
English gentlewoman who led a singular life on Mount Lebanon
in Syria, will be found in Kinglake's *Eothen*, chapter viii.

562. This *not unfeared, half-welcome guest* was Miss Harriet
Livermore, daughter of Judge Livermore of New Hampshire.
She was a woman of fine powers, but wayward, wild, and enthu-
siastic. She went on an independent mission to the Western
Indians, whom she, in common with some others, believed to be
remnants of the lost tribes of Israel. At the time of this narra-
tive she was about twenty-eight years old, but much of her life
afterward was spent in the Orient. She was at one time the
companion and friend of Lady Hester Stanhope, but finally
quarrelled with her about the use of the holy horses kept in the
stable in waiting for the Lord's ride to Jerusalem at the second
advent.

Where'er her troubled path may be,
　The Lord's sweet pity with her go!
The outward wayward life we see,
　The hidden springs we may not know.
Nor is it given us to discern
　What threads the fatal sisters spun,
　Through what ancestral years has run
The sorrow with the woman born,
What forged her cruel chain of moods,
What set her feet in solitudes,
　And held the love within her mute,
What mingled madness in the blood,
　A lifelong discord and annoy,
　Water of tears with oil of joy,
And hid within the folded bud
　Perversities of flower and fruit.
It is not ours to separate
The tangled skein of will and fate,
To show what metes and bounds should stand
Upon the soul's debatable land,
And between choice and Providence
Divide the circle of events ;
　But He who knows our frame is just,
Merciful and compassionate,
And full of sweet assurances
And hope for all the language is,
　That He remembereth we are dust!

At last the great logs, crumbling low,
Sent out a dull and duller glow,
The bull's-eye watch that hung in view,
Ticking its weary circuit through,
Pointed with mutely-warning sign
Its black hand to the hour of nine.

That sign the pleasant circle broke:
My uncle ceased his pipe to smoke,
Knocked from its bowl the refuse gray,
And laid it tenderly away,
Then roused himself to safely cover   600
The dull red brand with ashes over.
And while, with care, our mother laid
The work aside, her steps she stayed
One moment, seeking to express
Her grateful sense of happiness   605
For food and shelter, warmth and health,
And love's contentment more than wealth,
With simple wishes (not the weak,
Vain prayers which no fulfilment seek,
But such as warm the generous heart,   610
O'er-prompt to do with Heaven its part)
That none might lack, that bitter night,
For bread and clothing, warmth and light.

Within our beds awhile we heard
The wind that round the gables roared,   615
With now and then a ruder shock,
Which made our very bedsteads rock.
We heard the loosened clapboards tost,
The board-nails snapping in the frost;
And on us, through the unplastered wall,   620
Felt the light sifted snow-flakes fall,
But sleep stole on, as sleep will do
When hearts are light and life is new;
Faint and more faint the murmurs grew,
Till in the summer-land of dreams   625
They softened to the sound of streams,
Low stir of leaves, and dip of oars,
And lapsing waves on quiet shores.

Next morn we wakened with the shout
  Of merry voices high and clear ;   630
  And saw the teamsters drawing near
To break the drifted highways out.
Down the long hillside treading slow
We saw the half-buried oxen go,
Shaking the snow from heads uptost,   635
Their straining nostrils white with frost.
Before our door the straggling train
Drew up, an added team to gain.
The elders threshed their hands a-cold,
  Passed, with the cider-mug, their jokes   640
  From lip to lip ; the younger folks
Down the loose snow-banks, wrestling, rolled,
Then toiled again the cavalcade
  O'er windy hill, through clogged ravine,
  And woodland paths that wound between   645
Low drooping pine-boughs winter-weighed.
From every barn a team afoot,
At every house a new recruit,
Where, drawn by Nature's subtlest law,
Haply the watchful young men saw   650
Sweet doorway pictures of the curls
And curious eyes of merry girls,
Lifting their hands in mock defence
Against the snow-balls' compliments,
And reading in each missive tost   655
The charm with Eden never lost.

We heard once more the sleigh-bells' sound ;
  And, following where the teamsters led,
The wise old Doctor went his round,

659. The *wise old Doctor* was Dr. Weld of Haverhill, an able
man, who died at the age of ninety-six.

Just pausing at our door to say   660
In the brief autocratic way
Of one who, prompt at Duty's call,
Was free to urge her claim on all,
   That some poor neighbor sick abed
At night our mother's aid would need.   665
For, one in generous thought and deed,
   What mattered in the sufferer's sight
   The Quaker matron's inward light,
The Doctor's mail of Calvin's creed ?
All hearts confess the saints elect   670
   Who, twain in faith, in love agree,
And melt not in an acid sect
   The Christian pearl of charity !

So days went on : a week had passed
Since the great world was heard from last.   675
The Almanac we studied o'er,
Read and reread our little store
Of books and pamphlets, scarce a score ;
One harmless novel, mostly hid
From younger eyes, a book forbid,   680
And poetry, (or good or bad,
A single book was all we had,)
Where Ellwood's meek, drab-skirted Muse,
   A stranger to the heathen Nine,
   Sang, with a somewhat nasal whine,   685

683. Thomas Ellwood, one of the Society of Friends, a contemporary and friend of Milton, and the suggestor of *Paradise Regained*, wrote an epic poem in five books, called *Davideis*, the life of King David of Israel. He wrote the book, we are told, for his own diversion, so it was not necessary that others should be diverted by it. Ellwood's autobiography, a quaint and delightful book, is included in Howells's series of *Choice Autobiographies*.

The wars of David and the Jews.
At last the floundering carrier bore
The village paper to our door.
Lo! broadening outward as we read,
To warmer zones the horizon spread;　　690
In panoramic length unrolled
We saw the marvels that it told.
Before us passed the painted Creeks,
　And daft McGregor on his raids
　In Costa Rica's everglades.　　695
　And up Taygetus winding slow
Rode Ypsilanti's Mainote Greeks,
　A Turk's head at each saddle bow!
Welcome to us its week old news,
Its corner for the rustic Muse,　　700
　Its monthly gauge of snow and rain,
Its record, mingling in a breath
The wedding knell and dirge of death;
Jest, anecdote, and love-lorn tale,
The latest culprit sent to jail;　　705
Its hue and cry of stolen and lost,
Its vendue sales and goods at cost,
　And traffic calling loud for gain.
We felt the stir of hall and street,
The pulse of life that round us beat;　　710
The chill embargo of the snow

693. Referring to the removal of the Creek Indians from Georgia to beyond the Mississippi.

694. In 1822 Sir Gregor McGregor, a Scotchman, began an ineffectual attempt to establish a colony in Costa Rica.

697. Taygetus is a mountain on the Gulf of Messenia in Greece, and near by is the district of Maina, noted for its robbers and pirates. It was from these mountaineers that Ypsilanti, a Greek patriot, drew his cavalry in the struggle with Turkey which resulted in the independence of Greece.

Was melted in the genial glow ;
Wide swung again our ice-locked door,
And all the world was ours once more !

Clasp, Angel of the backward look   715
   And folded wings of ashen gray
   And voice of echoes far away,
The brazen covers of thy book ;
The weird palimpsest old and vast,
Wherein thou hid'st the spectral past ;   720
Where, closely mingling, pale and glow
The characters of joy and woe ;
The monographs of outlived years,
Or smile-illumed or dim with tears,
Green hills of life that slope to death,   725
   And haunts of home, whose vistaed trees
   Shade off to mournful cypresses
With the white amaranths underneath.
Even while I look, I can but heed
   The restless sands' incessant fall,   730
Importunate hours that hours succeed,
Each clamorous with its own sharp need,
   And duty keeping pace with all.
Shut down and clasp the heavy lids ;
I hear again the voice that bids   735
The dreamer leave his dream midway
   For larger hopes and graver fears :
   Life greatens in these later years,
The century's aloe flowers to-day !

Yet, haply, in some lull of life,   740
Some Truce of God which breaks its strife,

741. The name is drawn from a historic compact in 1040,
when the Church forbade barons to make any attack on each

The worldling's eyes shall gather dew,
  Dreaming in throngful city ways
Of winter joys his boyhood knew;
And dear and early friends — the few   745
Who yet remain — shall pause to view
  These Flemish pictures of old days;
Sit with me by the homestead hearth,
And stretch the hands of memory forth
  To warm them at the wood-fire's blaze!   750
And thanks untraced to lips unknown
Shall greet me like the odors blown
From unseen meadows newly mown,
Or lilies floating in some pond,
Wood-fringed, the wayside gaze beyond;   755
The traveller owns the grateful sense
Of sweetness near, he knows not whence,
And, pausing, takes with forehead bare
The benediction of the air.

THE SHIP-BUILDERS.

The sky is ruddy in the east,
  The earth is gray below,
And, spectral in the river-mist,
  The ship's white timbers show.
Then let the sounds of measured stroke   5
  And grating saw begin;

other between sunset on Wednesday and sunrise on the following
Monday, or upon any ecclesiastical fast or feast day. It also
provided that no man was to molest a laborer working in the
fields, or to lay hands on any implement of husbandry, on pain
of excommunication.

747. The Flemish school of painting was chiefly occupied with
homely interiors.

The broad-axe to the gnarléd oak,
  The mallet to the pin!

Hark! roars the bellows, blast on blast,
  The sooty smithy jars,   10
And fire-sparks, rising far and fast,
  Are fading with the stars.
All day for us the smith shall stand
  Beside that flashing forge;
All day for us his heavy hand   15
  The groaning anvil scourge.

From far-off hills, the panting team
  For us is toiling near;
For us the raftsmen down the stream
  Their island barges steer.   20
Rings out for us the axe-man's stroke
  In forests old and still;
For us the century-circled oak
  Falls crashing down his hill.

Up! up! in nobler toil than ours   25
  No craftsmen bear a part:
We make of Nature's giant powers
  The slaves of human Art.
Lay rib to rib and beam to beam,
  And drive the treenails free;   30
Nor faithless joint nor yawning seam
  Shall tempt the searching sea!

Where'er the keel of our good ship
  The sea's rough field shall plough;
Where'er her tossing spars shall drip   35
  With salt-spray caught below;

That ship must heed her master's beck,
　Her helm obey his hand,
And seamen tread her reeling deck
　As if they trod the land.

Her oaken ribs the vulture-beak
　Of Northern ice may peel;
The sunken rock and coral peak
　May grate along her keel;
And know we well the painted shell
　We give to wind and wave,
Must float, the sailor's citadel,
　Or sink, the sailor's grave!

Ho! strike away the bars and blocks,
　And set the good ship free!
Why lingers on these dusty rocks
　The young bride of the sea?
Look! how she moves adown the grooves,
　In graceful beauty now!
How lowly on the breast she loves
　Sinks down her virgin prow!

God bless her! wheresoe'er the breeze
　Her snowy wing shall fan,
Aside the frozen Hebrides,
　Or sultry Hindostan!
Where'er, in mart or on the main,
　With peaceful flag unfurled,
She helps to wind the silken chain
　Of commerce round the world!

Speed on the ship! But let her bear
　No merchandise of sin,

No groaning cargo of despair
  Her roomy hold within ;
No Lethean drug for Eastern lands,
  Nor poison-draught for ours ;   70
But honest fruits of toiling hands
  And Nature's sun and showers.

Be hers the Prairie's golden grain,
  The Desert's golden sand,
The clustered fruits of sunny Spain,   75
  The spice of Morning-land !
Her pathway on the open main
  May blessings follow free,
And glad hearts welcome back again
  Her white sails from the sea !   80

THE WORSHIP OF NATURE.

THE harp at Nature's advent strung
  Has never ceased to play ;
The song the stars of morning sung
  Has never died away.

And prayer is made, and praise is given,   5
  By all things near and far ;
The ocean looketh up to heaven,
  And mirrors every star.

Its waves are kneeling on the strand,
  As kneels the human knee,   10
Their white locks bowing to the sand,
  The priesthood of the sea !

They pour their glittering treasures forth,
  Their gifts of pearl they bring,

And all the listening hills of earth   15
  Take up the song they sing.

The green earth sends her incense up
  From many a mountain shrine;
From folded leaf and dewy cup
  She pours her sacred wine.   20

The mists above the morning rills
  Rise white as wings of prayer;
The altar-curtains of the hills
  Are sunset's purple air.

The winds with hymns of praise are loud,   25
  Or low with sobs of pain, —
The thunder-organ of the cloud,
  The dropping tears of rain.

With drooping head and branches crossed
  The twilight forest grieves,   30
Or speaks with tongues of Pentecost
  From all its sunlit leaves.

The blue sky is the temple's arch,
  Its transept earth and air,
The music of its starry march   35
  The chorus of a prayer.

So Nature keeps the reverent frame
  With which her years began,
And all her signs and voices shame
  The prayerless heart of man.   40

HENRY DAVID THOREAU.

BIOGRAPHICAL SKETCH.

THERE died at Concord, Massachusetts, in the year 1862, a man of forty-five who, if one were to take his word for it, need never have gone out of the little village of Concord to see all that was worth seeing in the world. Lowell, in his *My Garden Acquaintance*, reminds the reader of Gilbert White, who, in his *Natural History of Selborne*, gave minute details of a lively world found within the borders of a little English parish. Alphonse Karr, a French writer, has written a book which contracts the limit still further in *A Journey round my Garden*, but neither of these writers so completely isolated himself from the outside world as did Thoreau, who had a collegiate education at Harvard, made short journeys to Cape Cod, Maine, and Canada, acted for a little while as tutor in a family on Staten Island, but spent the best part of his life as a looker-on in Concord, and during two years of the time lived a hermit on the shores of Walden Pond. He made his living, as the phrase goes, by the occupation of a land surveyor, but he followed the profession only when it suited his convenience. He did not marry; he never went to church; he never voted; he refused to pay taxes; he sought no society; he declined companions when they were in his way, and when he had anything to say in public, went about from door to door and invited people to come to a hall to hear him deliver his word.

That he had something to say to the world at large is

pretty evident from the books which he has left, and it is intimated that the unpublished records of his observation and reflection are more extensive. Thus far his published writings are contained in ten volumes. The first in appearance was *A Week on the Concord and Merrimack Rivers.* It was published in 1849 and built upon the adventures of himself and brother ten years before, when, in a boat of their own construction, they had made their way from Concord down the Concord River to the Merrimack, up that to its source, and back to the starting point. It will readily be seen that such an excursion would not yield a bookful of observation, and though Thoreau notes in it many trivial incidents, a great part of the contents is in the reflections which he makes from day to day. He comes to the little river with its sparse border of population and meagre history, and insists upon measuring antiquity and fame by it. All of his reading he tests by the measure of this stream, and undertakes to show that the terms, big and little, are very much misapplied, and that here on this miniature scale one may read all that is worth knowing in life. His voyage is treated with the gravity which one might use in recording a journey to find the sources of the Nile.

Between the date of the journey and the publication of the book, Thoreau was engaged upon an experiment still more illustrative of his creed of individuality. In 1845 he built a hut in the woods by Walden Pond, and for two years lived a self-contained life there. It was not altogether a lonely life. He was within easy walking distance of Concord village, and the novelty of his housekeeping attracted many visitors, while his friends who valued his conversation sought him out in his hermitage. Besides and beyond this Thoreau had a genius for intercourse with humbler companions. There have been few instances in history of such perfect understanding as existed between him and the lower orders of creation. It has been said of him: " Every fact which occurs in the bed [of the Concord

Henry D. Thoreau.

River], on the banks, or in the air over it; the fishes, and their spawning and nests, their manners, their food; the shad-flies which fill the air on a certain evening once a year, and which are snapped at by the fishes so ravenously that many of these die of repletion, the conical heaps of small stones on the river-shallows, one of which heaps will sometimes overfill a cart, — these heaps the huge nests of small fishes, — the birds which frequent the stream, heron, duck, sheldrake, loon, osprey; the snake, muskrat, otter, woodchuck, and fox on the banks; the turtle, frog, hyla, and cricket which made the banks vocal, — were all known to him, and, as it were, townsmen and fellow-creatures. . . . His power of observation seemed to indicate additional senses. He saw as with microscrope, heard as with ear-trumpet, and his memory was a photographic register of all he saw and heard. . . . His intimacy with animals suggested what Thomas Fuller records of Butler the apiologist, that 'either he had told the bees things or the bees had told him;' snakes coiled round his leg; the fishes swam into his hand, and he took them out of the water; he pulled the woodchuck out of its hole by the tail, and took the foxes under his protection from the hunters." [1]

Walden, published in 1854, is the record of Thoreau's life in the woods, and inasmuch as that life was not exhausted in the bare provision against bodily wants, nor in the observation even of what lay under the eye and ear, but was busied about the questions which perplex all who would give an account of themselves, the record mingles common fact and personal experience, the world without and the world within. Thoreau records what he sees and hears in the woods, but these sights and sounds are the texts for sermons upon human life. He undertook to get at the elementary conditions of living, and to strip himself as far as he could of all that was unnecessary. In doing this he discovered many curious and ingenious things, and the unique

[1] Emerson's *Biographical Sketch.*

method which he took was pretty sure to give him glimpses of life not seen by others. But the method had its disadvantages, and chiefly this, that it was against the common order of things, and therefore the results reached could not be relied upon as sound and wholesome.

The great value of *Walden,* and indeed of all Thoreau's books, is not in the philosophy, which is often shrewd and often strained and arbitrary, but in the disclosure made of the common facts of the world about one. He used to say, " I think nothing is to be hoped from you, if this bit of mould under your feet is not sweeter to you to eat than any other in this world, or in any world ; " and the whole drift of his writing is toward the development of the individual in the place where he happens to be. Thoreau's protesting attitude, and the stout resistance which he made to all influences about him except the common ones of nature, betray themselves in the style of his writing. He has a way, almost insolent, of throwing out his thoughts, and growling forth his objections to the conventions of life, which renders his writing often crabbed and inartistic. There is a rudeness which seems sometimes affected, and a carelessness which is contemptuous. Yet often his indifference to style is a rugged insistence on the strongest thought, and in his effort to express himself unreservedly he reaches a force and energy which are refreshing.

A Week on the Concord and Merrimack Rivers and *Walden* were the only writings of Thoreau published in his lifetime. He printed contributions to the magazines from time to time, and out of these and his manuscripts have been gathered eight other volumes, *Excursions in Field and Forest, The Maine Woods, Cape Cod, Letters to Various Persons, A Yankee in Canada, Early Spring in Massachusetts, Summer* and *Winter.* To *Excursions* was prefixed a biographical sketch by R. W. Emerson, which gives one a very vivid portrait of this unique man. *Cape Cod,* which is the record of a walk taken the length of the

Cape, and *Walden* are likely to remain as the most finished and agreeable of Thoreau's books. All of his writings, however, will be searched for the evidence which they give of a mind singular for its independence, its resolute confronting of the problems of life, its insight into nature, its isolation, and its waywardness.

WILD APPLES.

THE HISTORY OF THE APPLE-TREE.

IT is remarkable how closely the history of the Apple-tree is connected with that of man. The geologist tells us that the order of the *Rosaceæ*, which includes the Apple, also the true Grasses, and the *Labiatæ*, or Mints, were introduced only a short time previous to the appearance of man on the globe.

It appears that apples made a part of the food of that unknown primitive people whose traces have lately been found at the bottom of the Swiss lakes, supposed to be older than the foundation of Rome, so old that they had no metallic implements. An entire black and shrivelled Crab-Apple has been recovered from their stores.

Tacitus says of the ancient Germans that they satisfied their hunger with wild apples, among other things.

Niebuhr[1] observes that " the words for a house, a field, a plough, ploughing, wine, oil, milk, sheep, apples, and others relating to agriculture and the gentler ways of life, agree in Latin and Greek, while the Latin words for all objects pertaining to war or the chase are utterly alien from the Greek." Thus the apple-tree may be considered a symbol of peace no less than the olive.

[1] A German historical critic of ancient life.

The apple was early so important, and so generally distributed, that its name traced to its root in many languages signifies fruit in general. Μῆλον [Mēlon], in Greek, means an apple, also the fruit of other trees, also a sheep and any cattle, and finally riches in general.

The apple-tree has been celebrated by the Hebrews, Greeks, Romans, and Scandinavians. Some have thought that the first human pair were tempted by its fruit. Goddesses are fabled to have contended for it, dragons were set to watch it, and heroes were employed to pluck it.[1]

The tree is mentioned in at least three places in the Old Testament, and its fruit in two or three more. Solomon sings, "As the apple-tree among the trees of the wood, so is my beloved among the sons." And again, "Stay me with flagons, comfort me with apples." The noblest part of man's noblest feature is named from this fruit, "the apple of the eye."

The apple-tree is also mentioned by Homer and Herodotus. Ulysses saw in the glorious garden of Alcinoüs "pears and pomegranates and apple-trees bearing beautiful fruit." And according to Homer, apples were among the fruits which Tantalus could not pluck, the wind ever blowing their boughs away from him. Theophrastus knew and described the apple-tree as a botanist.

According to the prose Edda,[2] "Iduna keeps in a box the apples which the gods, when they feel old age approaching, have only to taste of to become young again. It is in this manner that they will be kept in

---

[1] The Greek myths especially referred to are The Choice of Paris and The Apples of the Hesperides.

[2] The stories of the early Scandinavians.

renovated youth until Ragnarök " (or the destruction of the Gods).

I learn from Loudon[1] that "the ancient Welsh bards were rewarded for excelling in song by the token of the apple-spray; " and "in the Highlands of Scotland the apple-tree is the badge of the clan Lamont."

The apple-tree belongs chiefly to the northern temperate zone. Loudon says, that "it grows spontaneously in every part of Europe except the frigid zone, and throughout Western Asia, China and Japan." We have also two or three varieties of the apple indigenous in North America. The cultivated apple-tree was first introduced into this country by the earliest settlers, and is thought to do as well or better here than anywhere else. Probably some of the varieties which are now cultivated were first introduced into Britain by the Romans.

Pliny, adopting the distinction of Theophrastus, says, "Of trees there are some which are altogether wild, some more civilized." Theophrastus includes the apple among the last; and, indeed, it is in this sense the most civilized of all trees. It is as harmless as a dove, as beautiful as a rose, and as valuable as flocks and herds. It has been longer cultivated than any other, and so is more humanized; and who knows but, like the dog, it will at length be no longer traceable to its wild original? It migrates with man, like the dog and horse and cow; first, perchance, from Greece to Italy, thence to England, thence to America; and our Western emigrant is still marching steadily toward the setting sun with the seeds of the apple in

[1] An English authority on the culture of orchards and gardens.

his pocket, or perhaps a few young trees strapped to his load. At least a million apple-trees are thus set farther westward this year than any cultivated ones grew last year. Consider how the Blossom-Week, like the Sabbath, is thus annually spreading over the prairies; for when man migrates he carries with him not only his birds, quadrupeds, insects, vegetables, and his very sward, but his orchard also.

The leaves and tender twigs are an agreeable food to many domestic animals, as the cow, horse, sheep, and goat; and the fruit is sought after by the first, as well as by the hog. Thus there appears to have existed a natural alliance between these animals and this tree from the first. "The fruit of the Crab in the forests of France" is said to be "a great resource for the wild boar."

Not only the Indian, but many indigenous insects, birds, and quadrupeds, welcomed the apple-tree to these shores. The tent-caterpillar saddled her eggs on the very first twig that was formed, and it has since shared her affections with the wild cherry; and the canker-worm also in a measure abandoned the elm to feed on it. As it grew apace, the bluebird, robin, cherry-bird, king-bird, and many more, came with haste and built their nests and warbled in its boughs, and so became orchard-birds, and multiplied more than ever. It was an era in the history of their race. The downy woodpecker found such a savory morsel under its bark, that he perforated it in a ring quite round the tree before he left it, — a thing which he had never done before, to my knowledge. It did not take the partridge long to find out how sweet its buds were, and every winter eve she flew, and still flies, from the wood, to pluck them, much to the farmer's sorrow. The rabbit, too, was not slow to learn the taste of its twigs and bark; and when the fruit was ripe, the squirrel half-rolled, half-carried it to his hole; and even the musquash crept up the bank from the brook at evening, and greedily devoured it, until he had worn a path in the grass there; and when it was frozen and thawed, the crow and the jay were glad to taste it occasionally. The owl crept into the first apple-tree that became hollow, and fairly hooted with delight, finding it just the place for him; so, settling down into it, he has remained there ever since.

My theme being the Wild Apple, I will merely glance at some of the seasons in the annual growth of the cultivated apple, and pass on to my special province.

The flowers of the apple are perhaps the most beautiful of any tree, so copious and so delicious to both sight and scent. The walker is frequently tempted to turn and linger near some more than usually handsome one, whose blossoms are two thirds expanded. How superior it is in these respects to the pear, whose blossoms are neither colored nor fragrant!

By the middle of July, green apples are so large as to remind us of coddling, and of the autumn. The sward is commonly strewed with little ones which fall still-born, as it were, — Nature thus thinning them for us. The Roman writer Palladius said: "If apples are inclined to fall before their time, a stone placed in a split root will retain them." Some such notion, still surviving, may account for some of the stones which we see placed to be overgrown in the forks of trees. They have a saying in Suffolk, England, —

> "At Michaelmas time, or a little before,
> Half an apple goes to the core."

Early apples begin to be ripe about the first of August; but I think that none of them are so good to eat as some to smell. One is worth more to scent your handkerchief with than any perfume which they sell in the shops. The fragrance of some fruits is not to be forgotten, along with that of flowers. Some gnarly apple which I pick up in the road reminds me by its fragrance of all the wealth of Pomona,[1] — carrying me forward to those days when they will be collected in golden and ruddy heaps in the orchards and about the cider-mills.

A week or two later, as you are going by orchards or gardens, especially in the evenings, you pass through a little region possessed by the fragrance of ripe apples, and thus enjoy them without price, and without robbing anybody.

There is thus about all natural products a certain volatile and ethereal quality which represents their highest value, and which cannot be vulgarized, or bought and sold. No mortal has ever enjoyed the perfect flavor of any fruit, and only the godlike among men begin to taste its ambrosial qualities. For nectar and ambrosia are only those fine flavors of every earthly fruit which our coarse palates fail to perceive, — just as we occupy the heaven of the gods without knowing it. When I see a particularly mean man carrying a load of fair and fragrant early apples to market, I seem to see a contest going on between him and his horse, on the one side, and the apples on the other, and, to my mind, the apples always gain it. Pliny says that apples are the heaviest of all things, and that the oxen begin to sweat at the mere sight of a load of them. Our driver begins to lose his load

[1] The Roman goddess of fruit and fruit-trees.

the moment he tries to transport them to where they do not belong, that is, to any but the most beautiful. Though he gets out from time to time, and feels of them, and thinks they are all there, I see the stream of their evanescent and celestial qualities going to heaven from his cart, while the pulp and skin and core only are going to market. They are not apples, but pomace. Are not these still Iduna's apples, the taste of which keeps the gods forever young? and think you that they will let Loki or Thjassi carry them off to Jötunheim,[1] while they grow wrinkled and gray? No, for Ragnarök, or the destruction of the gods, is not yet.

There is another thinning of the fruit, commonly near the end of August or in September, when the ground is strewn with windfalls; and this happens especially when high winds occur after rain. In some orchards you may see fully three quarters of the whole crop on the ground, lying in a circular form beneath the trees, yet hard and green, — or, if it is a hillside, rolled far down the hill. However, it is an ill wind that blows nobody any good. All the country over, people are busy picking up the windfalls, and this will make them cheap for early apple-pies.

In October, the leaves falling, the apples are more distinct on the trees. I saw one year in a neighboring town some trees fuller of fruit than I remember to have ever seen before, small yellow apples hanging over the road. The branches were gracefully drooping with their weight, like a barberry-bush, so that

---

[1] Jötunheim (*Ye(r)t'-un-hime*) in Scandinavian mythology was the home of the Jötun or Giants. Loki was a descendant of the gods, and a companion of the Giants. Thjassi (*Tee-assy*) was a giant.

the whole tree acquired a new character. Even the topmost branches, instead of standing erect, spread and drooped in all directions; and there were so many poles supporting the lower ones, that they looked like pictures of banian-trees. As an old English manuscript says, "The mo appelen the tree bereth the more sche boweth to the folk."

Surely the apple is the noblest of fruits. Let the most beautiful or the swiftest have it. That should be the "going" price of apples.

Between the fifth and twentieth of October I see the barrels lie under the trees. And perhaps I talk with one who is selecting some choice barrels to fulfil an order. He turns a specked one over many times before he leaves it out. If I were to tell what is passing in my mind, I should say that every one was specked which he had handled; for he rubs off all the bloom, and those fugacious ethereal qualities leave it. Cool evenings prompt the farmers to make haste, and at length I see only the ladders here and there left leaning against the trees.

It would be well if we accepted these gifts with more joy and gratitude, and did not think it enough simply to put a fresh load of compost about the tree. Some old English customs are suggestive at least. I find them described chiefly in Brand's "Popular Antiquities." It appears that "on Christmas eve the farmers and their men in Devonshire take a large bowl of cider, with a toast in it, and carrying it in state to the orchard, they salute the apple-trees with much ceremony, in order to make them bear well the next season." This salutation consists in "throwing some of the cider about the roots of the tree, placing bits of the toast on the branches," and then, "encir-

cling one of the best bearing trees in the orchard,
they drink the following toast three several times : —

> "'Here 's to thee, old apple-tree,
> Whence thou mayst bud, and whence thou mayst blow,
> And whence thou mayst bear apples enow !
> Hats-full ! caps-full !
> Bushel, bushel, sacks-full !
> And my pockets full, too ! Hurra!'"

Also what was called "apple-howling" used to be
practised in various counties of England on New-
Year's eve. A troop of boys visited the different
orchards, and, encircling the apple-trees, repeated the
following words : —

> "Stand fast, root ! bear well, top !
> Pray God send us a good howling crop :
> Every twig, apples big ;
> Every bow, apples enow ! "

"They then shout in chorus, one of the boys accom-
panying them on a cow's horn. During this cere-
mony they rap the trees with their sticks." This is
called "wassailing" the trees, and is thought by some
to be "a relic of the heathen sacrifice to Pomona."

Herrick sings, —

> "Wassaile the trees that they may beare
> You many a plum and many a peare ;
> For more or less fruits they will bring
> As you so give them wassailing."

Our poets have as yet a better right to sing of cider
than of wine ; but it behooves them to sing better than
English Phillips did, else they will do no credit to
their Muse.

THE WILD APPLE.

So much for the more civilized apple-trees (*urba-
niores*, as Pliny calls them). I love better to go

through the old orchards of ungrafted apple-trees, at whatever season of the year, — so irregularly planted : sometimes two trees standing close together; and the rows so devious that you would think that they not only had grown while the owner was sleeping, but had been set out by him in a somnambulic state. The rows of grafted fruit will never tempt me to wander amid them like these. But I now, alas, speak rather from memory than from any recent experience, such ravages have been made !

Some soils, like a rocky tract called the Easter-brooks Country in my neighborhood, are so suited to the apple, that it will grow faster in them without any care, or if only the ground is broken up once a year, than it will in many places with any amount of care. The owners of this tract allow that the soil is excellent for fruit, but they say that it is so rocky that they have not patience to plough it, and that, together with the distance, is the reason why it is not cultivated. There are, or were recently, extensive orchards there standing without order. Nay, they spring up wild and bear well there in the midst of pines, birches, maples, and oaks. I am often surprised to see rising amid these trees the rounded tops of apple-trees glowing with red or yellow fruit, in harmony with the autumnal tints of the forest.

Going up the side of a cliff about the first of November, I saw a vigorous young apple-tree, which, planted by birds or cows, had shot up amid the rocks and open woods there, and had now much fruit on it, uninjured by the frosts, when all cultivated apples were gathered. It was a rank wild growth, with many green leaves on it still, and made an impression of thorniness. The fruit was hard and green, but looked as if it would be palatable in the winter. Some was dangling on the twigs, but more half-buried in the wet leaves under the tree, or rolled far down the hill amid the rocks. The owner knows nothing of it. The day was not observed when it first blossomed, nor when it first bore fruit, unless by the chickadee. There was no dancing on the green beneath it in its honor, and now there is no hand to pluck its fruit, — which is only gnawed by squirrels, as I perceive. It has done double duty, — not only borne this crop, but each twig has grown a foot into the air. And this is *such* fruit! bigger than many berries, we must admit, and carried home will be sound and palatable next spring. What care I for Iduna's apples so long as I can get these?

When I go by this shrub thus late and hardy, and see its dangling fruit, I respect the tree, and I am grateful for Nature's bounty, even though I cannot eat it. Here on this rugged and woody hillside has grown an apple-tree, not planted by man, no relic of a former orchard, but a natural growth, like the pines and oaks. Most fruits which we prize and use depend entirely on our care. Corn and grain, potatoes, peaches, melons, etc., depend altogether on our planting; but the apple emulates man's independence and enterprise. It is not simply carried, as I have said, but, like him, to some extent, it has migrated to this New World, and is even, here and there, making its way amid the aboriginal trees; just as the ox and dog and horse sometimes run wild and maintain themselves.

Even the sourest and crabbedest apple, growing in the most unfavorable position, suggests such thoughts as these, it is so noble a fruit.

THE CRAB.

Nevertheless, *our* wild apple is wild only like myself, perchance, who belong not to the aboriginal race here, but have strayed into the woods from the cultivated stock. Wilder still, as I have said, there grows elsewhere in this country a native and aboriginal Crab-Apple, "whose nature has not yet been modified by cultivation." It is found from Western New York to Minnesota and southward. Michaux[1] says that its ordinary height "is fifteen or eighteen feet, but it is sometimes found twenty-five or thirty feet high," and that the large ones "exactly resemble the common apple-tree." "The flowers are white mingled with rose-color, and are collected in corymbs." They are remarkable for their delicious odor. The fruit, according to him, is about an inch and a half in diameter, and is intensely acid. Yet they make fine sweetmeats, and also cider of them. He concludes, that "if, on being cultivated, it does not yield new and palatable varieties, it will at least be celebrated for the beauty of its flowers, and for the sweetness of its perfume."

I never saw the Crab-Apple till May, 1861. I had heard of it through Michaux, but more modern botanists, so far as I know, have not treated it as of any peculiar importance. Thus it was a half-fabulous tree to me. I contemplated a pilgrimage to the " Glades," a portion of Pennsylvania, where it was said to grow to perfection. I thought of sending to a nursery for it, but doubted if they had it, or would distinguish it from European varieties. At last I had occasion to go to Minnesota, and on entering Michigan I began

[1] Pronounced *mee-shŏ'* ; a French botanist and traveller.

to notice from the cars a tree with handsome rose-colored flowers. At first I thought it some variety of thorn; but it was not long before the truth flashed on me, that this was my long-sought Crab-Apple. It was the prevailing flowering shrub or tree to be seen from the cars at that season of the year, — about the middle of May. But the cars never stopped before one, and so I was launched on the bosom of the Mississippi without having touched one, experiencing the fate of Tantalus. On arriving at St. Anthony's Falls, I was sorry to be told that I was too far north for the Crab-Apple. Nevertheless I succeeded in finding it about eight miles west of the Falls; touched it and smelled it, and secured a lingering corymb of flowers for my herbarium. This must have been near its northern limit.

HOW THE WILD APPLE GROWS.

But though these are indigenous, like the Indians, I doubt whether they are any hardier than those back-woodsmen among the apple-trees, which, though descended from cultivated stocks, plant themselves in distant fields and forests, where the soil is favorable to them. I know of no trees which have more difficulties to contend with, and which more sturdily resist their foes. These are the ones whose story we have to tell. It oftentimes reads thus : —

Near the beginning of May, we notice little thickets of apple-trees just springing up in the pastures where cattle have been, — as the rocky ones of our Easterbrooks Country, or the top of Nobscot Hill in Sudbury. One or two of these perhaps survive the drought and other accidents, — their very birthplace defending them against the encroaching grass and some other dangers, at first.

In two years' time 't had thus
    Reached the level of the rocks,
Admired the stretching world,
    Nor feared the wandering flocks.

But at this tender age
    Its sufferings began :
There came a browsing ox
    And cut it down a span.

This time, perhaps, the ox does not notice it amid the
grass ; but the next year, when it has grown more
stout, he recognizes it for a fellow-emigrant from the
old country, the flavor of whose leaves and twigs he
well knows ; and though at first he pauses to welcome
it, and express his surprise, and gets for answer, " The
same cause that brought you here brought me," he
nevertheless browses it again, reflecting, it may be,
that he has some title to it.

Thus cut down annually, it does not despair ; but,
putting forth two short twigs for every one cut off, it
spreads out low along the ground in the hollows or
between the rocks, growing more stout and scrubby,
until it forms, not a tree as yet, but a little pyramidal,
stiff, twiggy mass, almost as solid and impenetrable
as a rock. Some of the densest and most impenetra-
ble clumps of bushes that I have ever seen, as well
on account of the closeness and stubbornness of their
branches as of their thorns, have been these wild-apple
scrubs. They are more like the scrubby fir and black
spruce on which you stand, and sometimes walk, on
the tops of mountains, where cold is the demon they
contend with, than anything else. No wonder they
are prompted to grow thorns at last, to defend them-
selves against such foes. In their thorniness, how-
ever, there is no malice, only some malic acid.

The rocky pastures of the tract I have referred to — for they maintain their ground best in a rocky field — are thickly sprinkled with these little tufts, reminding you often of some rigid gray mosses or lichens, and you see thousands of little trees just springing up between them, with the seed still attached to them.

Being regularly clipped all around each year by the cows, as a hedge with shears, they are often of a perfect conical or pyramidal form, from one to four feet high, and more or less sharp, as if trimmed by the gardener's art. In the pastures on Nobscot Hill and its spurs they make fine dark shadows when the sun is low. They are also an excellent covert from hawks for many small birds that roost and build in them. Whole flocks perch in them at night, and I have seen three robins' nests in one which was six feet in diameter.

No doubt many of these are already old trees, if you reckon from the day they were planted, but infants still when you consider their development and the long life before them. I counted the annual rings of some which were just one foot high, and as wide as high, and found that they were about twelve years old, but quite sound and thrifty! They were so low that they were unnoticed by the walker, while many of their contemporaries from the nurseries were already bearing considerable crops. But what you gain in time is perhaps in this case, too, lost in power, — that is, in the vigor of the tree. This is their pyramidal state.

The cows continue to browse them thus for twenty years or more, keeping them down and compelling them to spread, until at last they are so broad that they become their own fence, when some interior shoot, which their foes cannot reach, darts upward with joy: for it has not forgotten its high calling, and bears its own peculiar fruit in triumph.

Such are the tactics by which it finally defeats its bovine foes. Now, if you have watched the progress of a particular shrub, you will see that it is no longer a simple pyramid or cone, but out of its apex there rises a sprig or two, growing more lustily perchance than an orchard-tree, since the plant now devotes the whole of its repressed energy to these upright parts. In a short time these become a small tree, an inverted pyramid resting on the apex of the other, so that the whole has now the form of a vast hour-glass. The spreading bottom, having served its purpose, finally disappears, and the generous tree permits the now harmless cows to come in and stand in its shade, and rub against and redden its trunk, which has grown in spite of them, and even to taste a part of its fruit, and so disperse the seed.

Thus the cows create their own shade and food; and the tree, its hour-glass being inverted, lives a second life, as it were.

It is an important question with some nowadays, whether you should trim young apple-trees as high as your nose or as high as your eyes. The ox trims them up as high as he can reach, and that is about the right height, I think.

In spite of wandering kine and other adverse circumstance, that despised shrub, valued only by small birds as a covert and shelter from hawks, has its blossom-week at last, and in course of time its harvest, sincere, though small.

By the end of some October, when its leaves have

fallen, I frequently see such a central sprig, whose progress I have watched, when I thought it had forgotten its destiny, as I had, bearing its first crop of small green or yellow or rosy fruit, which the cows cannot get at over the bushy and thorny hedge which surrounds it; and I make haste to taste the new and undescribed variety. We have all heard of the numerous varieties of fruit invented by Van Mons [1] and Knight.[2] This is the system of Van Cow, and she has invented far more and more memorable varieties than both of them.

Through what hardships it may attain to bear a sweet fruit! Though somewhat small, it may prove equal, if not superior, in flavor to that which has grown in a garden, — will perchance be all the sweeter and more palatable for the very difficulties it has had to contend with. Who knows but this chance wild fruit, planted by a cow or a bird on some remote and rocky hillside, where it is as yet unobserved by man, may be the choicest of all its kind, and foreign potentates shall hear of it, and royal societies seek to propagate it, though the virtues of the perhaps truly crabbed owner of the soil may never be heard of, — at least, beyond the limits of his village? It was thus the Porter and the Baldwin grew.

Every wild-apple shrub excites our expectation thus, somewhat as every wild child. It is, perhaps, a prince in disguise. What a lesson to man! So are human beings, referred to the highest standard, the celestial fruit which they suggest and aspire to bear, browsed on by fate; and only the most persistent and strongest genius defends itself and prevails, sends a tender

---

[1] A Belgian chemist and horticulturist.

[2] An English vegetable physiologist.

scion upward at last, and drops its perfect fruit on the ungrateful earth. Poets and philosophers and statesmen thus spring up in the country pastures, and outlast the hosts of unoriginal men.

Such is always the pursuit of knowledge. The celestial fruits, the golden apples of the Hesperides, are ever guarded by a hundred-headed dragon which never sleeps, so that it is an herculean labor to pluck them.

This is one and the most remarkable way in which the wild apple is propagated ; but commonly it springs up at wide intervals in woods and swamps, and by the sides of roads, as the soil may suit it, and grows with comparative rapidity. Those which grow in dense woods are very tall and slender. I frequently pluck from these trees a perfectly mild and tamed fruit. As Palladius says, "And the ground is strewn with the fruit of an unbidden apple-tree."

It is an old notion, that, if these wild trees do not bear a valuable fruit of their own, they are the best stocks by which to transmit to posterity the most highly prized qualities of others. However, I am not in search of stocks, but the wild fruit itself, whose fierce gust has suffered no " inteneration." It is not my

> "highest plot
> To plant the Bergamot."

THE FRUIT, AND ITS FLAVOR.

The time for wild apples is the last of October and the first of November. They then get to be palatable, for they ripen late, and they are still, perhaps, as beautiful as ever. I make a great account of these fruits, which the farmers do not think it worth the while to gather, — wild flavors of the Muse, vivacious and inspiriting. The farmer thinks that he has better in his barrels; but he is mistaken, unless he has a walker's appetite and imagination, neither of which can he have.

Such as grow quite wild, and are left out till the first of November, I presume that the owner does not mean to gather. They belong to children as wild as themselves, — to certain active boys that I know, — to the wild-eyed woman of the fields, to whom nothing comes amiss, who gleans after all the world, — and, moreover, to us walkers. We have met with them, and they are ours. These rights, long enough insisted upon, have come to be an institution in some old countries, where they have learned how to live. I hear that " the custom of grippling, which may be called apple-gleaning, is, or was formerly, practised in Herefordshire. It consists in leaving a few apples, which are called the gripples, on every tree, after the general gathering, for the boys, who go with climbing-poles and bags to collect them."

As for those I speak of, I pluck them as a wild fruit, native to this quarter of the earth, — fruit of old trees that have been dying ever since I was a boy and are not yet dead, frequented only by the wood-pecker and the squirrel, deserted now by the owner, who has not faith enough to look under their boughs. From the appearance of the tree-top, at a little distance, you would- expect nothing but lichens to drop from it, but your faith is rewarded by finding the ground strewn with spirited fruit, — some of it, perhaps, collected at squirrel-holes, with the marks of their teeth by which they carried them, — some containing a cricket or two silently feeding within, and some, especially in damp days, a shelless snail. The very sticks and stones lodged in the tree-top might have convinced you of the savoriness of the fruit which has been so eagerly sought after in past years.

I have seen no account of these among the "Fruits and Fruit-Trees of America," though they are more memorable to my taste than the grafted kinds; more racy and wild American flavors do they possess, when October and November, when December and January, and perhaps February and March even, have assuaged them somewhat. An old farmer in my neighborhood, who always selects the right word, says that "they have a kind of bow-arrow tang."

Apples for grafting appear to have been selected commonly, not so much for their spirited flavor, as for their mildness, their size, and bearing qualities, — not so much for their beauty, as for their fairness and soundness. Indeed, I have no faith in the selected lists of pomological gentlemen. Their " Favorites " and " Non-suches " and " Seek-no-farthers," when I have fruited them, commonly turn out very tame and forgetable. They are eaten with comparatively little zest, and have no real *tang* nor *smack* to them.

What if some of these wildings are acrid and puckery, genuine *verjuice*, do they not still belong to the *Pomaceæ*, which are uniformly innocent and kind to our race? I still begrudge them to the cider-mill. Perhaps they are not fairly ripe yet.

No wonder that these small and high-colored apples are thought to make the best cider. Loudon quotes from the *Herefordshire Report* that " apples of a small size are always, if equal in quality, to be preferred to those of a larger size, in order that the rind and kernel may bear the greatest proportion to the pulp, which affords the weakest and most watery juice." And he says, that, " to prove this, Dr. Symonds of Hereford, about the year 1800, made one hogshead of cider entirely from the rinds and cores of apples, and another from the pulp only, when the first was found of extraordinary strength and flavor, while the latter was sweet and insipid."

Evelyn [1] says that the " Red-strake " was the favorite cider-apple in his day ; and he quotes one Dr. Newburg as saying, " In Jersey 't is a general observation, as I hear, that the more of red any apple has in its rind, the more proper it is for this use. Pale-faced apples they exclude as much as may be from their cider-vat." This opinion still prevails.

All apples are good in November. Those which the farmer leaves out as unsalable, and unpalatable to those who frequent the markets, are choicest fruit to the walker. But it is remarkable that the wild apple, which I praise as so spirited and racy when eaten in the fields or woods, being brought into the house, has frequently a harsh and crabbed taste. The Saunterer's Apple not even the saunterer can eat in the house. The palate rejects it there, as it does haws and acorns, and demands a tamed one ; for there you miss the November air, which is the sauce it is to be eaten with. Accordingly, when Tityrus, seeing the lengthening shadows, invites Melibœus to go home and pass the night with him, he promises him *mild* apples and soft chestnuts. I frequently pluck wild apples of so rich and spicy a flavor that I wonder all orchardists do not get a scion from that tree, and I fail not to bring home my pockets full. But perchance, when I take one out of my desk and taste it in my chamber I find it unexpectedly crude, — sour enough to set a squirrel's teeth on edge and make a jay scream.

[1] An English writer of the seventeenth century.

These apples have hung in the wind and frost and rain till they have absorbed the qualities of the weather or season, and thus are highly *seasoned,* and they *pierce* and *sting* and *permeate* us with their spirit. They must be eaten in *season,* accordingly, — that is, out-of-doors.

To appreciate the wild and sharp flavors of these October fruits, it is necessary that you be breathing the sharp October or November air. The out-door air and exercise which the walker gets give a different tone to his palate, and he craves a fruit which the sedentary would call harsh and crabbed. They must be eaten in the fields, when your system is all aglow with exercise, when the frosty weather nips your fingers, the wind rattles the bare boughs or rustles the few remaining leaves, and the jay is heard screaming around. What is sour in the house a bracing walk makes sweet. Some of these apples might be labelled, " To be eaten in the wind."

Of course no flavors are thrown away; they are intended for the taste that is up to them. Some apples have two distinct flavors, and perhaps one-half of them must be eaten in the house, the other out-doors. One Peter Whitney wrote from Northborough in 1782, for the Proceedings of the Boston Academy, describing an apple-tree in that town " producing fruit of opposite qualities, part of the same apple being frequently sour and the other sweet ; " also some all sour, and others all sweet, and this diversity on all parts of the tree.

There is a wild apple on Nawshawtuck Hill in my town which has to me a peculiarly pleasant bitter tang, not perceived till it is three-quarters tasted. It remains on the tongue. As you eat it, it smells exactly like a squash-bug.   It is a sort of triumph to eat and relish it.

I hear that the fruit of a kind of plum-tree in Provence is " called *Prunes sibarelles*, because it is impossible to whistle after having eaten them, from their sourness."   But perhaps they were only eaten in the house and in summer, and if tried out-of-doors in a stinging atmosphere, who knows but you could whistle an octave higher and clearer ?

In the fields only are the sours and bitters of Nature appreciated ; just as the wood-chopper eats his meal in a sunny glade, in the middle of a winter day, with content, basks in a sunny ray there, and dreams of summer in a degree of cold which, experienced in a chamber, would make a student miserable.   They who are at work abroad are not cold, but rather it is they who sit shivering in houses.   As with temperatures, so with flavors ; as with cold and heat, so with sour and sweet.   This natural raciness, the sours and bitters which the diseased palate refuses, are the true condiments.

Let your condiments be in the condition of your senses.   To appreciate the flavor of these wild apples requires vigorous and healthy senses, *papillæ* [1] firm and erect on the tongue and palate, not easily flattened and tamed.

From my experience with wild apples, I can understand that there may be reason for a savage's preferring many kinds of food which the civilized man rejects.   The former has the palate of an out-door man. It takes a savage or wild taste to appreciate a wild fruit.

[1] A Latin word, accent on the second syllable, meaning here the rough surface of the tongue and palate.

What a healthy out-of-door appetite it takes to relish the apple of life, the apple of the world, then !

"Nor is it every apple I desire,
    Nor that which pleases every palate best ;
'T is not the lasting Deuxan I require,
    Nor yet the red-cheeked Greening I request,
Nor that which first beshrewed the name of wife,
Nor that whose beauty caused the golden strife :
No, no ! bring me an apple from the tree of life."

So there is one *thought* for the field, another for the house. I would have my thoughts, like wild apples, to be food for walkers, and will not warrant them to be palatable, if tasted in the house.

THEIR BEAUTY.

Almost all wild apples are handsome. They cannot be too gnarly and crabbed and rusty to look at. The gnarliest will have some redeeming traits even to the eye. You will discover some evening redness dashed or sprinkled on some protuberance or in some cavity. It is rare that the summer lets an apple go without streaking or spotting it on some part of its sphere. It will have some red stains, commemorating the mornings and evenings it has witnessed ; some dark and rusty blotches, in memory of the clouds and foggy, mildewy days that have passed over it ; and a spacious field of green reflecting the general face of Nature, — green even as the fields ; or a yellow ground, which implies a milder flavor, — yellow as the harvest, or russet as the hills.

Apples, these I mean, unspeakably fair, — apples not of Discord, but Concord ! Yet not so rare but that the homeliest may have a share. Painted by the frosts, some a uniform clear bright yellow, or red, or crimson, as if their spheres had regularly revolved, and enjoyed the influence of the sun on all sides alike, — some with the faintest pink blush imaginable, — some brindled with deep red streaks like a cow, or with hundreds of fine blood-red rays running regularly from the stem-dimple to the blossom-end, like meridional lines, on a straw-colored ground, — some touched with a greenish rust, like a fine lichen, here and there, with crimson blotches or eyes more or less confluent and fiery when wet, — and others gnarly, and freckled or peppered all over on the stem side with fine crimson spots on a white ground, as if accidentally sprinkled from the brush of Him who paints the autumn leaves. Others, again, are sometimes red inside, perfused with a beautiful blush, fairy food, too beautiful to eat, — apple of the Hesperides, apple of the evening sky! But like shells and pebbles on the sea-shore, they must be seen as they sparkle amid the withering leaves in some dell in the woods, in the autumnal air, or as they lie in the wet grass, and not when they have wilted and faded in the house.

THE NAMING OF THEM.

It would be a pleasant pastime to find suitable names for the hundred varieties which go to a single heap at the cider-mill. Would it not tax a man's invention, — no one to be named after a man, and all in the *lingua vernacula?* [1] Who shall stand godfather at the christening of the wild apples? It would exhaust the Latin and Greek languages, if they were used, and make the *lingua vernacula* flag. We should have to call in the sunrise and the sunset, the rainbow and the autumn woods and the wild flowers,

----

[1] *Lingua vernac'ula,* common speech.

and the woodpecker and the purple finch, and the squirrel and the jay and the butterfly, the November traveller and the truant boy, to our aid.

In 1836 there were in the garden of the London Horticultural Society more than fourteen hundred distinct sorts. But here are species which they have not in their catalogue, not to mention the varieties which our Crab might yield to cultivation. Let us enumerate a few of these. I find myself compelled, after all, to give the Latin names of some for the benefit of those who live where English is not spoken, — for they are likely to have a world-wide reputation.

There is, first of all, the Wood-Apple (*Malus sylvatica*); the Blue-Jay Apple; the Apple which grows in Dells in the Woods (*sylvestrivallis*), also in Hollows in Pastures (*campestrivallis*); the Apple that grows in an old Cellar-Hole (*Malus cellaris*); the Meadow-Apple; the Partridge-Apple; the Truant's Apple (*Cessatoris*), which no boy will ever go by without knocking off some, however *late* it may be; the Saunterer's Apple, — you must lose yourself before you can find the way to that; the Beauty of the Air (*Decus Aëris*); December-Eating; the Frozen-Thawed (*gelato-soluta*), good only in that state; the Concord Apple, possibly the same with the *Musketaquidensis*; the Assabet Apple; the Brindled Apple; Wine of New England; the Chickaree Apple; the Green Apple (*Malus viridis*); — this has many synonyms; in an imperfect state, it is the *Cholera morbifera aut dysenterifera, puerulis dilectissima;*[1] — the Apple which Atalanta stopped to pick up; the Hedge - Apple (*Malus Sepium*); the Slug - Apple

---

[1] The apple that brings the disease of cholera and of dysentery, the fruit that small boys like best.

(*limacea*); the Railroad-Apple, which perhaps came
from a core thrown out of the cars; the Apple whose
Fruit we tasted in our Youth; our Particular Apple,
not to be found in any catalogue, — *Pedestrium So-
latium;* [1] also the Apple where hangs the Forgotten
Scythe; Iduna's Apples, and the Apples which Loki
found in the Wood; [2] and a great many more I have
on my list, too numerous to mention, — all of them
good.   As Bodæus exclaims, referring to the culti-
vated kinds, and adapting Virgil to his case, so I,
adapting Bodæus, —

> "Not if I had a hundred tongues, a hundred mouths,
> An iron voice, could I describe all the forms
> And reckon up all the names of these *wild apples.*"

THE LAST GLEANING.

By the middle of November the wild apples have
lost some of their brilliancy, and have chiefly fallen.
A great part are decayed on the ground, and the
sound ones are more palatable than before.   The
note of the chickadee sounds now more distinct, as
you wander amid the old trees, and the autumnal
dandelion is half-closed and tearful.   But still, if you
are a skilful gleaner, you may get many a pocket-full
even of grafted fruit, long after apples are supposed
to be gone out-of-doors.   I know a Blue-Pearmain
tree, growing within the edge of a swamp, almost as
good as wild.   You would not suppose that there was
any fruit left there, on the first survey, but you must
look according to system.   Those which lie exposed
are quite brown and rotten now, or perchance a few
still show one blooming cheek here and there amid
the wet leaves.   Nevertheless, with experienced eyes,

---

[1] The tramp's comfort.   [2] See p. 172.

I explore amid the bare alders and the huckleberry-bushes and the withered sedge, and in the crevices of the rocks, which are full of leaves, and pry under the fallen and decaying ferns, which, with apple and alder leaves, thickly strew the ground. For I know that they lie concealed, fallen into hollows long since and covered up by the leaves of the tree itself, — a proper kind of packing. From these lurking-places, anywhere within the circumference of the tree, I draw forth the fruit, all wet and glossy, maybe nibbled by rabbits and hollowed out by crickets and perhaps with a leaf or two cemented to it (as Curzon [1] an old manuscript from a monastery's mouldy cellar), but still with a rich bloom on it, and at least as ripe and well kept, if not better than those in barrels, more crisp and lively than they. If these resources fail to yield anything, I have learned to look between the bases of the suckers which spring thickly from some horizontal limb, for now and then one lodges there, or in the very midst of an alder-clump, where they are covered by leaves, safe from cows which may have smelled them out. If I am sharp-set, for I do not refuse the Blue-Pearmain, I fill my pockets on each side ; and as I retrace my steps in the frosty eve, being perhaps four or five miles from home, I eat one first from this side, and then from that, to keep my balance.

I learn from Topsell's Gesner, whose authority appears to be Albertus, that the following is the way in which the hedgehog collects and carries home his apples. He says: " His meat is apples, worms, or

---

[1] Robert Curzon was a traveller who searched for old manuscripts in the monasteries of the Levant. See his book, *Ancient Monasteries of the East.*

grapes : when he findeth apples or grapes on the earth, he rolleth himself upon them, until he have filled all his prickles, and then carrieth them home to his den, never bearing above one in his mouth ; and if it fortune that one of them fall off by the way, he likewise shaketh off all the residue, and walloweth upon them afresh, until they be all settled upon his back again. So, forth he goeth, making a noise like a cart-wheel ; and if he have any young ones in his nest, they pull off his load wherewithal he is loaded, eating thereof what they please, and laying up the residue for the time to come."

THE " FROZEN-THAWED " APPLE.

Toward the end of November, though some of the sound ones are yet more mellow and perhaps more edible, they have generally, like the leaves, lost their beauty, and are beginning to freeze. It is finger-cold, and prudent farmers get in their barrelled apples, and bring you the apples and cider which they have engaged ; for it is time to put them into the cellar. Perhaps a few on the ground show their red cheeks above the early snow, and occasionally some even preserve their color and soundness under the snow throughout the winter. But generally at the beginning of the winter they freeze hard, and soon, though undecayed, acquire the color of a baked apple.

Before the end of December, generally, they experience their first thawing. Those which a month ago were sour, crabbed, and quite unpalatable to the civilized taste, such at least as were frozen while sound, let a warmer sun come to thaw them, for they are extremely sensitive to its rays, are found to be filled with a rich, sweet cider, better than any bottled

cider that I know of, and with which I am better
acquainted than with wine. All apples are good in
this state, and your jaws are the cider-press. Others,
which have more substance, are a sweet and luscious
food, — in my opinion of more worth than the pine-
apples which are imported from the West Indies.
Those which lately even I tasted only to repent of it,
— for I am semi-civilized, — which the farmer will-
ingly left on the tree, I am now glad to find have the
property of hanging on like the leaves of the young
oaks. It is a way to keep cider sweet without boil-
ing. Let the frost come to freeze them first, solid as
stones, and then the rain or a warm winter day to
thaw them, and they will seem to have borrowed a
flavor from heaven through the medium of the air in
which they hang. Or perchance you find, when you
get home, that those which rattled in your pocket
have thawed, and the ice is turned to cider. But
after the third or fourth freezing and thawing they
will not be found so good.

What are the imported half-ripe fruits of the torrid
South to this fruit matured by the cold of the frigid
North? These are those crabbed apples with which
I cheated my companion, and kept a smooth face that
I might tempt him to eat. Now we both greedily fill
our pockets with them, — bending to drink the cup
and save our lappets from the overflowing juice, —
and grow more social with their wine. Was there
one that hung so high and sheltered by the tangled
branches that our sticks could not dislodge it?

It is a fruit never carried to market, that I am
aware of, — quite distinct from the apple of the
markets, as from dried apple and cider, — and it is
not every winter that produces it in perfection.

The era of the Wild Apple will soon be past. It is a fruit which will probably become extinct in New England. You may still wander through old orchards of native fruit of great extent, which for the most part went to the cider-mill, now all gone to decay. I have heard of an orchard in a distant town, on the side of a hill, where the apples rolled down and lay four feet deep against a wall on the lower side, and this the owner cut down for fear they should be made into cider. Since the temperance reform and the general introduction of grafted fruit, no native apple-trees, such as I see everywhere in deserted pastures, and where the woods have grown up around them, are set out. I fear that he who walks over these fields a century hence will not know the pleasure of knocking off wild apples. Ah, poor man, there are many pleasures which he will not know! Notwithstanding the prevalence of the Baldwin and the Porter, I doubt if so extensive orchards are set out to-day in my town as there were a century ago, when those vast straggling cider-orchards were planted, when men both ate and drank apples, when the pomace-heap was the only nursery, and trees cost nothing but the trouble of setting them out. Men could afford then to stick a tree by every wall-side and let it take its chance. I see nobody planting trees to-day in such out-of-the-way places, along the lonely roads and lanes, and at the bottom of dells in the wood. Now that they have grafted trees, and pay a price for them, they collect them into a plat by their houses, and fence them in, — and the end of it all will be that we shall be compelled to look for our apples in a barrel.

This is " The word of the Lord that came to Joel the son of Pethuel."

" Hear this, ye old men, and give ear, all ye inhabitants of the land ! Hath this been in your days, or even in the days of your fathers? . . .

" That which the palmer-worm hath left hath the locust eaten ; and that which the locust hath left hath the canker-worm eaten ; and that which the canker-worm hath left hath the caterpillar eaten.

" Awake, ye drunkards, and weep ! and howl, all ye drinkers of wine, because of the new wine ! for it is cut off from your mouth.

" For a nation is come up upon my land, strong, and without number, whose teeth are the teeth of a lion, and he hath the cheek-teeth of a great lion.

" He hath laid my vine waste, and barked my fig-tree ; he hath made it clean bare, and cast it away ; the branches thereof are made white. . . .

" Be ye ashamed, O ye husbandmen ! howl, O ye vine-dressers ! . . .

" The vine is dried up, and the fig-tree languisheth ; the pomegranate-tree, the palm-tree also, and the apple-tree, even all the trees of the field, are withered : because joy is withered away from the sons of men." [1]

[1] Joel, chapter i., verses 1–12.

JOHN BOYLE O'REILLY.

BIOGRAPHICAL SKETCH.[1]

JOHN BOYLE O'REILLY was born on June 28, 1844, in Dowth Castle, four miles above the town of Drogheda, Ireland. His parents were cultured and talented. He inherited a good constitution, and was passionately fond of out-of-door sports. Among the boys of his neighborhood no one was more daring or skilful than the handsome, rosy-cheeked, curly-haired, dark-eyed John. At the age of eleven he left home to become an apprentice in the printing-office of the *Drogheda Argus*, at a salary of two shillings and sixpence a week, which did not include board and lodging; his salary was increased sixpence a week every year.

After nearly four years of service the death of his employer released him from the obligations of his apprenticeship. In 1859 he went to Preston, England, the home of his uncle, Captain Watkinson, where he obtained a situation as an apprentice in the office of the *Guardian*. Three years later he graduated from the printer's case and became a reporter, having learned shorthand and otherwise equipped himself for the work of a journalist. In March, 1863, he obeyed a call from his father to return home to Ireland.

He had become deeply imbued with the revolutionary principles then so freely adopted by patriotic Irishmen. It

1 The information given in this brief sketch has been gleaned from the *Life of John Boyle O'Reilly*, by James Jeffrey Roche, published by the Cassell Publishing Company, of New York.

was hoped that disaffection would be sowed in the ranks of the British army, of which more than thirty per cent were Irishmen. Accordingly in May, 1863, O'Reilly enlisted as a trooper in the Tenth Hussars, where he became a model soldier, quick to learn and punctual to obey orders. In February, 1866, he was arrested on the charge of "having at Dublin in January, 1866, come to the knowledge of an intended mutiny in Her Majesty's Forces in Ireland, and not giving information of said intended mutiny to his commanding officer." On June 27th, of the same year, the day preceding his twenty-second birthday, his trial by court-martial began. On July 9, 1866, formal sentence of death was passed upon him. The same day the sentence was commuted to life imprisonment, and afterwards to twenty years' penal servitude. For about fifteen months he was confined in the prisons of Mountjoy, Pentonville, Millbank, Chatham, Portsmouth, Dartmoor, and Portland. He suffered intensely from poor food, hard work, foul air, and inhuman jailers. He made two unsuccessful attempts to escape, for which he was severely punished by solitary confinement and a diet of bread and water.

In October, 1867, he and sixty-two other political prisoners were embarked on the Hougoumont for Australia. His popularity among the guards secured for him kindly treatment on the voyage. He arrived at Freemantle on the morning of January 10, 1868, and four weeks later was sent to Bunbury, thirty miles away, where he led the life of a convict among some of the most degraded of humankind — murderers, burglars, offenders of every grade and color of vice. But ill fortune instead of blighting had nourished in him the growth of the instincts of pure humanity. He soon won the respect of the officer over him, became of assistance in clerical work, and was appointed a "constable," or aid to an officer in charge of a working party. Not long after the following advertisement appeared in the *Police Gazette* of Western Australia: —

John Boyle O'Reilly

ABSCONDERS.

20 — John B. O'Reilly, registered No. 9843, imperial convict; arrived in the colony per convict ship Hougoumont in 1868; sentenced to twenty years, 9th July, 1866. Description — Healthy appearance ; present age 25 years ; 5 feet 7½ inches high, black hair, brown eyes, oval visage, dark complexion : an Irishman. Absconded from Convict Road Party, Bunbury, on the 18th of February, 1869.

O'Reilly had escaped through the Bush to the seashore, and after a disappointing delay and much suffering from hunger and thirst he was taken on board the Gazelle, a New Bedford whaler commanded by Captain Gifford. Two months later, in the harbor of Roderique, he escaped capture through a well-planned ruse of his friend, Mr. Hathaway, the third mate of the Gazelle. To avoid the danger of capture at St. Helena, the next port for the Gazelle, O'Reilly was reluctantly transferred, by Captain Gifford, on July 29th, to the Sapphire, of Boston, bound for Liverpool. After a short stay at Liverpool he embarked as third mate on the Bombay, and on November 23, 1869, landed at Philadelphia. His first act after landing was to present himself before the United States District Court and take out his first naturalization papers. He soon went to New York, where by the invitation of the Fenians he delivered a lecture to over two thousand persons at the Cooper Institute, on December 16, 1869. We next find him in Boston as clerk in the office of the Inman Line Steamship Company. After four or five weeks of satisfactory work he was discharged by orders received from the general office of the company in England, whither news had been sent that John Boyle O'Reilly, an escaped convict, was in the employment of the company at Boston. In the spring of 1870, after having lectured successfully in Boston, Providence, Salem, Lawrence, and other places, he was employed by Mr. Donahoe, the editor and proprietor of the Boston *Pilot*, as a reporter and general writer. In June, 1870, he took part in the invasion of Canada by the Fenians, as war-correspondent of the *Pilot*. His frank criticism of friends and foes at this time, and his wise and temperate reports to the *Pilot* attracted much attention.

In February, 1876, O'Reilly, in his thirty-second year, became one of the proprietors of the *Pilot*. In 1879 he was President of the Papyrus Club, which he had helped to found, and also of the Boston Press Club. His literary work was not confined to the *Pilot*. He made many contributions, in both poetry and prose, to some of the leading magazines of the United States, and delivered a number of notable addresses on public occasions. A large part of his poems found a permanent form in the volumes entitled *Songs of the Southern Seas, The Statues in the Block* and *In Bohemia*. He also published *Moondyne*, a novel, and some other books. His reputation as an editor, lecturer, poet, and leader of the Irish-American people continued to increase until his death, which occurred on the night of August 9, 1890.

On August 15, 1872, he was married to Miss Mary Murphy, of Charlestown, Massachusetts. They had four daughters, all of whom survived their father.

Of the many noble poems written by Mr. O'Reilly, the *Pilgrim Fathers*, read August 1, 1889, at the dedication of the national monument to the Pilgrim Fathers at Plymouth, Massachusetts, is described as the crowning work of his life as an American singer. This poem is given in full in the following pages.

THE PILGRIM FATHERS.

ONE righteous word for Law — the common will;
One living truth of Faith — God regnant still;
One primal test of Freedom — all combined;
One sacred Revolution — change of mind;
One trust unfailing for the night and need —   5
The tyrant-flower shall cast the freedom-seed.

So held they firm, the Fathers aye to be,
From home to Holland, Holland to the sea;
Pilgrims for manhood, in their little ship,
Hope in each heart and prayer on every lip.   10
They could not live by king-made codes and creeds;
They chose the path where every footstep bleeds.
Protesting, not rebelling; scorned and banned;
Through pains and prisons harried from the land;
Through double exile, — till at last they stand   15
Apart from all, — unique, unworldly, true,
Selected grain to sow the earth anew;
A winnowed part, a saving remnant they;
Dreamers who work, adventurers who pray!

What vision led them? Can we test their prayers? 20
Who knows they saw no empire in the West?
The later Puritans sought land and gold,
And all the treasures that the Spaniard told;
What line divides the Pilgrims from the rest?

We know them by the exile that was theirs;   25
Their justice, faith, and fortitude attest;

And those long years in Holland, when their band
Sought humble living in a stranger's land.
They saw their England covered with a weed
Of flaunting lordship both in court and creed.   30
With helpless hands they watched the error grow,
Pride on the top and impotence below;
Indulgent nobles, privileged and strong,
A haughty crew to whom all rights belong;
The bishops arrogant, the courts impure,   35
The rich conspirators against the poor;
The peasant scorned, the artisan despised;
The all-supporting workers lowest prized.
They marked those evils deepen year by year:
The pensions grow, the freeholds disappear,
Till England meant but monarch, prelate, peer.
At last the Conquest!   Now they know the word:
The Saxon tenant and the Norman lord!
No longer Merrie England: now it meant
The payers and the takers of the rent;   45
And rent exacted not from lands alone —
All rights and hopes must centre in the throne:
Law-tithes for prayer — their souls were not their own!

Then o'er the brim the bitter waters welled;
The mind protested and the soul rebelled.   50
And yet, how deep the bowl, how slight the flow!
A few brave exiles from their country go;
A few strong souls whose rich affections cling,
Though cursed by clerics, hunted by the king;
Their last sad vision on the Grimsby strand   55
Their wives and children kneeling on the sand.

Then   twelve   slow   years   in   Holland — changing
      years —

Strange ways of life — strange voices in their ears;
The growing children learning foreign speech;
And growing, too, within the heart of each   60
A thought of further exile — of a home
In some far land — a home for life and death
By their hands built, in equity and faith.

And then the preparation — the heart-beat
Of wayfarers who may not rest their feet;   65
Their pastor's blessing — the farewells of some
Who stayed in Leyden. Then the sea's wide blue:
" They sailed," writ one, " and as they sailed they
       knew
That they were Pilgrims! "

                     On the wintry main
God flings their lives as farmers scatter grain.   70
His breath propels the wingéd seed afloat;   ,
His tempests swerve to spare the fragile boat;
Before his prompting terrors disappear;
He points the way while patient seamen steer;
Till port is reached, nor North, nor South, but
       HERE!   75

Here, where the shore was rugged as the waves,
Where frozen nature dumb and leafless lay,
And no rich meadows bade the Pilgrims stay,
Was spread the symbol of the life that saves:
To conquer first the outer things; to make   80
Their own advantage, unallied, unbound;
Their blood the mortar, building from the ground;
Their cares the statutes, making all anew;
To learn to trust the many, not the few;
To bend the mind to discipline; to break   85

The bonds of old convention, and forget
The claims and barriers of class ; to face
A desert land, a strange and hostile race,
And conquer both to friendship by the debt
That nature pays to justice, love, and toil.   90

Here, on this rock, and on this sterile soil,
Began the kingdom not of kings, but men :
Began the making of the world again.
Here centuries sank, and from the hither brink
A new world reached and raised an old-world link,   95
When English hands, by wider vision taught,
Threw down the feudal bars the Normans brought,
And here revived, in spite of sword and stake,
Their ancient freedom of the Wapentake !
Here struck the seed — the Pilgrims' roofless town,   100
Where equal rights and equal bonds were set,
Where all the people equal-franchised met ;
Where doom was writ of privilege and crown ;
Where human breath blew all the idols down ;
Where crests were nought, where vulture flags were
          furled,   105
And common men began to own the world !

All praise to others of the vanguard then !
To Spain, to France ; to Baltimore and Penn ;
To Jesuit, Quaker, Puritan and Priest ;
Their toil be crowned, their honors be increased !   110
We slight no true devotion, steal no fame
From other shrines to gild the Pilgrims' name.
As time selects, we judge their treasures heaped ;
Their deep foundations laid ; their harvests reaped ;
Their primal mode of liberty ; their rules   115
Of civil right ; their churches, courts, and schools ;

Their freedom's very secret here laid down, —
The spring of government is the little town!
They knew that streams must follow to a spring;
And no stream flows from township to a king.   120
Give praise to others, early-come or late,
For love and labor on our ship of state;
But this must stand above all fame and zeal:
The Pilgrim Fathers laid the ribs and keel.
On their strong lines we base our social health, —   125
The man — the home — the town — the commonwealth!

Unconscious builders?   Yea: the conscious fail!
Design is impotent if Nature frown.
No deathless pile has grown from intellect.
Immortal things have God for architect,   130
And men are but the granite he lays down.
Unconscious? Yea!   They thought it might avail
To build a gloomy creed about their lives,
To shut out all dissent; but naught survives
Of their poor structure; and we know to-day   135
Their mission was less pastoral than lay —
More Nation-seed than Gospel-seed were they!

The faith was theirs: the time had other needs.
The salt they bore must sweeten worldly deeds.
There was a meaning in the very wind   140
That blew them here, so few, so poor, so strong,
To grapple concrete work, not abstract wrong.
Their saintly Robinson was left behind
To teach by gentle memory; to shame
The bigot spirit and the word of flame;   145
To write dear mercy in the Pilgrims' law;
To lead to that wide faith his soul foresaw, —
That no rejected race in darkness delves;

There are no Gentiles, but they make themselves;
That men are one of blood and one of spirit;   150
That one is as the whole, and all inherit!

On all the story of a life or race,
The blessing of a good man leaves its trace.
Their Pastor's word at Leyden here sufficed:
"But follow me as I have followed Christ!"   155
And, "I believe there is more truth to come!"
O gentle soul, what future age shall sum
The sweet incentive of thy tender word!
Thy sigh to hear of conquest by the sword;
"How happy to convert, and not to slay!"   160
When valiant Standish killed the chief at bay.
To such as thee the fathers owe their fame;
The nation owes a temple to thy name.
Thy teaching made the Pilgrims kindly, free, —
All that the later Puritans should be.   165
Thy pious instinct marks their destiny.
Thy love won more than force or arts adroit, —
It writ and kept the deed with Massasoit;
It earned the welcome Samoset expressed;
It lived again in Eliot's loving breast;   170
It filled the Compact which the Pilgrims signed —
Immortal scroll! the first where men combined
From one deep lake of common blood to draw
All rulers, rights, and potencies of law.

When waves of ages have their motive spent   175
Thy sermon preaches in this Monument,
Where Virtue, Courage, Law, and Learning sit;
Calm Faith above them, grasping Holy Writ;
White hand upraised o'er beauteous, trusting eyes,
And pleading finger pointing to the skies!   180

The past is theirs, the future ours; and we
Must learn and teach.   Oh, may our record be
Like theirs, a glory, symbolled in a stone,
To speak as this speaks, of our labors done.
They had no model; but they left us one.   185

Severe they were; but let him cast the stone
Who Christ's dear love dare measure with his own.
Their strict professions were not cant nor pride.
Who calls them narrow, let his soul be wide!
Austere, exclusive — ay, but with their faults,   190
Their golden probity mankind exalts.
They never lied in practice, peace, or strife;
They were no hypocrites; their faith was clear;
They feared too much some sins men ought to fear:
The lordly arrogance and avarice,   195
And vain frivolity's besotting vice;
The stern enthusiasm of their life
Impelled too far, and weighed poor nature down;
They missed God's smile, perhaps, to watch his frown.
But he who digs for faults shall resurrect   200
Their manly virtues born of self-respect.
How sum their merits?   They were true and brave;
They broke no compact and they owned no slave.
They had no servile order, no dumb throat;
They trusted first the universal vote;   205
The first were they to practice and instil
The rule of law and not the rule of will;
They lived one noble test: who would be freed
Must give up all to follow duty's lead.
They made no revolution based on blows,   210
But taught one truth that all the planet knows,
That all men think of, looking on a throne --
The people may be trusted with their own!

In every land wherever might holds sway
The Pilgrims' leaven is at work to-day.   215
The Mayflower's cabin was the chosen womb
Of light predestined for the nations' gloom.
God grant that those who tend the sacred flame
May worthy prove of their Forefathers' name.
More light has come, — more dangers, too, perplex: 220
New prides, new greeds, our high condition vex.
The Fathers fled from feudal lords, and made
A freehold state; may we not retrograde
To lucre-lords and hierarchs of trade.
May we, as they did, teach in court and school,   225
There must be classes, but no class shall rule:
The sea is sweet, and rots not like the pool.
Though vast the token of our future glory,
Though tongue of man hath told not such a story, —
Surpassing Plato's dream, More's phantasy, — still
          we   230
Have no new principles to keep us free.
As Nature works with changeless grain on grain,
The truths the Fathers taught we need again.
Depart from this, though we may crowd our shelves,
With codes and precepts for each lapse and flaw,   235
And patch our moral leaks with statute law,
We cannot be protected from ourselves!
Still must we keep in every stroke and vote
The law of conscience that the Pilgrims wrote;
Our seal their secret: LIBERTY CAN BE;   240
THE STATE IS FREEDOM IF THE TOWN IS FREE.
The death of nations in their work began;
They sowed the seed of federated Man.
Dead nations were but robber-holds; and we
The first battalion of Humanity!   245
All living nations, while our eagles shine,

One after one, shall swing into our line ;
Our freeborn heritage shall be the guide
And bloodless order of their regicide;
The sea shall join, not limit; mountains stand　　250
Dividing farm from farm, not land from land.

O people's Voice ! when farthest thrones shall hear ;
When teachers own ; when thoughtful rabbis know ;
When artist minds in world-wide symbol show ;
When serfs and soldiers their mute faces raise ;　　255
When priests on grand cathedral altars praise ;
When pride and arrogance shall disappear,
The Pilgrims' Vision is accomplished here !

JAMES RUSSELL LOWELL.

BIOGRAPHICAL SKETCH.

JAMES RUSSELL LOWELL was born February 22, 1819, at Elmwood, Cambridge, Massachusetts, in the house where he died August 12, 1891. His early life was spent in Cambridge, and he has sketched many of the scenes in it very delightfully in *Cambridge Thirty Years Ago*, in his volume of *Fireside Travels*, as well as in his early poem, *An Indian Summer Reverie*. His father was a Congregationalist minister of Boston, and the family to which he belonged has had a strong representation in Massachusetts. His grandfather, John Lowell, was an eminent jurist, the Lowell Institute of Boston owes its endowment to John Lowell, a cousin of the poet, and the city of Lowell was named after Francis Cabot Lowell, an uncle, who was one of the first to begin the manufacturing of cotton in New England.

Lowell was a student at Harvard, and was graduated in 1838, when he gave a class poem, and in 1841 his first volume of poems, *A Year's Life*, was published. His bent from the beginning was more decidedly literary than that of any contemporary American poet. That is to say, the history and art of literature divided his interest with the production of literature, and he carries the unusual gift of rare critical power, joined to hearty, spontaneous creation. It may indeed be guessed that the keenness of judgment and incisiveness of wit which characterize his examination of literature have sometimes interfered with his poetic power,

and made him liable to question his art when he would
rather have expressed it unchecked.   In connection with
Robert Carter, a littérateur who has lately died, he began,
in 1843, the publication of *The Pioneer, a Literary and
Critical Magazine*, which lived a brilliant life of three
months.   A volume of poetry followed in 1844, and the
next year he published *Conversations on Some of the Old
Poets*, — a book which is now out of print, but interesting
as marking the enthusiasm of a young scholar, treading a
way then almost wholly neglected in America, and intimat-
ing a line of thought and study in which he afterward made
most noteworthy ventures.   Another series of poems fol-
lowed in 1848, and in the same year *The Vision of Sir
Launfal*.   Perhaps it was in reaction from the marked sen-
timent of his poetry that he issued now a *jeu d'esprit, A
Fable for Critics*, in which he hit off, with a rough and
ready wit, the characteristics of the writers of the day, not
forgetting himself in these lines : —

" There is Lowell, who 's striving Parnassus to climb
  With a whole bale of *isms* tied together with rhyme ;
  He might get on alone, spite of brambles and boulders,
  But he can't with that bundle he has on his shoulders ;
  The top of the hill he will ne'er come nigh reaching
  Till he learns the distinction 'twixt singing and preaching ;
  His lyre has some chords that would ring pretty well,
  But he 'd rather by half make a drum of the shell,
  And rattle away till he 's old as Methusalem,
  At the head of a march to the last new Jerusalem."

This, of course, is but a half serious portrait of himself,
and it touches but a single feature ; others can say better
that Lowell's ardent nature showed itself in the series of
satirical poems which made him famous, *The Biglow Pa-
pers*, written in a spirit of indignation and fine scorn, when
the Mexican War was causing many Americans to blush
with shame at the use of the country by a class for its own
ignoble ends.   The true patriotism which marked these and

other of his early poems burned with a steady glow in after years, and illumined poems of which we shall speak presently.

After a year and a half spent in travel, Lowell was appointed in 1855 to the Belles Lettres professorship at Harvard, previously held by Longfellow. When the *Atlantic Monthly* was established in 1857 he became its editor, and soon after relinquishing that post he assumed part editorship of the *North American Review.* In these two magazines, as also in *Putnam's Monthly,* he published poems, essays, and critical papers, which have been gathered into volumes. His prose writings, besides the volumes already mentioned, include two series of *Among my Books,* historical and critical studies, chiefly in English literature; and *My Study Windows,* including, with similar subjects, observations of nature and contemporary life. During the war for the Union he published a second series of the *Biglow Papers,* in which, with the wit and fun of the earlier series, there was mingled a deeper strain of feeling and a larger tone of patriotism. The limitations of his style in these satires forbade the fullest expression of his thought and emotion; but afterward in a succession of poems, occasioned by the honors paid to student-soldiers in Cambridge, the death of Agassiz, and the celebration of national anniversaries during the years 1875 and 1876, he sang in loftier, more ardent strains. The interest which readers have in Lowell is still divided between his rich, abundant prose, and his thoughtful, often passionate verse. The sentiment of his early poetry, always humane, was greatly enriched by larger experience; so that the themes which he chose for his later work demanded and received a broad treatment, full of sympathy with the most generous instincts of their time, and built upon historic foundations.

In 1877 he went to Spain as Minister Plenipotentiary. In 1880 he was transferred to England as Minister Plenipotentiary near the Court of St. James. His duties as

American Minister did not prevent him from producing occasional writings, chiefly in connection with public events. Notable among these are his address at the unveiling of a statue of Fielding, and his address on Democracy.

Mr. Lowell returned to the United States in 1885, and was not afterward engaged in public affairs, but passed the rest of his life quietly in his Cambridge home, prevented by failing health from doing much literary work. He made a collection of his later poems in 1888, under the title *Heartsease and Rue*, and carefully revised his complete works, published in ten volumes in 1890.

BOOKS AND LIBRARIES.

AN ADDRESS GIVEN AT THE OPENING OF THE FREE PUB-
LIC LIBRARY IN CHELSEA, MASS., 22 DECEMBER, 1885.

A FEW years ago my friend, Mr. Alexander Ire-
land, published a very interesting volume which he
called *The Book-Lover's Enchiridion*, the hand-
book,[1] that is to say, of those who love books. It
was made up of extracts from the writings of a great
variety of distinguished men, ancient and modern, in
praise of books. It was a chorus of many voices in
many tongues, a hymn of gratitude and praise, full
of such piety and fervor as can be paralleled only in
songs dedicated to the supreme Power, the supreme
Wisdom, and the supreme Love. Nay, there is a glow
of enthusiasm and sincerity in it which is often pain-
fully wanting in those other too commonly mechani-
cal compositions. We feel at once that here it is
out of the fulness of the heart, yes, and of the head
too, that the mouth speaketh. Here was none of that
compulsory commonplace which is wont to charac-
terize those " testimonials of celebrated authors," by
means of which publishers sometimes strive to linger
out the passage of a hopeless book toward its *requi-
escat*[2] in oblivion. These utterances which Mr. Ire-

---

[1] *Handbook* is a translation of the Greek word *enchiridion*.

[2] It was once more common than now to place upon tomb-
stones the Latin words *Requiescat in pace:* May he rest in
peace.

land has gathered lovingly together are stamped with
that spontaneousness which is the mint-mark of all
sterling speech.   It is true that they are mostly, as
is only natural, the utterances of literary men, and
there is a well-founded proverbial distrust of herring
that bear only the brand of the packer, and not that
of the sworn inspector.   But to this objection a cynic
might answer with the question, " Are authors so
prone, then, to praise the works of other people that
we are to doubt them when they do it unasked ? "
Perhaps the wisest thing I could have done to-night
would have been to put upon the stand some of the
more weighty of this cloud of witnesses.   But since
your invitation implied that I should myself say
something, I will endeavor to set before you a few of
the commonplaces of the occasion, as they may be
modified by passing through my own mind, or by hav-
ing made themselves felt in my own experience.

The greater part of Mr. Ireland's witnesses testify
to the comfort and consolation they owe to books, to
the refuge they have found in them from sorrow or
misfortune, to their friendship, never estranged and
outliving all others.   This testimony they volunteered.
Had they been asked, they would have borne evi-
dence as willingly to the higher and more general uses
of books in their service to the commonwealth, as well
as to the individual man.   Consider, for example,
how a single page of Burke may emancipate the
young student of politics from narrow views and
merely contemporaneous judgments.[1]   Our English
ancestors, with that common-sense which is one of the

[1] An interesting reference to Burke as a political thinker will
be found in Mr. Lowell's paper, *The Place of the Independent in
Politics*, in his volume of *Political Essays*.

most useful, though not one of the most engaging,
properties of the race, made a rhyming proverb, which
says that —

> " When land and goods are gone and spent
> *Then* learning is most excellent ; "

and this is true so far as it goes, though it goes per-
haps hardly far enough.   The law also calls only the
earth and what is immovably attached to it *real* [1]
property, but I am of opinion that those only are real
possessions which abide with a man after he has been
stripped of those others falsely so called, and which
alone save him from seeming and from being the mis-
erable forked radish to which the bitter scorn of Lear
degraded every child of Adam.[2]   The riches of schol-
arship, the benignities of literature, defy fortune and
outlive calamity.   They are beyond the reach of thief
or moth or rust.   As they cannot be inherited, so
they cannot be alienated.   But they may be shared,
they may be distributed, and it is the object and office
of a free public library to perform these beneficent
functions.

" Books," says Wordsworth, " are a real world," [3]
and he was thinking, doubtless, of such books as are
not merely the triumphs of pure intellect, however
supreme, but of those in which intellect infused with
the sense of beauty aims rather to produce delight
than conviction, or, if conviction, then through intui-
tion rather than formal logic, and, leaving what Donne
wisely calls —

---

[1] What is *personal* property or estate, as distinguished from
real ?

[2] See *King Lear*, Act III. sc. 4 ; but see *King Henry IV.,*
Part II., Act III. sc. 2.

[3] In what poem ?

"Unconcerning things, matters of fact," [1]

to science and the understanding, seeks to give ideal
expression to those abiding realities of the spiritual
world for which the outward and visible world serves
at best but as the husk and symbol. Am I wrong in
using the word realities? wrong in insisting on the
distinction between the real and the actual? in assum-
ing for the ideal an existence as absolute and self-
subsistent as that which appeals to our senses, nay,
so often cheats them, in the matter of fact? How
very small a part of the world we truly live in is
represented by what speaks to us through the senses
when compared with that vast realm of the mind
which is peopled by memory and imagination, and
with such shining inhabitants! These walls, these
faces, what are they in comparison with the countless
images, the innumerable population which every one
of us can summon up to the tiny show-box of the
brain, in material breadth scarce a span, yet infinite
as space and time? and in what, I pray, are those we
gravely call historical characters, of which each new
historian strains his neck to get a new and different
view, in any sense more real than the personages of
fiction? Do not serious and earnest men discuss

---

[1] A line in the poem *Of the Progress of the Soul*. The passage
should be read in full.

> "We see in authors, too stiff to recant,
> A hundred controversies of an ant;
> And yet one watches, starves, freezes, and sweats,
> To know but catechisms and alphabets
> Of unconcerning things, matters of fact,
> How others on our stage their parts did act,
> What Cæsar did, yea, and what Cicero said:
> Why grass is green, or why our blood is red,
> Are mysteries which none have reached unto;
> In this low form, poor soul, what wilt thou do?
> Oh! when wilt thou shake off this pedantry,
> Of being taught by sense and fantasy?"

Hamlet as they would Cromwell or Lincoln? Does Cæsar, does Alaric, hold existence by any other or stronger tenure than the Christian of Bunyan, or the Don Quixote of Cervantes, or the Antigone of Sophocles? Is not the history which is luminous because of an indwelling and perennial truth to nature, because of that light which never was on sea or land,[1] really *more* true, in the highest sense, than many a weary chronicle with names and date and place in which " an Amurath to Amurath succeeds " ? Do we know as much of any authentic Danish prince as of Hamlet?

But to come back a little nearer to Chelsea and the occasion that has called us together. The founders of New England, if sometimes, when they found it needful, an impracticable, were always a practical people. Their first care, no doubt, was for an adequate supply of powder, and they encouraged the manufacture of musket bullets by enacting that they should pass as currency at a farthing each, — a coinage nearer to its nominal value and not heavier than some with which we are familiar. Their second care was that " good learning should not perish from among us," and to this end they at once established the Grammar (Latin) School[2] in Boston, and soon after the college at Cambridge. The nucleus of this was, as you all know, the bequest in money by John Harvard. Hardly less important, however, was the legacy of his library, a collection of good books, inconsider-

---

[1] See Wordsworth's poem, *Elegiac Stanzas suggested by a Picture of Peele Castle in a Storm.*

[2] An interesting account of this school may be read in *The Oldest School in America,* containing a notable historical address by Phillips Brooks.

able measured by the standard of to-day, but very
considerable then as the possession of a private per-
son.   From that little acorn what an oak has sprung,
and from its acorns again what a vocal forest, as old
Howell would have called it!—old Howell, whom I
love to cite, because his name gave their title to the
Essays of Elia,[1] and is borne with slight variation
by one of the most delightful of modern authors.   It
was, in my judgment, those two foundations, more
than anything else, which gave to New England char-
acter its bent, and to Boston that literary supremacy
which, I am told, she is in danger of losing, but which
she will not lose till she and all the world lose Holmes.

The opening of a free public library,[2] then, is a
most important event in the history of any town.   A
college training is an excellent thing; but, after all,
the better part of every man's education is that which
he gives himself, and it is for this that a good library
should furnish the opportunity and the means.   I have
sometimes thought that our public schools undertook
to teach too much, and that the older system, which
taught merely the three R's, and taught them well,
leaving natural selection to decide who should go
farther, was the better.   However this may be, all

[1] Mr. Lowell here conjectures that Lamb, who was at home
in quaint English literature, adopted his signature of *Elia* from
the *Epistolæ Ho-Elianæ* of James Howell, a writer of the former
half of the seventeenth century; but Lamb himself, in a letter
to his publishers, states that he took the name of *Elia*, which he
tells them to pronounce *Ellia*, from a former fellow-clerk of his
at the India House, an Italian named *Elia*.

[2] It would be an interesting study for any one to trace the
rise and growth of public libraries in the United States.   Abun-
dant material will be found in a *Special Report* issued by the
Bureau of Education at Washington in 1876.

that is primarily needful in order to use a library is the ability to read. I say primarily, for there must also be the inclination, and, after that, some guidance in reading well. Formerly the duty of a librarian was considered too much that of a watch-dog, to keep people as much as possible away from the books, and to hand these over to his successor as little worn by use as he could. Librarians now, it is pleasant to see, have a different notion of their trust, and are in the habit of preparing, for the direction of the inexperienced, lists of such books as they think best worth reading. Cataloguing has also, thanks in great measure to American librarians, become a science, and catalogues, ceasing to be labyrinths without a clew, are furnished with finger-posts at every turn. Subject catalogues again save the beginner a vast deal of time and trouble by supplying him for nothing with one at least of the results of thorough scholarship, the knowing where to look for what he wants. I do not mean by this that there is or can be any short cut to learning, but that there may be, and is, such a short cut to information that will make learning more easily accessible.

But have you ever rightly considered what the mere ability to read means? That it is the key which admits us to the whole world of thought and fancy and imagination? to the company of saint and sage, of the wisest and the wittiest at their wisest and wittiest moment? That it enables us to see with the keenest eyes, hear with the finest ears, and listen to the sweetest voices of all time? More than that, it annihilates time and space for us; it revives for us without a miracle the Age of Wonder, endowing us with the shoes of swiftness and the cap of darkness, so that we

walk invisible like Fern-seed,[1] and witness unharmed
the plague [2] at Athens or Florence or London ; ac-
company Cæsar on his marches, or look in on Catiline
in council with his fellow-conspirators, or Guy Fawkes
in the cellar of St. Stephen's.   We often hear of peo-
ple who will descend to any servility, submit to any
insult, for the sake of getting themselves or their chil-
dren into what is euphemistically called good society.
Did it ever occur to them that there is a select society
of all the centuries to which they and theirs can be
admitted for the asking, a society, too, which will not
involve them in ruinous expense, and still more ruin-
ous waste of time and health and faculties ?

Southey tells us that, in his walk one stormy day,
he met an old woman, to whom, by way of greeting,
he made the rather obvious remark that it was dread-
ful weather.   She answered, philosophically, that, in
her opinion, " *any* weather was better than none ! "
I should be half inclined to say that any reading was
better than none, allaying the crudeness of the state-
ment by the Yankee proverb, which tells us that,
though " all deacons are good, there's odds in dea-
cons."   Among books, certainly, there is much variety
of company, ranging from the best to the worst, from
Plato to Zola ; and the first lesson in reading well is
that which teaches us to distinguish between litera-
ture and merely printed matter.   The choice lies
wholly with ourselves.   We have the key put into
our hands ; shall we unlock the pantry or the ora-

---

[1] Any good collection of fairy tales will enable one to re-
count the stories which make use of the shoes, the cap, and the
fern-seed.

[2] Thucydides describes the plague at Athens ; Defoe, the
plague at London.

tory? There is a Wallachian legend which, like
most of the figments of popular fancy, has a moral in
it. One Bakála, a good-for-nothing kind of fellow in
his way, having had the luck to offer a sacrifice espe-
cially well pleasing to God, is taken up into heaven.
He finds the Almighty sitting in something like the
best room of a Wallachian peasant's cottage — there
is always a profound pathos in the homeliness of the
popular imagination, forced, like the princess in the
fairy tale, to weave its semblance of gold tissue out
of straw. On being asked what reward he desires
for the good service he has done, Bakála, who had
always passionately longed to be the owner of a bag-
pipe, seeing a half worn-out one lying among some
rubbish in a corner of the room, begs eagerly that it
may be bestowed on him. The Lord, with a smile of
pity at the meanness of his choice, grants him his
boon, and Bakála goes back to earth delighted with
his prize. With an infinite possibility within his
reach, with the choice of wisdom, of power, of beauty
at-his tongue's end, he asked according to his kind,
and his sordid wish is answered with a gift as sordid.
Yes, there is a choice in books as in friends, and the
mind sinks or rises to the level of its habitual society,
is subdued, as Shakespeare says of the dyer's hand,
to what it works in.[1] Cato's advice, *cum bonis am-
bula* (consort with the good), is quite as true if we
extend it to books, for they, too, insensibly give away
their own nature to the mind that converses with
them. They either beckon upwards or drag down.
Du gleichst dem Geist den du begreifst,[2] says the
World Spirit to Faust, and this is true of the ascend-

[1] Sonnet cxi.
[2] Thou 'rt like the Spirit whom thou conceivest.

ing no less than of the descending scale. Every book we read may be made a round in the ever-lengthening ladder by which we climb to knowledge, and to that temperance and serenity of mind which, as it is the ripest fruit of Wisdom, is also the sweetest. But this can only be if we read such books as make us think, and read them in such a way as helps them to do so, that is, by endeavoring to judge them, and thus to make them an exercise rather than a relaxation of the mind. Desultory reading, except as conscious pastime, hebetates the brain and slackens the bowstring of Will. It communicates as little intelligence as the messages that run along the telegraph wire to the birds that perch on it. Few men learn the highest use of books. After lifelong study many a man discovers too late that to have had the philosopher's stone availed nothing without the philosopher to use it. Many a scholarly life, stretched like a talking wire to bring the wisdom of antiquity into communion with the present, can at last yield us no better news that the true accent of a Greek verse, or the translation of some filthy nothing scrawled · on the walls of a brothel by some Pompeian idler. And it is certainly true that the material of thought reacts upon the thought itself. Shakespeare himself would have been commonplace had he been paddocked in a thinly-shaven vocabulary, and Phidias, had he worked in wax, only a more inspired Mrs. Jarley. A man is known, says the proverb, by the company he keeps, and not only so, but made by it. Milton makes his fallen angels grow small to enter the infernal council room,[1] but the soul, which God meant to be the spacious chamber where high thoughts and generous aspi-

[1] See *Paradise Lost*, Book I. lines 775–798.

rations might commune together, shrinks and narrows itself to the measure of the meaner company that is wont to gather there, hatching conspiracies against our better selves. We are apt to wonder at the scholarship of the men of three centuries ago, and at a certain dignity of phrase that characterizes them. They were scholars because they did not read so many things as we. They had fewer books, but these were of the best. Their speech was noble because they lunched with Plutarch and supped with Plato. We spend as much time over print as they did, but instead of communing with the choice thoughts of choice spirits, and unconsciously acquiring the grand manner of that supreme society, we diligently inform ourselves, and cover the continent with a cobweb of telegraphs to inform us, of such inspiring facts as that a horse belonging to Mr. Smith ran away on Wednesday, seriously damaging a valuable carryall; that a son of Mr. Brown swallowed a hickory nut on Thursday; and that a gravel bank caved in and buried Mr. Robinson alive on Friday. Alas, it is we ourselves that are getting buried alive under this avalanche of earthy impertinences! It is we who, while we might each in his humble way be helping our follows into the right path, or adding one block to the climbing spire of a fine soul, are willing to become mere sponges saturated from the stagnant goose-pond of village gossip. This is the kind of news we compass the globe to catch, fresh from Bungtown Centre, when we might have it fresh from heaven by the electric lines of poet or prophet![1] It is

[1] It might not be uninstructive for one to make such computations as these: How much time does it take to read my customary local newspaper? What is the shortest time I can give

bad enough that we should be compelled to know so many nothings, but it is downright intolerable that we must wash so many barrow-loads of gravel to find a grain of mica after all. And then to be told that the ability to read makes us all shareholders in the Bonanza Mine of Universal Intelligence!

One is sometimes asked by young people to recommend a course of reading. My advice would be that they should confine themselves to the supreme books in whatever literature, or still better to choose some one great author, and make themselves thoroughly familiar with him. For, as all roads lead to Rome, so do they likewise lead away from it, and you will find that, in order to understand perfectly and weigh exactly any vital piece of literature, you will be gradually and pleasantly persuaded to excursions and explorations of which you little dreamed when you began, and will find yourselves scholars before you are aware. For remember that there is nothing less profitable than scholarship for the mere sake of scholarship, nor anything more wearisome in the attainment. But the moment you have a definite aim, attention is quickened, the mother of memory, and all that you acquire groups and arranges itself in an order that is lucid, because everywhere and always it is in intelligent relation to a central object of constant and growing interest. This method also forces upon us the necessity of thinking, which is, after all,

to it and get the really important things out of it? How many numbers of my newspaper would correspond in time of reading with Shakespeare's *Tempest?* How much should I remember of the papers a month afterward? how much of *The Tempest?* But newspapers are not to be despised; only we are to study economy in the using of them.

the highest result of all education. For what we want is not learning, but knowledge; that is, the power to make learning answer its true end as a quickener of intelligence and a widener of our intellectual sympathies. I do not mean to say that every one is fitted by nature or inclination for a definite course of study, or indeed for serious study in any sense. I am quite willing that these should " browse in a library," as Dr. Johnson called it, to their hearts' content. It is, perhaps, the only way in which time may be profitably wasted. But desultory reading will not make a " full man," as Bacon understood it, of one who has not Johnson's memory, his power of assimilation, and, above all, his comprehensive view of the relations of things. " Read not," says Lord Bacon in his *Essay of Studies*,[1] " to contradict and confute; nor to believe and take for granted; nor to find talk and discourse; but to weigh and consider. Some books are to be tasted, others to be swallowed, and some few to be chewed and digested; that is, some books are to be read only in parts; others to be read, but not curiously [carefully], and some few to be read wholly and with diligence and attention. *Some books also may be read by deputy.*" This is weighty and well said, and I would call your attention especially to the wise words with which the passage closes. The best books are not always those which lend themselves to discussion and comment, but those (like Montaigne's *Essays*) which discuss and comment ourselves.

I have been speaking of such books as should be

---

[1] It is in this essay that the reference to the "full man" occurs, and as the essay is not long, it would be a good one to commit to memory.

chosen for profitable reading. A public library, of course, must be far wider in its scope. It should contain something for all tastes, as well as the material for a thorough grounding in all branches of knowledge. It should be rich in books of reference, in encyclopædias,[1] where one may learn without cost of research what things are generally known. For it is far more useful to know these than to know those that are *not* generally known. Not to know them is the defect of those half-trained and therefore hasty men who find a mare's nest on every branch of the tree of knowledge. A library should contain ample stores of history, which, if it do not always deserve the pompous title which Bolingbroke gave it, of philosophy teaching by example,[2] certainly teaches many things profitable for us to know and lay to heart; teaches, among other things, how much of the present is still held in mortmain by the past; teaches that, if there be no controlling purpose, there is, at least, a sternly logical sequence in human affairs, and that chance has but a trifling dominion over them; teaches why things are and must be so and not otherwise, and that, of all hopeless contests, the most hopeless is that which fools are most eager to challenge, — with the Nature of Things; teaches, perhaps more than anything else, the value of personal character as a chief factor in what used to be called destiny, for that cause is strong

[1] A capital subject for discussion would be on the comparative merits of the many encyclopædias to be found in a good public library; not to determine which was the best, but what was the characteristic of each.

[2] There is another suggestive definition of history made by the English historian E. A. Freeman, and used as a motto on the title-page of the various *Johns Hopkins University Studies in Historical and Political Science.*

which has not a multitude but one strong man behind
it. History is, indeed, mainly the biography of a few
imperial men, and forces home upon us the useful
lesson how infinitesimally important our own private
affairs are to the universe in general. History is
clarified experience, and yet how little do men profit
by it; nay, how should we expect it of those who so
seldom are taught anything by their own! Delusions,
especially economical delusions, seem the only things
that have any chance of an earthly immortality. I
would have plenty of biography. It is no insignificant
fact that eminent men have always loved their Plu-
tarch, since example, whether for emulation or avoid-
ance, is never so poignant as when presented to us in
a striking personality. Autobiographies are also in-
structive reading to the student of human nature,
though generally written by men who are more inter-
esting to themselves than to their fellow-men. I have
been told that Emerson and George Eliot agreed in
thinking Rousseau's *Confessions* the most interesting
book they had ever read.

A public library should also have many and full
shelves of political economy, for the dismal science,
as Carlyle called it, if it prove nothing else, will go
far towards proving that theory is the bird in the
bush, though she sing more sweetly than the night-
ingale, and that the millennium will not hasten its
coming in deference to the most convincing string of
resolutions that were ever unanimously adopted in
public meeting. It likewise induces in us a profound
and wholesome distrust of social panaceas.

I would have a public library abundant in transla-
tions of the best books in all languages, for, though
no work of genius can be adequately translated, be-

cause every word of it is permeated with what Milton calls " the precious life-blood of a master spirit " which cannot be transfused into the veins of the best translation, yet some acquaintance with foreign and ancient literatures has the liberalizing effect of foreign travel.[1] He who travels by translation travels more hastily and superficially, but brings home something that is worth having, nevertheless. Translations properly used, by shortening the labor of acquisition, add as many years to our lives as they subtract from the processes of our education. Looked at from any but the æsthetic point of view, translations retain whatever property was in their originals to enlarge, liberalize, and refine the mind. At the same time I would have also the originals of these translated books, as a temptation to the study cf languages, which has a special use and importance of its own in teaching us to understand the niceties of our mother-tongue. The practice of translation, by making us deliberate in the choice of the best equivalent of the foreign word in our own language, has likewise the advantage of continually schooling us in one of the main elements of a good style, — precision ; and precision of thought is not only exemplified by precision of language, but is largely dependent on the habit of it.

In such a library the sciences should be fully represented, that men may at least learn to know in what a marvellous museum they live, what a wonder-worker is giving them an exhibition daily for nothing. Nor let Art be forgotten in all its many forms, not as the antithesis of Science, but as her elder or fairer sister,

[1] Emerson, in his essay entitled *Books*, in the volume *Society and Solitude*, has something to say about translations, and his remark often is quoted.

,whom we love all the more that her usefulness cannot be demonstrated in dollars and cents. I should be thankful if every day-laborer among us could have his mind illumined, as those of Athens and of Florence had, with some image of what is best in architecture, painting, and sculpture, to train his crude perceptions and perhaps call out latent faculties. I should like to see the works of Ruskin within the reach of every artisan among us. For I hope some day that the delicacy of touch and accuracy of eye that have made our mechanics in some departments the best in the world, may give us the same supremacy in works of wider range and more purely ideal scope.

Voyages and travels I would also have, good store, especially the earlier, when the world was fresh and unhackneyed and men saw things invisible to the modern eye. They are fast-sailing ships to waft away from present trouble to the Fortunate Isles.

To wash down the drier morsels that every library must necessarily offer at its board, let there be plenty of imaginative literature, and let its range be not too narrow to stretch from Dante to the elder Dumas. The world of the imagination is not the world of abstraction and nonentity, as some conceive, but a world formed out of chaos by a sense of the beauty that is in man and the earth on which he dwells. It is the realm of Might-be, our haven of refuge from the shortcomings and disillusions of life. It is, to quote Spenser, who knew it well, —

"The world's sweet inn from care and wearisome turmoil."

Do we believe, then, that God gave us in mockery this splendid faculty of sympathy with things that are

a joy forever? [1] For my part, I believe that the love·
and study of works of imagination is of practical
utility in a country so profoundly material (or, as we
like to call it, practical) in its leading tendencies as
ours. The hunger after purely intellectual delights,
the content with ideal possessions, cannot but be good
for us in maintaining a wholesome balance of the
character and of the faculties. I for one shall never
be persuaded that Shakespeare left a less useful leg-
acy to his countrymen than Watt. We hold all the
deepest, all the highest satisfactions of life as tenants
of imagination. Nature will keep up the supply of
what are called hard-headed people without our help,
and, if it come to that, there are other as good uses
for heads as at the end of battering rams.

I know that there are many excellent people who
object to the reading of novels as a waste of time, if
not as otherwise harmful. But I think they are try-
ing to outwit nature, who is sure to prove cunninger
than they. Look at children. One boy shall want a
chest of tools, and one a book, and of those who want
books one shall ask for a botany, another for a ro-
mance. They will be sure to get what they want,
and we are doing a grave wrong to their morals by
driving them to do things on the sly, to steal that
food which their constitution craves and which is
wholesome for them, instead of having it freely and
frankly given them as the wisest possible diet. If
we cannot make a silk purse out of a sow's ear, so
neither can we hope to succeed with the opposite
experiment. But we may spoil the silk for its legiti-
mate uses. I can conceive of no healthier reading

---

[1] The first line of Keats's poem *Endymion* suggested this
phrase.

for a boy, or girl either, than Scott's novels, or Cooper's, to speak only of the dead. I have found them very good reading at least for one young man, for one middle-aged man, and for one who is growing old. No, no — banish the *Antiquary*, banish *Leather Stocking*, and banish all the world![1] Let us not go about to make life duller than it is.

But I must shut the doors of my imaginary library or I shall never end. It is left for me to say a few words of cordial acknowledgment to Mr. Fitz for his judicious and generous gift. I have great pleasure in believing that the custom of giving away money during their lifetime (and there is nothing harder for most men to part with, except prejudice) is more common with Americans than with any other people. It is a still greater pleasure to see that the favorite direction of their beneficence is towards the founding of colleges and libraries. My observation has led me to believe that there is no country in which wealth is so sensible of its obligations as our own. And, as most of our rich men have risen from the ranks, may we not fairly attribute this sympathy with their kind to the benign influence of democracy rightly understood? My dear and honored friend, George William Curtis, told me that he was sitting in front of the late Mr. Ezra Cornell in a convention, where one of the speakers made a Latin quotation. Mr. Cornell leaned forward and asked for a translation of it, which Mr. Curtis gave him. Mr. Cornell thanked him, and added, "If I can help it, no young man shall grow up in New York hereafter without the

[1] In Shakespeare's *King Henry IV., Part I.*, Act II. sc. 4, will be found the phrase which was in Mr. Lowell's mind when he wrote this.

chance, at least, of knowing what a Latin quotation means when he hears it." This was the germ of Cornell University,[1] and it found food for its roots in that sympathy and thoughtfulness for others of which I just spoke. This is the healthy side of that good nature which democracy tends to foster, and which is so often harmful when it has its root in indolence or indifference; especially harmful where our public affairs are concerned, and where it is easiest, because there we are giving away what belongs to other people. It should be said, however, that in this country it is as laudably easy to procure signatures to a subscription paper as it is shamefully so to obtain them for certificates of character and recommendations to office. And is not this public spirit a national evolution from that frame of mind in which New England was colonized, and which found expression in these grave words of Robinson and Brewster,[2] "We are knit together as a body in a most strict and sacred bond and covenant of the Lord, of the violation of which we make great conscience, and by virtue whereof we hold ourselves strictly tied to all care of each other's good and of the whole"? Let us never forget the deep and solemn import of these words. The problem before us is to make a whole of our many discordant parts, our many foreign elements; and I know of no way in which this can better be done than by providing a common system of education, and a common door of access to the best books by which that education may be continued, broadened,

---

[1] The motto about the seal of Cornell University indicates Mr. Cornell's conception of that institution.

[2] In a letter signed jointly by them to Sir Edwin Sandys, to be found in Bradford's *History of Plymouth Plantation*, page 20.

and made fruitful. For it is certain that, whatever we do or leave undone, those discordant parts and foreign elements are to be, whether we will or no, members of that body which Robinson and Brewster had in mind, bone of our bone, and flesh of our flesh, for good or ill. I am happy in believing that democracy has enough vigor of constitution to assimilate these seemingly indigestible morsels, and transmute them into strength of muscle and symmetry of limb.[1]

There is no way in which a man can build so secure and lasting a monument for himself as in a public library. Upon that he may confidently allow " Resurgam "[2] to be carved, for, through his good deed, he will rise again in the grateful remembrance and in the lifted and broadened minds and fortified characters of generation after generation. The pyramids may forget their builders, but memorials such as this have longer memories.

Mr. Fitz has done his part in providing your library with a dwelling. It will be for the citizens of Chelsea to provide it with worthy habitants. So shall they, too, have a share in the noble eulogy of the ancient wise man: " The teachers shall shine as the firmament, and they that turn many to righteousness as the stars forever and ever."

[1] For a fuller statement of Mr. Lowell's faith, see his address *Democracy.*

[2] This Latin word, " I shall rise again," reappears in the word *resurrection.*

ABRAHAM LINCOLN.[1]

THERE have been many painful crises since the impatient vanity of South Carolina hurried ten prosperous Commonwealths into a crime whose assured retribution was to leave them either at the mercy of the nation they had wronged, or of the anarchy they had summoned but could not control, when no thoughtful American opened his morning paper without dreading to find that he had no longer a country to love and honor. Whatever the result of the convulsion whose first shocks were beginning to be felt, there would still be enough square miles of earth for elbow-room; but that ineffable sentiment made up of memory and hope, of instinct and tradition, which swells every man's heart and shapes his thought, though perhaps never present to his consciousness, would be gone from it, leaving it common earth and nothing more. Men might gather rich crops from it, but that ideal harvest of priceless associations would be reaped no longer; that fine virtue which sent up messages of courage and security from every sod of it would have evaporated beyond recall. We should be irrevocably cut off from our past, and be forced to splice the ragged ends of our lives upon whatever new conditions chance might leave dangling for us.

We confess that we had our doubts at first whether the patriotism of our people were not too narrowly provincial to embrace the proportions of national

---

[1] This paper was published by Mr. Lowell originally in the *North American Review* for January, 1864. When he reprinted it in his volume, *My Study Windows*, he added the final paragraph, and inserted a few sentences elsewhere.

peril. We felt an only too natural distrust of immense public meetings and enthusiastic cheers.

That a reaction should follow the holiday enthusiasm with which the war was entered on, that it should follow soon, and that the slackening of public spirit should be proportionate to the previous over-tension, might well be foreseen by all who had studied human nature or history. Men acting gregariously are always in extremes; as they are one moment capable of higher courage, so they are liable, the next, to baser depression, and it is often a matter of chance whether numbers shall multiply confidence or discouragement. Nor does deception lead more surely to distrust of men, than self-deception to suspicion of principles. The only faith that wears well and holds its color in all weathers is that which is woven of conviction and set with the sharp mordant of experience. Enthusiasm is good material for the orator, but the statesman needs something more durable to work in, — must be able to rely on the deliberate reason and consequent firmness of the people, without which that presence of mind, no less essential in times of moral than of material peril, will be wanting at the critical moment. Would this fervor of the Free States hold out? Was it kindled by a just feeling of the value of constitutional liberty? Had it body enough to withstand the inevitable dampening of checks, reverses, delays? Had our population intelligence enough to comprehend that the choice was between order and anarchy, between the equilibrium of a government by law and the tussle of misrule by *pronunciamiento?* Could a war be maintained without the ordinary stimulus of hatred and plunder, and with the impersonal loyalty of principle? Those were serious questions, and with no precedent to aid in answering them.

At the beginning of the war there was, indeed, occasion for the most anxious apprehension. A president known to be infected with the political heresies, and suspected of sympathy with the treason, of the Southern conspirators, had just surrendered the reins, we will not say of power, but of chaos, to a successor known only as the representative of a party whose leaders, with long training in opposition, had none in the conduct of affairs; an empty treasury was called on to supply resources beyond precedent in the history of finance; the trees were yet growing and the iron unmined with which a navy·was to be built and armored; officers without discipline were to make a mob into an army; and, above all, the public opinion of Europe, echoed and reinforced with every vague hint and every specious argument of despondency by a powerful faction at home, was either contemptuously sceptical or actively hostile. It would be hard to overestimate the force of this latter element of disintegration and discouragement among a people where every citizen at home, and every soldier in the field, is a reader of newspapers. The pedlers of rumor in the North were the most effective allies of the rebellion. A nation can be liable to no more insidious treachery than that of the telegraph, sending hourly its electric thrill of panic along the remotest nerves of the community, till the excited imagination makes every real danger loom heightened with its unreal double.

And even if we look only at more palpable difficulties, the problem to be solved by our civil war was so vast, both in its immediate relations and its future consequences; the conditions of its solution were so intricate and so greatly dependent on incalculable and uncontrollable contingencies; so·many of the data, whether for hope or fear, were, from their novelty, incapable of arrangement under any of the categories of historical precedent, that there were moments of crisis when the firmest believer in the strength and sufficiency of the democratic theory of government might well hold his breath in vague apprehension of disaster. Our teachers of political philosophy, solemnly arguing from the precedent of some petty Grecian, Italian, or Flemish city, whose long periods of aristocracy were broken now and then by awkward parentheses of mob, had always taught us that democracies were incapable of the sentiment of loyalty, of concentrated and prolonged effort, of far-reaching conceptions; were absorbed in material interests; impatient of regular, and much more of exceptional restraint; had no natural nucleus of gravitation, nor any forces but centrifugal; were always on the verge of civil war, and slunk at last into the natural almshouse of bankrupt popular government, a military despotism. Here was indeed a dreary outlook for persons who knew democracy, not by rubbing shoulders with it lifelong, but merely from books, and America only by the report of some fellow-Briton, who, having eaten a bad dinner or lost a carpet-bag here, had written to *The Times* demanding redress, and drawing a mournful inference of democratic instability. Nor were men wanting among ourselves who had so steeped their brains in London literature as to mistake Cockneyism for European culture, and contempt of their country for cosmopolitan breadth of view, and who, owing all they had and all they were to democracy, thought it had an air of high-breeding to join in the shallow epicedium that our bubble had burst.

But beside any disheartening influences which might

affect the timid or the despondent, there were reasons enough of settled gravity against any over-confidence of hope. A war — which, whether we consider the expanse of the territory at stake, the hosts brought into the field, or the reach of the principles involved, may fairly be reckoned the most momentous of modern times — was to be waged by a people divided at home, unnerved by fifty years of peace, under a chief magistrate without experience and without reputation, whose every measure was sure to be cunningly hampered by a jealous and unscrupulous minority, and who, while dealing with unheard-of complications at home, must soothe a hostile neutrality abroad, waiting only a pretext to become war. All this was to be done without warning and without preparation, while at the same time a social revolution was to be accomplished in the political condition of four millions of people, by softening the prejudices, allaying the fears, and gradually obtaining the coöperation, of their unwilling liberators. Surely, if ever there were an occasion when the heightened imagination of the historian might see Destiny visible intervening in human affairs, here was a knot worthy of her shears. Never, perhaps, was any system of government tried by so continuous and searching a strain as ours during the last three years; never has any shown itself stronger; and never could that strength be so directly traced to the virtue and intelligence of the people, — to that general enlightenment and prompt efficiency of public opinion possible only under the influence of a political framework like our own. We find it hard to understand how even a foreigner should be blind to the grandeur of the combat of ideas that has been going on here, — to the heroic energy, persistency, and self-reliance of a nation proving that it knows how much dearer greatness is than mere power ; and we own that it is impossible for us to conceive the mental and moral condition of the American who does not feel his spirit braced and heightened by being even a spectator of such qualities and achievements. That a steady purpose and a definite aim have been given to the jarring forces which, at the beginning of the war, spent themselves in the discussion of schemes which could only become operative, if at all, after the war was over; that a popular excitement has been slowly intensified into an earnest national will ; that a somewhat impracticable moral sentiment has been made the unconscious instrument of a practical moral end ; that the treason of covert enemies, the jealousy of rivals, the unwise zeal of friends, have been made not only useless for mischief, but even useful for good ; that the conscientious sensitiveness of England to the horrors of civil conflict has been prevented from complicating a domestic with a foreign war ; — all these results, any one of which might suffice to prove greatness in a ruler, have been mainly due to the good sense, the good-humor, the sagacity, the large-mindedness, and the unselfish honesty of the unknown man whom a blind fortune, as it seemed, had lifted from the crowd to the most dangerous and difficult eminence of modern times. It is by presence of mind in untried emergencies that the native metal of a man is tested ; it is by the sagacity to see, and the fearless honesty to admit, whatever of truth there may be in an adverse opinion, in order more convincingly to expose the fallacy that lurks behind it, that a reasoner at length gains for his mere statement of a fact the force of argument ; it is by a wise forecast which allows hostile combinations to go so far as by the in. evitable reaction to become elements of his own power, that a politician proves his genius for state-craft; and especially it is by so gently guiding public sentiment that he seems to follow it, by so yielding doubtful points that he can be firm without seeming obstinate in essential ones, and thus gain the advantages of compromise without the weakness of concession; by so instinctively comprehending the temper and prejudices of a people as to make them gradually conscious of the superior wisdom of his freedom from temper and prejudice, — it is by qualities such as these that a magistrate shows himself worthy to be chief in a commonwealth of freemen. And it is for qualities such as these that we firmly believe History will rank Mr. Lincoln among the most prudent of statesmen and the most successful of rulers. If we wish to appreciate him, we have only to conceive the inevitable chaos in which we should now be weltering had a weak man or an unwise one been chosen in his stead.

"Bare is back," says the Norse proverb, "without brother behind it;" and this is, by analogy, true of an elective magistracy. The hereditary ruler in any critical emergency may reckon on the inexhaustible resources of *prestige*, of sentiment, of superstition, of dependent interest, while the new man must slowly and painfully create all these out of the unwilling material around him, by superiority of character, by patient singleness of purpose, by sagacious presentiment of popular tendencies and instinctive sympathy with the national character. Mr. Lincoln's task was one of peculiar and exceptional difficulty. Long habit had accustomed the American people to the notion of a party in power, and of a President as its creature and organ, while the more vital fact, that the executive for the time being represents the abstract idea of government as a permanent principle superior to all party and all private interest, had gradually become unfamiliar. They had so long seen the public policy more or less directed by views of party, and often even of personal advantage, as to be ready to suspect the motives of a chief magistrate compelled, for the first time in our history, to feel himself the head and hand of a great nation, and to act upon the fundamental maxim, laid down by all publicists, that the first duty of a government is to defend and maintain its own existence. Accordingly, a powerful weapon seemed to be put into the hands of the opposition by the necessity under which the administration found itself of applying this old truth to new relations. Nor were the opposition his only nor his most dangerous opponents.

The Republicans had carried the country upon an issue in which ethics were more directly and visibly mingled with politics than usual. Their leaders were trained to a method of oratory which relied for its effect rather on the moral sense than the understanding. Their arguments were drawn, not so much from experience as from general principles of right and wrong. When the war came, their system continued to be applicable and effective, for here again the reason of the people was to be reached and kindled through their sentiments. It was one of those periods of excitement, gathering, contagious, universal, which, while they last, exalt and clarify the minds of men, giving to the mere words *country, human rights, democracy,* a meaning and a force beyond that of sober and logical argument. They were convictions, main-

tained and defended by the supreme logic of passion.
That penetrating fire ran in and roused those primary
instincts that make their lair in the dens and caverns
of the mind. What is called the great popular heart
was awakened, that indefinable something which may
be, according to circumstances, the highest reason or
the most brutish unreason. But enthusiasm, once cold,
can never be warmed over into anything better than
cant, — and phrases, when once the inspiration that
filled them with beneficent power has ebbed away,
retain only that semblance of meaning which enables
them to supplant reason in hasty minds. Among the
lessons taught by the French Revolution there is none
sadder or more striking than this, that you may make
everything else out of the passions of men except a
political system that will work, and that there is no-
thing so pitilessly and unconsciously cruel as sincerity
formulated into dogma. It is always demoralizing to
extend the domain of sentiment over questions where
it has no legitimate jurisdiction; and perhaps the se-
verest strain upon Mr. Lincoln was in resisting a ten-
dency of his own supporters which chimed with his
own private desires while wholly opposed to his con-
victions of what would be wise policy.

The change which three years have brought about
is too remarkable to be passed over without comment,
too weighty in its lesson not to be laid to heart.
Never did a President enter upon office with less
means at his command, outside his own strength of
heart and steadiness of understanding, for inspiring
confidence in the people, and so winning it for him-
self, than Mr. Lincoln. All that was known of him
was that he was a good stump-speaker, nominated for
his *availability*, — that is, because he had no history,

— and chosen by a party with whose more extreme opinions he was not in sympathy. It might well be feared that a man past fifty, against whom the ingenuity of hostile partisans could rake up no accusation, must be lacking in manliness of character, in decision of principle, in strength of will; that a man who was at best only the representative of a party, and who yet did not fairly represent even that, would fail of political, much more of popular, support. And certainly no one ever entered upon office with so few resources of power in the past, and so many materials of weakness in the present, as Mr. Lincoln. Even in that half of the Union which acknowledged him as President, there was a large, and at that time dangerous minority, that hardly admitted his claim to the office, and even in the party that elected him there was also a large minority that suspected him of being secretly a communicant with the church of Laodicea.[1] All that he did was sure to be virulently attacked as ultra by one side; all that he left undone, to be stigmatized as proof of lukewarmness and backsliding by the other. Meanwhile he was to carry on a truly colossal war by means of both; he was to disengage the country from diplomatic entanglements of unprecedented peril undisturbed by the help or the hinderance of either, and to win from the crowning dangers of his administration, in the confidence of the people, the means of his safety and their own. He has contrived to do it, and perhaps none of our Presidents since Washington has stood so firm in the confidence of the people as he does after three years of stormy administration.

Mr. Lincoln's policy was a tentative one, and rightly so. He laid down no programme which must

---

[1] See the *Book of Revelation*, chapter 3, verse 15.

compel him to be either inconsistent or unwise, no cast-iron theorem to which circumstances must be fitted as they rose, or else be useless to his ends. He seemed to have chosen Mazarin's motto, *Le temps et moi.*[1] The *moi*, to be sure, was not very prominent at first; but it has grown more and more so, till the world is beginning to be persuaded that it stands for a character of marked individuality and capacity for affairs. Time was his prime-minister, and, we began to think, at one period, his general-in-chief also. At first he was so slow that he tired out all those who see no evidence of progress but in blowing up the engine; then he was so fast that he took the breath away from those who think there is no getting on safely while there is a spark of fire under the boilers. God is the only being who has time enough; but a prudent man, who knows how to seize occasion, can commonly make a shift to find as much as he needs. Mr. Lincoln, as it seems to us in reviewing his career, though we have sometimes in our impatience thought otherwise, has always waited, as a wise man should, till the right moment brought up all his reserves. *Semper nocuit differre paratis,*[2] is a sound axiom, but the really efficacious man will also be sure to know when he is *not* ready, and be firm against all persuasion and reproach till he is.

One would be apt to think, from some of the criticisms made on Mr. Lincoln's course by those who mainly agree with him in principle, that the chief object of a statesman should be rather to proclaim his adhesion to certain doctrines, than to achieve their

[1] Time and I. Cardinal Mazarin was prime-minister of Louis XIV. of France. Time, Mazarin said, was his prime-minister.

[2] It is always bad for those who are ready to put off action.

triumph by quietly accomplishing his ends. In our opinion, there is no more unsafe politician than a conscientiously rigid *doctrinaire*, nothing more sure to end in disaster than a theoretic scheme of policy that admits of no pliability for contingencies. True, there is a popular image of an impossible He, in whose plastic hands the submissive destinies of mankind become as wax, and to whose commanding necessity the toughest facts yield with the graceful pliancy of fiction; but in real life we commonly find that the men who control circumstances, as it is called, are those who have learned to allow for the influence of their eddies, and have the nerve to turn them to account at the happy instant. Mr. Lincoln's perilous task has been to carry a rather shaky raft through the rapids, making fast the unrulier logs as he could snatch opportunity, and the country is to be congratulated that he did not think it his duty to run straight at all hazards, but cautiously to assure himself with his setting-pole where the main current was, and keep steadily to that. He is still in wild water, but we have faith that his skill and sureness of eye will bring him out right at last.

A curious, and, as we think, not inapt parallel, might be drawn between Mr. Lincoln and one of the most striking figures in modern history, — Henry IV. of France. The career of the latter may be more picturesque, as that of a daring captain always is; but in all its vicissitudes there is nothing more romantic than that sudden change, as by a rub of Aladdin's lamp, from the attorney's office in a country town of Illinois to the helm of a great nation in times like these. The analogy between the characters and circumstances of the two men is in many respects singularly close. Succeeding to a rebellion rather than a crown, Henry's chief material dependence was the Huguenot party, whose doctrines sat upon him with a looseness distasteful certainly, if not suspicious to the more fanatical among them.   King only in name over the greater part of France, and with his capital barred against him, it yet gradually became clear to the more far-seeing even of the Catholic party that he was the only centre of order and legitimate authority round which France could reorganize itself.   While preachers who held the divine right of kings made the churches of Paris ring with declamations in favor of democracy rather than submit to the heretic dog of a Béarnois,[1] — much as our *soi-disant* Democrats have lately been preaching the divine right of slavery, and denouncing the heresies of the Declaration of Independence, — Henry bore both parties in hand till he was convinced that only one course of action could possibly combine his own interests and those of France. Meanwhile the Protestants believed somewhat doubtfully that he was theirs, the Catholics hoped somewhat doubtfully that he would be theirs, and Henry himself turned aside remonstrance, advice, and curiosity alike with a jest or a proverb (if a little *high*, he liked them none the worse), joking continually as his manner was. We have seen Mr. Lincoln contemptuously compared to Sancho Panza by persons incapable of appreciating one of the deepest pieces of wisdom in the profoundest romance ever written ; namely, that while Don Quixote was incomparable in theoretic and ideal statesmanship, Sancho, with his stock of proverbs, the ready money of human experience, made the best possible practical governor.   Henry IV. was as full of

---

[1] One of Henry's titles was Prince of Béarn, that being the old province of France from which he came.

wise saws and modern instances as Mr. Lincoln, but
beneath all this was the thoughtful, practical, humane,
and thoroughly earnest man, around whom the frag-
ments of France were to gather themselves till she
took her place again as a planet of the first magnitude
in the European system. In one respect Mr. Lincoln
was more fortunate than Henry. However some may
think him wanting in zeal, the most fanatical can find
no taint of apostasy in any measure of his, nor can
the most bitter charge him with being influenced by
motives of personal interest. The leading distinction
between the policies of the two is one of circumstances.
Henry went over to the nation ; Mr. Lincoln has stead-
ily drawn the nation over to him. One left a united
France ; the other, we hope and believe, will leave a
reunited America. We leave our readers to trace the
further points of difference and resemblance for them-
selves, merely suggesting a general similarity which
has often occurred to us. One only point of melan-
choly interest we will allow ourselves to touch upon.
That Mr. Lincoln is not handsome nor elegant, we
learn from certain English tourists who would consider
similar revelations in regard to Queen Victoria as
thoroughly American in their want of *bienséance*. It
is no concern of ours, nor does it affect his fitness for
the high place he so worthily occupies ; but he is
certainly as fortunate as Henry in the matter of good
looks, if we may trust contemporary evidence. Mr.
Lincoln has also been reproached with Americanism
by some not unfriendly British critics ; but, with all
deference, we cannot say that we like him any the
worse for it, or see in it any reason why he should
govern Americans the less wisely.

People of more sensitive organizations may be

shocked, but we are glad that in this, our true war of independence, which is to free us forever from the Old World, we have had at the head of our affairs a man whom America made, as God made Adam, out of the very earth, unancestried, unprivileged, unknown, to show us how much truth, how much magnanimity, and how much statecraft await the call of opportunity in simple manhood when it believes in the justice of God and the worth of man. Conventionalities are all very well in their proper place, but they shrivel at the touch of nature like stubble in the fire. The genius that sways a nation by its arbitrary will seems less august to us than that which multiplies and reinforces itself in the instincts and convictions of an entire people. Autocracy may have something in it more melodramatic than this, but falls far short of it in human value and interest.

Experience would have bred in us a rooted distrust of improvised statesmanship, even if we did not believe politics to be a science, which, if it cannot always command men of special aptitude and great powers, at least demands the long and steady application of the best powers of such men as it can command to master even its first principles. It is curious, that, in a country which boasts of its intelligence, the theory should be so generally held that the most complicated of human contrivances, and one which every day becomes more complicated, can be worked at sight by any man able to talk for an hour or two without stopping to think.

Mr. Lincoln is sometimes claimed as an example of a ready-made ruler. But no case could well be less in point; for, besides that he was a man of such fair-mindedness as is always the raw material of wisdom,

he had in his profession a training precisely the oppo-
site of that to which a partisan is subjected. His ex-
perience as a lawyer compelled him not only to see
that there is a principle underlying every phenomenon
in human affairs, but that there are always two sides
to every question, both of which must be fully under-
stood in order to understand either, and that it is of
greater advantage to an advocate to appreciate the
strength than the weakness of his antagonist's position.
Nothing is more remarkable than the unerring tact
with which, in his debate with Mr. Douglas, he went
straight to the reason of the question; nor have we
ever had a more striking lesson in political tactics than
the fact, that opposed to a man exceptionally adroit in
using popular prejudice and bigotry to his purpose,
exceptionally unscrupulous in appealing to those baser
motives that turn a meeting of citizens into a mob of
barbarians, he should yet have won his case before a
jury of the people. Mr. Lincoln was as far as possi-
ble from an impromptu politician. His wisdom was
made up of a knowledge of things as well as of men;
his sagacity resulted from a clear perception and hon-
est acknowledgment of difficulties, which enabled him
to see that the only durable triumph of political opin-
ion is based, not on any abstract right, but upon so
much of justice, the highest attainable at any given
moment in human affairs, as may be had in the bal-
ance of mutual concession. Doubtless he had an
ideal, but it was the ideal of a practical statesman, —
to aim at the best, and to take the next best, if he is
lucky enough to get even that. His slow, but singu-
larly masculine intelligence taught him that precedent
is only another name for embodied experience, and
that it counts for even more in the guidance of com-

munities of men than in that of the individual life.
He was not a man who held it good public economy to
pull down on the mere chance of rebuilding better.
Mr. Lincoln's faith in God was qualified by a very
well-founded distrust of the wisdom of man. Perhaps
it was his want of self-confidence that more than any-
thing else won him the unlimited confidence of the
people, for they felt that there would be no need of
retreat from any position he had deliberately taken.
The cautious, but steady, advance of his policy during
the war was like that of a Roman army. He left be-
hind him a firm road on which public confidence could
follow; he took America with him where he went;
what he gained he occupied, and his advanced posts
became colonies. The very homeliness of his genius
was its distinction. His kingship was conspicuous by
its workday homespun. Never was ruler so absolute
as he, nor so little conscious of it; for he was the in-
carnate common-sense of the people. With all that
tenderness of nature whose sweet sadness touched
whoever saw him with something of its own pathos,
there was no trace of sentimentalism in his speech or
action. He seems to have had but one rule of con-
duct, always that of practical and successful politics,
to let himself be guided by events, when they were
sure to bring him out where he wished to go, though
by what seemed to unpractical minds, which let go the
possible to grasp at the desirable, a longer road.

Undoubtedly the highest function of statesmanship
is by degrees to accommodate the conduct of commu-
nities to ethical laws, and to subordinate the conflict-
ing self-interests of the day to higher and more per-
manent concerns. But it is on the understanding,
and not on the sentiment, of a nation that all safe

legislation must be based. Voltaire's saying, that " a consideration of petty circumstances is the tomb of great things," may be true of individual men, but it certainly is not true of governments. It is by a multitude of such considerations, each in itself trifling, but all together weighty, that the framers of policy can alone divine what is practicable and therefore wise. The imputation of inconsistency is one to which every sound politician and every honest thinker must sooner or later subject himself. The foolish and the dead alone never change their opinion. The course of a great statesman resembles that of navigable rivers, avoiding immovable obstacles with noble bends of concession, seeking the broad levels of opinion on which men soonest settle and longest dwell, following and marking the almost imperceptible slopes of national tendency, yet always aiming at direct advances, always recruited from sources nearer heaven, and sometimes bursting open paths of progress and fruitful human commerce through what seem the eternal barriers of both. It is loyalty to great ends, even though forced to combine the small and opposing motives of selfish men to accomplish them; it is the anchored cling to solid principles of duty and action, which knows how to swing with the tide, but is never carried away by it, — that we demand in public men, and not sameness of policy, or a conscientious persistency in what is impracticable. For the impracticable, however theoretically enticing, is always politically unwise, sound statesmanship being the application of that prudence to the public business which is the safest guide in that of private men.

No doubt slavery was the most delicate and embarrassing question with which Mr. Lincoln was called

on to deal, and it was one which no man in his posi-
tion, whatever his opinions, could evade ; for, though
he might withstand the clamor of partisans, he must
sooner or later yield to the persistent importunacy of
circumstances, which .thrust the problem upon him at
every turn and in every shape.

It has been brought against us as an accusation
abroad, and repeated here by people who measure
their country rather by what is thought of it than by
what it is, that our war has not been distinctly and
avowedly for the extinction of slavery, but a war rather
for the preservation of our national power and great-
ness, in which the emancipation of the negro has been
forced upon us by circumstances and accepted as a
necessity.   We are very far from denying this ; nay,
we, admit that it is so far true that we were slow to
renounce our constitutional obligations even toward
those who had absolved us by their own act from the
letter of our duty.   We are speaking of the govern-
ment which, legally installed for the whole country,
was bound, so long as it was possible, not to overstep
the limits of orderly prescription, and could not, with-
out abnegating its own very nature, take the lead in
making rebellion an excuse for revolution.   There
were, no doubt, many ardent and sincere persons who
seemed to think this as simple a thing to do as to lead
off a Virginia reel.   They forgot, what should be for-
gotten least of all in a system like ours, that the ad-
ministration for the time being represents not only
the majority which elects it, but the minority as well,
— a minority in this case powerful, and so little ready
for emancipation that it was opposed even to war.
Mr. Lincoln had not been chosen as general agent of
an anti-slavery society, but President of the United

States, to perform certain functions exactly defined by law. Whatever were his wishes, it was no less duty than policy to mark out for himself a line of action that would not further distract the country, by raising before their time questions which plainly would soon enough compel attention, and for which every day was making the answer more easy.

Meanwhile he must solve the riddle of this new Sphinx, or be devoured. Though Mr. Lincoln's policy in this critical affair has not been such as to satisfy those who demand an heroic treatment for even the most trifling occasion, and who will not cut their coat according to their cloth, unless they can borrow the scissors of Atropos,[1] it has been at least not unworthy of the long-headed king of Ithaca.[2] Mr. Lincoln had the choice of Bassanio[3] offered him. Which of the three caskets held the prize that was to redeem the fortunes of the country? There was the golden one whose showy speciousness might have tempted a vain man; the silver of compromise, which might have decided the choice of a merely acute one; and the leaden, — dull and homely-looking, as prudence always is, — yet with something about it sure to attract the eye of practical wisdom. Mr. Lincoln dallied with his decision perhaps longer than seemed needful to those on whom its awful responsibility was not to rest, but when he made it, it was worthy of his cautious but sure-footed understanding. The moral of the Sphinx-riddle, and it is a deep one, lies in the childish simplicity of the solution. Those who fail in guessing it, fail because they are over-ingenious, and

---

[1] One of the three Fates.

[2] Odysseus, or Ulysses, the hero of Homer's Odyssey.

[3] See Shakespeare's *Merchant of Venice*.

cast about for an answer that shall suit their own notion of the gravity of the occasion and of their own dignity, rather than the occasion itself.

In a matter which must be finally settled by public opinion, and in regard to which the ferment of prejudice and passion on both sides has not yet subsided to that equilibrium of compromise from which alone a sound public opinion can result, it is proper enough for the private citizen to press his own convictions with all possible force of argument and persuasion ; but the popular magistrate, whose judgment must become action, and whose action involves the whole country, is bound to wait till the sentiment of the people is so far advanced toward his own point of view, that what he does shall find support in it, instead of merely confusing it with new elements of division. It was not unnatural that men earnestly devoted to the saving of their country, and profoundly convinced that slavery was its only real enemy, should demand a decided policy round which all patriots might rally, — and this might have been the wisest course for an absolute ruler. But in the then unsettled state of the public mind, with a large party decrying even resistance to the slaveholders' rebellion as not only unwise, but even unlawful ; with a majority, perhaps, even of the would-be loyal so long accustomed to regard the Constitution as a deed of gift conveying to the South their own judgment as to policy and instinct as to right, that they were in doubt at first whether their loyalty were due to the country or to slavery ; and with a respectable body of honest and influential men who still believed in the possibility of conciliation, — Mr. Lincoln judged wisely, that, in laying down a policy in deference to one party, he should be giving to the other the very fulcrum for which their disloyalty had been waiting.

It behooved a clear-headed man in his position not to yield so far to an honest indignation against the brokers of treason in the North as to lose sight of the materials for misleading which were their stock in trade, and to forget that it is not the falsehood of sophistry which is to be feared, but the grain of truth mingled with it to make it specious, — that it is not the knavery of the leaders so much as the honesty of the followers they may seduce, that gives them power for evil. It was especially his duty to do nothing which might help the people to forget the true cause of the war in fruitless disputes about its inevitable consequences.

The doctrine of State rights can be so handled by an adroit demagogue as easily to confound the distinction between liberty and lawlessness in the minds of ignorant persons, accustomed always to be influenced by the sound of certain words, rather than to reflect upon the principles which give them meaning. For, though Secession involves the manifest absurdity of denying to a State the right of making war against any foreign power while permitting it against the United States; though it supposes a compact of mutual concessions and guaranties among States without any arbiter in case of dissension; though it contradicts common-sense in assuming that the men who framed our government did not know what they meant when they substituted Union for Confederation; though it falsifies history, which shows that the main opposition to the adoption of the Constitution was based on the argument that it did not allow that independence in the several States which alone would justify them in seceding; — yet, as slavery was universally admitted to be a reserved right, an inference could be drawn from any direct attack upon it (though only in self-defence) to a natural right of resistance, logical enough to satisfy minds untrained to detect fallacy, as the majority of men always are, and now too much disturbed by the disorder of the times, to consider that the order of events had any legitimate bearing on the argument.   Though Mr. Lincoln was too sagacious to give the Northern allies of the Rebels the occasion they desired and even strove to provoke, yet from the beginning of the war the most persistent efforts have been made to confuse the public mind as to its origin and motives, and to drag the people of the loyal States down from the national position they had instinctively taken to the old level of party squabbles and antipathies.   The wholly unprovoked rebellion of an oligarchy proclaiming negro slavery the corner-stone of free institutions, and in the first flush of over-hasty confidence venturing to parade the logical sequence of their leading dogma, "that slavery is right in principle, and has nothing to do with difference of complexion," has been represented as a legitimate and gallant attempt to maintain the true principles of democracy.   The rightful endeavor of an established government, the least onerous that ever existed, to defend itself against a treacherous attack on its very existence, has been cunningly made to seem the wicked effort of a fanatical clique to force its doctrines on an oppressed population.

Even so long ago as when Mr. Lincoln, not yet convinced of the danger and magnitude of the crisis, was endeavoring to persuade himself of Union majorities at the South, and to carry on a war that was half peace

in the hope of a peace that would have been all war, —
while he was still enforcing the Fugitive Slave Law,
under some theory that Secession, however it might
absolve States from their obligations, could not es-
cheat them of their claims under the Constitution, and
that slaveholders in rebellion had alone among mortals
the privilege of having their cake and eating it at the
same time, — the enemies of free government were
striving to persuade the people that the war was an
Abolition crusade. To rebel without reason was pro-
claimed as one of the rights of man, while it was care-
fully kept out of sight that to suppress rebellion is the
first duty of government. All the evils that have
come upon the country have been attributed to the
Abolitionists, though it is hard to see how any party
can become permanently powerful except in one of
two ways, either by the greater truth of its princi-
ples, or the extravagance of the party opposed to it.
To fancy the ship of state, riding safe at her constitu-
tional moorings, suddenly engulfed by a huge kraken
of Abolitionism, rising from unknown depths and
grasping it with slimy tentacles, is to look at the nat-
ural history of the matter with the eyes of Pontop-
pidan.[1] To believe that the leaders in the Southern
treason feared any danger from Abolitionism, would
be to deny them ordinary intelligence, though there
can be little doubt that they made use of it to stir the
passions and excite the fears of their deluded accom-
plices. They rebelled, not because they thought slav-
ery weak, but because they believed it strong enough,
not to overthrow the government, but to get posses-
sion of it ; for it becomes daily clearer that they used
rebellion only as a means of revolution, and if they

[1] A Danish antiquary and theologian.

got revolution, though not in the shape they looked
for, is the American people to save them from its con-
sequences at the cost of its own existence? The elec-
tion of Mr. Lincoln, which it was clearly in their
power to prevent had they wished, was the occasion
merely, and not the cause of their revolt. Abolition-
ism, till within a year or two, was the despised heresy
of a few earnest persons, without political weight
enough to carry the election of a parish constable;
and their cardinal principle was disunion, because
they were convinced that within the Union the posi-
tion of slavery was impregnable. In spite of the
proverb, great effects do not follow from small causes,
— that is, disproportionately small, — but from ade-
quate causes acting under certain required conditions.
To contrast the size of the oak with that of the parent
acorn, as if the poor seed had paid all costs from its
slender strong-box, may serve for a child's wonder;
but the real miracle lies in that divine league which
bound all the forces of nature to the service of the
tiny germ in fulfilling its destiny. Everything has
been at work for the past ten years in the cause of
anti-slavery, but Garrison and Phillips have been far
less successful propagandists than the slaveholders
themselves, with the constantly growing arrogance of
their pretensions and encroachments. They have
forced the question upon the attention of every voter
in the Free States, by defiantly putting freedom and
democracy on the defensive. But, even after the
Kansas outrages, there was no wide-spread desire on
the part of the North to commit aggressions, though
there was a growing determination to resist them.
The popular unanimity in favor of the war three years
ago was but in small measure the result of anti-slavery

sentiment, far less of any zeal for abolition. But every month of the war, every movement of the allies of slavery in the Free States, has been making Abolitionists by the thousand. The masses of any people, however intelligent, are very little moved by abstract principles of humanity and justice, until those principles are interpreted for them by the stinging commentary of some infringement upon their own rights, and then their instincts and passions, once aroused, do indeed derive an incalculable reinforcement of impulse and intensity from those higher ideas, those sublime traditions, which have no motive political force till they are allied with a sense of immediate personal wrong or imminent peril. Then at last the stars in their courses begin to fight against Sisera. Had any one doubted before that the rights of human nature are unitary, that oppression is of one hue the world over, no matter what the color of the oppressed, — had any one failed to see what the real essence of the contest was, — the efforts of the advocates of slavery among ourselves to throw discredit upon the fundamental axioms of the Declaration of Independence and the radical doctrines of Christianity, could not fail to sharpen his eyes.

While every day was bringing the people nearer to the conclusion which all thinking men saw to be inevitable from the beginning, it was wise in Mr. Lincoln to leave the shaping of his policy to events. In this country, where the rough and ready understanding of the people is sure at last to be the controlling power, a profound common-sense is the best genius for statesmanship. Hitherto the wisdom of the President's measures has been justified by the fact that they have always resulted in more firmly uniting public opinion.

One of the things particularly admirable in the public utterances of President Lincoln is a certain tone of familiar dignity, which, while it is perhaps the most difficult attainment of mere style, is also no doubtful indication of personal character. There must be something essentially noble in an elective ruler who can descend to the level of confidential ease without' losing respect, something very manly in one who can break through the etiquette of his conventional rank and trust himself to the reason and intelligence of those who have elected him. No higher compliment was ever paid to a nation than the simple confidence, the fireside plainness, with which Mr. Lincoln always addresses himself to the reason of the American people. This was, indeed, a true democrat, who grounded himself on the assumption that a democracy can think. "Come, let us reason together about this matter," has been the tone of all his addresses to the people; and accordingly we have never had a chief magistrate who so won to himself the love and at the same time the judgment of his countrymen. To us, that simple confidence of his in the right-mindedness of his fellow-men is very touching, and its success is as strong an argument as we have ever seen in favor of the theory that men can govern themselves. He never appeals to any vulgar sentiment, he never alludes to the humbleness of his origin; it probably never occurred to him, indeed, that there was anything higher to start from than manhood; and he put himself on a level with those he addressed, not by going down to them, but only by taking it for granted that they had brains and would come up to a common ground of reason. In an article lately printed in *The Nation*, Mr. Bayard Taylor mentions the striking fact, that in the foulest dens of the Five Points he found the portrait of Lincoln. The wretched population that makes its hive there threw all its votes and more against him, and yet paid this instinctive tribute to the sweet humanity of his nature. Their ignorance sold its vote and took its money, but all that was left of manhood in them recognized its saint and martyr.

Mr. Lincoln is not in the habit of saying, "This is *my* opinion, or *my* theory," but "This is the conclusion to which, in my judgment, the time has come, and to which, accordingly, the sooner we come the better for us." His policy has been the policy of public opinion based on adequate discussion and on a timely recognition of the influence of passing events in shaping the features of events to come.

One secret of Mr. Lincoln's remarkable success in captivating the popular mind is undoubtedly an unconsciousness of self which enables him, though under the necessity of constantly using the capital *I*, to do it without any suggestion of egotism. There is no single vowel which men's mouths can pronounce with such difference of effect. That which one shall hide away, as it were, behind the substance of his discourse, or, if he bring it to the front, shall use merely to give an agreeable accent of individuality to what he says, another shall make an offensive challenge to the self-satisfaction of all his hearers, and an unwarranted intrusion upon each man's sense of personal importance, irritating every pore of his vanity, like a dry northeast wind, to a goose-flesh of opposition and hostility. Mr. Lincoln has never studied Quintilian;[1] but he has, in the earnest simplicity and unaffected Americanism of his own character, one art

[1] A famous Latin writer on the *Art of Oratory.*

of oratory worth all the rest. He forgets himself so entirely in his object as to give his *I* the sympathetic and persuasive effect of *We* with the great body of his countrymen. Homely, dispassionate, showing all the rough-edged process of his thought as it goes along, yet arriving at his conclusions with an honest kind of every-day logic, he is so eminently our representative man, that, when he speaks, it seems as if the people were listening to their own thinking aloud. The dignity of his thought owes nothing to any ceremonial garb of words, but to the manly movement that comes of settled purpose and an energy of reason that knows not what rhetoric means. There has been nothing of Cleon, still less of Strepsiades [1] striving to underbid him in demagogism, to be found in the public utterances of Mr. Lincoln. He has always addressed the intelligence of men, never their prejudice, their passion, or their ignorance.

On the day of his death, this simple Western attorney, who according to one party was a vulgar joker, and whom the *doctrinaires* among his own supporters accused of wanting every element of statesmanship, was the most absolute ruler in Christendom, and this solely by the hold his good-humored sagacity had laid on the hearts and understandings of his countrymen. Nor was this all, for it appeared that he had drawn the great majority, not only of his fellow-citizens, but of mankind also, to his side. So strong and so persuasive is honest manliness without a single quality of romance or unreal sentiment to help it! A civilian

---

[1] Two Athenian demagogues, satirized by the dramatist Aristophanes.

during times of the most captivating military achieve-
ment, awkward, with no skill in the lower technicali-
ties of manners, he left behind him a fame beyond
that of any conqueror, the memory of a grace higher
than that of outward person, and of a gentlemanliness
deeper than mere breeding. Never before that star-
tled April morning did such multitudes of men shed
tears for the death of one they had never seen, as if
with him a friendly presence had been taken away from
their lives, leaving them colder and darker. Never
was funeral panegyric so eloquent as the silent look
of sympathy which strangers exchanged when they
met on that day. Their common manhood had lost a
kinsman.

ABRAHAM LINCOLN'S SPEECH

AT THE DEDICATION OF THE NATIONAL CEMETERY, GET-
TYSBURG, PENNSYLVANIA, NOVEMBER 19, 1863.

[THE great battles fought at Gettysburg, Pennsylvania,
in July, 1863, made that spot historic ground. It was early
perceived that the battles were critical, and they are now
looked upon by many as the turning-point of the war for the
Union. The ground where the fiercest conflict raged was
taken for a national cemetery, and the dedication of the
place was made an occasion of great solemnity. The ora-
tor of the day was Edward Everett, who was regarded as
the most finished public speaker in the country. Mr. Ever-
ett made a long and eloquent address, and was followed by
the President in a little speech which instantaneously af-
fected the country, whether people were educated or unlet-
tered, as a great speech. The impression created has deep-
ened with time. Ralph Waldo Emerson in his essay on
Eloquence says: "I believe it to be true that when any

orator at the bar or the Senate rises in his thought, he descends in his language, that is, when he rises to any height of thought or passion, he comes down to a language level with the ear of all his audience. It is the merit of John Brown and of Abraham Lincoln — one at Charlestown, one at Gettysburg — in the two best specimens of eloquence we have had in this country."

It is worth while to listen to Mr. Lincoln's own account of the education which prepared him for public speaking. Before he was nominated for the presidency he had attracted the notice of people by a remarkable contest in debate with a famous Illinois statesman, Stephen Arnold Douglas. As a consequence Mr. Lincoln received a great many invitations to speak in the Eastern States, and made, among others, a notable speech at the Cooper Union, New York. Shortly after, he spoke also at New Haven, and the Rev. J. P. Gulliver, in a paper in the *New York Independent*, Sept. 1, 1864, thus reports a conversation which he held with him when travelling in the same railroad car : —

"'Ah, that reminds me,' he said, 'of a most extraordinary circumstance, which occurred in New Haven, the other day. They told me that the Professor of Rhetoric in Yale College — a very learned man, is n't he?' 'Yes, sir, and a very fine critic, too.' 'Well, I suppose so; he ought to be, at any rate — They told me that he came to hear me and took notes of my speech, and gave a lecture on it to his class the next day; and, not satisfied with that, he followed me up to Meriden the next evening, and heard me again for the same purpose. Now, if this is so, it is to my mind very extraordinary. I have been sufficiently astonished at my success in the West. It has been most unexpected. But I had no thought of any marked success at the East, and least of all that I should draw out such commendations from literary and learned men!'

"'That suggests, Mr. Lincoln, an inquiry which has several times been upon my lips during this conversation. I want very much to know how you got this unusual power of " putting things." It must have been a matter of education. No man has it by nature alone. What has your education been?'

"'Well, as to education, the newspapers are correct. I never went to school more than six months in my life. But, as you say, this must be a product of culture in some form. I have been putting the question you ask me to myself while you have been talking. I say this, that among my earliest recollections, I remember how, when a mere child, I used to get irritated when anybody talked to me in a way I could not understand. I don't think I ever got angry at anything else in my life. But that always disturbed my temper, and has ever since. I can remember going to my little bedroom, after hearing the neighbors talk of an evening with my father, and spending no small part of the night walking up and down, and trying to make out what was the exact meaning of some of their, to me, dark sayings. I could not sleep, though I often tried to, when I got on such a hunt after an idea, until I had caught it; and when I thought I had got it, I was not satisfied until I had repeated it over and over, until I had put it in language plain enough, as I thought, for any boy I knew to comprehend. This was a kind of passion with me, and it has stuck by me, for I am never easy now, when I am handling a thought, till I have bounded it north and bounded it south and bounded it east and bounded it west. Perhaps that accounts for the characteristic you observe in my speeches, though I never put the two things together before.'" But to the speech itself.]

FOURSCORE and seven years ago, our fathers brought forth on this continent a new nation, conceived in liberty, and dedicated to the proposition that all men are created equal. Now we are engaged in a great civil war, testing whether that nation, or any nation so conceived and so dedicated, can long endure. We are met on a great battlefield of that war. We have come to dedicate a portion of that field as a final resting-place for those who here gave their lives that that nation might live. It is altogether fitting and proper that we should do this. But in a larger sense we cannot dedicate, we cannot consecrate, we cannot hallow this ground. The brave men, living and dead, who struggled here, have consecrated it far above our poor power to add or detract. The world will little note, nor long remember, what we say here, but it can never forget what they did here. It is for us, the living, rather to be dedicated here to the unfinished work which they who fought here have thus far so nobly advanced. /It is rather for us to be here dedicated to the great task remaining before us,—that from these honored dead we take increased devotion to that cause for which they gave the last full measure of devotion,—that we here highly resolve that these dead shall not have died in vain,—that this nation, under God, shall have a new birth of freedom,—and that government of the people, by the people, for the people, shall not perish from the earth.

THE VISION OF SIR LAUNFAL.

[AUTHOR'S NOTE.—According to the mythology of the Romancers, the San Greal, or Holy Grail, was the cup out of which Jesus Christ partook of the last supper with his disciples. It was brought into England by Joseph of Arimathea, and remained there, an object of pilgrimage and adoration, for many years, in the keeping of his lineal descendants. It was incumbent upon those who had charge of it

to be chaste in thought, word, and deed ; but one of the
keepers having broken this condition, the Holy Grail dis-
appeared.   From that time it was a favorite enterprise of
the Knights of Arthur's court to go in search of it.   Sir
Galahad was at last successful in finding it, as may be read
in the seventeenth book of the Romance of King Arthur.
Tennyson has made Sir Galahad the subject of one of the
most exquisite of his poems.

The plot (if I may give that name to anything so slight)
of the following poem is my own, and, to serve its purposes,
I have enlarged the circle of competition in search of the
miraculous cup in such a manner as to include not only other
persons than the heroes of the Round Table, but also a
period of time subsequent to the date of King Arthur's
reign.]

PRELUDE TO PART FIRST.

OVER his keys the musing organist,
   Beginning doubtfully and far away,
First lets his fingers wander as they list,
   And builds a bridge from Dreamland for his lay:
Then, as the touch of his loved instrument   5
   Gives hope and fervor, nearer draws his theme,
First guessed by faint auroral flushes sent
   Along the wavering vista of his dream.

Not only around our infancy
Doth heaven with all its splendors lie ;   10

. 9. In allusion to Wordsworth's
     "Heaven lies about us in our infancy,"
in his ode, *Intimations of Immortality from Recollections of Early
Childhood.*

Daily, with souls that cringe and plot,
We Sinais climb and know it not.

Over our manhood bend the skies ;
   Against our fallen and traitor lives
The great winds utter prophecies :   15
   With our faint hearts the mountain strives ;
Its arms outstretched, the druid wood
   Waits with its benedicite ;
And to our age's drowsy blood
   Still shouts the inspiring sea.   20

Earth gets its price for what Earth gives us ;
   The beggar is taxed for a corner to die in,
The priest hath his fee who comes and shrives us,
   We bargain for the graves we lie in ;
At the Devil's booth are all things sold,   25
Each ounce of dross costs its ounce of gold ;
   For a cap and bells our lives we pay,
Bubbles we buy with a whole soul's tasking :
   'T is heaven alone that is given away,
'T is only God may be had for the asking ;   30
No price is set on the lavish summer ;
June may be had by the poorest comer.

And what is so rare as a day in June ?
   Then, if ever, come perfect days ;
Then Heaven tries the earth if it be in tune,   35
   And over it softly her warm ear lays :

27. In the Middle Ages kings and noblemen had in their
courts jesters to make sport for the company ; as every one
then wore a dress indicating his rank or occupation, so the jester
wore a cap hung with bells. The fool of Shakespeare's plays is
the king's jester at his best.

Whether we look, or whether we listen,
We hear life murmur, or see it glisten ;
Every clod feels a stir of might,
    An instinct within it that reaches and towers,   40
And, groping blindly above it for light,
    Climbs to a soul in grass and flowers ;
The flush of life may well be seen
    Thrilling back over hills and valleys ;
The cowslip startles in meadows green,   45
    The buttercup catches the sun in its chalice,
And there 's never a leaf nor a blade too mean
    To be some happy creature's palace ;
The little bird sits at his door in the sun,
    Atilt like a blossom among the leaves,   50
And lets his illumined being o'errun
    With the deluge of summer it receives ;
His mate feels the eggs beneath her wings,
And the heart in her dumb breast flutters and sings ;
He sings to the wide world, and she to her nest, —   55
In the nice ear of Nature which song is the best ?

Now is the high-tide of the year,
    And whatever of life hath ebbed away
Comes flooding back with a ripply cheer,
    Into every bare inlet and creek and bay ;   60
Now the heart is so full that a drop overfills it,
We are happy now because God wills it ;
No matter how barren the past may have been,
'T is enough for us now that the leaves are green ;
We sit in the warm shade and feel right well   65
How the sap creeps up and blossoms swell ;
We may shut our eyes, but we cannot help knowing
That skies are clear and grass is growing ;
The breeze comes whispering in our ear,

That dandelions are blossoming near, 70
 That maize has sprouted, that streams are flowing,
That the river is bluer than the sky,
That the robin is plastering his house hard by;
And if the breeze kept the good news back,
For other couriers we should not lack; 75
 We could guess it all by yon heifer's lowing, —
And hark! how clear bold chanticleer,
Warmed with the new wine of the year,
 Tells all in his lusty crowing!

Joy comes, grief goes, we know not how; 80
Everything is happy now,
 Everything is upward striving;
'T is as easy now for the heart to be true
As for grass to be green or skies to be blue, —
 'T is the natural way of living: 85
Who knows whither the clouds have fled?
 In the unscarred heaven they leave no wake;
And the eyes forget the tears they have shed,
 The heart forgets its sorrow and ache;
The soul partakes of the season's youth, 90
 And the sulphurous rifts of passion and woe
Lie deep 'neath a silence pure and smooth,
 Like burnt-out craters healed with snow.
What wonder if Sir Launfal now
Remembered the keeping of his vow? 95

PART FIRST.

. I.

" My golden spurs now bring to me,
 And bring to me my richest mail,

For to-morrow I go over land and sea
  In search of the Holy Grail;
Shall never a bed for me be spread,   100
Nor shall a pillow be under my head,
Till I begin my vow to keep;
Here on the rushes will I sleep,
And perchance there may come a vision true
Ere day create the world anew."   105
  Slowly Sir Launfal's eyes grew dim,
  Slumber fell like a cloud on him,
And into his soul the vision flew.

II.

The crows flapped over by twos and threes,
In the pool drowsed the cattle up to their knees,   110
  The little birds sang as if it were
  The one day of summer in all the year,
And the very leaves seemed to sing on the trees:
The castle alone in the landscape lay
Like an outpost of winter, dull and gray: 115
'T was the proudest hall in the North Countree,
And never its gates might opened be,
Save to lord or lady of high degree;
Summer besieged it on every side,
But the churlish stone her assaults defied;   120
She could not scale the chilly wall,
Though around it for leagues her pavilions tall
Stretched left and right,
Over the hills and out of sight;
  Green and broad was every tent,   125
  And out of each a murmur went
Till the breeze fell off at night.

III.

The drawbridge dropped with a surly clang,
And through the dark arch a charger sprang,
Bearing Sir Launfal, the maiden knight,   130
In his gilded mail, that flamed so bright
It seemed the dark castle had gathered all
Those shafts the fierce sun had shot over its wall
   In his siege of three hundred summers long,
And, binding them all in one blazing sheaf,   135
   Had cast them forth: so, young and strong,
And lightsome as a locust-leaf,
Sir Launfal flashed forth in his unscarred mail,
To seek in all climes for the Holy Grail.

IV.

It was morning on hill and stream and tree,   140
   And morning in the young knight's heart;
Only the castle moodily
Rebuffed the gifts of the sunshine free,
   And gloomed by itself apart;
The season brimmed all other things up   145
Full as the rain fills the pitcher-plant's cup.

V.

As Sir Launfal made morn through the darksome gate,
   He was 'ware of a leper, crouched by the same,
Who begged with his hand and moaned as he sate;
   And a loathing over Sir Launfal came;   150
The sunshine went out of his soul with a thrill,
   The flesh 'neath his armor 'gan shrink and crawl,
And midway its leap his heart stood still
   Like a frozen waterfall;
For this man, so foul and bent of stature,   155

Rasped harshly against his dainty nature,
And seemed the one blot on the summer morn, —
So he tossed him a piece of gold in scorn.

VI.

The leper raised not the gold from the dust:
" Better to me the poor man's crust,   160
Better the blessing of the poor,
Though I turn me empty from his door;
That is no true alms which the hand can hold;
He gives nothing but worthless gold
    Who gives from a sense of duty;   165
But he who gives but a slender mite,
And gives to that which is out of sight,
    That thread of the all-sustaining Beauty
Which runs through all and doth all unite, —
The hand cannot clasp the whole of his alms,   170
The heart outstretches its eager palms,
For a god goes with it and makes it store
To the soul that was starving in darkness before."

PRELUDE TO PART SECOND.

Down swept the chill wind from the mountain peak,
    From the snow five thousand summers old;   175
On open wold and hill-top bleak
    It had gathered all the cold,
And whirled it like sleet on the wanderer's cheek:
It carried a shiver everywhere

174. Note the different moods that are indicated by the two
preludes. The one is of June, the other of snow and winter.
By these preludes the poet, like an organist, strikes a key which
he holds in the subsequent parts.

From the unleafed boughs and pastures bare;   180
The little brook heard it and built a roof
'Neath which he could house him, winter-proof;
All night by the white stars' frosty gleams
He groined his arches and matched his beams;
Slender and clear were his crystal spars   185
As the lashes of light that trim the stars;
He sculptured every summer delight
In his halls and chambers out of sight;
Sometimes his tinkling waters slipt
Down through a frost-leaved forest-crypt,   190
Long, sparkling aisles of steel-stemmed trees
Bending to counterfeit a breeze;
Sometimes the roof no fretwork knew
But silvery mosses that downward grew;
Sometimes it was carved in sharp relief   195
With quaint arabesques of ice-fern leaf;
Sometimes it was simply smooth and clear
For the gladness of heaven to shine through, and
        here
He had caught the nodding bulrush-tops
And hung them thickly with diamond-drops,   200
That crystalled the beams of moon and sun,
And made a star of every one:
No mortal builder's most rare device
Could match this winter-palace of ice;
'T was as if every image that mirrored lay   205
In his depths serene through the summer day,
Each fleeting shadow of earth and sky,
    Lest the happy model should be lost,

203. The Empress of Russia, Catherine II., in a magnificent
freak, built a palace of ice, which was a nine-days' wonder.
Cowper has given a poetical description of it in *The Task*, Book
V. lines 131-176.

Had been mimicked in fairy masonry
   By the elfin builders of the frost.   210

Within the hall are song and laughter,
   The cheeks of Christmas grow red and jolly,
And sprouting is every corbel and rafter
   With lightsome green of ivy and holly;
Through the deep gulf of the chimney wide   215
Wallows the Yule-log's roaring tide;
The broad flame-pennons droop and flap
   And belly and tug as a flag in the wind;
Like a locust shrills the imprisoned sap,
   Hunted to death in its galleries blind;   220
And swift little troops of silent sparks,
   Now pausing, now scattering away as in fear,
Go threading the soot-forest's tangled darks
   Like herds of startled deer.
But the wind without was eager and sharp,   225
Of Sir Launfal's gray hair it makes a harp,
    And rattles and wrings
    The icy strings,
Singing, in dreary monotone,
A Christmas carol of its own,   230
   Whose burden still, as he might guess,
Was — "Shelterless, shelterless, shelterless!"
The voice of the seneschal flared like a torch
As he shouted the wanderer away from the porch,

---

216. The Yule-log was anciently a huge log burned at the feast of Juul (pronounced Yule) by our Scandinavian ancestors in honor of the god Thor. Juul-tid (Yule-time) corresponded in time to Christmas tide, and when Christian festivities took the place of pagan, many ceremonies remained. The great log, still called the Yule-log, was dragged in and burned in the fireplace after Thor had been forgotten.

And he sat in the gateway and saw all night
  The great hall-fire, so cheery and bold,
  Through the window-slits of the castle old,
Build out its piers of ruddy light,
  Against the drift of the cold.

PART SECOND.

I.

THERE was never a leaf on bush or tree,
The bare boughs rattled shudderingly;
The river was dumb and could not speak,
  For the weaver Winter its shroud had spun.
A single crow on the tree-top bleak
  From his shining feathers shed off the cold sun;
Again it was morning, but shrunk and cold,
As if her veins were sapless and old,
And she rose up decrepitly
For a last dim look at earth and sea.

II.

Sir Launfal turned from his own hard gate,
For another heir in his earldom sate;
An old, bent man, worn out and frail,
He came back from seeking the Holy Grail;
Little he recked of his earldom's loss,
No more on his surcoat was blazoned the cross,
But deep in his soul the sign he wore,
The badge of the suffering and the poor.

III.

Sir Launfal's raiment thin and spare
Was idle mail 'gainst the barbéd air,

For it was just at the Christmas time;   260
So he mused, as he sat, of a sunnier clime,
And sought for a shelter from cold and snow
In the light and warmth of long-ago ;
He sees the snake-like caravan crawl
O'er the edge of the desert, black and small,   265
Then nearer and nearer, till, one by one,
He can count the camels in the sun,
As over the red-hot sands they pass
To where, in its slender necklace of grass,
The little spring laughed and leapt in the shade,   270
And with its own self like an infant played,
And waved its signal of palms.

IV.

" For Christ's sweet sake, I beg an alms ; " —
The happy camels may reach the spring,
But Sir Launfal sees only the grewsome thing,   275
The leper, lank as the rain-blanched bone,
That cowers beside him, a thing as lone
And white as the ice-isles of Northern seas
In the desolate horror of his disease.

V.

And Sir Launfal said, — " I behold in thee   280
An image of Him who died on the tree;
Thou also hast had thy crown of thorns, —
Thou also hast had the world's buffets and scorns, —
And to thy life were not denied
The wounds in the hands and feet and side :   285
Mild Mary's Son, acknowledge me ;
Behold, through him, I give to Thee ! "

VI.

Then the soul of the leper stood up in his eyes
    And looked at Sir Launfal, and straightway he
Remembered in what a haughtier guise   290
    He had flung an alms to leprosie,
When he girt his young life up in gilded mail
And set forth in search of the Holy Grail.
The heart within him was ashes and dust;
He parted in twain his single crust,   295
He broke the ice on the streamlet's brink,
And gave the leper to eat and drink:
'T was a mouldy crust of coarse brown bread,
    'T was water out of a wooden bowl, —
Yet with fine wheaten bread was the leper fed,   300
    And 't was red wine he drank with his thirsty soul.

VII.

As Sir Launfal mused with a downcast face,
A light shone round about the place;
The leper no longer crouched at his side,
But stood before him glorified,   305
Shining and tall and fair and straight
As the pillar that stood by the Beautiful Gate, —
Himself the Gate whereby men can
Enter the temple of God in Man.

VIII.

His words were shed softer than leaves from the
      pine,   310
And they fell on Sir Launfal as snows on the brine,
That mingle their softness and quiet in one
With the shaggy unrest they float down upon;
And the voice that was calmer than silence said,

" Lo, it is I, be not afraid ! ₃₁₅
In many climes, without avail,
Thou hast spent thy life for the Holy Grail;
Behold, it is here, — this cup which thou
Didst fill at the streamlet for Me but now ;
This crust is My body broken for thee, ₃₂₀
This water His blood that died on the tree ;
The Holy Supper is kept, indeed,
In whatso we share with another's need :
Not what we give, but what we share, —
For the gift without the giver is bare ; ₃₂₅
Who gives himself with his alms feeds three, —
Himself, his hungering neighbor, and Me."

IX.

Sir Launfal awoke as from a swound : —
" The Grail in my castle here is found !
Hang my idle armor up on the wall, ₃₃₀
Let it be the spider's banquet-hall ;
He must be fenced with stronger mail
Who would seek and find the Holy Grail."

X.

The castle gate stands open now,
    And the wanderer is welcome to the hall ₃₃₅
As the hangbird is to the elm-tree bough :
    No longer scowl the turrets tall,
The Summer's long siege at last is o'er ;
When the first poor outcast went in at the door,
She entered with him in disguise, ₃₄₀
And mastered the fortress by surprise ;
There is no spot she loves so well on ground,
She lingers and smiles there the whole year round ;

The meanest serf on Sir Launfal's land
Has hall and bower at his command ;
And there's no poor man in the North Countree
But is lord of the earldom as much as he.

RALPH WALDO EMERSON.

BIOGRAPHICAL SKETCH.

RALPH WALDO EMERSON was born in Boston, May 25, 1803. His father, his grandfather, and his great-grand-father were all ministers, and, indeed, on both his father's and mother's side he belongs to a continuous line of minis-terial descent from the seventeenth century. At the time of his birth, his father, the Rev. William Emerson, was minis-ter of the First Church congregation, but on his death a few years afterward, Ralph Waldo Emerson, a boy of seven, went to live in the old manse at Concord, where his grand-father had lived when the Concord fight occurred. The old manse was afterward the home at one time of Hawthorne, who wrote there the stories which he gathered into the vol-ume, *Mosses from an Old Manse.*

Emerson was graduated at Harvard in 1821, and after teaching a year or two gave himself to the study of divinity. From 1827 to 1832 he preached in Unitarian churches, and was for four years a colleague pastor in the Second Church in Boston. He then left the ministry and afterward devoted himself to literature. He travelled abroad in 1833, in 1847, and again in 1872, making friends among the leading think-ers during his first journey, and confirming the friendships when again in Europe; with the exception of these three journeys and occasional lecturing tours in the United States, he lived quietly at Concord until his death, April 27, 1882.

He had delivered several special addresses, and in his early manhood was an important lecturer in the Lyceum courses which were so popular, especially in New England, forty years ago, but his first published book was *Nature*, in 1839. Subsequent prose writings were his *Essays*, under that title, and in several volumes with specific titles, *Representative Men*, and *English Traits*. In form the prose is either the oration or the essay, with one exception. *English Traits* records the observations of the writer after his first two journeys to England ; and while it may loosely be classed among essays, it has certain distinctive features which separate it from the essays of the same writer; there is in it narrative, reminiscence, and description, which make it more properly the note-book of a philosophic traveller.

It may be said of his essays as well as of his deliberate orations that the writer never was wholly unmindful of an audience; he was conscious always that he was not merely delivering his mind, but speaking directly to men. One is aware of a certain pointedness of speech which turns the writer into a speaker, and the printed words into a sounding voice.

He wrote poems when in college, but his first publication of verse was through *The Dial*, a magazine established in 1840, and the representative of a knot of men and women of whom Emerson was the acknowledged or unacknowledged leader. The first volume of his poems was published in 1847, and included those by which he is best known, as *The Problem, The Sphinx, The Rhodora, The Humble Bee, Hymn Sung at the Completion of the Concord Monument*. After the establishment of the *Atlantic Monthly* in 1857, he contributed to it both prose and poetry, and verses published in the early numbers, mere enigmas to some, profound revelations to others, were fruitful of discussion and thought; his second volume of poems, *May Day and other Pieces*, was not issued until 1867. Since then a volume of his collected poetry has appeared, containing most of those published in the two volumes, and a few in addition. We are told, however, that the published writings of

Emerson bear but small proportion to the unpublished. Many lectures have been delivered, but not printed ; many poems written, and a few read, which have never been published. The inference from this, borne out by the marks upon what has been published, is that Mr. Emerson set a high value upon literature, and was jealous of the prerogative of the poet. He is frequently called a seer, and this old word, indicating etymologically its original intention, is applied well to a poet who saw into nature and human life with a spiritual power which made him a marked man in his own time, and one destined to an unrivalled place in literature. He fulfilled Wordsworth's lines : —

> " With an eye made quiet by the power
> Of harmony, and the deep power of joy,
> We see into the life of things."

BEHAVIOR.

GRACE, Beauty, and Caprice
Build this golden portal ;
Graceful women, chosen men,
Dazzle every mortal :
Their sweet and lofty countenance
His enchanting food ;
He need not go to them, their forms
Beset his solitude.
He looketh seldom in their face,
His eyes explore the ground,
The green grass is a looking-glass
Whereon their traits are found.
Little he says to them,
So dances his heart in his breast,
Their tranquil mien bereaveth him
Of wit, of words, of rest.
Too weak to win, too fond to shun
The tyrants of his doom,
The much-deceived Endymion
Slips behind a tomb.

THE soul which animates Nature is not less signifi-
cantly published in the figure, movement, and gesture
of animated bodies, than in its last vehicle of articulate
speech. This silent and subtile language is Manners ;
not *what*, but *how*. Life expresses. A statue has no
tongue, and needs none. Good tableaux do not need
declamation. Nature tells every secret once. Yes,
but in man she tells it all the time, by form, attitude,
gesture, mien, face, and parts of the face, and by the
whole action of the machine. The visible carriage or
action of the individual, as resulting from his organi-
zation and his will combined, we call manners. What
are they but thought entering the hands and feet, con-
trolling the movements of the body, the speech and
behavior ?

R. Waldo Emerson

There is always a best way of doing everything, if it be to boil an egg. Manners are the happy ways of doing things; each, once a stroke of genius or of love, — now repeated and hardened into usage. They form at last a rich varnish, with which the routine of life is washed, and its details adorned. If they are superficial, so are the dewdrops which give such a depth to the morning meadows. Manners are very communicable; men catch them from each other. Consuelo, in the romance,[1] boasts of the lessons she had given the nobles in manners, on the stage; and, in real life, Talma[2] taught Napoleon the arts of behavior. Genius invents fine manners, which the baron and the baroness copy very fast, and, by the advantage of a palace, better the instruction. They stereotype the lesson they have learned into a mode.

The power of manners is incessant, — an element as unconcealable as fire. The nobility cannot in any country be disguised, and no more in a republic or a democracy than in a kingdom. No man can resist their influence. There are certain manners which are learned in good society, of that force, that, if a person have them, he or she must be considered, and is everywhere welcome, though without beauty, or wealth, or genius. Give a boy address and accomplishments, and you give him the mastery of palaces and fortunes where he goes. He has not the trouble of earning or owning them; they solicit him to enter and possess. We send girls of a timid, retreating disposition to the boarding-school, to the riding-school, to the ball-room, or wheresoever they can come into acquaintance and nearness of leading persons of their own sex; where

---

[1] Of the same name, by George Sand.
[2] A celebrated actor.

they might learn address, and see it near at hand. The power of a woman of fashion to lead, and also to daunt and repel, derives from their belief that she knows resources and behaviors not known to them; but when these have mastered her secret, they learn to confront her, and recover their self-possession.

Every day bears witness to their gentle rule. People who would obtrude, now do not obtrude. The mediocre circle learns to demand that which belongs to a high state of nature or of culture. Your manners are always under examination, and by committees little suspected, — a police in citizens' clothes, — but are awarding or denying you very high prizes when you least think of it.

We talk much of utilities, but 't is our manners that associate us. In hours of business, we go to him who knows, or has, or does this or that which we want, and we do not let our taste or feeling stand in the way. But this activity over, we return to the indolent state, and wish for those we can be at ease with; those who will go where we go, whose manners do not offend us, whose social tone chimes with ours. When we reflect on their persuasive and cheering force; how they recommend, prepare, and draw people together; how, in all clubs, manners make the members; how manners make the fortune of the ambitious youth; that, for the most part, his manners marry him, and, for the most part, he marries manners; when we think what keys they are, and to what secrets; what high lessons and inspiring tokens of character they convey; and what divination is required in us, for the reading of this fine telegraph, we see what range the subject has, and what relations to convenience, power, and beauty.

Their first service is very low, — when they are the

minor morals: but 't is the beginning of civility, — to make us, I mean, endurable to each other. We prize them for their rough-plastic, abstergent force; to get people out of the quadruped state; to get them washed, clothed, and set up on end; to slough their animal husks and habits; compel them to be clean; overawe their spite and meanness, teach them to stifle the base, and choose the generous expression, and make them know how much happier the generous behaviors are.

Bad behavior the laws cannot reach. Society is infested with rude, cynical, restless, and frivolous persons who prey upon the rest, and whom a public opinion concentrated into good manners — forms accepted by the sense of all — can reach: the contradictors and railers at public and private tables, who are like terriers, who conceive it the duty of a dog of honor to growl at any passer-by, and do the honors of the house by barking him out of sight; — I have seen men who neigh like a horse when you contradict them, or say something which they do not understand: — then the overbold, who make their own invitation to your hearth; the persevering talker, who gives you his society in large, saturating doses; the pitiers of themselves, — a perilous class; the frivolous Asmodeus, who relies on you to find him in ropes of sand to twist; the monotones; in short, every stripe of absurdity; — these are social inflictions which the magistrate cannot cure or defend you from, and which must be intrusted to the restraining force of custom, and proverbs, and familiar rules of behavior impressed on young people in their school-days.

In the hotels on the banks of the Mississippi, they print, or used to print, among the rules of the house, that " no gentleman can be permitted to come to the

public table without his coat; " and in the same coun-
try, in the pews of the churches, little placards plead
with the worshipper against the fury of expectoration.
Charles Dickens self-sacrificingly undertook the refor-
mation of our American manners in unspeakable par-
ticulars. I think the lesson was not quite lost; that
it held bad manners up, so that the churls could see
the deformity. Unhappily, the book had its own de-
formities. It ought not to need to print in a reading-
room a caution to strangers not to speak loud; nor to
persons who look over fine engravings, that they
should be handled like cobwebs and butterflies' wings;
nor to persons who look at marble statues, that they
shall not smite them with canes. But, even in the
perfect civilization of this city, such cautions are not
quite needless in the Athenæum and City Library.

Manners are factitious, and grow out of circum-
stance as well as out of character. If you look at the
pictures of patricians and of peasants, of different
periods and countries, you will see how well they
match the same classes in our towns. The modern
aristocrat not only is well drawn in Titian's Venetian
doges, and in Roman coins and statues, but also in the
pictures which Commodore Perry brought home of
dignitaries in Japan. Broad lands and great interests
not only arrive to such heads as can manage them, but
form manners of power. A keen eye, too, will see
nice gradations of rank, or see in the manners the
degree of homage the party is wont to receive. A
prince who is accustomed every day to be courted and
deferred to by the highest grandees, acquires a corre-
sponding expectation, and a becoming mode of receiv-
ing and replying to this homage.

There are always exceptional people and modes.

English grandees affect to be farmers. Claverhouse is a fop, and, under the finish of dress, and levity of behavior, hides the terror of his war. But Nature and Destiny are honest, and never fail to leave their mark, to hang out a sign for each and for every quality. It is much to conquer one's face, and perhaps the ambitious youth thinks he has got the whole secret when he has learned that disengaged manners are commanding. Don't be deceived by a facile exterior. Tender men sometimes have strong wills. We had, in Massachusetts, an old statesman, who had sat all his life in courts and in chairs of state, without overcoming an extreme irritability of face, voice, and bearing; when he spoke, his voice would not serve him; it cracked, it broke, it wheezed, it piped : little cared he; he knew that it had got to pipe, or wheeze, or screech his argument and his indignation. When he sat down, after speaking, he seemed in a sort of fit, and held on to his chair with both hands; but underneath all this irritability was a puissant will, firm and advancing, and a memory in which lay in order and method like geologic strata every fact of his history, and under the control of his will.

Manners are partly factitious, but, mainly, there must be capacity for culture in the blood. Else all culture is vain. The obstinate prejudice in favor of blood, which lies at the base of the feudal and monarchical fabrics of the Old World, has some reason in common experience. Every man — mathematician, artist, soldier, or merchant — looks with confidence for some traits and talents in his own child, which he would not dare to presume in the child of a stranger. The Orientalists are very orthodox on this point. "Take a thorn-bush," said the emir Abdel-Kader, "and sprinkle it for a whole year with water; it will yield nothing but thorns. Take a date-tree, leave it without culture, and it will always produce dates. Nobility is the date-tree, and the Arab populace is a bush of thorns."

A main fact in the history of manners is the wonderful expressiveness of the human body. If it were made of glass, or of air, and the thoughts were written on steel tablets within, it could not publish more truly its meaning than now. Wise men read very sharply all your private history in your look and gait and behavior. The whole economy of nature is bent on expression. The tell-tale body is all tongues. Men are like Geneva watches with crystal faces which expose the whole movement. They carry the liquor of life flowing up and down in these beautiful bottles, and announcing to the curious how it is with them. The face and eyes reveal what the spirit is doing, how old it is, what aims it has. The eyes indicate the antiquity of the soul, or through how many forms it has already ascended. It almost violates the proprieties, if we say above the breath here, what the confessing eyes do not hesitate to utter to every street passenger.

Man cannot fix his eye on the sun, and so far seems imperfect. In Siberia, a late traveller found men who could see the satellites of Jupiter with their unarmed eye. In some respects the animals excel us. The birds have a longer sight, beside the advantage by their wings of a higher observatory. A cow can bid her calf, by secret signal, probably of the eye, to run away, or to lie down and hide itself. The jockeys say of certain horses, that "they look over the whole ground." The out-door life, and hunting, and labor, give equal vigor to the human eye. A farmer looks

out at you as strong as the horse ; his eye-beam is like
the stroke of a staff. An eye can threaten like a
loaded and levelled gun, or can insult like hissing or
kicking ; or, in its altered mood, by beams of kind-
ness, it can make the heart dance with joy.

The eye obeys exactly the action of the mind.
When a thought strikes us, the eyes fix, and remain
gazing at a distance ; in enumerating the names of
persons or of countries, as France, Germany, Spain,
Turkey, the eyes wink at each new name. There
is no nicety of learning sought by the mind which
the eyes do not vie in acquiring. "An artist," said
Michel Angelo, "must have his measuring tools not
in the hand, but in the eye ;" and there is no end to
the catalogue of its performances, whether in indolent
vision (that of health and beauty), or in strained vi-
sion (that of art and labor).

Eyes are bold as lions, — roving, running, leaping,
here and there, far and near. They speak all lan-
guages. They wait for no introduction ; they are no
Englishmen ; ask no leave of age or rank ; they re-
spect neither poverty nor riches, neither learning nor
power, nor virtue, nor sex, but intrude, and come
again, and go through and through you, in a moment
of time. What inundation of life and thought is dis-
charged from one soul into another, through them !
The glance is natural magic. The mysterious com-
munication established across a house between two
entire strangers, moves all the springs of wonder.
The communication by the glance is in the greatest
part not subject to the control of the will. It is the
bodily symbol of identity of nature. We look into
the eyes to know if this other form is another self,
and the eyes will not lie, but make a faithful confes-

sion what inhabitant is there. The revelations are sometimes terrific. The confession of a low, usurping devil is there made, and the observer shall seem to feel the stirring of owls, and bats, and horned hoofs, where he looked for innocence and simplicity. 'T is remarkable, too, that the spirit that appears at the windows of the house does at once invest himself in a new form of his own, to the mind of the beholder.

The eyes of men converse as much as their tongues, with the advantage, that the ocular dialect needs no dictionary, but is understood all the world over. When the eyes say one thing, and the tongue another, a practised man relies on the language of the first. If the man is off his centre, the eyes show it. You can read in the eyes of your companion, whether your argument hits him, though his tongue will not confess it. There is a look by which a man shows he is going to say a good thing, and a look when he has said it. Vain and forgotten are all the fine offers and offices of hospitality, if there is no holiday in the eye. How many furtive inclinations avowed by the eye, though dissembled by the lips! One comes away from a company, in which, it may easily happen, he has said nothing, and no important remark has been addressed to him, and yet, if in sympathy with the society, he shall not have a sense of this fact, such a stream of life has been flowing into him, and out from him, through the eyes. There are eyes, to be sure, that give no more admission into the man than blueberries. Others are liquid and deep, — wells that a man might fall into ; — others are aggressive and devouring, seem to call out the police, take all too much notice, and require crowded Broadways, and the security of millions, to protect individuals against them.

The military eye I meet, now darkly sparkling under clerical, now under rustic, brows. 'T is the city of Lacedæmon; 't is a stack of bayonets. There are asking eyes, asserting eyes, prowling eyes; and eyes full of fate, — some of good, and some of sinister, omen. The alleged power to charm down insanity, or ferocity in beasts, is a power behind the eye. It must be a victory achieved in the will, before it can be signified in the eye. 'T is very certain that each man carries in his eye the exact indication of his rank in the immense scale of men, and we are always learning to read it. A complete man should need no auxiliaries to his personal presence. Whoever looked on him would consent to his will, being certified that his aims were generous and universal. The reason why men do not obey us, is because they see the mud at the bottom of our eye.

If the organ of sight is such a vehicle of power, the other features have their own. A man finds room in the few square inches of the face for the traits of all his ancestors; for the expression of all his history, and his wants. The sculptor, and Winckelmann, and Lavater, will tell you how significant a feature is the nose; how its form expresses strength or weakness of will and good or bad temper. The nose of Julius Cæsar, of Dante, and of Pitt suggest " the terrors of the beak." What refinement, and what limitations, the teeth betray! " Beware you don't laugh," said the wise mother, " for then you show all your faults."

Balzac left in manuscript a chapter, which he called " *Théorie de la démarche,*" in which he says: " The look, the voice, the respiration, and the attitude or walk are identical. But, as it has not been given to

man, the power to stand guard, at once, over these
four different simultaneous expressions of his thought,
watch that one which speaks out the truth, and you
will know the whole man."

Palaces interest us mainly in the exhibition of man-
ners, which in the idle and expensive society dwelling
in them are raised to a high art. The maxim of
courts is that manner is power. A calm and resolute
bearing, a polished speech, and embellishment of tri-
fles, and the art of hiding all uncomfortable feeling,
are essential to the courtier, and Saint Simon, and
Cardinal de Retz, and Roederer, and an encyclopædia
of *Mémoires* will instruct you, if you wish, in those
potent secrets. Thus, it is a point of pride with kings
to remember faces and names. It is reported of one
prince, that his head had the air of leaning down-
wards, in order not to humble the crowd. There are
people who come in ever like a child with a piece of
good news. It was said of the late Lord Holland,
that he always came down to breakfast with the air
of a man who had just met with some signal good for-
tune. In *Notre Dame* the grandee took his place
on the dais, with the look of one who is thinking of
something else. But we must not peep and eavesdrop
at palace-doors.

Fine manners need the support of fine manners in
others. A scholar may be a well-bred man, or he may
not. The enthusiast is introduced to polished scholars
in society, and is chilled and silenced by finding him-
self not in their element. They all have somewhat
which he has not, and, it seems, ought to have. But
if he finds the scholar apart from his companions, it
is then the enthusiast's turn, and the scholar has no
defence, but must deal on his terms. Now they must

fight the battle out on their private strength. What
is the talent of that character so common, — the suc-
cessful man of the world, — in all marts, senates, and
drawing-rooms? Manners: manners of power; sense
to see his advantage, and manners up to it. See him
approach his man. He knows that troops behave as
they are handled at first; — that is his cheap secret;
just what happens to every two persons who meet on
any affair, one instantly perceives that he has the key
of the situation, that his will comprehends the other's
will, as the cat does the mouse, and he has only to use
courtesy, and furnish good-natured reasons to his vic-
tim to cover up the chain, lest he be shamed into re-
sistance.

The theatre in which this science of manners has a
formal importance is not with us a court, but dress-
circles, wherein, after the close of the day's business,
men and women meet at leisure, for mutual entertain-
ment, in ornamented drawing-rooms. Of course, it
has every variety of attraction and merit; but, to
earnest persons, to youths or maidens who have great
objects at heart, we cannot extol it highly. A well-
dressed, talkative company, where each is bent to
amuse the other, — yet the high-born Turk who came
hither fancied that every woman seemed to be suffer-
ing for a chair; that all talkers were brained and ex-
hausted by the de-oxygenated air; it spoiled the best
persons: it put all on stilts. Yet here are the secret
biographies written and read. The aspect of that
man is repulsive; I do not wish to deal with him.
The other is irritable, shy, and on his guard. The
youth looks humble and manly: I choose him. Look
on this woman. There is not beauty, nor brilliant say-
ings, nor distinguished power to serve you; but all see

her gladly; her whole air and impression are healthful. Here come the sentimentalists, and the invalids. Here is Elise, who caught cold in coming into the world, and has always increased it since. Here are creep-mouse manners; and thievish manners. "Look at Northcote," said Fuseli; "he looks like a rat that has seen a cat." In the shallow company, easily excited, easily tired, here is the columnar Bernard: the Alleghanies do not express more repose than his behavior. Here are the sweet, following eyes of Cecile: it seemed always that she demanded the heart. Nothing can be more excellent in kind than the Corinthian grace of Gertrude's manners, and yet Blanche, who has no manners, has better manners than she; for the movements of Blanche are the sallies of a spirit which is sufficient for the moment, and she can afford to express every thought by instant action.

Manners have been somewhat cynically defined to be a contrivance of wise men to keep fools at a distance. Fashion is shrewd to detect those who do not belong to her train, and seldom wastes her attentions. Society is very swift in its instincts, and, if you do not belong to it, resists and sneers at you; or quietly drops you. The first weapon enrages the party attacked; the second is still more effective, but is not to be resisted, as the date of the transaction is not easily found. People grow up and grow old under this infliction, and never suspect the truth, ascribing the solitude which acts on them very injuriously to any cause but the right one.

The basis of good manners is self-reliance. Necessity is the law of all who are not self-possessed. Those who are not self-possessed obtrude and pain us. Some men appear to feel that they belong to a Pariah caste.

They fear to offend, they bend and apologize, and walk through life with a timid step.

As we sometimes dream that we are in a well-dressed company without any coat, so Godfrey acts ever as if he suffered from some mortifying circumstance. The hero should find himself at home, wherever he is; should impart comfort by his own security and good-nature to all beholders. The hero is suffered to be himself. A person of strong mind comes to perceive that for him an immunity is secured so long as he renders to society that service which is native and proper to him, — an immunity from all the observances, yea, and duties, which society so tyrannically imposes on the rank and file of its members. "Euripides," says Aspasia, "has not the fine manners of Sophocles: "but," she adds, good-humoredly, "the movers and masters of our souls have surely a right to throw out their limbs as carelessly as they please on the world that belongs to them, and before the creatures they have animated." [1]

Manners require time, as nothing is more vulgar than haste. Friendship should be surrounded with ceremonies and respects, and not crushed into corners. Friendship requires more time than poor busy men can usually command. Here comes to me Roland, with a delicacy of sentiment leading and inwrapping him like a divine cloud or holy ghost. 'T is a great destitution to both that this should not be entertained with large leisures, but contrariwise should be balked by importunate affairs.

But through this lustrous varnish, the reality is ever shining. 'T is hard to keep the *what* from breaking through this pretty painting of the *how.* The core

[1] Landor, *Pericles and Aspasia.*

will come to the surface. Strong will and keen perception overpower old manners, and create new; and the thought of the present moment has a greater value than all the past. In persons of character we do not remark manners, because of their instantaneousness. We are surprised by the thing done, out of all power to watch the way of it. Yet nothing is more charming than to recognize the great style which runs through the action of such. People masquerade before us in their fortunes, titles, offices, and connections, as academic or civil presidents, or senators, or professors, or great lawyers, and impose on the frivolous, and a good deal on each other, by these fames. At least, it is a point of prudent good manners to treat these reputations tenderly, as if they were merited. But the sad realist knows these fellows at a glance, and they know him; as when in Paris the chief of the police enters a ball-room, so many diamonded pretenders shrink and make themselves as inconspicuous as they can, or give him a supplicating look as they pass. "I had received," said a sibyl, — "I had received at birth the fatal gift of penetration;" and these Cassandras are always born.

Manners impress as they indicate real power. A man who is sure of his point carries a broad and contented expression, which everybody reads. And you cannot rightly train one to an air and manner except by making him the kind of man of whom that manner is the natural expression. Nature forever puts a premium on reality. What is done for effect is seen to be done for effect; what is done for love is felt to be done for love. A man inspires affection and honor, because he was not lying in wait for these. The things of a man for which we visit him, were done in the dark and the cold. A little integrity is better than any career. So deep are the sources of this surface-action, that even the size of your companion seems to vary with his freedom of thought. Not only is he larger, when at ease, and his thoughts generous, but everything around him becomes variable with expression. No carpenter's rule, no rod and chain, will measure the dimensions of any house or house-lot: go into the house: if the proprietor is constrained and deferring, 't is of no importance how large his house, how beautiful his grounds, — you quickly come to the end of all; but if the man is self-possessed, happy, and at home, his house is deep-founded, indefinitely large and interesting, the roof and dome buoyant as the sky. Under the humblest roof, the commonest person in plain clothes sits there massive, cheerful, yet formidable like the Egyptian colossi.

Neither Aristotle, nor Leibnitz, nor Junius, nor Champollion has set down the grammar-rules of this dialect, older than Sanscrit; but they who cannot yet read English, can read this. Men take each other's measure, when they meet for the first time, — and every time they meet. How do they get this rapid knowledge, even before they speak, of each other's power and dispositions? One would say that the persuasion of their speech is not in what they say, — or, that men do not convince by their argument, — but by their personality, by who they are, and what they said and did heretofore. A man already strong is listened to, and everything he says is applauded. Another opposes him with sound argument, but the argument is scouted, until by and by it gets into the mind of some weighty person; then it begins to tell on the community.

Self-reliance is the basis of behavior, as it is the guaranty that the powers are not squandered in too much demonstration. In this country, where school education is universal, we have a superficial culture, and a profusion of reading and writing and expression. We parade our nobilities in poems and orations, instead of working them up into happiness. There is a whisper out of the ages to him who can understand it, — "Whatever is known to thyself alone has always very great value." There is some reason to believe that, when a man does not write his poetry, it escapes by other vents through him, instead of the one vent of writing; clings to his form and manners, whilst poets have often nothing poetical about them except their verses. Jacobi said, that "when a man has fully expressed his thought, he has somewhat less possession of it." One would say, the rule is, — What a man is irresistibly urged to say, helps him and us. In explaining his thought to others, he explains it to himself: but when he opens it for show, it corrupts him.

Society is the stage on which manners are shown; novels are their literature. Novels are the journal or record of manners; and the new importance of these books derives from the fact that the novelist begins to penetrate the surface, and treat this part of life more worthily. The novels used to be all alike, and had a quite vulgar tone. The novels used to lead us on to a foolish interest in the fortunes of the boy and girl they described. The boy was to be raised from a humble to a high position. He was in want of a wife and a castle, and the object of the story was to supply him with one or both. We watched sympathetically, step by step, his climbing, until, at last, the point is gained, the wedding day is fixed, and we follow the gala procession home to the bannered portal, when the doors are slammed in our face, and the poor reader is left outside in the cold, not enriched by so much as an idea, or a virtuous impulse.

But the victories of character are instant, and victories for all. Its greatness enlarges all. We are fortified by every heroic anecdote. The novels are as useful as Bibles, if they teach you the secret, that the best of life is conversation, and the greatest success is confidence, or perfect understanding between sincere people. 'T is a French definition of friendship, *rien que s'entendre*, good understanding. The highest compact we can make with our fellow is, — "Let there be truth between us two for evermore." That is the charm in all good novels, as it is the charm in all good histories, that the heroes mutually understand, from the first, and deal loyally and with a profound trust in each other. It is sublime to feel and say of another, I need never meet, or speak, or write to him: we need not reinforce ourselves, or send tokens of remembrance: I rely on him as on myself: if he did thus, or thus, I know it was right.

In all the superior people I have met, I notice directness, truth spoken more truly, as if everything of obstruction, of malformation, had been trained away. What have they to conceal? What have they to exhibit? Between simple and noble persons there is always a quick intelligence: they recognize at sight, and meet on a better ground than the talents and skills they may chance to possess, namely, on sincerity and uprightness. For, it is not what talents or genius a man has, but how he is to his talents, that constitutes friendship and character. The man that stands

by himself, the universe stands by him also.   It is re-
lated of the monk Basle, that, being excommunicated
by the Pope, he was, at his death, sent in charge of an
angel to find a fit place of suffering in hell; but, such
was the eloquence and good-humor of the monk, that
wherever he went he was received gladly, and civilly
treated, even by the most uncivil angels: and, when
he came to discourse with them, instead of contradict-
ing or forcing him, they took his part, and adopted
his manners; and even good angels came from far, to
see him, and take up their abode with him.   The an-
gel that was sent to find a place of torment for him
attempted to remove him to a worse pit, but with no
better success; for such was the contented spirit of the
monk, that he found something to praise in every
place and company, though in hell, and made a kind
of heaven of it.   At last the escorting angel returned
with his prisoner to them that sent him, saying that
no phlegethon could be found that would burn him;
for that in whatever condition, Basle remained incor-
rigibly Basle.   The legend says, his sentence was re-
mitted, and he was allowed to go into heaven, and
was canonized as a saint.

There is a stroke of magnanimity in the correspon-
dence of Bonaparte with his brother Joseph, when the
latter was King of Spain, and complained that he
missed in Napoleon's letters the affectionate tone
which had marked their childish correspondence.   " I
am sorry," replies Napoleon, " you think you shall
find your brother again only in the Elysian Fields.
It is natural, that at forty, he should not feel towards
you as he did at twelve.   But his feelings towards you
have greater truth and strength.   His friendship has
the features of his mind."

How much we forgive in those who yield us the rare spectacle of heroic manners! We will pardon them the want of books, of arts, and even of the gentler virtues. How tenaciously we remember them! Here is a lesson which I brought along with me in boyhood from the Latin School, and which ranks with the best of Roman anecdotes. Marcus Scaurus was accused by Quintus Varius Hispanus, that he had excited the allies to take arms against the Republic. But he, full of firmness and gravity, defended himself in this manner: "Quintus Varius Hispanus alleges that Marcus Scaurus, President of the Senate, excited the allies to arms: Marcus Scaurus, President of the Senate, denies it. There is no witness. Which do you believe, Romans?" "*Utri creditis, Quirites?*" When he had said these words, he was absolved by the assembly of the people.

I have seen manners that make a similar impression with personal beauty; that give the like exhilaration, and refine us like that; and, in memorable experiences, they are suddenly better than beauty, and make that superfluous and ugly. But they must be marked by fine perception, the acquaintance with real beauty. They must always show self-control: you shall not be facile, apologetic, or leaky, but king over your word; and every gesture and action shall indicate power at rest. Then they must be inspired by the good heart. There is no beautifier of complexion, or form, or behavior, like the wish to scatter joy and not pain around us. 'T is good to give a stranger a meal, or a night's lodging. 'T is better to be hospitable to his good meaning and thought, and give courage to a companion. We must be as courteous to a man as we are to a picture, which we are willing to give the

advantage of a good light. Special precepts are not
to be thought of: the talent of well-doing contains
them all. Every hour will show a duty as paramount
as that of my whim just now; and yet I will write it,
— that there is one topic peremptorily forbidden to
all well-bred, to all rational mortals, namely, their
distempers. If you have not slept, or if you have
slept, or if you have headache, or sciatica, or leprosy,
or thunder-stroke, I beseech you, by all angels, to hold
your peace, and not pollute the morning, to which all
the housemates bring serene and pleasant thoughts, by
corruption and groans. Come out of the azure.
Love the day. Do not leave the sky out of your land-
scape. The oldest and the most deserving person
should come very modestly into any newly awaked
company, respecting the divine communications, out of
which all must be presumed to have newly come. An
old man, who added an elevating culture to a large
experience of life, said to me: " When you come into
the room, I think I will study how to make humanity
beautiful to you."

As respects the delicate question of culture, I do
not think that any other than negative rules can be
laid down. For positive rules, for suggestion, Nature
alone inspires it. Who dare assume to guide a youth,
a maid, to perfect manners? — the golden mean is so
delicate, difficult, — say frankly, unattainable. What
finest hands would not be clumsy to sketch the genial
precepts of the young girl's demeanor? The chances
seem infinite against success; and yet success is con-
tinually attained. There must not be secondariness,
and 't is a thousand to one that her air and manner
will at once betray that she is not primary, but that
there is some other one or many of her class, to whom

she habitually postpones herself. But Nature lifts her easily, and without knowing it, over these impossibilities, and we are continually surprised with graces and felicities not only unteachable, but undescribable.

BOSTON HYMN.

READ IN MUSIC HALL, JANUARY 1, 1863.

THE word of the Lord by night
To the watching Pilgrims came,
As they sat by the seaside,
And filled their hearts with flame.

God said, I am tired of kings,   5
I suffer them no more ;
Up to my ear the morning brings
The outrage of the poor.

Think ye I made this ball
A field of havoc and war,   10
Where tyrants great and tyrants small
Might harry the weak and poor ?

My angel, — his name is Freedom, —
Choose him to be your king ;
He shall cut pathways east and west   15
And fend you with his wing.

Lo ! I uncover the land
Which I hid of old time in the West,
As the sculptor uncovers the statue
When he has wrought his best ;   20

I show Columbia, of the rocks
Which dip their foot in the seas
And soar to the air-borne flocks
Of clouds and the boreal fleece.

I will divide my goods;
Call in the wretch and slave:
None shall rule but the humble,
And none but Toil shall have.

I will have never a noble,
No lineage counted great;
Fishers and choppers and ploughmen
Shall constitute a state.

Go, cut down trees in the forest
And trim the straightest boughs;
Cut down trees in the forest
And build me a wooden house.

Call the people together,
The young men and the sires,
The digger in the harvest field,
Hireling and him that hires;

And here in a pine state-house
They shall choose men to rule
In every needful faculty,
In church and state and school.

Lo, now! if these poor men
Can govern the land and sea
And make just laws below the sun,
As planets faithful be.

And ye shall succor men ;
'T is nobleness to serve ;   50
Help them who cannot help again :
Beware from right to swerve.

I break your bonds and masterships,
And I unchain the slave :
Free be his heart and hand henceforth   55
As wind and wandering wave.

I cause from every creature
His proper good to flow :
As much as he is and doeth,
So much he shall bestow.   60

But, laying hands on another
To coin his labor and sweat,
He goes in pawn to his victim
For eternal years in debt.

To-day unbind the captive,   65
So only are ye unbound ;
Lift up a people from the dust,
Trump of their rescue, sound !

Pay ransom to the owner
And fill the bag to the brim.   70
Who is the owner? The slave is owner,
And ever was. Pay him.

O North ! give him beauty for rags,
And honor, O South ! for his shame :
Nevada ! coin thy golden crags   75
With Freedom's image and name.

Up! and the dusky race
That sat in darkness long, —
Be swift their feet as antelopes,
And as behemoth strong.

Come, East and West and North,
By races, as snow-flakes,
And carry my purpose forth,
Which neither halts nor shakes.

My will fulfilled shall be,
For, in daylight or in dark,
My thunderbolt has eyes to see
His way home to the mark.

DANIEL WEBSTER.

BIOGRAPHICAL SKETCH.

" In the last year of the Revolutionary War, on the 18th of January, 1782, Daniel Webster was born, in the home which his father had established on the outskirts of civilization.[1] If the character and situation of the place, and the circumstances under which he passed the first years of his life, might seem adverse to the early cultivation of his extraordinary talent, it still cannot be doubted that they possessed influences favorable to elevation and strength of character. The hardships of an infant settlement and border life, the traditions of a long series of Indian wars, and of two mighty national contests, in which an honored parent had borne his part, the anecdotes of Fort William Henry, of Quebec, of Bennington, of West Point, of Wolfe and Stark and Washington, the great Iliad and Odyssey of American Independence, — this was the fireside entertainment. of the long winter evenings of the secluded village home. . . .

" Something that was called a school was kept for two or three months in the winter, frequently by an itinerant, too often a pretender, claiming only to teach a little reading, writing, and ciphering, and wholly incompetent to give any valuable assistance to a clever youth in learning either.

" Such as the village school was, Mr. Webster enjoyed its advantages, if they could be called by that name. It was,

[1] Salisbury (now Franklin), N. H.

314 *DANIEL WEBSTER.*

however, of a migratory character. When it was near his father's residence it was easy to attend; but it was sometimes in a distant part of the town, and sometimes in another town. . . . Poor as these opportunities of education were, they were bestowed on Mr. Webster more liberally than on his brothers. He showed a greater eagerness for learning; and he was thought of too frail a constitution for any robust pursuit. . . . It is probable that the best part of his education was derived from the judicious and experienced father, and the strong-minded, affectionate, and ambitious mother." [1]

His attitude toward books is well shown by the following extract from his *Autobiography:* "I remember that my father brought home from some of the lower towns Pope's *Essay on Man*, published in a sort of pamphlet. I took it, and very soon could repeat it from beginning to end. We had so few books, that to read them once or twice was nothing. We thought they were all to be got by heart."

In 1796 Webster went to Exeter Academy, but poverty at home caused his withdrawal in February, 1797. He then studied in the neighboring town of Boscawen, under the Rev. Samuel Wood, whose entire charge for board and instruction was $1.00 a week. In 1797 he entered Dartmouth College, where he was graduated in 1801, after four years of hard and telling work; his winter vacations were spent in teaching school.

Webster next studied law, but the need of money by himself and his brother Ezekiel compelled him to accept an offer to take charge of an academy at Fryeburg, Maine, at a salary of about a dollar a day; he supported himself by copying deeds, and thus was able to save all his salary as a fund for the further education of himself and his brother.

[1] See *Biographical Memoir*, by Edward Everett. From this Memoir, and from Lodge's *Life of Webster*, in the American Statesmen Series, most of the material of this sketch has been taken.

Danl Webster

He resumed the study of law in September, 1802, and in the spring of 1805 was admitted to the bar at Boston. He opened an office at Boscawen, N. H., but in September, 1807, moved to Portsmouth, where he at once rose to the head of his profession, and for nine successive years had a large though not very lucrative practice.

In 1808 he was married to Miss Grace Fletcher of Hopkinton, N. H.

In November, 1812, he was elected a member of the National House of Representatives, where his great talents were at once recognized ; he was reëlected in 1814. From 1823 until his death in 1852, with the exception of about two years, he was constantly in public life, as congressman, senator, and secretary of state.

In 1816 he moved to Boston, and soon took a commanding position in his profession of the law. He had a choice of the best business of the whole country. He distinguished himself especially in the realm of Constitutional Law, by which the rights of States and individuals under the Constitution were defined. In 1818 he argued the famous Dartmouth College case, and secured a decision declaring unconstitutional, on the ground of impairing the obligation of a contract, an act of the New Hampshire Legislature altering the charter of the college. He was thereafter retained in almost every important case argued before the Supreme Court at Washington.

On December 22, 1820, the two hundredth anniversary of the landing of the Pilgrims, he delivered his famous *Plymouth Oration*, the first of a series of noble, patriotic addresses which showed him to be the greatest orator America ever produced. On June 17, 1825, he delivered an oration at the laying of the corner-stone of the Bunker Hill Monument, and on August 2, 1826, his eulogy on the Ex-Presidents John Adams and Thomas Jefferson, who died within a few hours of each other, on July 4, 1826, the fiftieth anniversary of the Declaration of Independence. In

1830, he made, in the United States Senate, his celebrated *Reply to Hayne*, in which he repelled insinuations against New England, and argued against the right of nullification.

In 1850 he delivered in the Senate Chamber, at Washington, what is known as his *Seventh of March Speech*. Henry Cabot Lodge says, in his *Life of Webster*, that at this time Webster's place was at the head of a new party based on the principles which he had himself formulated against the extension of slavery ; that he did not change his party, and therefore had to change his opinions. In the *Seventh of March Speech*, he spoke in favor of enforcing the Fugitive Slave Law, and against the Wilmot Proviso, by which slavery was to be excluded from all territory thereafter acquired. He depicted at length the grievances of the South, and said but little about those of the North. Mr. George T. Curtis, in his Biography, says that a great majority of Webster's constituents, if not of the whole North, disapproved of this speech. The judgment of many was summed up in Whittier's great poem, *Ichabod*. In connection with this should be read the same poet's verses, *The Lost Occasion*. Both of these poems refer to Webster.

Webster as an orator had no equal, and as a lawyer no superior. His reputation as a statesman, though for the most part grand and glorious, was, in the eyes of many, dimmed by his change of base on the slavery question. His personal appearance was very remarkable ; he had a swarthy complexion and straight black hair; his head was large and of noble shape, with a broad and lofty brow; his features were finely cut and full of massive strength, and his eyes were dark and deep set. Mr. Lodge says, " There is no man in all history who came into the world so equipped physically for speech."

Webster died at Marshfield, Mass., October 24, 1852, while holding the office of secretary of state under President Fillmore.

THE BUNKER HILL MONUMENT.

AN ADDRESS DELIVERED AT THE LAYING OF THE CORNER-
STONE OF THE BUNKER HILL MONUMENT AT CHARLES-
TOWN, MASS., ON THE 17TH OF JUNE, 1825.

[As early as 1776, some steps were taken toward the com-
memoration of the Battle of Bunker Hill and the fall of
General Warren, who was buried upon the hill the day after
the action. The Massachusetts Lodge of Masons, over
which Warren had presided, applied to the provisional gov-
ernment of Massachusetts for permission to take up his re-
mains and to bury them with the usual solemnities. The
council granted this request, on condition that it should be
carried into effect in such a manner that the government of
the Colony might have an opportunity to erect a monument
to his memory. A funeral procession was had, and a eulogy
on General Warren was delivered by Perez Morton, but no
measures were taken toward building a monument.

A resolution was adopted by the Congress of the United
States on the 8th of April, 1777, directing that monuments
should be erected to the memory of General Warren, in
Boston, and of General Mercer, at Fredericksburg; but this
resolution has remained to the present time unexecuted.

On the 11th of November, 1794, a committee was ap-
pointed by King Solomon's Lodge, at Charlestown,[1] to take
measures for the erection of a monument to the memory of
General Joseph Warren, at the expense of the lodge. This
resolution was promptly carried into effect. The land for

---

[1] General Warren, at the time of his decease, was Grand
Master of the Masonic Lodges in America.

this purpose was presented to the lodge by the Hon. James Russell, of Charlestown, and it was dedicated with appropriate ceremonies on the 2d of December, 1794. It was a wooden pillar of the Tuscan order, eighteen feet in height, raised on a pedestal eight feet square, and of an elevation of ten feet from the ground. The pillar was surmounted by a gilt urn. An appropriate inscription was placed on the south side of the pedestal.

In February, 1818, a committee of the legislature of Massachusetts was appointed to consider the expediency of building a monument of American marble to the memory of General Warren, but this proposal was not carried into effect.

As the half-century from the date of the battle drew toward a close, a stronger feeling of the duty of commemorating it began to be awakened in the community. Among those who from the first manifested the greatest interest in the subject was the late William Tudor, Esq. He expressed the wish, in a letter still preserved, to see upon the battle-ground " the noblest monument in the world," and he was so ardent and persevering in urging the project, that it has been stated that he first conceived the idea of it. The steps taken in execution of the project, from the earliest private conferences among the gentlemen first engaged in it to its final completion, are accurately sketched by Mr. Richard Frothingham, Jr., in his valuable *History of the Siege of Boston.* All the material facts contained in this note are derived from his chapter on the Bunker Hill Monument. After giving an account of the organization of the society, the measures adopted for the collection of funds, and the deliberations on the form of the monument, Mr. Frothingham proceeds as follows : —

" It was at this stage of the enterprise that the directors proposed to lay the corner-stone of the monument, and ground was broken (June 7th) for this purpose. As a mark of respect to the liberality and patriotism of King

Solomon's Lodge, they invited the Grand Master of the Grand Lodge of Massachusetts to perform the ceremony. They also invited General Lafayette to accompany the President of the Association, Hon. Daniel Webster, and assist in it.

"This celebration was unequalled in magnificence by anything of the kind that had been seen in New England. The morning proved propitious. The air was cool, the sky was clear, and timely showers the previous day had brightened the vesture of nature into its loveliest hue. Delighted thousands flocked into Boston to bear a part in the proceedings, or to witness the spectacle. At about ten o'clock a procession moved from the State House towards Bunker Hill. The military, in their fine uniforms, formed the van. About two hundred veterans of the Revolution, of whom forty were survivors of the battle, rode in barouches next to the escort. These venerable men, the relics of a past generation, with emaciated frames, tottering limbs, and trembling voices, constituted a touching spectacle. Some wore, as honorable decorations, their old fighting equipments, and some bore the scars of still more honorable wounds. Glistening eyes constituted their answer to the enthusiastic cheers of the grateful multitudes who lined their pathway and cheered their progress. To this patriot band succeeded the Bunker Hill Monument Association. Then the Masonic fraternity, in their splendid regalia, thousands in number. Then Lafayette, continually welcomed by tokens of love and gratitude, and the invited guests. Then a long array of societies, with their various badges and banners. It was a splendid procession, and of such length that the front nearly reached Charlestown Bridge ere the rear had left Boston Common. It proceeded to Breed's Hill, where the Grand Master of the Freemasons, the President of the Monument Association, and General Lafayette performed the ceremony of laying the corner-stone, in the presence of a vast concourse of people."

The procession then moved to a spacious amphitheatre on the northern declivity of the hill, where the following address was delivered by Mr. Webster, in the presence of as great a multitude perhaps as was ever assembled within the sound of a human voice.]

THIS uncounted multitude before me and around me proves the feeling which the occasion has excited. These thousands of human faces, glowing with sympathy and joy, and from the impulses of a common gratitude turned reverently to heaven in this spacious temple of the firmament, proclaim that the day, the place, and the purpose of our assembling have made a deep impression on our hearts.

If, indeed, there be anything in local association fit to affect the mind of man, we need not strive to repress the emotions which agitate us here. We are among the sepulchres of our fathers. We are on ground distinguished by their valor, their constancy, and the shedding of their blood. We are here, not to fix an uncertain date in our annals, nor to draw into notice an obscure and unknown spot. If our humble purpose had never been conceived, if we ourselves had never been born, the 17th of June, 1775, would have been a day on which all subsequent history would have poured its light, and the eminence where we stand a point of attraction to the eyes of successive generations. But we are Americans. We live in what may be called the early age of this great continent; and we know that our posterity, through all time, are here to enjoy and suffer the allotments of humanity. We see before us a probable train of great events; we know that our own fortunes have been happily cast; and it is natural, therefore, that we should be moved by the contemplation of occurrences which have guided our destiny before many of us were born, and settled the condition in which we should pass that portion of our existence which God allows to men on earth.

We do not read even of the discovery of this continent, without feeling something of a personal interest in the event; without being reminded how much it has affected our own fortunes and our own existence. It would be still more unnatural for us, therefore, than for others, to contemplate with unaffected minds that interesting, I may say that most touching and pathetic scene, when the great discoverer of America stood on the deck of his shattered bark, the shades of night falling on the sea, yet no man sleeping; tossed on the billows of an unknown ocean, yet the stronger billows of alternate hope and despair tossing his own troubled thoughts; extending forward his harassed frame, straining westward his anxious and eager eyes, till Heaven at last granted him a moment of rapture and ecstasy, in blessing his vision with the sight of the unknown world.

Nearer to our times, more closely connected with our fates, and therefore still more interesting to our feelings and affections, is the settlement of our own country by colonists from England. We cherish every memorial of these worthy ancestors; we celebrate their patience and fortitude; we admire their daring enterprise; we teach our children to venerate their piety; and we are justly proud of being descended from men who have set the world an example of founding civil institutions on the great and united principles of human freedom and human knowledge. To us, their children, the story of their labors and sufferings can

never be without interest. We shall not stand un-
moved on the shore of Plymouth, while the sea con-
tinues to wash it; nor will our brethren in another
early and ancient Colony forget the place of its first
establishment, till their river shall cease to flow by it.[1]
No vigor of youth, no maturity of manhood, will lead
the nation to forget the spots where its infancy was
cradled and defended.

But the great event in the history of the continent,
which we are now met here to commemorate, that
prodigy of modern times, at once the wonder and the
blessing of the world, is the American Revolution.
In a day of extraordinary prosperity and happiness,
of high national honor, distinction, and power, we are
brought together, in this place, by our love of country,
by our admiration of exalted character, by our grati-
tude for signal services and patriotic devotion.

The Society whose organ I am [2] was formed for the
purpose of rearing some honorable and durable monu-
ment to the memory of the early friends of American
Independence. They have thought that for this ob-
ject no time could be more propitious than the present
prosperous and peaceful period; that no place could

---

[1] An interesting account of the voyage of the early emigrants
to the Maryland Colony, and of its settlement, is given in the
official report of Father White, written probably within the first
month after the landing at St. Mary's. The original Latin man-
uscript is still preserved among the archives of the Jesuits at
Rome. The Ark and the Dove are remembered with scarcely
less interest by the descendants of the sister colony, than is the
Mayflower in New England, which thirteen years earlier, at the
same season of the year, bore thither the Pilgrim Fathers.

[2] Mr. Webster was at this time President of the Bunker Hill
Monument Association, chosen on the death of Governor John
Brooks, the first President.

claim preference over this memorable spot; and that no day could be more auspicious to the undertaking, than the anniversary of the battle which was here fought. The foundation of that monument we have now laid. With solemnities suited to the occasion, with prayers to Almighty God for his blessing, and in the midst of this cloud of witnesses, we have begun the work. We trust it will be prosecuted, and that, springing from a broad foundation, rising high in massive solidity and unadorned grandeur, it may remain as long as Heaven permits the works of man to last, a fit emblem, both of the events in memory of which it is raised, and of the gratitude of those who have reared it.

We know, indeed, that the record of illustrious actions is most safely deposited in the universal remembrance of mankind. We know, that if we could cause this structure to ascend, not only till it reached the skies, but till it pierced them, its broad surfaces could still contain but part of that which, in an age of knowledge, hath already been spread over the earth, and which history charges itself with making known to all future times. We know that no inscription on entablatures less broad than the earth itself can carry information of the events we commemorate where it has not already gone; and that no structure, which shall not outlive the duration of letters and knowledge among men, can prolong the memorial. But our object is, by this edifice, to show our own deep sense of the value and importance of the achievements of our ancestors; and, by presenting this work of gratitude to the eye, to keep alive similar sentiments, and to foster a constant regard for the principles of the Revolution. Human beings are composed, not of reason only, but of imagination also, and sentiment; and that is neither wasted nor misapplied which is appropriated to the purpose of giving right direction to sentiments, and opening proper springs of feeling in the heart. Let it not be supposed that our object is to perpetuate national hostility, or even to cherish a mere military spirit. It is higher, purer, nobler. We consecrate our work to the spirit of national independence, and we wish that the light of peace may rest upon it for ever. We rear a memorial of our conviction of that unmeasured benefit which has been conferred on our own land, and of the happy influences which have been produced, by the same events, on the general interests of mankind. We come, as Americans, to mark a spot which must forever be dear to us and our posterity. We wish that whosoever, in all coming time, shall turn his eye hither, may behold that the place is not undistinguished where the first great battle of the Revolution was fought. We wish that this structure may proclaim the magnitude and importance of that event to every class and every age. We wish that infancy may learn the purpose of its erection from maternal lips, and that weary and withered age may behold it, and be solaced by the recollections which it suggests. We wish that labor may look up here, and be proud, in the midst of its toil. We wish that, in those days of disaster, which, as they come upon all nations, must be expected to come upon us also, desponding patriotism may turn its eyes hitherward, and be assured that the foundations of our national power are still strong. We wish that this column, rising towards heaven among the pointed spires of so many temples dedicated to God, may contribute also to produce, in all minds, a pious feeling of dependence and gratitude. We wish, finally, that the last object to the sight of him who leaves his native shore, and the first to gladden him who revisits it, may be something which shall remind him of the liberty and the glory of his country. Let it rise! let it rise, till it meet the sun in his coming; let the earliest light of the morning gild it, and parting day linger and play on its summit.

We live in a most extraordinary age. Events so various and so important that they might crowd and distinguish centuries are, in our times, compressed within the compass of a single life. When has it happened that history has had so much to record, in the same term of years, as since the 17th of June, 1775? Our own revolution, which, under other circumstances, might itself have been expected to occasion a war of half a century, has been achieved; twenty-four sovereign and independent States erected; and a general government established over them, so safe, so wise, so free, so practical, that we might well wonder its establishment should have been accomplished so soon, were it not far the greater wonder that it should have been established at all. Two or three millions of people have been augmented to twelve, the great forests of the West prostrated beneath the arm of successful industry, and the dwellers on the banks of the Ohio and the Mississippi become the fellow-citizens and neighbors of those who cultivate the hills of New England.[1] We have a commerce

[1] That which was spoken of figuratively in 1825 has, in the lapse of a quarter of a century, by the introduction of railroads and telegraphic lines, become a reality. It is an interesting circumstance, that the first railroad on the Western Continent was constructed for the purpose of accelerating the erection of this monument. — *Edward Everett, in* 1851.

that leaves no sea unexplored ; navies which take no law from superior force ; revenues adequate to all the exigencies of government, almost without taxation ; and peace with all nations, founded on equal rights and mutual respect.

Europe, within the same period, has been agitated by a mighty revolution, which, while it has been felt in the individual condition and happiness of almost every man, has shaken to the centre her political fabric, and dashed against one another thrones which had stood tranquil for ages. On this, our continent, our own example has been followed, and colonies have sprung up to be nations. Unaccustomed sounds of liberty and free government have reached us from beyond the track of the sun ; and at this moment the dominion of European power in this continent, from the place where we stand to the south pole, is annihilated for ever.[1]

In the mean time, both in Europe and America, such has been the general progress of knowledge, such the improvement in legislation, in commerce, in the arts, in letters, and, above all, in liberal ideas and the general spirit of the age, that the whole world seems changed.

Yet, notwithstanding that this is but a faint abstract of the things which have happened since the day of the battle of Bunker Hill, we are but fifty years removed from it ; and we now stand here to enjoy all the blessings of our own condition, and to look abroad on the brightened prospects of the world, while we still have among us some of those who were active agents in the scenes of 1775, and who are now here,

[1] This has special reference to the Monroe Doctrine, then fresh in the minds of Mr. Webster and his hearers.

from every quarter of New England, to visit once more, and under circumstances so affecting, I had almost said so overwhelming, this renowned theatre of their courage and patriotism.

VENERABLE MEN ! you have come down to us from a former generation. Heaven has bounteously lengthened out your lives, that you might behold this joyous day. You are now where you stood fifty years ago, this very hour, with your brothers and your neighbors, shoulder to shoulder, in the strife for your country. Behold, how altered ! The same heavens are indeed over your heads; the same ocean rolls at your feet; but all else how changed ! You hear now no roar of hostile cannon, you see no mixed volumes of smoke and flame rising from burning Charlestown. The ground strewed with the dead and the dying; the impetuous charge; the steady and successful repulse; the loud call to repeated assault; the summoning of all that is manly to repeated resistance ; a thousand bosoms freely and fearlessly bared in an instant to whatever of terror there may be in war and death; — all these you have witnessed, but you witness them no more. All is peace. The heights of yonder metropolis, its towers and roofs, which you then saw filled with wives and children and countrymen in distress and terror, and looking with unutterable emotions for the issue of the combat, have presented you to-day with the sight of its whole happy population, come out to welcome and greet you with a universal jubilee. Yonder proud ships, by a felicity of position appropriately lying at the foot of this mount, and seeming fondly to cling around it, are not means of annoyance to you, but your country's own means of distinction and defence.[1] All is peace; and God has granted you this sight of your country's happiness, ere you slumber in the grave. He has allowed you to behold and to partake the reward of your patriotic toils; and he has allowed us, your sons and countrymen, to meet you here, and in the name of the present generation, in the name of your country, in the name of liberty, to thank you!

But, alas! you are not all here! Time and the sword have thinned your ranks. Prescott, Putnam, Stark, Brooks, Read, Pomeroy, Bridge! our eyes seek for you in vain amid this broken band. You are gathered to your fathers, and live only to your country in her grateful remembrance and your own bright example. But let us not too much grieve, that you have met the common fate of men. You lived at least long enough to know that your work had been nobly and successfully accomplished. You lived to see your country's independence established, and to sheathe your swords from war. On the light of Liberty you saw arise the light of Peace, like

> "another morn,
> Risen on mid-noon;"

and the sky on which you closed your eyes was cloudless.

But, ah! Him! the first great martyr in this great cause! Him! the premature victim of his own self-devoting heart! Him! the head of our civil councils, and the destined leader of our military bands, whom nothing brought hither but the unquenchable fire of his own spirit! Him! cut off by Providence in the

---

[1] It is necessary to inform those only who are unacquainted with the localities, that the United States Navy Yard at Charlestown is situated at the base of Bunker Hill.

hour of overwhelming anxiety and thick gloom; falling ere he saw the star of his country rise; pouring out his generous blood like water, before he knew whether it would fertilize a land of freedom or of bondage! — how shall I struggle with the emotions that stifle the utterance of thy name![1] Our poor work may perish; but thine shall endure! This monument may moulder away; the solid ground it rests upon may sink down to a level with the sea; but thy memory shall not fail! Wheresoever among men a heart shall be found that beats to the transports of patriotism and liberty, its aspirations shall be to claim kindred with thy spirit.

But the scene amidst which we stand does not permit us to confine our thoughts or our sympathies to those fearless spirits who hazarded or lost their lives on this consecrated spot. We have the happiness to rejoice here in the presence of a most worthy representation of the survivors of the whole Revolutionary army.

VETERANS! you are the remnant of many a well-fought field. You bring with you marks of honor from Trenton and Monmouth, from Yorktown, Camden, Bennington, and Saratoga. VETERANS OF HALF A CENTURY! when in your youthful days you put every thing at hazard in your country's cause, good as that cause was, and sanguine as youth is, still your fondest hopes did not stretch onward to an hour like this! At a period to which you could not reasonably have expected to arrive, at a moment of national prosperity such as you could never have foreseen, you are now met here to enjoy the fellowship of old soldiers, and to receive the overflowings of a universal gratitude.

[1] The name of Joseph Warren was very dear to Americans of Webster's day.

But your agitated countenances and your heaving breasts inform me that even this is not an unmixed joy. I perceive that a tumult of contending feelings rushes upon you. The images of the dead, as well as the persons of the living, present themselves before you. The scene overwhelms you, and I turn from it. May the Father of all mercies smile upon your declining years, and bless them! And when you shall here have exchanged your embraces, when you shall once more have pressed the hands which have been so often extended to give succor in adversity, or grasped in the exultation of victory, then look abroad upon this lovely land which your young valor defended, and mark the happiness with which it is filled; yea, look abroad upon the whole earth, and see what a name you have contributed to give to your country, and what a praise you have added to freedom, and then rejoice in the sympathy and gratitude which beam upon your last days from the improved condition of mankind!

The occasion does not require of me any particular account of the battle of the 17th of June, 1775, nor any detailed narrative of the events which immediately preceded it. These are familiarly known to all. In the progress of the great and interesting controversy, Massachusetts and the town of Boston had become early and marked objects of the displeasure of the British Parliament. This had been manifested in the act for altering the government of the Province, and in that for shutting up the port of Boston. Nothing sheds more honor on our early history, and nothing better shows how little the feelings and sentiments of the Colonies were known or regarded in England, than the impression which these measures everywhere produced in America. It had been anticipated, that while the Colonies in general would be terrified by the severity of the punishment inflicted on Massachusetts, the other seaports would be governed by a mere spirit of gain; and that, as Boston was now cut off from all commerce, the unexpected advantage which this blow on her was calculated to confer on other towns would be greedily enjoyed. How miserably such reasoners deceived themselves! How little they knew of the depth, and the strength, and the intenseness of that feeling of resistance to illegal acts of power, which possessed the whole American people! Everywhere the unworthy boon was rejected with scorn. The fortunate occasion was seized, everywhere, to show to the whole world that the Colonies were swayed by no local interest, no partial interest, no selfish interest. The temptation to profit by the punishment of Boston was strongest to our neighbors of Salem. Yet Salem was precisely the place where this miserable proffer was spurned, in a tone of the most lofty self-respect and the most indignant patriotism. "We are deeply affected," said its inhabitants, "with the sense of our public calamities; but the miseries that are now rapidly hastening on our brethren in the capital of the Province greatly excite our commiseration. By shutting up the port of Boston some imagine that the course of trade might be turned hither and to our benefit; but we must be dead to every idea of justice, lost to all feelings of humanity, could we indulge a thought to seize on wealth and raise our fortunes on the ruin of our suffering neighbors." These noble sentiments were not confined to our immediate vicinity. In that day of general affection and brotherhood, the blow given to Boston smote on every patriotic heart from one end of the country to the other. Virginia and the Carolinas, as well as Connecticut and New Hampshire, felt and proclaimed the cause to be their own. The Continental Congress, then holding its first session in Philadelphia, expressed its sympathy for the suffering inhabitants of Boston, and addresses were received from all quarters, assuring them that the cause was a common one, and should be met by common efforts and common sacrifices. The Congress of Massachusetts responded to these assurances ; and in an address to the Congress at Philadelphia, bearing the official signature, perhaps among the last, of the immortal Warren, notwithstanding the severity of its suffering and the magnitude of the dangers which threatened it, it was declared that this Colony " is ready, at all times, to spend and to be spent in the cause of America."

But the hour drew nigh which was to put professions to the proof, and to determine whether the authors of these mutual pledges were ready to seal them in blood. The tidings of Lexington and Concord had no sooner spread, than it was universally felt that the time was at last come for action. A spirit pervaded all ranks, not transient, not boisterous, but deep, solemn, determined, —

> " Totamque infusa per artus
> Mens agitat molem, et magno se corpore miscet." [1]

War on their own soil and at their own doors, was, indeed, a strange work to the yeomanry of New England ; but their consciences were convinced of its necessity, their country called them to it, and they did not withhold themselves from the perilous trial. The

---

[1] " And a Mind, diffused throughout the members, gives energy to the whole mass, and mingles with the vast body."

ordinary occupations of life were abandoned ; the plough was stayed in the unfinished furrow ; wives gave up their husbands, and mothers gave up their sons, to the battles of a civil war. Death might come in honor, on the field ; it might come, in disgrace, on the scaffold. For either and for both they were prepared. The sentiment of Quincy was full in their hearts. " Blandishments," said that distinguished son of genius and patriotism, " will not fascinate us, nor will threats of a halter intimidate ; for, under God, we are determined, that, wheresoever, whensoever, or howsoever, we shall be called to make our exit, we will die free men."

The 17th of June saw the four New England Colonies standing here, side by side, to triumph or to fall together ; and there was with them from that moment to the end of the war, what I hope will remain with them for ever, — one cause, one country, one heart.

The battle of Bunker Hill was attended with the most important effects beyond its immediate results as a military engagement. It created at once a state of open, public war. There could now be no longer a question of proceeding against individuals, as guilty of treason or rebellion. That fearful crisis was past. The appeal lay to the sword, and the only question was, whether the spirit and the resources of the people would hold out till the object should be accomplished. Nor were its general consequences confined to our own country. The previous proceedings of the Colonies, their appeals, resolutions, and addresses, had made their cause known to Europe. Without boasting, we may say, that in no age or country has the public cause been maintained with more force of argument, more power of illustration, or more of that persuasion which excited feeling and elevated principle can alone bestow, than the Revolutionary state papers exhibit. These papers will forever deserve to be studied, not only for the spirit which they breathe, but for the ability with which they were written.

To this able vindication of their cause, the Colonies had now added a practical and severe proof of their own true devotion to it, and given evidence also of the power which they could bring to its support. All now saw, that if America fell, she would not fall without a struggle. Men felt sympathy and regard, as well as surprise, when they beheld these infant states, remote, unknown, unaided, encounter the power of England, and, in the first considerable battle, leave more of their enemies dead on the field, in proportion to the number of combatants, than had been recently known to fall in the wars of Europe.

Information of these events, circulating throughout the world, at length reached the ears of one who now hears me.[1] He has not forgotten the emotion which the fame of Bunker Hill, and the name of Warren, excited in his youthful breast.

Sir, we are assembled to commemorate the establishment of great public principles of liberty, and to do honor to the distinguished dead. The occasion is too severe for eulogy of the living. But, Sir, your interesting relation to this country, the peculiar circumstances which surround you and surround us, call on me to express the happiness which we derive from your presence and aid in this solemn commemoration.

---

[1] Among the earliest of the arrangements for the celebration of the 17th of June, 1825, was the invitation to General Lafayette to be present ; and he had so timed his progress through the other States as to return to Massachusetts in season for the great occasion.

Fortunate, fortunate man! with what measure of devotion will you not thank God for the circumstances of your extraordinary life! You are connected with both hemispheres and with two generations. Heaven saw fit to ordain that the electric spark of liberty should be conducted, through you, from the New World to the Old; and we, who are now here to perform this duty of patriotism, have all of us long ago received it in charge from our fathers to cherish your name and your virtues. You will account it an instance of your good fortune, Sir, that you crossed the seas to visit us at a time which enables you to be present at this solemnity. You now behold the field, the renown of which reached you in the heart of France, and caused a thrill in your ardent bosom. You see the lines of the little redoubt thrown up by the incredible diligence of Prescott; defended, to the last extremity, by his lion-hearted valor; and within which the corner-stone of our monument has now taken its position. You see where Warren fell, and where Parker, Gardner, McCleary, Moore, and other early patriots fell with him. Those who survived that day, and whose lives have been prolonged to the present hour, are now around you. Some of them you have known in the trying scenes of the war. Behold! they now stretch forth their feeble arms to embrace you. Behold! they raise their trembling voices to invoke the blessing of God on you and yours forever.

Sir, you have assisted us in laying the foundation of this structure. You have heard us rehearse, with our feeble commendation, the names of departed patriots. Monuments and eulogy belong to the dead. We give then this day to Warren and his associates. On other occasions they have been given to your more immediate companions in arms, to Washington, to Greene, to Gates, to Sullivan, and to Lincoln. We have become reluctant to grant these, our highest and last honors, further. We would gladly hold them yet back from the little remnant of that immortal band. " *Serus in cœlum redeas.*"[1] Illustrious as are your merits, yet far, O, very far distant be the day, when any inscription shall bear your name, or any tongue pronounce its eulogy!

The leading reflection to which this occasion seems to invite us, respects the great changes which have happened in the fifty years since the battle of Bunker Hill was fought. And it peculiarly marks the character of the present age, that, in looking at these changes, and in estimating their effect on our condition, we are obliged to consider, not what has been done in our country only, but in others also. In these interesting times, while nations are making separate and individual advances in improvement, they make, too, a common progress; like vessels on a common tide, propelled by the gales at different rates, according to their several structure and management, but all moved forward by one mighty current, strong enough to bear onward whatever does not sink beneath it.

A chief distinction of the present day is a community of opinions and knowledge amongst men in different nations, existing in a degree heretofore unknown. Knowledge has, in our time, triumphed, and is triumphing, over distance, over difference of languages, over diversity of habits, over prejudice, and over bigotry. The civilized and Christian world is fast learning the great lesson, that difference of nation does not imply necessary hostility, and that all contact need not

[1] "Late may you return to heaven."

be war. The whole world is becoming a common field for intellect to act in. Energy of mind, genius, power, wheresoever it exists, may speak out in any tongue, and the world will hear it. A great chord of sentiment and feeling runs through two continents, and vibrates over both. Every breeze wafts intelligence from country to country, every wave rolls it; all give it forth, and all in turn receive it. There is a vast commerce of ideas; there are marts and exchanges for intellectual discoveries, and a wonderful fellowship of those individual intelligences which make up the mind and opinion of the age. Mind is the great lever of all things; human thought is the process by which human ends are ultimately answered; and the diffusion of knowledge, so astonishing in the last half-century, has rendered innumerable minds, variously gifted by nature, competent to be competitors or fellow-workers on the theatre of intellectual operation.

From these causes important improvements have taken place in the personal condition of individuals. Generally speaking, mankind are not only better fed and better clothed, but they are able also to enjoy more leisure; they possess more refinement and more self-respect. A superior tone of education, manners, and habits prevails. This remark, most true in its application to our own country, is also partly true when applied elsewhere. It is proved by the vastly augmented consumption of those articles of manufacture and of commerce which contribute to the comforts . and the decencies of life; an augmentation which has far outrun the progress of population. And while the unexampled and almost incredible use of machinery would seem to supply the place of labor, labor still finds its occupation and its reward; so wisely has

Providence adjusted men's wants and desires to their condition and their capacity.

Any adequate survey, however, of the progress made during the last half-century in the polite and the mechanic arts, in machinery and manufactures, in commerce and agriculture, in letters and in science, would require volumes. I must abstain wholly from these subjects, and turn for a moment to the contemplation of what has been done on the great question of politics and government. This is the master topic of the age; and during the whole fifty years it has intensely occupied the thoughts of men. The nature of civil government, its ends and uses, have been canvassed and investigated; ancient opinions attacked and defended; new ideas recommended and resisted, by whatever power the mind of man could bring to the controversy. From the closet and the public halls the debate has been transferred to the field; and the world has been shaken by wars of unexampled magnitude, and the greatest variety of fortune. A day of peace has at length succeeded; and now that the strife has subsided, and the smoke cleared away, we may begin to see what has actually been done, permanently changing the state and condition of human society. And, without dwelling on particular circumstances, it is most apparent, that, from the before-mentioned causes of augmented knowledge and improved individual condition, a real, substantial, and important change has taken place, and is taking place, highly favorable, on the whole, to human liberty and human happiness.

The great wheel of political revolution began to move in America. Here its rotation was guarded, regular, and safe. Transferred to the other continent, from unfortunate but natural causes, it received an irregular and violent impulse ; it whirled, along with a fearful celerity ; till at length, like the chariot-wheels in the races of antiquity, it took fire from the rapidity of its own motion, and blazed onward, spreading conflagration and terror around.

We learn from the result of this experiment, how fortunate was our own condition, and how admirably the character of our people was calculated for setting the great example of popular governments. The possession of power did not turn the heads of the Amercan people, for they had long been in the habit of exercising a great degree of self-control. Although the paramount authority of the parent state existed over them, yet a large field of legislation had always been open to our Colonial assemblies. They were accustomed to representative bodies and the forms of free government ; they understood the doctrine of the division of power among different branches, and the necessity of checks on each. The character of our countrymen, moreover, was sober, moral, and religious ; and there was little in the change to shock their feelings of justice and humanity, or even to disturb an honest prejudice. We had no domestic throne to overturn, no privileged orders to cast down, no violent changes of property to encounter. In the American Revolution, no man sought or wished for more than to defend and enjoy his own. None hoped for plunder or for spoil. Rapacity was unknown to it ; the axe was not among the instruments of its accomplishment ; and we all know that it could not have lived a single day under any well-founded imputation of possessing a tendency adverse to the Christian religion.

It need not surprise us, that, under circumstances

less auspicious, political revolutions elsewhere, even when well intended, have terminated differently. It is, indeed, a great achievement, it is the masterwork of the world, to establish governments entirely popular on lasting foundations; nor is it easy, indeed, to introduce the popular principle at all into governments to which it has been altogether a stranger. It cannot be doubted, however, that Europe has come out of the contest, in which she has been so long engaged, with greatly superior knowledge, and, in many respects, in a highly improved condition. Whatever benefit has been acquired is likely to be retained, for it consists mainly in the acquisition of more enlightened ideas. And although kingdoms and provinces may be wrested from the hands that hold them, in the same manner they were obtained; although ordinary and vulgar power may, in human affairs, be lost as it has been won; yet it is the glorious prerogative of the empire of knowledge, that what it gains it never loses. On the contrary, it increases by the multiple of its own power; all its ends become means; all its attainments, helps to new conquests. Its whole abundant harvest is but so much seed wheat, and nothing has limited, and nothing can limit, the amount of ultimate product.

Under the influence of this rapidly increasing knowledge, the people have begun, in all forms of government, to think, and to reason, on affairs of state. Regarding government as an institution for the public good, they demand a knowledge of its operations, and a participation in its exercise. A call for the representative system, wherever it is not enjoyed, and where there is already intelligence enough to estimate its value, is perseveringly made. Where men may speak out, they demand it; where the bayonet is at their throats, they pray for it.

When Louis the Fourteenth said, "I am the State," he expressed the essence of the doctrine of unlimited power. By the rules of that system, the people are disconnected from the state; they are its subjects, it is their lord. These ideas, founded in the love of power, and long supported by the excess and the abuse of it, are yielding, in our age, to other opinions; and the civilized world seems at last to be proceeding to the conviction of that fundamental and manifest truth, that the powers of government are but a trust, and that they cannot be lawfully exercised but for the good of the community. As knowledge is more and more extended, this conviction becomes more and more general. Knowledge, in truth, is the great sun in the firmament. Life and power are scattered with all its beams. The prayer of the Grecian champion, when enveloped in unnatural clouds and darkness, is the appropriate political supplication for the people of every country not yet blessed with free institutions : —

> "Dispel this cloud, the light of heaven restore,
> Give me TO SEE, — and Ajax asks no more."

We may hope that the growing influence of enlightened sentiment will promote the permanent peace of the world. Wars to maintain family alliances, to uphold or to cast down dynasties, and to regulate successions to thrones, which have occupied so much room in the history of modern times, if not less likely to happen at all, will be less likely to become general and involve many nations, as the great principle shall be more and more established, that the interest of the world is peace, and its first great statute, that every nation possesses the power of establishing a government for itself.   But public opinion has attained also an influence over governments which do not admit the popular principle into their organization.   A necessary respect for the judgment of the world operates, in some measure, as a control over the most unlimited forms of authority.   It is owing, perhaps, to this truth, that the interesting struggle of the Greeks has been suffered to go on so long, without a direct interference, either to wrest that country from its present masters, or to execute the system of pacification by force ; and, with united strength, lay the neck of Christian and civilized Greek at the foot of the barbarian Turk.   Let us thank God that we live in an age when something has influence besides the bayonet, and when the sternest authority does not venture to encounter the scorching power of public reproach. Any attempt of the kind I have mentioned should be met by one universal burst of indignation ; the air of the civilized world ought to be made too warm to be comfortably breathed by any one who would hazard it.

It is, indeed, a touching reflection, that, while, in the fulness of our country's happiness, we rear this monument to her honor, we look for instruction in our undertaking to a country which is now in fearful contest, not for works of art or memorials of glory, but for her own existence.   Let her be assured, that she is not forgotten in the world ; that her efforts are applauded, and that constant prayers ascend for her success.   And let us cherish a confident hope for her final triumph.   If the true spark of religious and civil liberty be kindled, it will burn.   Human agency cannot extinguish it.   Like the earth's central fire, it may be smothered for a time ; the ocean may overwhelm it ; mountains may press it down ; but its inherent and unconquerable force will heave both the ocean and the land, and at some time or other, in some place or other, the volcano will break out and flame up to heaven.

Among the great events of the half-century, we must reckon, certainly, the revolution of South America; and we are not likely to overrate the importance of that revolution, either to the people of the country itself or to the rest of the world. The late Spanish colonies, now independent states, under circumstances less favorable, doubtless, than attended our own revolution, have yet successfully commenced their national existence. They have accomplished the great object of establishing their independence; they are known and acknowledged in the world; and although in regard to their systems of government, their sentiments on religious toleration, and their provision for public instruction, they may have yet much to learn, it must be admitted that they have risen to the condition of settled and established states more rapidly than could have been reasonably anticipated. They already furnish an exhilarating example of the difference between free governments and despotic misrule. Their commerce, at this moment, creates a new activity in all the great marts of the world. They show themselves able, by an exchange of commodities, to bear a useful part in the intercourse of nations.

A new spirit of enterprise and industry begins to prevail; all the great interests of society receive a salutary impulse; and the progress of information not only testifies to an improved condition, but itself constitutes the highest and most essential improvement.

When the battle of Bunker Hill was fought, the existence of South America was scarcely felt in the civilized world. The thirteen little colonies of North America habitually called themselves the "continent." Borne down by colonial subjugation, monopoly, and bigotry, these vast regions of the South were hardly visible above the horizon. But in our day there has been, as it were, a new creation. The southern hemisphere emerges from the sea. Its lofty mountains begin to lift themselves into the light of heaven; its broad and fertile plains stretch out, in beauty, to the eye of civilized man, and at the mighty bidding of the voice of political liberty the waters of darkness retire.

And now, let us indulge an honest exultation in the conviction of the benefit which the example of our country has produced, and is likely to produce, on human freedom and human happiness. Let us endeavor to comprehend in all its magnitude, and to feel in all its importance, the part assigned to us in the great drama of human affairs. We are placed at the head of the system of representative and popular governments. Thus far our example shows that such governments are compatible, not only with respectability and power, but with repose, with peace, with security of personal rights, with good laws, and a just administration.

We are not propagandists. Wherever other systems are preferred, either as being thought better in themselves, or as better suited to existing conditions, we leave the preference to be enjoyed. Our history hitherto proves, however, that the popular form is practicable, and that with wisdom and knowledge men may govern themselves; and the duty incumbent on us is to preserve the consistency of this cheering example, and take care that nothing may weaken its authority with the world. If, in our case, the representative system ultimately fail, popular governments must be pronounced impossible. No combination of circumstances more favorable to the experiment can ever be expected to occur. The last hopes of mankind, therefore, rest with us; and if it should be proclaimed, that our example had become an argument against the experiment, the knell of popular liberty would be sounded throughout the earth.

These are excitements to duty; but they are not suggestions of doubt. Our history and our condition, all that is gone before us, and all that surrounds us, authorize the belief, that popular governments, though subject to occasional variations, in form perhaps not always for the better, may yet, in their general character, be as durable and permanent as other systems. We know, indeed, that in our country any other is impossible. The principle of free governments adheres to the American soil. It is bedded in it, immovable as its mountains.

And let the sacred obligations which have devolved on this generation, and on us, sink deep into our hearts. Those who established our liberty and our government are daily dropping from among us. The great trust now descends to new hands. Let us apply ourselves to that which is presented to us, as our appropriate object. We can win no laurels in a war for independence. Earlier and worthier hands have gathered them all. Nor are there places for us by the side of Solon, and Alfred, and other founders of states. Our fathers have filled them. But there remains to us a great duty of defence and preservation; and there is opened to us, also, a noble pursuit, to which the spirit of the times strongly invites us. Our proper business is improvement. Let our age be the age of improvement. In a day of peace, let us advance the arts of peace and the works of peace. Let us develop the resources of our land, call forth its powers, build up its institutions, promote all its great interests, and see whether we also, in our day and generation, may not perform something worthy to be remembered. Let us cultivate a true spirit of union and harmony. In pursuing the great objects which our condition points out to us, let us act under a settled conviction, and an habitual feeling, that these twenty-four States are one country. Let our conceptions be enlarged to the circle of our duties. Let us extend our ideas over the whole of the vast field in which we are called to act. Let our object be, OUR COUNTRY, OUR WHOLE COUNTRY, AND NOTHING BUT OUR COUNTRY. And, by the blessing of God, may that country itself become a vast and splendid monument, not of oppression and terror, but of Wisdom, of Peace, and of Liberty, upon which the world may gaze with admiration forever!

EDWARD EVERETT.

BIOGRAPHICAL SKETCH.

EDWARD EVERETT was born at Dorchester, Mass., April 11, 1794. At the age of eight he was, for a short time, a pupil of Daniel Webster, who was twelve years his senior. The acquaintance then begun between these embryo orators ripened into a lasting friendship.

His son, Dr. William Everett, says in a speech made at the Harvard Commencement Dinner of 1891: " My father's connection with Harvard College began eighty-seven years ago, when he was a child of ten. His older brother was in college, living in the south entry of Hollis. The child was to begin the study of Greek in the winter vacation. The family were too poor to afford two Greek grammars; and little Edward had to walk in the depth of winter from the corner of Essex and Washington streets in Boston over the then most lonely road to the college and secure the prized volume. From that day his connection with Harvard College was scarcely broken till his death. He was four years an undergraduate, . . . two years a tutor, nine years a professor, three years president, and at two different times an overseer; at his death he held an appointment as college lecturer."

The older brother referred to above was Alexander Hill Everett, who was graduated with the highest honors at the age of fourteen. Five years later (in 1811) Edward was graduated with the highest honors at the age of seventeen; he was regarded in college as a prodigy of youthful genius.

In 1812 he became a tutor at Harvard, and at the same time a student of theology.   On February 9, 1814, at the youthful age of nineteen, he was ordained as pastor of the Brattle Street Church, at Boston, where he immediately rose to distinction as an eloquent and impressive pulpit orator.

In March, 1815, he accepted the Eliot Professorship of Greek at Harvard College.   In order to become better prepared for the duties of the position he travelled and studied in Europe until 1819.   While abroad he pursued an extensive range of study at the principal centres of learning, and he took the degree of Ph. D. at the University of Göttingen. His return to Cambridge was hailed with delight, and gave a wonderful impulse to American scholarship.   In addition to his duties as professor he took charge of the *North American Review*, which he conducted for five years.

In 1824 he delivered his celebrated Phi Beta Kappa oration at Cambridge, Mass., to an immense audience, including General Lafayette, in which he portrayed in eloquent and patriotic terms the political, social, and literary future of our country.   In the same year he was elected a member of the National House of Representatives ; after four re-elections and a valuable service of ten years as Congressman he was chosen Governor of Massachusetts.   He was annually reëlected Governor until 1839, when he was defeated by a majority of one vote.

In 1841, after nearly a year's sojourn in Europe, he was appointed Minister Plenipotentiary to Great Britain, under General Harrison as President and his friend Daniel Webster as Secretary of State.   In 1845 he returned to America and became for three years President of Harvard College. In 1850 he published his speeches and orations in two volumes, and at about the same time edited Daniel Webster's works in six volumes, for which he prepared an elaborate memoir.   Upon the death of Webster in 1852, Everett took his place as Secretary of State under President Fillmore.

Edward Everett.

From March, 1853, to May, 1854, he was in the United States Senate.

On February 22, 1856, he delivered in Boston an address, on the *Character of Washington,* which he repeated in different cities and towns nearly one hundred and fifty times. He gave the entire proceeds of this address toward the purchase of Mt. Vernon, the home of Washington, for the general government. He also gave for the same purpose $10,000 received for articles written for the *New York Ledger,* thus raising the entire amount contributed by him to over $100,000. In 1857 and 1858 he gave to different charitable associations the proceeds of other addresses, amounting to nearly $20,000.

In 1860 he was nominated for the Vice-Presidency on the ticket with John Bell, of Tennessee, but was defeated. Though anxious for peace while there was a chance to avoid war, he threw the whole weight of his powers into a support of the Union after the War of Secession began, and won the gratitude of his countrymen by the fervent, patriotic eloquence of his speeches in all the principal cities of the North. His death occurred on January 15, 1865, and resulted from a cold caught on the evening of January 9, while delivering an address in aid of the suffering inhabitants of Savannah, which had just been captured by Gen. Sherman.

Edward Everett's life of seventy-one years spanned a large portion of the youth of our nation. Born in the administration of Washington, he lived to see the War of Secession practically ended under Lincoln. Although thirty-six years old before the first locomotive engine made its appearance in the United States, he lived to see our country covered with a network of over thirty-five thousand miles of railways. During his life the population of the United States increased from about four to thirty millions, and the number of States from fifteen to thirty-six.

It is not to be wondered at that he was fired with an intense feeling of patriotism, or that his noble utterances struck responsive chords in the hearts of his listeners. He had a theory that man can do fairly well anything that he honestly tries to do; his own practice was to undertake whatever work lay before him, and so extraordinary was the versatility of his great mental power that he did remarkably well whatever he undertook. He achieved distinction as an orator, a man of letters, a statesman, and a diplomatist, but the single title which describes him best is that of *orator*. Had he labored continuously in some chosen field he would have left behind him even a greater monument of his remarkable power than is to be found in his numerous speeches and orations.

COMMON sense was eminently a characteristic of Washington; so called, not because it is so very common a trait of character of public men, but because it is the final judgment on great practical questions to which the mind of the community is pretty sure eventually to arrive. Few qualities of character in those who influence the fortunes of nations are so conducive both to stability and progress. But it is a quality which takes no hold of the imagination; it inspires no enthusiasm, it wins no favor; it is well if it can stand its ground against the plausible absurdities, the hollow pretences, the stupendous impostures of the day.

But, however these unobtrusive and austere virtues may be overlooked in the popular estimate, they belong unquestionably to the true type of sterling greatness, reflecting as far as it can be done within the narrow limits of humanity that deep repose and silent equilibrium of mental and moral power which governs the universe. To complain of the character of Washington that it is destitute of brilliant qualities, is to complain of a circle that it has no salient points and no sharp angles in its circumference; forgetting that it owes all its wonderful properties to the unbroken curve of which every point is equidistant from the centre.[1] Instead, therefore, of being a mark of infe-

[1] I was not aware, when I wrote this sentence, that I had ever read Dryden's "Heroic Stanzas consecrated to the Memory of his Highness Oliver, late Lord Protector of this Commonwealth,

riority, this sublime adjustment of powers and virtues in the character of Washington is in reality its glory. It is this which chiefly puts him in harmony with more than human greatness. The higher we rise in the scale of being, — material, intellectual, and moral, — the more certainly we quit the region of the brilliant eccentricities and dazzling contrasts which belong to a vulgar greatness. Order and proportion characterize the primordial constitution of the terrestrial system; ineffable harmony rules the heavens. All the great eternal forces act in solemn silence. The brawling torrent that dries up in summer deafens you with its roaring whirlpools in March; while the vast earth on which we dwell, with all its oceans and all its continents and its thousand millions of inhabitants, revolves unheard upon its soft axle at the rate of a thousand miles an hour, and rushes noiselessly on its orbit a million and a half miles a day. Two storm-clouds encamped upon opposite hills on a sultry summer's evening, at the expense of no more electricity, according to Mr. Faraday, than is evolved in the decomposition of a single drop of water, will shake the surrounding atmosphere with their thunders, which, loudly as they rattle on the spot, will yet not be heard at the distance of twenty miles; while those tremendous and unutterable forces which ever issue from the throne of God, and drag the chariot-wheels of Uranus and Neptune along the uttermost pathways of the solar system, pervade the illimitable universe in silence.

written after celebrating his funeral," one of which is as follows : —

"How shall I then begin or where conclude,
    To draw a fame so truly circular,
For in a round what order can be shewed,
    When all the parts so equal perfect are ? "

This calm and well-balanced temperament of Washington's character is not badly shadowed forth in the poet's description of Cicero: —

> " This magistrate hath struck an awe into me,
> And by his sweetness won a more regard
> Unto his place, than all the boisterous moods
> That ignorant greatness practiseth to fill
> The large unfit authority it wears.
> How easy is a noble spirit discerned
> From harsh and sulphurous matter, that flies out
> In contumelies, makes a noise, and bursts." [1]

And did I say, my friends, that I was unable to furnish an entirely satisfactory answer to the question, in what the true excellence of the character of Washington consists? Let me recall the word as unjust to myself and unjust to you. The answer is plain and simple enough; it is this, that all the great qualities of disposition and action, which so eminently fitted him for the service of his fellow-men, were founded on the basis of a pure Christian morality, and derived their strength and energy from that vital source. He was great as he was good; he was great because he was good; and I believe, as I do in my existence, that it was an important part in the design of Providence in raising him up to be the leader of the Revolutionary struggle, and afterwards the first President of the United States, to rebuke prosperous ambition and successful intrigue; to set before the people of America, in the morning of their national existence, a living example to prove that armies may be best conducted, and governments most ably and honorably administered, by men of sound moral principle; to teach to gifted and aspiring individuals, and the parties they lead, that, though a hundred crooked paths may con-

[1] Ben Jonson's *Catiline.*

duct to a temporary success, the one plain and straight path of public and private virtue can alone lead to a pure and lasting fame and the blessings of posterity.

Born beneath an humble but virtuous roof, brought up at the knees of a mother not unworthy to be named with the noblest matrons of Rome or Israel, the "good boy," as she delighted to call him, passed uncorrupted through the temptations of the solitary frontier, the camp, and the gay world, and grew up into the good man. Engaging in early youth in the service of the country, rising rapidly to the highest trusts, office and influence and praise passing almost the bounds of human desert did nothing to break down the austere simplicity of his manners or to shake the solid basis of his virtues. Placed at the head of the suffering and discontented armies of his country, urged by the tempter to change his honest and involuntary dictatorship of influence into a usurped dictatorship of power, reluctantly consenting to one reëlection to the Presidency and positively rejecting a second, no suspicion ever crossed the mind of an honest man, — let the libellers say what they would, for libellers I am sorry to say there were in that day as in this, — men who pick their daily dishonorable bread out of the characters of men as virtuous as themselves, — and they spared not Washington, — but the suspicion never entered into the mind of an honest man, that his heart was open to the seductions of ambition or interest; or that he was capable in the slightest degree, by word or deed, of shaping his policy with a view to court popular favor or serve a selfish end; that a wish or purpose ever entered his mind inconsistent with the spotless purity of his character.

" No veil
He needed, virtue proof, no thought infirm
Altered his cheek."

And is the judgment of mankind so depraved, is their perception of moral worth so dull, that they can withhold their admiration from such a character and bestow it, for instance, upon the hard-hearted, wondrous youth of ancient renown, who when he had trampled the effeminate rabble of the East under the iron feet of his Macedonian Phalanx, and that world which he wept to conquer was in fact grovelling at his footstool; when he might have founded a dynasty at Babylon which would have crushed the Roman domination in the bud, and changed the history of the world from that time to this, could fool away the sceptre of universal dominion which Providence was forcing into his hand in one night's debauch, and quench power and glory and reason and life in the poisonous cup of wine and harlotry?

Can men coldly qualify their applause of the patriot hero of the American Revolution, who never drew his sword but in a righteous defensive war, and magnify the name of the great Roman Dictator who made the " bravo's trade " the merciless profession of his life, and trained his legions in the havoc of unoffending foreign countries for the " more than civil wars " in which he prostrated the liberties of his own?

Can they seriously disparage our incorruptible Washington, who would not burden the impoverished treasury of the Union by accepting even the frugal pay of his rank; whose entire expenditure charged to the public for the whole war was less than the cost of the stationery of Congress for a single year; whom all the gold of California and Australia could not have

bribed to a mean act, — can they seriously disparage
him in comparison with such a man as the hero of
Blenheim, the renowned English commander, the ablest
general, the most politic statesman, the most adroit
negotiator of the day, — of whom it has been truly
said that he never formed the plan of a campaign
which he failed to execute, never besieged a city which
he did not take, never fought a battle which he did
not gain, and who, alas! caused the muster-rolls of his
victorious army to be fraudently made out, and pock-
eted the pay which he drew in the names of men who
had fallen in his own sight four years before.

There is a splendid monumental pile in England,
the most magnificent perhaps of her hundred palaces,
founded in the time of Queen Anne at the public cost,
to perpetuate the fame of Marlborough. The grand
building, with its vast wings and spacious courts, cov-
ers seven acres and a half of land. It is approached
on its various sides by twelve gates or bridges, some
of them triumphal gates, in a circumference of thirteen
miles, enclosing the noble park of twenty-seven hun-
dred acres (Boston Common has forty-three), in which
the castle stands, surrounded by the choicest beauties
of forest and garden and fountain and lawn and
stream. All that gold could buy, or the bounty of
his own or foreign princes could bestow, or taste de-
vise, or art execute, or ostentation could lavish, to per-
fect and adorn the all but regal structure, without
and within, is there. Its saloons and its galleries, its
library and its museum, among the most spacious in
England for a private mansion, are filled with the
rarities and wonders of ancient and modern art. Elo-
quent inscriptions from the most gifted pens of the
age — the English by Lord Bolingbroke, the Latin, I

believe, by Bishop Hoadley — set forth on triumphal arches and columns the exploits of him to whom the whole edifice and the domains which surround it are one gorgeous monument. Lest human adulation should prove unequal to the task, Nature herself has been called in to record his achievements. They have been planted, rooted in the soil. Groves and coppices, curiously disposed, represent the position, the numbers, the martial array of the hostile squadrons at Blenheim. Thus, with each returning year, Spring hangs out his triumphant banners. May's Æolian lyre sings of his victories through her gorgeous foliage; and the shrill trump of November sounds " Malbrook " through her leafless branches.

Twice in my life I have visited the magnificent residence, — not as a guest; once when its stately porticos afforded a grateful shelter from the noonday sun, and again, after thirty years' interval, when the light of a full harvest moon slept sweetly on the bank once shaded by fair Rosamond's bower, — so says tradition, — and poured its streaming bars of silver through the branches of oaks which were growing before Columbus discovered America. But to me, at noontide or in the evening, the gorgeous pile was as dreary as death, its luxurious grounds as melancholy as a churchyard. It seemed to me, not a splendid palace, but a dismal mausoleum, in which a great and blighted name lies embalmed like some old Egyptian tyrant, black and ghastly in the asphaltic contempt of ages, serving but to rescue from an enviable oblivion the career and character of the magnificent peculator and miser and traitor to whom it is dedicated; needy in the midst of his ill-gotten millions; mean at the head of his victorious armies: despicable under the shadow of his thick-woven laurels ; and poor and miserable and blind and naked amidst the lying shams of his tinsel greatness. The eloquent inscriptions in Latin and English as I strove to read them seemed to fade from arch and column, and three dreadful words of palimpsestic infamy came out in their stead, like those which caused the knees of the Chaldean tyrant to smite together, as he beheld them traced by no mortal fingers on the vaulted canopy which spread like a sky over his accursed revels ; and those dreadful words were, —

Avarice, Plunder, Eternal Shame !

There is a modest private mansion on the bank of the Potomac, the abode of George Washington and Martha his beloved, his loving, faithful wife. It boasts no spacious portal nor gorgeous colonnade, nor massy elevation, nor storied tower. The porter's lodge at Blenheim Castle, nay, the marble dog-kennels, were not built for the entire cost of Mount Vernon. No arch nor column, in courtly English or courtlier Latin, sets forth the deeds and the worth of the Father of his Country ; he needs them not ; the unwritten benedictions of millions cover all the walls. No gilded dome swells from the lowly roof to catch the morning or evening beam ; but the love and gratitude of united America settle upon it in one eternal sunshine. From beneath that humble roof went forth the intrepid and unselfish warrior, — the magistrate who knew no glory but his country's good ; to that he returned happiest when his work was done. There he lived in noble simplicity ; there he died in glory and peace. While it stands the latest generations of the grateful children of America will make their pilgrimage to it as to a shrine ; and when it shall fall, if fall it must, the memory and the name of Washington shall shed an eternal glory on the spot.

Yes, my friends, it is the pure morality of Washington's character in which its peculiar excellence resides; and it is this which establishes its intimate relations with general humanity. On this basis he ceases to be the hero of America, and becomes the hero of mankind. I have seen it lately maintained by a respectable foreign writer, that he could not have led the mighty host which Napoleon marched into Russia in 1812; not so much one army as thirteen armies, each led by its veteran chief, some of them by tributary kings, and all conducted to their destination across continental Europe without confusion and without mutual interference, by the master mind, the greatest military array the world has ever seen. That Washington, who never proved unequal to any task, however novel or arduous, *could* not have led that gigantic army into Russia I am slow to believe. I see not why he who did great things with small means is to be supposed to be incompetent to do great things with large means. That he *would* not, if it depended on him, have plunged France and Europe into that dreadful war, I readily grant. But allowing what cannot be shown, that he was not as a strategist equal to the task in question, I do not know that his military reputation is more impeached by this gratuitous assumption, that he could not have got that mighty host into Russia, than Napoleon's by the historical fact that he could not and did not get it out of Russia.

At any rate, whatever idle comparisons between Napoleon and Washington, unfavorable to the military genius of the latter, may be instituted, Washington himself, modest as he was, deriving conscious strength from the pure patriotism which formed the great motive of his conduct, did not fear to place himself in a position which he must have thought would, in all human probability, bring him into collision with the youthful conqueror of Italy, fresh from the triumphs of his first, and, all things considered, his most brilliant campaigns. The United States, I need not remind you, were on the verge of a war with France in 1798. The command of the armies of the Union was pressed by President Adams on Washington, and he consented to take command in the event of an invasion. In a very remarkable letter written in July, 1798, he mentions the practice " adopted by the French (with whom we are now to contend), and with great and astonishing success, to appoint generals of juvenile years to command their armies."[1] He had every reason at that time to suppose, and no doubt did suppose, that in the event of a French invasion, the armies of France would have been commanded by the youngest and most successful of those youthful generals.

A recent judicious French writer (M. Edouard Laboulaye), though greatly admiring the character of Washington, denies him the brilliant military genius of Julius Cæsar. For my own part, considering the disparity of the means at their command respectively and of their scale of operations, I believe that after times will, on the score of military capacity, assign as high a place to the patriot chieftain who founded the Republic of America, as to the ambitious usurper who overturned the liberties of Rome. Washington would not most certainly have carried an unprovoked and

[1] *Washington's Works*, vol. xi. p. 249.

desolating war into the provinces of Gallia, chopping off the right hands of whole populations guilty of no crime but that of defending their homes; he would not have thrown his legions into Britain as Cæsar did, though the barbarous natives had never heard of his name. Though, to meet the invaders of his country, he could push his way across the broad Delaware, through drifting masses of ice in a December night, he could not, I grant, in defiance of the laws of his country, have spurred his horse across the " little Rubicon" beneath the mild skies of an Ausonian winter.[1] It was not talent which he wanted for brilliant military achievement; he wanted a willingness to shed the blood of fellow-men for selfish ends; he wanted unchastened ambition; he wanted an ear deaf as the adder's to the cry of suffering humanity; he wanted a remorseless thirst for false glory; he wanted an iron heart.

But it is time, my friends, to draw these contemplations to a close. When the decease of this illustrious and beloved commander-in-chief, in 1799, was officially announced to the army of the United States by General Hamilton, who of all his honored and trusted associates stood highest, I think, in his affections and confidence, it was truly said by him in his general orders, that "the voice of praise would in vain endeavor to exalt a name unrivalled in the lists of true glory." It is for us, citizens of the country which he lived but to serve, children of parents who saw him face to face, enjoying ourselves the inestimable blessings which he did so much to secure and perpetuate, to reflect lustre upon his memory in the only way in which it is possible for us to do so, by showing

[1] Ut ventum est parvi Rubicontis ad undam. — Lucan, i. 185.

that his example and his counsels, instead of losing their influence by the lapse of years, are possessed of an ever-during vitality. Born into the family of nations in these latter days, inheriting from ancient times and from foreign countries the bright and instructive example of all their honored sons, it has been the privilege of America, in the first generation of her national existence, to give back to the world many names whose lustre will never fade, one of which the whole family of Christendom is willing to acknowledge the preëminence; a name of which neither Greece nor Rome, nor republican Italy, Switzerland nor Holland, nor constitutional England can boast the rival. "A character of virtues so happily tempered by one another" (I use the words of Charles James Fox), "and so wholly unalloyed with any vices as that of Washington, is hardly to be found on the pages of history."

HENRY WADSWORTH LONGFELLOW.

BIOGRAPHICAL SKETCH.

HENRY WADSWORTH LONGFELLOW was born in Portland, Maine, February 27, 1807. He was a classmate of Hawthorne at Bowdoin College, graduating there in the class of 1825. He began the study of law in the office of his father, Hon. Stephen Longfellow; but receiving shortly the appointment of professor of modern languages at Bowdoin, he devoted himself after that to literature, and to teaching in connection with literature. Before beginning his work at Bowdoin he increased his qualifications by travel and study in Europe, where he stayed three years. Upon his return he gave his lectures on modern languages and literature at the college, and wrote occasionally for the *North American Review* and other periodicals. The first volume which he published was an *Essay on the Moral and Devotional Poetry of Spain*, accompanied by translations from Spanish verse. This was issued in 1833, but has not been kept in print as a separate work. It appears as a chapter in *Outre-Mer*, a reflection of his European life and travel, the first of his prose writings. In 1835 he was invited to succeed Mr. George Ticknor as professor of modern languages and literature at Harvard College, and again went to Europe for preparatory study, giving especial attention to Switzerland and the Scandinavian countries. He held his professorship until 1854, but continued to live in Cambridge until his death, March 24, 1882, occupying a house known from a former occupant as the Craigie house, and also as Washington's headquarters, that general having so used it while organizing the army that held Boston in siege at the beginning of the Revolution. Everett, Sparks, and Worcester, the lexicographer, at one time or another lived in this house, and here Longfellow wrote most of his works.

In 1839 appeared *Hyperion, a Romance,* which, with more narrative form than *Outre-Mer,* like that gave the results of a poet's entrance into the riches of the Old World life. In the same year was published *Voices of the Night,* a little volume containing chiefly poems and translations which had been printed separately in periodicals. *The Psalm of Life,* perhaps the best known of Longfellow's short poems, was in this volume, and here too were *The Beleaguered City* and *Footsteps of Angels. Ballads and other Poems* and *Poems on Slavery* appeared in 1842; *The Spanish Student,* a play in three acts, in 1843; *The Belfry of Bruges and other Poems* in 1846; *Evangeline* in 1847; *Kavanagh, a Tale,* in prose, in 1849. Besides the various volumes comprising short poems, the list of Mr. Longfellow's works includes *The Golden Legend, The Song of Hiawatha, The Courtship of Miles Standish, Tales of a Wayside Inn, The New England Tragedies,* and a translation of Dante's *Divina Commedia.* Mr. Longfellow's literary life began in his college days, and he wrote poems almost to the day of his death. A classification of his poems and longer works would be an interesting task, and would help to disclose the wide range of his sympathy and taste; a collection of the metres which he has used would show the versatility of his art, and similar studies would lead one to discover the many countries and ages to which he went for subjects. It would not be difficult to gather from the volume of Longfellow's poems hints of personal experience, that biography of the heart which is of more worth to us than any record, however full, of external change and adventure. Such hints may be found, for example, in the early lines, *To the River Charles,* which may be compared with his recent *Three Friends of Mine*, IV., V. ; in *A Gleam of Sunshine, To a Child, The Day is Done, The Fire of Driftwood, Resignation, The Open Window, The Ladder of St. Augustine, My Lost Youth, The Children's Hour, Weariness,* and other poems ; not that we are to take all sentiments and statements made in the first person as the poet's, for often the form of the poem is so far dramatic that the poet is assuming a character not necessarily his own, but the recurrence of certain strains, joined with personal allusions, helps one to penetrate the slight veil with which the poet, here as elsewhere, half conceals and half reveals himself. The friendly associations of the poet may also be discovered in several poems directly addressed to persons or distinctively alluding to them, and the reader will find it pleasant to construct the companionship of the poet out of such poems as *The Herons of Elmwood, To William E. Channing, The Fiftieth Birthday of Agassiz, To Charles Sumner,* the *Prelude* to *Tales of a Wayside Inn, Hawthorne,* and other poems. An interesting study of Mr. Longfellow's writings will be found in a paper by W. D. Howells, in the *North American Review,* vol. civ.

EVANGELINE: A TALE OF ACADIE.

HISTORICAL INTRODUCTION.

[THE country now known as Nova Scotia, and called formerly Acadie by the French, was in the hands of the French and English by turns until the year 1713, when, by the Peace of Utrecht, it was ceded by France to Great Britain, and has ever since remained in the possession of the English. But in 1713 the inhabitants of the peninsula were mostly French farmers and fishermen, living about Minas Basin and on Annapolis River, and the English government exercised only a nominal control over them. It was not till 1749 that the English themselves began to make settlements in the country, and that year they laid the foundations of the town of Halifax. A jealousy soon sprang up between the English and French settlers, which was deepened by the great conflict which was impending between the two mother countries; for the treaty of peace at Aix-la-Chapelle in 1748, which confirmed the English title to Nova Scotia, was scarcely more than a truce between the two powers which had been struggling for ascendency during the beginning of the century. The French engaged in a long controversy with the English respecting the boundaries of Acadie, which had been defined by the treaties in somewhat general terms, and intrigues were carried on with the Indians, who were generally in sympathy with the French, for the annoyance of the English settlers. The Acadians were allied to the French by blood and by religion, but they claimed to have the rights of neutrals, and that these rights had been

Henry W. Longfellow

granted to them by previous English officers of the crown. The one point of special dispute was the oath of allegiance demanded of the Acadians by the English. This they refused to take, except in a form modified to excuse them from bearing arms against the French. The demand was repeatedly made, and evaded with constant ingenuity and persistency. Most of the Acadians were probably simple-minded and peaceful people, who desired only to live undisturbed upon their farms ; but there were some restless spirits, especially among the young men, who compromised the reputation of the community, and all were very much under the influence of their priests, some of whom made no secret of their bitter hostility to the English, and of their determination to use every means to be rid of them.

As the English interests grew and the critical relations between the two countries approached open warfare, the question of how to deal with the Acadian problem became the commanding one of the colony. There were some who coveted the rich farms of the Acadians ; there were some who were inspired by religious hatred ; but the prevailing spirit was one of fear for themselves from the near presence of a community which, calling itself neutral, might at any time offer a convenient ground for hostile attack. Yet to require these people to withdraw to Canada or Louisburg would be to strengthen the hands of the French, and make these neutrals determined enemies. The colony finally resolved, without consulting the home government, to remove the Acadians to other parts of North America, distributing them through the colonies in such a way as to preclude any concert amongst the scattered families by which they should return to Acadia. To do this required quick and secret preparations. There were at the service of the English governor a number of New England troops, brought thither for the capture of the forts lying in the debatable land about the head of the Bay of Fundy. These were under the command of Lieutenant-Colonel John Winslow, of Massachusetts, a great-grandson of Governor Edward Winslow, of Plymouth, and to this gentleman and Captain Alexander Murray was intrusted the task of removal. They were instructed to use stratagem, if possible, to bring together the various families, but to prevent any from escaping to the woods. On the 2d of September, 1755, Winslow issued a written order, addressed to the inhabitants of Grand-Pré, Minas, River Canard, etc., " as well ancient as young men and lads," — a proclamation summoning all the males to attend him in the church at Grand-Pré on the 5th instant, to hear a communication which the governor had sent. As there had been negotiations respecting the oath of allegiance, and much discussion as to the withdrawal of the Acadians from the country, though none as to their removal and dispersal, it was understood that this was an important meeting, and upon the day named four hundred and eighteen men and boys assembled in the church. Winslow, attended by his officers and men, caused a guard to be placed round the church, and then announced to the people his majesty's decision that they were to be removed with their families out of the country. The church became at once a guard-house, and all the prisoners were under strict surveillance. At the same time similar plans had been carried out at Pisiquid under Captain Murray, and less successfully at Chignecto. Meanwhile there were whispers of a rising among the prisoners, and although the transports which had been ordered from Boston had not yet arrived, it was determined to make use of the vessels which had conveyed the troops, and remove the men to these for safer keeping. This was done on the 10th of September, and the men remained on the vessels in the harbor until the arrival of the transports, when these were made use of, and about three thousand souls sent out of the country to North Carolina, Virginia, Maryland, Pennsylvania, New York, Connecticut, and Massachusetts. In the haste and confusion of sending them off, — a haste which was increased by the anxiety of the officers to be rid of the distasteful business, and a confusion which was greater from the difference of tongues, — many families were separated, and some at least never came together again.

The story of Evangeline is the story of such a separation. The removal of the Acadians was a blot upon the government of Nova Scotia and upon that of Great Britain, which never disowned the deed, although it was probably done without direct permission or command from England. It proved to be unnecessary, but it must also be remembered that to many men at that time the English power seemed trembling before France, and that the colony at Halifax regarded the act as one of self-preservation.

The authorities for an historical inquiry into this subject are best seen in a volume published by the government of Nova Scotia at Halifax in 1869, entitled *Selections from the Public Documents of the Province of Nova Scotia*, edited by Thomas B. Akins, D. C. L., Commissioner of Public Records ; and in a manuscript journal kept by Colonel Winslow, now in the cabinet of the Massachusetts Historical Society in Boston. At the State House in Boston are two volumes of records, entitled *French Neutrals*, which contain voluminous papers relating to the treatment of the Acadians who were sent to Massachusetts. Probably the work used by the poet in writing *Evangeline* was *An Historical and Statistical Account of Nova Scotia*, by Thomas C. Haliburton, who is best known as the author of *The Clock-Maker, or The Sayings and Doings of Samuel Slick of Slickville*, a book which, written apparently to prick the Nova Scotians into more enterprise, was for a long while the chief representative of Yankee smartness. Judge Haliburton's history was published in 1829. A later history, which takes advantage more freely of historical documents, is *A History of Nova Scotia, or Acadie*, by Beamish Murdock, Esq., Q. C., Halifax, 1866. Still more recent is a smaller, well-written work, entitled *The History of Acadia from its*

First Discovery to its Surrender to England by the Treaty of Paris, by James Hannay, St. John, N. B., 1879. W. J. Anderson published a paper in the *Transactions* of the Literary and Historical Society of Quebec, New Series, part 7, 1870, entitled *Evangeline and the Archives of Nova Scotia,* in which he examines the poem by the light of the volume of Nova Scotia *Archives,* edited by T. B. Akins. The sketches of travellers in Nova Scotia, as *Acadia, or a Month among the Blue Noses,* by F. S. Cozzens, and *Baddeck,* by C. D. Warner, give the present appearance of the country and inhabitants.

The measure of *Evangeline* is what is commonly known as English dactylic hexameter. The hexameter is the measure used by Homer in the *Iliad* and the *Odyssey,* and by Virgil in the *Æneid,* but the difference between the English language and the Latin or Greek is so great, especially when we consider that in English poetry every word must be accented according to its customary pronounciation, while in scanning Greek and Latin verse accent follows the quantity of the vowels, that in applying this term of hexameter to *Evangeline* it must not be supposed by the reader that he is getting the effect of Greek hexameters. It is the Greek hexameter translated into English use, and some have maintained that the verse of the *Iliad* is better represented in the English by the trochaic measure of fifteen syllables, of which an excellent illustration is in Tennyson's *Locksley Hall ;* others have compared the Greek hexameter to the ballad metre of fourteen syllables, used notably by Chapman in his translation of Homer's *Iliad.* The measure adopted by Mr. Longfellow has never become very popular in English poetry, but has repeatedly been attempted by other poets. The reader will find the subject of hexameters discussed by Matthew Arnold in his lectures *On Translating Homer ;* by James Spedding in *English . Hexameters,* in his recent volume, *Reviews and Discussions, Literary, Political and Historical, not relating to*

Bacon; and by John Stuart Blackie in *Remarks on English Hexameters,* contained in his volume *Horæ Hellenicæ.*

The measure lends itself easily to the lingering melancholy which marks the greater part of the poem, and the poet's fine sense of harmony between subject and form is rarely better shown than in this poem. The fall of the verse at the end of the line and the sharp recovery at the beginning of the next will be snares to the reader, who must beware of a jerking style of delivery. The voice naturally seeks a rest in the middle of the line, and this rest, or cæsural pause, should be carefully regarded; a little practice will enable one to acquire that habit of reading the hexameter, which we may liken, roughly, to the climbing of a hill, resting a moment on the summit, and then descending the other side. The charm in reading *Evangeline* aloud, after a clear understanding of the sense, which is the essential in all good reading, is found in this gentle labor of the former half of the line, and gentle acceleration of the latter half.]

THIS is the forest primeval. The murmuring pines
    and the hemlocks,
Bearded with moss, and in garments green, indistinct
    in the twilight,
Stand like Druids of eld, with voices sad and prophetic,

1. A primeval forest is, strictly speaking, one which has never been disturbed by the axe.

3. *Druids* were priests of the Celtic inhabitants of ancient Gaul and Britain. The name was probably of Celtic origin, but its form may have been determined by the Greek word *drûs,* an oak, since their places of worship were consecrated groves of oak. Perhaps the choice of the image was governed by the analogy of a religion and tribe that were to disappear before a stronger power.

Stand like harpers hoar, with beards that rest on their
   bosoms.
Loud from its rocky caverns, the deep-voiced neigh-
   boring ocean   5
Speaks, and in accents disconsolate answers the wail
   of the forest.

   This is the forest primeval; but where are the
      hearts that beneath it
Leaped like the roe, when he hears in the woodland
   the voice of the huntsman?
Where is the thatch-roofed village, the home of Aca-
   dian farmers, —
Men whose lives glided on like rivers that water the
   woodlands,   10
Darkened by shadows of earth, but reflecting an image
   of heaven?
Waste are those pleasant farms, and the farmers for-
   ever departed!
Scattered like dust and leaves, when the mighty blasts
   of October
Seize them, and whirl them aloft, and sprinkle them
   far o'er the ocean.
Naught but tradition remains of the beautiful village
   of Grand-Pré.   15

   Ye who believe in affection that hopes, and endures,
      and is patient,

4. A poetical description of an ancient harper will be found
in the *Introduction* to the *Lay of the Last Minstrel,* by Sir Walter
Scott.

8. Observe how the tragedy of the story is anticipated by this
picture of the startled roe.

Ye who believe in the beauty and strength of woman's
    devotion,
List to the mournful tradition still sung by the pines
    of the forest ;
List to a Tale of Love in Acadie, home of the happy.

PART THE FIRST.

I.

In the Acadian land, on the shores of the Basin of
    Minas,   ²⁰
Distant, secluded, still, the little village of Grand-Pré
Lay in the fruitful valley. Vast meadows stretched
    to the eastward,
Giving the village its name, and pasture to flocks
    without number.
Dikes, that the hands of the farmers had raised with
    labor incessant,

19. In the earliest records *Acadie* is called Cadie ; it after-
wards was called Arcadia, Accadia, or L'Acadie. The name is
probably a French adaptation of a word common among the
Micmac Indians living there, signifying place or region, and used
as an affix to other words as indicating the place where various
things, as cranberries, eels, seals, were found in abundance. The
French turned this Indian term into Cadie or Acadie ; the Eng-
lish into Quoddy, in which form it remains when applied to the
Quoddy Indians, to Quoddy Head, the last point of the United
States next to Acadia, and in the compound Passamaquoddy, or
Pollock-Ground.

21. Compare, for effect, the first line of Goldsmith's *The
Traveller*. Grand-Pré will be found on the map as part of the
township of Horton.

24. The people of Acadia are mainly the descendants of the
colonists who were brought out to La Have and Port Royal by
Isaac de Razilly and Charnisay between the years 1633 and 1638.

Shut out the turbulent tides; but at stated seasons the
flood-gates   25
Opened and welcomed the sea to wander at will o'er
the meadows.
West and south there were fields of flax, and orchards
and cornfields
Spreading afar and unfenced o'er the plain; and away
to the northward
Blomidon rose, and the forests old, and aloft on the
mountains
Sea-fogs pitched their tents, and mists from the mighty
Atlantic   30
Looked on the happy valley, but ne'er from their sta-
tion descended.
There, in the midst of its farms, reposed the Acadian
village.
Strongly built were the houses, with frames of oak and
of hemlock,
Such as the peasants of Normandy built in the reign
of the Henries.

These colonists came from Rochelle, Saintonge, and Poitou, so
that they were drawn from a very limited area on the west coast
of France, covered by the modern departments of Vendée and
Charente Inférieure. This circumstance had some influence on
their mode of settling the lands of Acadia, for they came from a
country of marshes, where the sea was kept out by artificial
dikes, and they found in Acadia similar marshes, which they dealt
with in the same way that they had been accustomed to practise
in France. Hannay's *History of Acadia*, pp. 282, 283. An excel-
lent account of dikes and the flooding of lowlands, as practised
in Holland, may be found in *A Farmer's Vacation*, by George E.
Waring, Jr.

29. *Blomidon* is a mountainous headland of red sandstone, sur-
mounted by a perpendicular wall of basaltic trap, the whole about
four hundred feet in height, at the entrance of the Basin of
Minas.

Thatched were the roofs, with dormer-windows; and
    gables projecting   35
Over the basement below protected and shaded the
    doorway.
There in the tranquil evenings of summer, when
    brightly the sunset
Lighted the village street, and gilded the vanes on the
    chimneys,
Matrons and maidens sat in snow-white caps and·in
    kirtles
Scarlet and blue and green, with distaffs spinning the
    golden   40
Flax for the gossiping looms, whose noisy shuttles
    within doors
Mingled their sound with the whir of the wheels and
    the songs of the maidens.
Solemnly down the street came the parish priest, and
    the children
Paused in their play to kiss the hand he extended to
    bless them.
Reverend walked he among them; and up rose ma-
    trons and maidens,   45
Hailing his slow approach with words of affectionate
    welcome.
Then came the laborers home from the field, and se-
    renely the sun sank

36. The characteristics of a Normandy village may be further
learned by reference to a pleasant little sketch-book, published
a few years since, called *Normandy Picturesque,* by Henry Black-
burn, and to *Through Normandy,* by Katharine S. Macquoid.

39. The term *kirtle* was sometimes applied to the jacket only,
sometimes to the train or upper petticoat attached to it. A full
kirtle was always both; a half kirtle was a term applied to
either. A man's jacket was sometimes called a kirtle; here the
reference is apparently to the full kirtle worn by women.

Down to his rest, and twilight prevailed.   Anon from
the belfry
Softly the Angelus sounded, and over the roofs of the
village
Columns of pale blue smoke, like clouds of incense
ascending,   50
Rose from a hundred hearths, the homes of peace and
contentment.
Thus dwelt together in love these simple Acadian
farmers, —
Dwelt in the love of God and of man.   Alike were
they free from
Fear, that reigns with the tyrant, and envy, the vice
of republics.
Neither locks had they to their doors, nor bars to their
windows ;   55
But their dwellings were open as day and the hearts
of the owners ;
There the richest was poor, and the poorest lived in
abundance.

Somewhat apart from the village, and nearer the
Basin of Minas,
Benedict Bellefontaine, the wealthiest farmer of
Grand-Pré,
Dwelt on his goodly acres; and with him, directing
his household,   60
Gentle Evangeline lived, his child, and the pride of
the village.

49. *Angelus Domini* is the full name given to the bell which, at
morning, noon, and night, called the people to prayer, in com-
memoration of the visit of the angel of the Lord to the Virgin
Mary.   It was introduced into France in its modern form in the
sixteenth century.

Stalworth and stately in form was the man of seventy
    winters ;

Hearty and hale was he, an oak that is covered with
    snow-flakes ;

White as the snow were his locks, and his cheeks as
    brown as the oak-leaves.

Fair was she to behold, that maiden of seventeen sum-
    mers ;   65

Black were her eyes as the berry that grows on the
    thorn by the wayside,

Black, yet how softly they gleamed beneath the brown
    shade of her tresses !

Sweet was her breath as the breath of kine that feed
    in the meadows.

When in the harvest heat she bore to the reapers at
    noontide

Flagons of home-brewed ale, ah ! fair in sooth was the
    maiden.   70

Fairer was she when, on Sunday morn, while the bell
    from its turret

Sprinkled with holy sounds the air, as the priest with
    his hyssop

Sprinkles the congregation, and scatters blessings upon
    them,

Down the long street she passed, with her chaplet of
    beads and her missal,

Wearing her Norman cap and her kirtle of blue, and
    the ear-rings   75

Brought in the olden time from France, and since, as
    an heirloom,

Handed down from mother to child, through long gen-
    erations.

But a celestial brightness — a more ethereal beauty —

Shone on her face and encircled her form, when, after
    confession,

Homeward serenely she walked with God's benediction upon her. 80

When she had passed, it seemed like the ceasing of exquisite music.

Firmly builded with rafters of oak, the house of the farmer

Stood on the side of a hill commanding the sea; and a shady

Sycamore grew by the door, with a woodbine wreathing around it.

Rudely carved was the porch, with seats beneath; and a footpath 85

Led through an orchard wide, and disappeared in the meadow.

Under the sycamore-tree were hives overhung by a penthouse,

Such as the traveller sees in regions remote by the roadside,

Built o'er a box for the poor, or the blessed image of Mary.

Farther down, on the slope of the hill, was the well with its moss-grown 90

Bucket, fastened with iron, and near it a trough for the horses.

Shielding the house from storms, on the north, were the barns and the farm-yard;

There stood the broad-wheeled wains and the antique ploughs and the harrows;

There were the folds for the sheep; and there, in his feathered seraglio,

93. The accent is on the first syllable of *antique,* where it remains in the form *antic,* which once had the same general meaning.

Strutted the lordly turkey, and crowed the cock, with
    the selfsame   95
Voice that in ages of old had startled the penitent
    Peter.
Bursting with hay were the barns, themselves a vil-
    lage. In each one
Far o'er the gable projected a roof of thatch ; and a
    staircase,
Under the sheltering eaves, led up to the odorous corn-
    loft.
There too the dove-cot stood, with its meek and inno-
    cent inmates   100
Murmuring ever of love; while above in the variant
    breezes
Numberless noisy weathercocks rattled and sang of
    mutation.

Thus, at peace with God and the world, the farmer
    of Grand-Pré
Lived on his sunny farm, and Evangeline governed
    his household.
Many a youth, as he knelt in the church and opened
    his missal,   105
Fixed his eyes upon her as the saint of his deepest
    devotion ;

99. *Odorous.* The accent here, as well as in line 403, is upon
the first syllable, where it is commonly placed ; but Milton, who
of all poets had the most refined ear, writes

> " So from the root
> Springs lighter the green stalk, from thence the leaves
> More airy, last the bright consummate flower
> Spirits odorous breathes."
> *Par. Lost*, Book V., lines 479–482.

But he also uses the more familiar accent in other passages,
as, " An amber scent of ódorous perfume," in *Samson Agonistes*,
line 720.

Happy was he who might touch her hand or the hem
of her garment!

Many a suitor came to her door, by the darkness be-
friended,

And, as he knocked and waited to hear the sound of
her footsteps,

Knew not which beat the louder, his heart or the
knocker of iron;   110

Or, at the joyous feast of the Patron Saint of the vil-
lage,

Bolder grew, and pressed her hand in the dance as he
whispered

Hurried words of love, that seemed a part of the
music.

But among all who came young Gabriel only was
welcome;

Gabriel Lajeunesse, the son of Basil the black-
smith,   115

Who was a mighty man in the village, and honored
of all men;

For since the birth of time, throughout all ages and
nations,

Has the craft of the smith been held in repute by the
people.

Basil was Benedict's friend. Their children from
earliest childhood

Grew up together as brother and sister; and Father
Felician,   120

Priest and pedagogue both in the village, had taught
them their letters

Out of the selfsame book, with the hymns of the
church and the plain-song.

122. The *plain-song* is a monotonic recitative of the collects.

But when the hymn was sung, and the daily lesson
    completed,
Swiftly they hurried away to the forge of Basil the
    blacksmith.
There at the door they stood, with wondering eyes to
    behold him   125
Take in his leathern lap the hoof of the horse as a
    plaything,
Nailing the shoe in its place ; while near him the tire
    of the cart-wheel
Lay like a fiery snake, coiled round in a circle of
    cinders.
Oft on autumnal eves, when without in the gathering
    darkness
Bursting with light seemed the smithy, through every
    cranny and crevice,   130
Warm by the forge within they watched the laboring
    bellows,
And as its panting ceased, and the sparks expired in
    the ashes,
Merrily laughed, and said they were nuns going into
    the chapel.
Oft on sledges in winter, as swift as the swoop of the
    eagle,
Down the hillside bounding, they glided away o'er the
    meadow.   135
Oft in the barns they climbed to the populous nests
    on the rafters,
Seeking with eager eyes that wondrous stone, which
    the swallow
Brings from the shore of the sea to restore the sight
    of its fledglings ;

133. The French have another saying similar to this, that they
were guests going into the wedding.

Lucky was he who found that stone in the nest of the
　　swallow !

Thus passed a few swift years, and they no longer
　.　were children.　　　　　　　　'　　　　　140

He was a valiant youth, and his face, like the face of
　　the morning,

Gladdened the earth with its light, and ripened
　　thought into action.

She was a woman now, with the heart and hopes of a
　　woman.

" Sunshine of Saint Eulalie " was she called ; for that
　　was the sunshine

Which, as the farmers believed, would load their
　　orchards with apples ;　　　　　　　　　145

She too would bring to her husband's house delight
　　and abundance,

Filling it full of love and the ruddy faces of children.

II.

Now had the season returned, when the nights grow
　　colder and longer,

And the retreating sun the sign of the Scorpion en-
　　ters.

139. In Pluquet's *Contes Populaires* we are told that if one of
a swallow's young is blind the mother bird seeks on the shore of
the ocean a little stone, with which she restores its sight ; and
he adds, " He who is fortunate enough to find that stone in a
swallow's nest holds a wonderful remedy." Pluquet's book
treats of Norman superstitions and popular traits.

144. Pluquet also gives this proverbial saying : —

> " Si le soleil rit le jour Sainte-Eulalie,
> Il y aura pommes et cidre à folie."

(If the sun smiles on Saint Eulalie's day, there will be plenty
of apples, and cider enough.)

Saint Eulalie's day is the 12th of February.

Birds of passage sailed through the leaden air, from
    the ice-bound,   150
Desolate northern 'bays to the shores of tropical is-
    lands.
Harvests were gathered in ; and wild with the winds
    of September .
Wrestled the trees of the forest, as Jacob of old with
    the angel.
All the signs foretold a winter long and inclement.
Bees, with prophetic instinct of want, had hoarded
    their honey   155
Till the hives overflowed; and the Indian hunters as-
    serted
Cold would the winter be, for thick was the fur of the
    foxes.
Such was the advent of autumn. Then followed that
    beautiful season,
Called by the pious Acadian peasants the Summer of
    All-Saints !
Filled was the air with a dreamy and magical light ;
    and the landscape   160
Lay as if new-created in all the freshness of child-
    hood.
Peace seemed to reign upon earth, and the restless
    heart of the ocean
Was for a moment consoled. All sounds were in
    harmony blended.
Voices of children at play, the crowing of cocks in the
    farm-yards,

159. The Summer of All-Saints is our Indian Summer, All-
Saints Day being November 1st. The French also give this sea-
son the name of Saint Martin's Summer, Saint Martin's Day
being November 11th.

Whir of wings in the drowsy air, and the cooing of
    pigeons,   165
All were subdued and low as thê murmurs of love,
    and the great sun
Looked with the eye of love through the golden va-
    pors around him;
While arrayed in its robes of russet and scarlet and
    yellow,
Bright with the sheen of the dew, each glittering tree
    of the forest
Flashed like the plane-tree the Persian adorned with
    mantles and jewels.   170

Now recommenced the region of rest and affection
    and stillness.
Day with its burden and heat had departed, and twi-
    light descending
Brought back the evening star to the sky, and the
    herds to the homestead.
Pawing the ground they came, and resting their necks
    on each other,
And with their nostrils distended inhaling the fresh-
    ness of evening.   175
Foremost, bearing the bell, Evangeline's beautiful
    heifer,
Proud of her snow-white hide, and the ribbon that
    waved from her collar,
Quietly paced and slow, as if conscious of human
    affection.

170. Herodotus, in his account of Xerxes' expedition against
Greece, tells of a beautiful plane-tree which Xerxes found, and
was so enamored with that he dressed it as one might a woman,
and placed it under the care of a guardsman (vii. 31). Another
writer, Ælian, improving on this, says he adorned it with a neck-
lace and bracelets.

Then came the shepherd back with his bleating flocks
    from the seaside,
Where was their favorite pasture. Behind them fol-
    lowed the watch-dog,   180
Patient, full of importance, and grand in the pride of
    his instinct,
Walking from side to side with a lordly air, and
    superbly
Waving his bushy tail, and urging forward the strag-
    glers;
Regent of flocks was he when the shepherd slept;
    their protector,
When from the forest at night, through the starry
    silence, the wolves howled.   185
Late, with the rising moon, returned the wains from
    the marshes,
Laden with briny hay, that filled the air with its odor.
Cheerily neighed the steeds, with dew on their manes
    and their fetlocks,
While aloft on their shoulders the wooden and pon-
    derous saddles,
Painted with brilliant dyes, and adorned with tassels
    of crimson,   190
Nodded in bright array, like hollyhocks heavy with
    blossoms.
Patiently stood the cows meanwhile, and yielded their
    udders
Unto the milkmaid's hand; whilst loud and in regular
    cadence

---

193. There is a charming milkmaid's song in Tennyson's drama
of *Queen Mary*, Act III., Scene 5, where the streaming of the
milk into the sounding pails is caught in the tinkling *k*'s of such
lines as

    "And you came and kissed me, milking the cow."

Into the sounding pails the foaming streamlets descended.

Lowing of cattle and peals of laughter were heard in the farm-yard, 195

Echoed back by the barns. Anon they sank into stillness ;

Heavily closed, with a jarring sound, the valves of the barn-doors,

Rattled the wooden bars, and all for a season was silent.

In-doors, warm by the wide-mouthed fireplace, idly the farmer

Sat in his elbow-chair, and watched how the flames and the smoke-wreaths 200

Struggled together like foes in a burning city. Behind him,

Nodding and mocking along the wall with gestures fantastic,

Darted his own huge shadow, and vanished away into darkness.

Faces, clumsily carved in oak, on the back of his arm-chair

Laughed in the flickering light, and the pewter plates on the dresser 205

Caught and reflected the flame, as shields of armies the sunshine.

Fragments of song the old man sang, and carols of Christmas,

Such as at home, in the olden time, his fathers before him

Sang in their Norman orchards and bright Burgundian vineyards.

Close at her father's side was the gentle Evangeline seated, 210

Spinning flax for the loom that stood in the corner
    behind her.
Silent awhile were its treadles, at rest was its diligent
    shuttle,
While the monotonous drone of the wheel, like the
    drone of a bagpipe,
Followed the old man's song, and united the fragments
    together.
As in a church, when the chant of the choir at inter-
    vals ceases,   215
Footfalls are heard in the aisles, or words of the priest
    at the altar,
So, in each pause of the song, with measured motion
    the clock clicked.

   Thus as they sat, there were footsteps heard, and,
    suddenly lifted,
Sounded the wooden latch, and the door swung back
    on its hinges.
Benedict knew by the hob-nailed shoes it was Basil
    the blacksmith,   220
And by her beating heart Evangeline knew who was
    with him.
" Welcome ! " the farmer exclaimed, as their footsteps
    paused on the threshold,
" Welcome, Basil, my friend ! Come, take thy place
    on the settle
Close by the chimney-side, which is always empty
    without thee ;
Take from the shelf overhead thy pipe and the box of
    tobacco ;   225
Never so much thyself art thou as when, through the
    curling
Smoke of the pipe or the forge, thy friendly and jovial
    face gleams

Round and red as the harvest moon through the mist
  of the marshes."
Then, with a smile of content, thus answered Basil the
  blacksmith,
Taking with easy air the accustomed seat by the fire-
  side : —   230
" Benedict Bellefontaine, thou hast ever thy jest and
  thy ballad !
Ever in cheerfullest mood art thou, when others are
  filled with
Gloomy forebodings of ill, and see only ruin before
  them.
Happy art thou, as if every day thou hadst picked up
  a horseshoe."
Pausing a moment, to take the pipe that Evangeline
  brought him,   235
And with a coal from the embers had lighted, he
  slowly continued : —
" Four days now are passed since the English ships
  at their anchors
Ride in the Gaspereau's mouth, with their cannon
  pointed against us.
What their design may be is unknown ; but all are
  commanded
On the morrow to meet in the church, where his
  Majesty's mandate   240
Will be proclaimed as law in the land.   Alas ! in the
  mean time
Many surmises of evil alarm the hearts of the peo-
  ple."
Then made answer the farmer : — " Perhaps some
  friendlier purpose

239. The text of Colonel Winslow's proclamation will be found
in *Haliburton,* i. 175.

Brings these ships to our shores. Perhaps the har-
    vests in England
By untimely rains or untimelier heat have been
    blighted,   245
And from our bursting barns they would feed their
    cattle and children."
"Not so thinketh the folk in the village," said warmly
    the blacksmith,
Shaking his head as in doubt; then, heaving a sigh,
    he continued : —
" Louisburg is not forgotten, nor Beau Séjour, nor
    Port Royal.
Many already have fled to the forest, and lurk on its
    outskirts,   250
Waiting with anxious hearts the dubious fate of to-
    morrow.
Arms have been taken from us, and warlike weapons
    of all kinds;
Nothing is left but the blacksmith's sledge and the
    scythe of the mower."
Then with a pleasant smile made answer the jovial
    farmer : —

249. Louisburg, on Cape Breton, was built by the French as a
military and naval station early in the eighteenth century, but
was taken by an expedition from Massachusetts under General
Pepperell in 1745. It was restored by England to France in the
treaty of Aix-la-Chapelle, and recaptured by the English in
1757. Beau Séjour was a French fort upon the neck of land
connecting Acadia with the mainland which had just been cap-
tured by Winslow's forces. Port Royal, afterwards called Anna-
polis Royal, at the outlet of Annapolis River into the Bay of
Fundy, had been disputed ground, being occupied alternately by
French and English, but in 1710 was attacked by an expedition
from New England, and after that held by the English govern-
ment and made a fortified place.

" Safer are we unarmed, in the midst of our flocks
    and our cornfields,   255
Safer within these peaceful dikes besieged by the ocean,
Than our fathers in forts, besieged by the enemy's
    cannon.
Fear no evil, my friend, and to-night may no shadow
    of sorrow
Fall on this house and hearth; for this is the night
    of the contract.
Built are the house and the barn.   The merry lads of
    the village   260
Strongly have built them and well; and, breaking the
    glebe round about them,
Filled the barn with hay, and the house with food for
    a twelvemonth.
René Leblanc will be here anon, with his papers and
    inkhorn.
Shall we not then be glad, and rejoice in the joy of
    our children ? "
As apart by the window she stood, with her hand in
    her lover's,   265
Blushing Evangeline heard the words that her father
    had spoken,
And, as they died on his lips, the worthy notary en-
    tered.

III.

Bent like a laboring oar, that toils in the surf of
    the ocean,

267. A *notary* is an officer authorized to attest contracts or
writings of any kind. His authority varies in different coun-
tries; in France he is the necessary maker of all contracts where
the subject-matter exceeds 150 francs, and his instruments,
which are preserved and registered by himself, are the origi-
nals, the parties preserving only copies.

Bent, but not broken, by age was the form of the no-
    tary public ;

Shocks of yellow hair, like the silken floss of the
    maize, hung   270

Over his shoulders; his forehead was high; and
    glasses with horn bows

Sat astride on his nose, with a look of wisdom supernal.

Father of twenty children was he, and more than a
    hundred

Children's children rode on his knee, and heard his
    great watch tick.

Four long years in the times of the war had he lan-
    guished a captive,   275

Suffering much in an old French fort as the friend of
    the English.

Now, though warier grown, without all guile or sus-
    picion,

Ripe in wisdom was he, but patient, and simple, and
    childlike.

He was beloved by all, and most of all by the chil-
    dren ;

For he told them tales of the Loup-garou in the for-
    est,   280

275. King George's War, which broke out in 1744 in Cape
Breton, in an attack by the French upon an English garrison,
and closed with the peace of Aix-la-Chapelle in 1748 ; or, the
reference may possibly be to Queen Anne's war, 1702-1713,
when the French aided the Indians in their warfare with the col-
onists.

280. The *Loup-garou*, or were-wolf, is, according to an old su-
perstition especially prevalent in France, a man with power to
turn himself into a wolf, which he does that he may devour chil-
dren. In later times the superstition passed into the more inno-
cent one of men having a power to charm wolves.

And of the goblin that came in the night to water the
    horses,'

And of the white Létiche, the ghost of a child who
    unchristened

Died, and was doomed to haunt unseen the chambers
    of children;

And how on Christmas eve the oxen talked in the
    stable,

And how the fever was cured by a spider shut up in
    a nutshell,   285

And of the marvellous powers of four-leaved clover
    and horseshoes,

With whatsoever else was writ in the lore of the village.

Then up rose from his seat by the fireside Basil the
    blacksmith,

Knocked from his pipe the ashes, and slowly extend-
    ing his right hand,

"Father Leblanc," he exclaimed, "thou hast heard
    the talk in the village,   290

And, perchance, canst tell us some news of these ships
    and their errand."

Then with modest demeanor made answer the notary
    public, —

"Gossip enough have I heard, in sooth, yet am never
    the wiser;

282. Pluquet relates this superstition, and conjectures that the
white, fleet ermine gave rise to it.

284. A belief still lingers among the peasantry of England, as
well as on the Continent, that at midnight, on Christmas eve, the
cattle in the stalls fall down on their knees in adoration of the
infant Saviour, as the old legend says was done in the stable at
Bethlehem.

285. In like manner a popular superstition prevailed in Eng-
land that ague could be cured by sealing a spider in a goose-
quill and hanging it about the neck.

And what their errand may be I know no better than
    others.
Yet am I not of those who imagine some evil inten-
    tion   295
Brings them here, for we are at peace; and why then
    molest us ? "
"God's name !" shouted the hasty and somewhat iras-
    cible blacksmith ;
" Must we in all things look for the how, and the why,
    and the wherefore ?
Daily injustice is done, and might is the right of the
    strongest ! "
But, without heeding his warmth, continued the notary
    public, —   300
" Man is unjust, but God is just ; and finally justice
Triumphs ; and well I remember a story, that often
    consoled me,
When as a captive I lay in the old French fort at
    Port Royal."
This was the old man's favorite tale, and he loved to
    repeat it
When his neighbors complained that any injustice was
    done them.   305
" Once in an ancient city, whose name I no longer re-
    member,
Raised aloft on a column, a brazen statue of Justice
Stood in the public square, upholding the scales in its
    left hand,
And in its right a sword, as an emblem that justice
    presided
Over the laws of the land, and the hearts and homes
    of the people.   310

302. This is an old Florentine story ; in an altered form it is
the theme of Rossini's opera of *La Gazza Ladra.*

Even the birds had built their nests in the scales of
    the balance,
Having no fear of the sword that flashed in the sun-
    shine above them.
But in the course of time the laws of the land were
    corrupted;
Might took the place of right, and the weak were
    oppressed, and the mighty
Ruled with an iron rod.   Then it chanced in a noble-
    man's palace   315
That a necklace of pearls was lost, and ere long a sus-
    picion
Fell on an orphan girl who lived as maid in the house-
    hold.
She, after form of trial condemned to die on the scaf-
    fold,
Patiently met her doom at the foot of the statue of
    Justice.
As to her Father in heaven her innocent spirit as-
    cended,   320
Lo! o'er the city a tempest rose; and the bolts of the
    thunder
Smote the statue of bronze, and hurled in wrath from
  · its left hand
Down on the pavement below the clattering scales of
    the balance,
And in the hollow thereof was found the nest of a
    magpie,
Into whose clay-built walls the necklace of pearls was
    inwoven."   325
Silenced, but not convinced, when the story was ended,
    the blacksmith
Stood like a man who fain would speak, but findeth
    no language;

All his thoughts were congealed into lines on his face, as the vapors
Freeze in fantastic shapes on the window-panes in the winter.

   Then Evangeline lighted the brazen lamp on the table,   330
Filled, till it overflowed, the pewter tankard with home-brewed
Nut-brown ale, that was famed for its strength in the village of Grand-Pré;
While from his pocket the notary drew his papers and inkhorn,
Wrote with a steady hand the date and the age of the parties,
Naming the dower of the bride in flocks of sheep and in cattle.   335
Orderly all things proceeded, and duly and well were completed,
And the great seal of the law was set like a sun on the margin.
Then from his leathern pouch the farmer threw on the table
Three times the old man's fee in solid pieces of silver;
And the notary rising, and blessing the bride and bridegroom,   340
Lifted aloft the tankard of ale and drank to their welfare.
Wiping the foam from his lip, he solemnly bowed and departed,
While in silence the others sat and mused by the fireside,

Till Evangeline brought the draught-board out of its
    corner.
Soon was the game begun. In friendly contention
    the old men   . 345
Laughed at each lucky hit, or unsuccessful manœuvre,
Laughed when a man was crowned, or a breach was
    made in the king-row.
Meanwhile apart, in the twilight gloom of a window's
    embrasure,
Sat the lovers and whispered together, beholding the
    moon rise
Over the pallid sea and the silvery mist of the mead-
    ows.   350
Silently one by one, in the infinite meadows of heaven,
Blossomed the lovely stars, the forget-me-nots of the
    angels.

    Thus was the evening passed. Anon the bell from
    the belfry
Rang out the hour of nine, the village curfew, and
    straightway
Rose the guests and departed ; and silence reigned in
    the household.   355

344. The word *draughts* is derived from the circumstance of
drawing the men from one square to another.

354. *Curfew* is a corruption of *couvre-feu,* or cover fire. In
the Middle Ages, when police patrol at night was almost un-
known, it was attempted to lessen the chances of crime by mak-
ing it an offence against the laws to be found in the streets in
the night, and the curfew bell was tolled, at various hours, ac-
cording to the custom of the place, from seven to nine o'clock in
the evening. It warned honest people to lock their doors, cover
their fires, and go to bed. The custom still lingers in many
places, even in America, of ringing a bell at nine o'clock in the
evening.

Many a farewell word and sweet good-night on the
    door-step
Lingered long in Evangeline's heart, and filled it with
    gladness.
Carefully then were covered the embers that glowed
    on the hearth-stone,
And on the oaken stairs resounded the tread of the
    farmer.
Soon with a soundless step the foot of Evangeline fol-
    lowed.   360
Up the staircase moved a luminous space in the dark-
    ness,
Lighted less by the lamp than the shining face of the
    maiden.
Silent she passed through the hall, and entered the
    door of her chamber.
Simple that chamber was, with its curtains of white,
    and its clothes-press
Ample and high, on whose spacious shelves were care-
    fully folded   365
Linen and woollen stuffs, by the hand of Evangeline
    woven.
This was the precious dower she would bring to her
    husband in marriage,
Better than flocks and herds, being proofs of her skill
    as a housewife.
Soon she extinguished her lamp, for the mellow and
    radiant moonlight
Streamed through the windows, and lighted the room,
    till the heart of the maiden   370
Swelled and obeyed its power, like the tremulous tides
    of the ocean.
Ah! she was fair, exceeding fair to behold, as she
    stood with

Naked snow-white feet on the gleaming floor of her
    chamber !

Little she dreamed that below, among the trees of the
    orchard,

Waited her lover and watched for the gleam of her
    lamp and her shadow.   375

Yet were her thoughts of him, and at times a feeling
    of sadness

Passed o'er her soul, as the sailing shade of clouds in
    the moonlight

Flitted across the floor and darkened the room for a
    moment.

And, as she gazed from the window, she saw serenely
    the moon pass

Forth from the folds of a cloud, and one star follow
    her footsteps,   380

As out of Abraham's tent young Ishmael wandered
    with Hagar.

IV.

Pleasantly rose next morn the sun on the village
    of Grand-Pré.

Pleasantly gleamed in the soft, sweet air the Basin of
    Minas,

Where the ships, with their wavering shadows, were
    riding at anchor.

Life had long been astir in the village, and clamorous
    labor   385

Knocked with its hundred hands at the golden gates
    of the morning.

Now from the country around, from the farms and
    neighboring hamlets,

Came in their holiday dresses the blithe Acadian
    peasants.

Many a glad good-morrow and jocund laugh from the
    young folk
Made the bright air brighter, as up from the numer-
    ous meadows,   390
Where no path could be seen but the track of wheels
    in the greensward,
Group after group appeared, and joined, or passed on
    the highway.
Long ere noon, in the village all sounds of labor were
    silenced.
Thronged were the streets with people; and noisy
    groups at the house-doors
Sat in the cheerful sun, and rejoiced and gossiped to-
    gether.   395
Every house was an inn, where all were welcomed and
    feasted ;
For with this simple people, who lived like brothers
    together,
All things were held in common, and what one had
    was another's.
Yet under Benedict's roof hospitality seemed more
    abundant:

396. " Real misery was wholly unknown, and benevolence
anticipated the demands of poverty.   Every misfortune was re-
lieved as it were before it could be felt, without ostentation on
the one hand, and without meanness-on the other.   It was, in
short, a society of brethren, every individual of which was
equally ready to give and to receive what he thought the com-
mon right of mankind." — From the Abbé Raynal's account of
the Acadians.   The Abbé Guillaume Thomas Francis Raynal
was a French writer (1711–1796), who published *A Philosophi-
cal History of the Settlements and Trade of the Europeans in the
East and West Indies,* in which he included also some account of
Canada and Nova Scotia.   His picture of life among the Aca-
dians, somewhat highly colored, is the source from which after
writers have drawn their knowledge of Acadian manners.

For Evangeline stood among the guests of her
    father;   400
Bright was her face with smiles, and words of wel-
    come and gladness
Fell from her beautiful lips, and blessed the cup as
    she gave it.

Under the open sky, in the odorous air of the
    orchard,
Stript of its golden fruit, was spread the feast of be-
    trothal.
There in the shade of the porch were the priest and
    the notary seated;   405
There good Benedict sat, and sturdy Basil the black-
    smith.
Not far withdrawn from these, by the cider-press and
    the beehives,
Michael the fiddler was placed, with the gayest of
    hearts and of waistcoats.
Shadow and light from the leaves alternately played
    on his snow-white
Hair, as it waved in the wind; and the jolly face of
    the fiddler   410
Glowed like a living coal when the ashes are blown
    from the embers.
Gayly the old man sang to the vibrant sound of his
    fiddle,
Tous les Bourgeois de Chartres, and *Le Carillon de
    Dunkerque*,

---

413. *Tous les Bourgeois de Chartres* was a song written by
Ducauroi, *maître de chapelle* of Henri IV., the words of which
are : —

> Vous connaissez Cybèle,
> Qui sut fixer le Temps ;
> On la disait fort belle,
> Même dans ses vieux ans.

And anon with his wooden shoes beat time to the
  music.
Merrily, merrily whirled the wheels of the dizzying
  dances   415
Under the orchard-trees and down the path to the
  meadows;
Old folk and young together, and children mingled
  among them.
Fairest of all the maids was Evangeline, Benedict's
  daughter!
Noblest of all the youths was Gabriel, son of the
  blacksmith!

So passed the morning away. And lo! with a sum-
  mons sonorous   420
Sounded the bell from its tower, and over the mead-
  ows a drum beat.
Thronged ere long was the church with men. With-
  out, in the churchyard,

CHORUS.

Cette divinité, quoique déjà grand' mere
  Avait les yeux doux, le teint frais,
  Avait même certains attraits
  Fermes comme la Terre.

Le Carillon de Dunkerque was a popular song to a tune played
on the Dunkirk chimes. The words are : —

Imprudent, téméraire
A l'instant, je l'espère
Dans mon juste courroux,
Tu vas tomber sous mes coups!
  — Je brave ta menace.
  — Etre moi! quelle audace!
  Avance donc, poltron!
  Tu trembles? non, non, non.
  — J'étouffe de colère !
  — Je ris de ta colère.

The music to which the old man sang these songs will be found
in *La Clé du Caveau*, by Pierre Capelle, Nos. 564 and 739.
Paris : A. Cotelle.

Waited the women. They stood by the graves, and
　　hung on the headstones
Garlands of autumn-leaves and evergreens fresh from
　　the forest.
Then came the guard from the ships, and marching
　　proudly among them　　　　　　　　　　　　425
Entered the sacred portal. With loud and dissonant
　　clangor
Echoed the sound of their brazen drums from ceiling
　　and casement, —
Echoed a moment only, and slowly the ponderous por-
　　tal
Closed, and in silence the crowd awaited the will of
　　the soldiers.
Then uprose their commander, and spake from the
　　steps of the altar,　　　　　　　　　　　　430
Holding aloft in his hands, with its seals, the royal
　　commission.
" You are convened this day," he said, " by his Maj-
　　esty's orders.
Clement and kind has he been ; but how you have
　　answered his kindness
Let your own hearts reply ! To my natural make and
　　my temper
Painful the task is I do, which to you I know must
　　be grievous.　　　　　　　　　　　　　　　435
Yet must I bow and obey, and deliver the will of our
　　monarch :
Namely, that all your lands, and dwellings, and cattle
　　of all kinds
Forfeited be to the crown ; and that you yourselves
　　from this province

432. Colonel Winslow has preserved in his Diary the speech
which he delivered to the assembled Acadians, and it is copied
by Haliburton in his *History of Nova Scotia,* i. 166, 167.

Be transported to other lands.   God grant you may
  dwell there
Ever as faithful subjects, a happy and peaceable peo-
  ple !   440
Prisoners now I declare you, for such is his Majesty's
  pleasure ! "
As, when the air is serene in the sultry solstice of
  summer,
Suddenly gathers a storm, and the deadly sling of the
  hailstones
Beats down the farmer's corn in the field, and shatters
  his windows,
Hiding the sun, and strewing the ground with thatch
  from the house-roofs,   445
Bellowing fly the herds, and seek to break their en-
  closures ;
So on the hearts of the people descended the words of
  the speaker.
Silent a moment they stood in speechless wonder, and
  then rose
Louder and ever louder a wail of sorrow and anger,
And, by one impulse moved, they madly rushed to the
  door-way.   450
Vain was the hope of escape; and cries and fierce
  imprecations
Rang through the house of prayer ; and high o'er the
  heads of the others
Rose, with his arms uplifted, the figure of Basil the
  blacksmith,
As, on a stormy sea, a spar is tossed by the billows.
Flushed was his face and distorted with passion ; and
  wildly he shouted, —   455
" Down with the tyrants of England ! we never have
  sworn them allegiance !

Death to these foreign soldiers, who seize on our
    homes and our harvests!"
More he fain would have said, but the merciless hand
    of a soldier
Smote him upon the mouth, and dragged him down to
    the pavement.

In the midst of the strife and tumult of angry con-
    tention,   460
Lo! the door of the chancel opened, and Father Feli-
    cian
Entered, with serious mien, and ascended the steps of
    the altar.
Raising his reverend hand, with a gesture he awed
    into silence
All that clamorous throng; and thus he spake to his
    people;
Deep were his tones and solemn; in accents measured
    and mournful   465
Spake he, as, after the tocsin's alarum, distinctly the
    clock strikes.
"What is this that ye do, my children? what madness
    has seized you?
Forty years of my life have I labored among you, and
    taught you,
Not in word alone, but in deed, to love one another!
Is this the fruit of my toils, of my vigils and prayers
    and privations?   470
Have you so soon forgotten all lessons of love and
    forgiveness?
This is the house of the Prince of Peace, and would
    you profane it
Thus with violent deeds and hearts overflowing with
    hatred?

Lo! where the crucified Christ from His cross is gaz-
    ing upon you!

See! in those sorrowful eyes what meekness and holy
    compassion! 475

Hark! how those lips still repeat the prayer, 'O
    Father, forgive them!'

Let us repeat that prayer in the hour when the wicked
    assail us,

Let us repeat it now, and say, 'O Father, forgive
    them!'"

Few were his words of rebuke, but deep in the hearts
    of his people

Sank they, and sobs of contrition succeeded the pas-
    sionate outbreak, 480

While they repeated his prayer, and said, "O Father,
    forgive them!"

Then came the evening service. The tapers gleamed
    from the altar;

Fervent and deep was the voice of the priest, and the
    people responded,

Not with their lips alone, but their hearts; and the
    Ave Maria

Sang they, and fell on their knees, and their souls,
    with devotion translated, 485

Rose on the ardor of prayer, like Elijah ascending to
    heaven.

Meanwhile had spread in the village the tidings of
    ill, and on all sides

Wandered, wailing, from house to house the women
    and children.

Long at her father's door Evangeline stood, with her
    right hand

Shielding her eyes from the level rays of the sun,
    that, descending,   490
Lighted the village street with mysterious splendor,
    and roofed each
Peasant's cottage with golden thatch, and emblazoned
    its windows.
Long within had been spread the snow-white cloth on
    the table;
There stood the wheaten loaf, and the honey fragrant
    with wild flowers;
There stood the tankard of ale, and the cheese fresh
    brought from the dairy;   495
And at the head of the board the great arm-chair of
    the farmer.
Thus did Evangeline wait at her father's door, as the
    sunset
Threw the long shadows of trees o'er the broad am-
    brosial meadows.
Ah! on her spirit within a deeper shadow had fallen,
And from the fields of her soul a fragrance celestial
    ascended, —   500
Charity, meekness, love, and hope, and forgiveness,
    and patience!
Then, all forgetful of self, she wandered into the vil-
    lage,
Cheering with looks and words the mournful hearts of
    the women,
As o'er the darkening fields with lingering steps they
    departed,
Urged by their household cares, and the weary feet of
    their children.   505

492. To emblazon is literally to adorn anything with ensigns
armorial. It was often the custom to work these ensigns into
the design of painted windows.

Down sank the great red sun, and in golden, glimmer-
ing vapors
Veiled the light of his face, like the Prophet descend-
ing from Sinai.
Sweetly over the village the bell of the Angelus
sounded.

Meanwhile, amid the gloom, by the church Evange-
line lingered.
All was silent within; and in vain at the door and the
windows   510
Stood she, and listened and looked, until, overcome by
emotion,
"Gabriel!" cried she aloud with tremulous voice;
but no answer
Came from the graves of the dead, nor the gloomier
grave of the living.
Slowly at length she returned to the tenantless house
of her father.
Smouldered the fire on the hearth, on the board was
the supper untasted.   515
Empty and drear was each room, and haunted with
phantoms of terror.
Sadly echoed her step on the stair and the floor of her
chamber.
In the dead of the night she heard the disconsolate
rain fall
Loud on the withered leaves of the sycamore-tree by
the window.
Keenly the lightning flashed; and the voice of the
echoing thunder   520
Told her that God was in heaven, and governed the
world He created!

Then she remembered the tale she had heard of the
    justice of Heaven;
Soothed was her troubled soul, and she peacefully
    slumbered till morning.

V.

Four times the sun had risen and set; and now on
    the fifth day
Cheerily called the cock to the sleeping maids of the
    farm-house.   525
Soon o'er the yellow fields, in silent and mournful pro-
    cession,
Came from the neighboring hamlets and farms the
    Acadian women,
Driving in ponderous wains their household goods to
    the sea-shore,
Pausing and looking back to gaze once more on their
    dwellings,
Ere they were shut from sight by the winding road and
    the woodland.   530
Close at their sides their children ran, and urged on
    the oxen,
While in their little hands they clasped some frag-
    ments of playthings.

Thus to the Gaspereau's mouth they hurried; and
    there on the sea-beach
Piled in confusion lay the household goods of the
    peasants.
All day long between the shore and the ships did the
    boats ply;   535
All day long the wains came laboring down from the
    village.
Late in the afternoon, when the sun was near to his
    setting,

Echoed far o'er the fields came the roll of drums from
    the churchyard.
Thither the women and children thronged. On a sud-
    den the church-doors
Opened, and forth came the guard, and marching in
    gloomy procession   540
Followed the long-imprisoned, but patient, Acadian
    farmers.
Even as pilgrims, who journey afar from their homes
    and their country,
Sing as they go, and in singing forget they are weary
    and wayworn,
So with songs on their lips the Acadian peasants de-
    scended
Down from the church to the shore, amid their wives
    and their daughters.   545
Foremost the young men came; and, raising together
    their voices,
Sang with tremulous lips a chant of the Catholic
    Missions: —
"Sacred heart of the Saviour! O inexhaustible foun-
    tain!
Fill our hearts this day with strength and submission
    and patience!"
Then the old men, as they marched, and the women
    that stood by the wayside   550
Joined in the sacred psalm, and the birds in the sun-
    shine above them
Mingled their notes therewith, like voices of spirits
    departed.

    Half-way down to the shore Evangeline waited in
    silence,
Not overcome with grief, but strong in the hour of
    affliction, —

Calmly and sadly she waited, until the procession ap-
    proached her,   555
And she beheld the face of Gabriel pale with emotion.
Tears then filled her eyes, and, eagerly running to
    meet him,
Clasped she his hands, and laid her head on his
    shoulder, and whispered, —
"Gabriel! be of good cheer! for if we love one
    another
Nothing, in truth, can harm us, whatever mischances
    may happen!"   560
Smiling she spake these words; then suddenly paused,
    for her father
Saw she, slowly advancing. Alas! how changed was
    his aspect!
Gone was the glow from his cheek, and the fire from
    his eye, and his footstep
Heavier seemed with the weight of the heavy heart
    in his bosom.
But with a smile and a sigh, she clasped his neck and
    embraced him,   565
Speaking words of endearment where words of com-
    fort availed not.
Thus to the Gaspereau's mouth moved on that mourn-
    ful procession.

    There disorder prevailed, and the tumult and stir of
        embarking.
Busily plied the freighted boats; and in the confusion
Wives were torn from their husbands, and mothers,
    too late, saw their children   570
Left on the land, extending their arms, with wildest
    entreaties.
So unto separate ships were Basil and Gabriel carried,

While in despair on the shore Evangeline stood with
    her father.

Half the task was not done when the sun went down,
    and the twilight

Deepened and darkened around; and in haste the
    refluent ocean   575

Fled away from the shore, and left the line of the
    sand-beach

Covered with waifs of the tide, with kelp and the slip-
    pery sea-weed.

Farther back in the midst of the household goods and
    the wagons,

Like to a gypsy camp, or a leaguer after a battle,

All escape cut off by the sea, and the sentinels near
    them,   580

Lay encamped for the night the houseless Acadian
    farmers.

Back to its nethermost caves retreated the bellowing
    ocean,

Dragging adown the beach the rattling pebbles, and
    leaving

Inland and far up the shore the stranded boats of the
    sailors.

Then, as the night descended, the herds returned from
    their pastures;   585

Sweet was the moist still air with the odor of milk
    from their udders;

Lowing they waited, and long, at the well-known bars
    of the farm-yard, —

Waited and looked in vain for the voice and the hand
    of the milkmaid.

Silence reigned in the streets; from the church no
    Angelus sounded,

Rose no smoke from the roofs, and gleamed no lights
    from the windows.   590

But on the shores meanwhile the evening fires had
    been kindled,
Built of the drift-wood thrown on the sands from
    wrecks in the tempest.
Round them shapes of gloom and sorrowful faces were
    gathered,
Voices of women were heard, and of men, and the
    crying of children.
Onward from fire to fire, as from hearth to hearth in
    his parish,   595
Wandered the faithful priest, consoling and blessing
    and cheering,
Like unto shipwrecked Paul on Melita's desolate sea-
    shore.
Thus he approached the place where Evangeline sat
    with her father,
And in the flickering light beheld the face of the old
    man,
Haggard and hollow and wan, and without either
    thought or emotion,   600
E'en as the face of a clock from which the hands have
    been taken.
Vainly Evangeline strove with words and caresses to
    cheer him,
Vainly offered him food ; yet he moved not, he looked
    not, he spake not,
But, with a vacant stare, ever gazed at the flickering
    fire-light.
" *Benedicite !* " murmured the priest, in tones of com-
    passion.   605
More he fain would have said, but his heart was full,
    and his accents
Faltered and paused on his lips, as the feet of a child
    on a threshold,

Hushed by the scene he beholds, and the awful presence of sorrow.

Silently, therefore, he laid his hand on the head of the maiden,

Raising his tearful eyes to the silent stars that above them   610

Moved on their way, unperturbed by the wrongs and sorrows of mortals.

Then sat he down at her side, and they wept together in silence.

Suddenly rose from the south a light, as in autumn the blood-red

Moon climbs the crystal walls of heaven, and o'er the horizon

Titan-like stretches its hundred hands upon mountain and meadow,   615

Seizing the rocks and the rivers, and piling huge shadows together.

Broader and ever broader it gleamed on the roofs of the village,

Gleamed on the sky and the sea, and the ships that lay in the roadstead.

Columns of shining smoke uprose, and flashes of flame were

Thrust through their folds and withdrawn, like the quivering hands of a martyr.   620

---

615. The Titans were giant deities in Greek mythology who attempted to deprive Saturn of the sovereignty of heaven, and were driven down into Tartarus by Jupiter, the son of Saturn, who hurled thunderbolts at them. Briareus, the hundred-handed giant, was in mythology of the same parentage as the Titans, but was not classed with them.

Then as the wind seized the gleeds and the burning
    thatch, and, uplifting,
Whirled them aloft through the air, at once from a
    hundred house-tops
Started the sheeted smoke with flashes of flame inter-
    mingled.

These things beheld in dismay the crowd on the
    shore and on shipboard.
Speechless at first they stood, then cried aloud in their
    anguish,   625
" We shall behold no more our homes in the village of
    Grand-Pré ! "
Loud on a sudden the cocks began to crow in the farm-
    yards,
Thinking the day had dawned ; and anon the lowing
    of cattle
Came on the evening breeze, by the barking of dogs
    interrupted.
Then rose a sound of dread, such as startles the sleep-
    ing encampments   630
Far in the western prairies of forests that skirt the
    Nebraska,
When the wild horses affrighted sweep by with the
    speed of the whirlwind,

    621. *Gleeds.* Hot, burning coals ; a Chaucerian word : —
        " And wafres piping hoot out of the gleede."
                             Canterbury Tales, l. 3379.
    The burning of the houses was in accordance with the instruc-
tions of the Governor to Colonel Winslow, in case he should fail
in collecting all the inhabitants : "You must proceed by the most
vigorous measures possible, not only in compelling them to em-
bark, but in depriving those who shall escape of all means of
shelter or support, by burning their houses and by destroying
everything that may afford them the means of subsistence in the
country."

Or the loud bellowing herds of buffaloes rush to the
  river.
Such was the sound that arose on the night, as the
  herds and the horses
Broke through their folds and fences, and madly
  rushed o'er the meadows.   635

  Overwhelmed with the sight, yet speechless, the
    priest and the maiden
Gazed on the scene of terror that reddened and
  widened before them ;
And as they turned at length to speak to their silent
  companion,
Lo ! from his seat he had fallen, and stretched abroad
  on the seashore
Motionless lay his form, from which the soul had de-
  parted.   640
Slowly the priest uplifted the lifeless head, and the
  maiden
Knelt at her father's side, and wailed aloud in her
  terror.
Then in a swoon she sank, and lay with her head on
  his bosom.
Through the long night she lay in deep, oblivious
  slumber ;
And when she woke from the trance, she beheld a
  multitude near her.   645
Faces of friends she beheld, that were mournfully gaz-
  ing upon her,
Pallid, with tearful eyes, and looks of saddest com-
  passion.
Still the blaze of the burning village illumined the
  landscape,

Reddened the sky overhead, and gleamed on the faces
    around her,

And like the day of doom it seemed to her wavering
    senses.   650

Then a familiar voice she heard, as it said to the peo-
    ple, —

"Let us bury him here by the sea. When a happier
    season

Brings us again to our homes from the unknown land
    of our exile,

Then shall his sacred dust be piously laid in the
    churchyard."

Such were the words of the priest. And there in
    haste by the sea-side,   655

Having the glare of the burning village for funeral
    torches,

But without bell or book, they buried the farmer of
    Grand-Pré.

And as the voice of the priest repeated the service of
    sorrow,

Lo! with a mournful sound like the voice of a vast
    congregation,

Solemnly answered the sea, and mingled its roar with
    the dirges.   660

'T was the returning tide, that afar from the waste of
    the ocean,

With the first dawn of the day, came heaving and hur-
    rying landward.

Then recommenced once more the stir and noise of
    embarking;

657. The bell was tolled to mark the passage of the soul into
the other world; the book was the service book. The phrase
"bell, book, or candle" was used in referring to excommunica-
tion.

And with the ebb of the tide the ships sailed out of
 the harbor,
Leaving behind them the dead on the shore, and the
 village in ruins. 665

PART THE SECOND.

I.

MANY a weary year had passed since the burning of
 Grand-Pré,
When on the falling tide the freighted vessels de-
 parted,
Bearing a nation, with all its household gods, into
 exile,
Exile without an end, and without an example in
 story.
Far asunder, on separate coasts, the Acadians
 landed; 670
Scattered were they, like flakes of snow, when the
 wind from the northeast
Strikes aslant through the fogs that darken the Banks
 of Newfoundland.
Friendless, homeless, hopeless, they wandered from
 city to city,
From the cold lakes of the North to sultry Southern
 savannas, —
From the bleak shores of the sea to the lands where
 the Father of Waters 675
Seizes the hills in his hands, and drags them down to
 the ocean,
Deep in their sands to bury the scattered bones of the
 mammoth.

677. Bones of the mastodon, or mammoth, have been found

Friends they sought and homes; and many, despairing,
　　heart-broken,
Asked of the earth but a grave, and no longer a friend
　　nor a fireside.
Written their history stands on tablets of stone in the
　　churchyards.　　　　　　　　　　　　　　680
Long among them was seen a maiden who waited and
　　wandered,
Lowly and meek in spirit, and patiently suffering all
　　things.
Fair was she and young; but, alas! before her ex-
　　tended,
Dreary and vast and silent, the desert of life, with its
　　pathway
Marked by the graves of those who had sorrowed and
　　suffered before her,　　　　　　　　　　　685
Passions long extinguished, and hopes long dead and
　　abandoned,
As the emigrant's way o'er the Western desert is
　　marked by
Camp-fires long consumed, and bones that bleach in
　　the sunshine.
Something there was in her life incomplete, imperfect,
　　unfinished;
As if a morning of June, with all its music and sun-
　　shine,　　　　　　　　　　　　　　690
Suddenly paused in the sky, and, fading, slowly de-
　　scended
Into the east again, from whence it late had arisen.
Sometimes she lingered in towns, till, urged by the
　　fever within her,

scattered all over the territory of the United States and Canada,
but the greatest number have been collected in the Salt Licks of
Kentucky, and in the States of Ohio, Mississippi, Missouri, and
Alabama.

Urged by a restless longing, the hunger and thirst of
    the spirit,

She would commence again her endless search and en-
    deavor;   695

Sometimes in churchyards strayed, and gazed on the
    crosses and tombstones,

Sat by some nameless grave, and thought that perhaps
    in its bosom

He was already at rest, and she longed to slumber be-
    side him.

Sometimes a rumor, a hearsay, an inarticulate whis-
    per,

Came with its airy hand to point and beckon her for-
    ward.   700

Sometimes she spake with those who had seen her be-
    loved and known him,

But it was long ago, in some far-off place or forgot-
    ten.

" Gabriel Lajeunesse ! " they said ; " Oh, yes ! we have
    seen him.

He was with Basil the blacksmith, and both have gone
    to the prairies ;

Coureurs-des-bois are they, and famous hunters and
    trappers."   705

699. Observe the diminution in this line, by which one is led
to the *airy hand* in the next.

705. The *coureurs-des-bois* formed a class of men, very early in
Canadian history, produced by the exigencies of the fur-trade.
They were French by birth, but by long affiliation with the In-
dians and adoption of their customs had become half-civilized
vagrants, whose chief vocation was conducting the canoes of the
traders along the lakes and rivers of the interior. *Bushrangers*
is the English equivalent. They played an important part in the
Indian wars, but were nearly as lawless as the Indians them-
selves. The reader will find them frequently referred to in

" Gabriel Lajeunesse ! ", said others ; " Oh, yes ! we
    have seen him.
He is a voyageur in the lowlands of Louisiana."
Then would they say, " Dear child ! why dream and
    wait for him longer ?
Are there not other youths as fair as Gabriel ? others
Who have hearts as tender and true, and spirits as
    loyal ?   710
Here is Baptiste Leblanc, the notary's son, who has
    loved thee
Many a tedious year ; come, give him thy hand and be
    happy !
Thou art too fair to be left to braid St. Catherine's
    tresses."
Then would Evangeline answer, serenely but sadly,
    " I cannot !
Whither my heart has gone, there follows my hand,
    and not elsewhere.   715
For when the heart goes before, like a lamp, and
    illumines the pathway,
Many things are made clear, that else lie hidden in
    darkness."
Thereupon the priest, her friend and father confessor,
Said, with a smile, " O daughter ! thy God thus
    speaketh within thee !
Talk not of wasted affection, affection never was
    wasted ;   720

Parkman's histories, especially in *The Conspiracy of Pontiac,
The Discovery of the Great West,* and *Frontenac and New France
under Louis XIV.*

   707. A *voyageur* is a river boatman, and is a term applied
usually to Canadians.

   713. St. Catherine of Alexandria and St. Catherine of Siena
were both celebrated for their vows of virginity. Hence the say-
ing *to braid St. Catherine's tresses,* of one devoted to a single life.

If it enrich not the heart of another, its waters, re-
　　turning
Back to their springs, like the rain, shall fill them full
　　of refreshment ;
That which the fountain sends forth returns again to
　　the fountain.
Patience ; accomplish thy labor ; accomplish thy work
　　of affection !
Sorrow and silence are strong, and patient endurance
　　is godlike.　　　　　　　　　　　　　　　　　725
Therefore accomplish thy labor of love, till the heart
　　is made godlike,
Purified, strengthened, perfected, and rendered more
　　worthy of heaven ! "
Cheered by the good man's words, Evangeline labored
　　and waited.
Still in her heart she heard the funeral dirge of the
　　ocean,
But with its sound there was mingled a voice that
　　whispered, " Despair not ! "　　　　　　　　730
Thus did that poor soul wander in want and cheer-
　　less discomfort,
Bleeding, barefooted, over the shards and thorns of
　　existence.
Let me essay, O Muse ! to follow the wanderer's foot-
　　steps ; —
Not through each devious path, each changeful year
　　of existence ;
But as a traveller follows a streamlet's course through
　　the valley :　　　　　　　　　　　　　　735
Far from its margin at times, and seeing the gleam of
　　its water
Here and there, in some open space, and at intervals
　　only ;

Then drawing nearer its banks, through sylvan glooms
    that conceal it,
Though he behold it not, he can hear its continuous
    murmur;
Happy, at length, if he find a spot where it reaches
    an outlet.   740

II.

It was the month of May.   Far down the Beautiful
    River,
Past the Ohio shore and past the mouth of the Wa-
    bash,
Into the golden stream of the broad and swift Mis-
    sissippi,
Floated a cumbrous boat, that was rowed by Acadian
    boatmen.
It was a band of exiles: a raft, as it were, from the
    shipwrecked   745
Nation, scattered along the coast, now floating to-
    gether,
Bound by the bonds of a common belief and a com-
    mon misfortune;
Men and women and children, who, guided by hope
    or by hearsay,
Sought for their kith and their kin among the few-
    acred farmers
On the Acadian coast, and the prairies of fair Ope-
    lousas.   750

741. The Iroquois gave to this river the name of Ohio, or the
Beautiful River, and La Salle, who was the first European to
discover it, preserved the name, so that it was transferred to
maps very early.

750. Between the 1st of January and the 13th of May, 1765,
about six hundred and fifty Acadians had arrived at New Or-

With them Evangeline went, and her guide, the
    Father Felician.
Onward o'er sunken sands, through a wilderness
    sombre with forests,
Day after day they glided adown the turbulent river;
Night after night, by their blazing fires, encamped on
    its borders.
Now through rushing chutes, among green islands,
    where plumelike   755
Cotton-trees nodded their shadowy crests, they swept
    with the current,
Then emerged into broad lagoons, where silvery sand-
    bars
Lay in the stream, and along the wimpling waves of
    their margin,
Shining with snow-white plumes, large flocks of pel-
    icans waded.
Level the landscape grew, and along the shores of the
    river,   760
Shaded by china-trees, in the midst of luxuriant gar-
    dens,
Stood the houses of planters, with negro cabins and
    dove-cots.
They were approaching the region where reigns per-
    petual summer,

leans. Louisiana had been ceded by France to Spain in 1762, but did not really pass under the control of the Spanish until 1769. The existence of a French population attracted the wandering Acadians, and they were sent by the authorities to form settlements in Attakapas and Opelousas. They afterward formed settlements on both sides of the Mississippi from the German Coast up to Baton Rouge, and even as high as Pointe Coupée. Hence the name of Acadian Coast, which a portion of the banks of the river still bears. See Gayarré's *History of Louisiana: The French Dominion,* vol. ii.

Where through the Golden Coast, and groves of
orange and citron,
Sweeps with majestic curve the river away to the east-
ward.   765
They, too, swerved from their course; and, entering
the Bayou of Plaquemine,
Soon were lost in a maze of sluggish and devious
waters,
Which, like a network of steel, extended in every
direction.
Over their heads the towering and tenebrous boughs
of the cypress
Met in a dusky arch, and trailing mosses in mid-
air   770
Waved like banners that hang on the walls of ancient
cathedrals.
Deathlike the silence seemed, and unbroken, save by
the herons
Home to their roosts in the cedar-trees returning at
sunset,
Or by the owl, as he greeted the moon with demoniac
laughter.
Lovely the moonlight was as it glanced and gleamed
on the water,   775
Gleamed on the columns of cypress and cedar sustain-
ing the arches,
Down through whose broken vaults it fell as through
chinks in a ruin.
Dreamlike, and indistinct, and strange were all things
around them;
And o'er their spirits there came a feeling of wonder
and sadness, —
Strange forebodings of ill, unseen and that cannot be
compassed.   780

As, at the tramp of a horse's hoof on the turf of the
    prairies,
Far in advance are closed the leaves of the shrinking
    mimosa,
So, at the hoof-beats of fate, with sad forebodings of
    evil,
Shrinks and closes the heart, ere the stroke of doom
    has attained it.
But Evangeline's heart was sustained by a vision, that
    faintly   785
Floated before her eyes, and beckoned her on through
    the moonlight.
It was the thought of her brain that assumed the
    shape of a phantom.
Through those shadowy aisles had Gabriel wandered
    before her,
And every stroke of the oar now brought him nearer
    and nearer.

   Then in his place, at the prow of the boat, rose one
    of the oarsmen,   790
And, as a signal sound, if others like them peradven-
    ture
Sailed on those gloomy and midnight streams, blew a
    blast on his bugle.
Wild through the dark colonnades and corridors leafy
    the blast rang,
Breaking the seal of silence and giving tongues to the
    forest.
Soundless above them the banners of moss just stirred
    to the music.   795
Multitudinous echoes awoke and died in the distance,
Over the watery floor, and beneath the reverberant
    branches;

But not a voice replied ; no answer came from the
    darkness ;
And when the echoes had ceased, like a sense of pain
    was the silence.
Then Evangeline slept ; but the boatmen rowed
    through the midnight,   800
Silent at times, then singing familiar Canadian boat-
    songs,
Such as they sang of old on their own Acadian rivers,
While through the night were heard the mysterious
    sounds of the desert,
Far off, — indistinct, — as of wave or wind in the
    forest,
Mixed with the whoop of the crane and the roar of
    the grim alligator.   805

    Thus ere another noon they emerged from the
    shades ; and before them
Lay, in the golden sun, the lakes of the Atchafalaya.
Water-lilies in myriads rocked on the slight undula-
    tions
Made by the passing oars, and, resplendent in beauty,
    the lotus
Lifted her golden crown above the heads of the boat-
    men.   810
Faint was the air with the odorous breath of magno-
    lia blossoms,
And with the heat of noon ; and numberless sylvan
    islands,
Fragrant and thickly embowered with blossoming
    hedges of roses,
Near to whose shores they glided along, invited to
    slumber.
Soon by the fairest of these their weary oars were sus-
    pended.   815

Under the boughs of Wachita willows, that grew by
    the margin,
Safely their boat was moored; and scattered about on
    the greensward,
Tired with their midnight toil, the weary travellers
    slumbered.
Over them vast and high extended the cope of a
    cedar.
Swinging from its great arms, the trumpet-flower and
    the grapevine   820
Hung their ladder of ropes aloft like the ladder of
    Jacob,
On whose pendulous stairs the angels ascending, de-
    scending,
Were the swift humming-birds, that flitted from blos-
    som to blossom.
Such was the vision Evangeline saw as she slumbered
    beneath it.
Filled was her heart with love, and the dawn of an
    opening heaven   825
Lighted her soul in sleep with the glory of regions
    celestial.

  Nearer, ever nearer, among the numberless islands,
Darted a light, swift boat, that sped away o'er the
    water,
Urged on its course by the sinewy arms of hunters
    and trappers.
Northward its prow was turned, to the land of the
    bison and beaver.   830
At the helm sat a youth, with countenance thoughtful
    and careworn.
Dark and neglected locks overshadowed his brow, and
    a sadness

Somewhat beyond his years on his face was legibly
     written.

Gabriel was it, who, weary with waiting, unhappy and
     restless,

Sought in the Western wilds oblivion of self and of
     sorrow.   835

Swiftly they glided along, close under the lee of the
     island,

But by the opposite bank, and behind a screen of pal-
     mettos ;

So that they saw not the boat, where it lay concealed
     in the willows ;

All undisturbed by the dash of their oars, and unseen,
     were the sleepers ;

Angel of God was there none to awaken the slumber-
     ing maiden.   840

Swiftly they glided away, like the shade of a cloud on
     the prairie.

After the sound of their oars on the tholes had died
     in the distance,

As from a magic trance the sleepers awoke, and the
     maiden

Said with a sigh to the friendly priest, "O Father
     Felician !

Something says in my heart that near me Gabriel
     wanders.   845

Is it a foolish dream, an idle and vague superstition ?

Or has an angel passed, and revealed the truth to my
     spirit ? "

Then, with a blush, she added, "Alas for my credu-
     lous fancy !

Unto ears like thine such words as these have no
     meaning."

But made answer the reverend man, and he smiled as
     he answered, —   850

" Daughter, thy words are not idle; nor are they to
  me without meaning,
Feeling is deep and still; and the word that floats on
  the surface
Is as the tossing buoy, that betrays where the anchor
  is hidden.
Therefore trust to thy heart, and to what the world
  calls illusions.
Gabriel truly is near thee; for not far away to the
  southward,   855
On the banks of the Têche, are the towns of St. Maur
  and St. Martin.
There the long-wandering bride shall be given again
  to her bridegroom,
There the long-absent pastor regain his flock and his
  sheepfold.
Beautiful is the land, with its prairies and forests of
  fruit-trees;
Under the feet a garden of flowers, and the bluest of
  heavens   860
Bending above, and resting its dome on the walls of
  the forest.
They who dwell there have named it the Eden of
  Louisiana."

  With these words of cheer they arose and continued
    their journey.
Softly the evening came. The sun from the western
  horizon
Like a magician extended his golden wand o'er the
  landscape;   865
Twinkling vapors arose; and sky and water and forest
Seemed all on fire at the touch, and melted and min-
  gled together.

Hanging between two skies, a cloud with edges of
    silver,

Floated the boat, with its dripping oars, on the mo-
    tionless water.

Filled was Evangeline's heart with inexpressible sweet-
    ness.   870

Touched by the magic spell, the sacred fountains of
    feeling

Glowed with the light of love, as the skies and waters
    around her.

Then from a neighboring thicket the mocking-bird,
    wildest of singers,

Swinging aloft on a willow spray that hung o'er the
    water,

Shook from his little throat such floods of delirious
    music,   875

That the whole air and the woods and the waves
    seemed silent to listen.

Plaintive at first were the tones and sad; then soaring
    to madness

Seemed they to follow or guide the revel of frenzied
    Bacchantes.

Single notes were then heard, in sorrowful, low lam-
    entation;

Till, having gathered them all, he flung them abroad
    in derision,   880

As when, after a storm, a gust of wind through the
    tree-tops

Shakes down the rattling rain in a crystal shower on
    the branches.

878. The Bacchantes were worshippers of the god Bacchus,
who in Greek mythology presided over the vine and its fruits.
They gave themselves up to all manner of excess, and their
songs and dances were to wild, intoxicating measures.

With such a prelude as this, and hearts that throbbed
    with emotion,
Slowly they entered the Têche, where it flows through
    the green Opelousas,
And, through the amber air, above the crest of the
    woodland, 885
Saw the column of smoke that arose from a neighbor-
    ing dwelling ; —
Sounds of a horn they heard, and the distant lowing
    of cattle.

III.

Near to the bank of the river, o'ershadowed by oaks
    from whose branches
Garlands of Spanish moss. and of mystic mistletoe
    flaunted,
Such as the Druids cut down with golden hatchets at
    Yule-tide, 890
Stood, secluded and still, the house of the herdsman.
    A garden
Girded it round about with a belt of luxuriant blos-
    soms,
Filling the air with fragrance.   The house itself was
    of timbers
Hewn from the cypress-tree, and carefully fitted to-
    gether.
Large and low was the roof ; and on slender columns
    supported, 895
Rose-wreathed, vine-encircled, a broad and spacious
    veranda,
Haunt of the humming-bird and the bee, extended
    around it.
At each end of the house, amid the flowers of the
    garden,

Stationed the dove-cots were, as love's perpetual sym-
   bol,
Scenes of endless wooing, and endless contentions of
   rivals.   900
Silence reigned o'er the place. The line of shadow
   and sunshine
Ran near the tops of the trees; but the house itself
   was in shadow,
And from its chimney-top, ascending and slowly ex-
   panding
Into the evening air, a thin blue column of smoke
   rose.
In the rear of the house, from the garden gate, ran a
   pathway   905
Through the great groves of oak to the skirts of the
   limitless prairie,
Into whose sea of flowers the sun was slowly descend-
   ing.
Full in his track of light, like ships with shadowy
   canvas
Hanging loose from their spars in a motionless calm
   in the tropics,
Stood a cluster of trees, with tangled cordage of
   grapevines.   910

   Just where the woodlands met the flowery surf of
      the prairie,
Mounted upon his horse, with Spanish saddle and
   stirrups,
Sat a herdsman, arrayed in gaiters and doublet of
   deerskin.
Broad and brown was the face that from under the
   Spanish sombrero
Gazed on the peaceful scene, with the lordly look of
   its master.   915

Round about him were numberless herds of kine that
    were grazing
Quietly in the meadows, and breathing the vapory
    freshness
That uprose from the river, and spread itself over the
    landscape.
Slowly lifting the horn that hung at his side, and ex-
    panding
Fully his broad, deep chest, he blew a blast, that re-
    sounded   920
Wildly and sweet and far, through the still damp air
    of the evening.
Suddenly out of the grass the long white horns of the
    cattle
Rose like flakes of foam on the adverse currents of
    ocean.
Silent a moment they gazed, then bellowing rushed
    o'er the prairie,
And the whole mass became a cloud, a shade in the
    distance.   925
Then, as the herdsman turned to the house, through
    the gate of the garden
Saw he the forms of the priest and the maiden ad-
    vancing to meet him.
Suddenly down from his horse he sprang in amaze-
    ment, and forward
Pushed with extended arms and exclamations of won-
    der;
When they beheld his face, they recognized Basil the
    blacksmith.   930
Hearty his welcome was, as he led his guests to the
    garden.
There in an arbor of roses with endless question and
    answer

Gave they vent to their hearts, and renewed their
    friendly embraces,
Laughing and weeping by turns, or sitting silent and
    thoughtful.
Thoughtful, for Gabriel came not; and now dark
    doubts and misgivings   935
Stole o'er the maiden's heart; and Basil, somewhat
    embarrassed,
Broke the silence and said, "If you came by the
    Atchafalaya,
How have you nowhere encountered my Gabriel's
    boat on the bayous?"
Over Evangeline's face at the words of Basil a shade
    passed.
Tears came into her eyes, and she said, with a trem-
    ulous accent,   940
"Gone? is Gabriel gone?" and, concealing her face
    on his shoulder,
All her o'erburdened heart gave way, and she wept
    and lamented.
Then the good Basil said, — and his voice grew blithe
    as he said it, —
"Be of good cheer, my child; it is only to-day he
    departed.
Foolish boy! he has left me alone with my herds and
    my horses.   945
Moody and restless grown, and tried and troubled, his
    spirit
Could no longer endure the calm of this quiet exis-
    tence.
Thinking ever of thee, uncertain and sorrowful ever,
Ever silent, or speaking only of thee and his troubles,
He at length had become so tedious to men and to
    maidens,   950

Tedious even to me, that at length I bethought me, and sent him

Unto the town of Adayes to trade for mules with the Spaniards.

Thence he will follow the Indian trails to the Ozark Mountains,

Hunting for furs in the forests, on rivers trapping the beaver.

Therefore be of good cheer; we will follow the fugitive lover;   955

He is not far on his way, and the Fates and the streams are against him.

Up and away to-morrow, and through the red dew of the morning,

We will follow him fast, and bring him back to his prison."

Then glad voices were heard, and up from the banks of the river,

Borne aloft on his comrades' arms, came Michael the fiddler.   960

Long under Basil's roof had he lived, like a god on Olympus,

Having no other care than dispensing music to mortals.

Far renowned was he for his silver locks and his fiddle.

"Long live Michael," they cried, "our brave Acadian minstrel!"

As they bore him aloft in triumphal procession; and straightway   965

Father Felician advanced with Evangeline, greeting the old man

Kindly and oft, and recalling the past, while Basil, enraptured,

Hailed with hilarious joy his old companions and gos-
    sips,
Laughing loud and long, and embracing mothers and
    daughters.
Much they marvelled to see the wealth of the ci-devant
    blacksmith,   970
All his domains and his herds, and his patriarchal
    demeanor;
Much they marvelled to hear his tales of the soil and
    the climate,
And of the prairies, whose numberless herds were his
    who would take them;
Each one thought in his heart, that he, too, would go
    and do likewise.
Thus they ascended the steps, and, crossing the breezy
    veranda,   975
Entered the hall of the house, where already the sup-
    per of Basil
Waited his late return; and they rested and feasted
    together.

Over the joyous feast the sudden darkness de-
    scended.
All was silent without, and, illuming the landscape
    with silver,
Fair rose the dewy moon and the myriad stars; but
    within doors,   980
Brighter than these, shone the faces of friends in the
    glimmering lamplight.
Then from his station aloft, at the head of the table,
    the herdsman
Poured forth his heart and his wine together in endless
    profusion.
Lighting his pipe, that was filled with sweet Natchi-
    toches tobacco,

Thus he spake to his guests, who listened, and smiled
    as they listened : —   985
" Welcome once more, my friends, who long have been
    friendless and homeless,
Welcome once more to a home, that is better per-
    chance than the old one !
Here no hungry winter congeals our blood like the
    rivers ;
Here no stony ground provokes the wrath of the
    farmer ;
Smoothly the ploughshare runs through the soil, as a
    keel through the water.   990
All the year round the orange-groves are in blossom ;
    and grass grows
More in a single night than a whole Canadian summer.
Here, too, numberless herds run wild and unclaimed
    in the prairies ;
Here, too, lands may be had for the asking, and
    forests of timber
With a few blows of the axe are hewn and framed
    into houses.   995
After your houses are built, and your fields are yellow
    with harvests,
No King George of England shall drive you away from
    your homesteads,
Burning your dwellings and barns, and stealing your
    farms and your cattle."
Speaking these words, he blew a wrathful cloud from
    his nostrils,
While his huge, brown hand came thundering down
    on the table,   1000
So that the guests all started ; and Father Felician,
    astounded,
Suddenly paused, with a pinch of snuff half-way to
    his nostrils.

But the brave Basil resumed, and his words were
    milder and gayer : —
"Only beware of the fever, my friends, beware of the
    fever!
For it is not like that of our cold Acadian climate, 1005
Cured by wearing a spider hung round one's neck in a
    nutshell!"
Then there were voices heard at the door, and foot-
    steps approaching
Sounded upon the stairs and the floor of the breezy
    veranda.
It was the neighboring Creoles and small Acadian
    planters,
Who had been summoned all to the house of Basil the
    herdsman.   1010
Merry the meeting was of ancient comrades and
    neighbors :
Friend clasped friend in his arms; and they who
    before were as strangers,
Meeting in exile, became straightway as friends to each
    other,
Drawn by the gentle bond of a common country
    together.
But in the neighboring hall a strain of music, pro-
    ceeding   1015
From the accordant strings of Michael's melodious
    fiddle,
Broke up all further speech. Away, like children
    delighted,
All things forgotten beside, they gave themselves to
    the maddening
Whirl of the dizzy dance, as it swept and swayed to
    the music,
Dreamlike, with beaming eyes and the rush of flutter-
    ing garments.   1020

Meanwhile, apart, at the head of the hall, the priest
  and the herdsman

Sat, conversing together of past and present and
  future;

While Evangeline stood like one entranced, for within
  her

Olden memories rose, and loud in the midst of the
  music

Heard she the sound of the sea, and an irrepres-
  sible sadness   1025

Came o'er her heart, and unseen she stole forth into
  the garden.

Beautiful was the night. Behind the black wall of
  the forest,

Tipping its summit with silver, arose the moon. On
  the river

Fell here and there through the branches a tremulous
  gleam of the moonlight,

Like the sweet thoughts of love on a darkened and
  devious spirit.   1030

Nearer and round about her, the manifold flowers
  of the garden

Poured out their souls in odors, that were their prayers
  and confessions

Unto the night, as it went its way, like a silent
  Carthusian.

1033. The Carthusians are a monastic order founded in the
twelfth century, perhaps the most severe in its rules of all reli-
gious societies. Almost perpetual silence is one of the vows; the
monks can talk together but once a week; the labor required of
them is unremitting and the discipline exceedingly rigid. The
first monastery was established at Chartreux near Grenoble in
France, and the Latinized form of the name has given us the
word Carthusian.

Fuller of fragrance than they, and as heavy with
    shadows and night-dews,
Hung the heart of the maiden. The calm and the
    magical moonlight   1035
Seemed to inundate her soul with indefinable long-
    ings,
As, through the garden gate, and beneath the shade
    of the oak-trees,
Passed she along the path to the edge of the measure-
    less prairie.
Silent it lay, with a silvery haze upon it, and fire-flies
Gleaming and floating away in mingled and infinite
    numbers.   1040
Over her head the stars, the thoughts of God in the
    heavens,
Shone on the eyes of man, who had ceased to marvel
    and worship,
Save when a blazing comet was seen on the walls of
    that temple,
As if a hand had appeared and written upon them,
    " Upharsin."
And the soul of the maiden, between the stars and
    the fire-flies,   1045
Wandered alone, and she cried, " O Gabriel! O my
    beloved!
Art thou so near unto me, and yet I cannot behold
    thee?
Art thou so near unto me, and yet thy voice does not
    reach me?
Ah! how often thy feet have trod this path to the
    prairie!
Ah! how often thine eyes have looked on the wood-
    lands around me!   1050
Ah! how often beneath this oak, returning from labor,

Thou hast lain down to rest, and to dream of me in
thy slumbers!
When shall these eyes behold, these arms be folded
about thee?"
Loud and sudden and near the note of a whippoor-
will sounded
Like a flute in the woods; and anon, through the
neighboring thickets, 1055
Farther and farther away it floated and dropped into
silence.
"Patience!" whispered the oaks from oracular cav-
erns of darkness;
And, from the moonlit meadow, a sigh responded,
"To-morrow!"

Bright rose the sun next day; and all the flowers
of the garden
Bathed his shining feet with their tears, and anointed
his tresses 1060
With the delicious balm that they bore in their vases
of crystal.
"Farewell!" said the priest, as he stood at the
shadowy threshold;
"See that you bring us the Prodigal Son from his
fasting and famine,
And, too, the Foolish Virgin, who slept when the
bridegroom was coming."
"Farewell!" answered the maiden, and, smiling, with
Basil descended 1065
Down to the river's brink, where the boatmen already
were waiting.
Thus beginning their journey with morning, and sun-
shine, and gladness,
Swiftly they followed the flight of him who was speed-
ing before them,

Blown by the blast of fate like a dead leaf over the
    desert.

Not that day, nor the next, nor yet the day that suc-
    ceeded,   1070

Found they trace of his course, in lake or forest or
    river,

Nor, after many days, had they found him ; but vague
    and uncertain

Rumors alone were their guides through a wild and
    desolate country ;

Till, at the little inn of the Spanish town of Adayes,

Weary and worn, they alighted, and learned from the
    garrulous landlord   1075

That on the day before, with horses and guides and
    companions,

Gabriel left the village,. and took the road of the
    prairies.

IV.

Far in the West there lies a desert land, where the
    mountains

Lift, through perpetual snows, their lofty and lumi-
    nous summits.

Down from their jagged, deep ravines, where the
    gorge, like a gateway,   1080

Opens a passage rude to the wheels of the emigrant's
    wagon,

Westward the Oregon flows and the Walleway and
    Owyhee.

Eastward, with devious course, among the Wind-river
    Mountains,

Through the Sweet-water Valley precipitate leaps the
    Nebraska ;

And to the south, from Fontaine-qui-bout and the
    Spanish sierras,   1085

Fretted with sands and rocks, and swept by the wind
    of the desert,
Numberless torrents, with ceaseless sound, descend to
    the ocean,
Like the great chords of a harp, in loud and solemn
    vibrations.
Spreading between these streams are the wondrous,
    beautiful prairies,
Billowy bays of grass ever rolling in shadow and sun-
    shine,   1090
Bright with luxuriant clusters of roses and purple
    amorphas.
Over them wandered the buffalo herds, and the elk
    and the roebuck;
Over them wandered the wolves, and herds of rider-
    less horses;
Fires that blast and blight, and winds that are weary
    with travel;
Over them wander the scattered tribes of Ishmael's
    children,   1095
Staining the desert with blood; and above their terri-
    ble war-trails
Circles and sails aloft, on pinions majestic, the vul-
    ture,
Like the implacable soul of a chieftain slaughtered
    in battle,
By invisible stairs ascending and scaling the heav-
    ens.
Here and there rise smokes from the camps of these
    savage marauders;   1100
Here and there rise groves from the margins of swift-
    running rivers;
And the grim, taciturn bear, the anchorite monk of
    the desert,

Climbs down their dark ravines to dig for roots by
the brook-side,
And over all is the sky, the clear and crystalline
heaven,
Like the protecting hand of God inverted above
them.   1105

Into this wonderful land, at the base of the Ozark
Mountains,
Gabriel far had entered, with hunters and trappers
behind him.
Day after day, with their Indian guides, the maiden
and Basil
Followed his flying steps, and thought each day to
o'ertake him.
Sometimes they saw, or thought they saw, the smoke
of his camp-fire   1110
Rise in the morning air from the distant plain; but
at nightfall,
When they had reached the place, they found only
embers and ashes.
And, though their hearts were sad at times and their
bodies were weary,
Hope still guided them on, as the magic Fata Morgana
Showed them her lakes of light, that retreated and
vanished before them.   1115

1114. The Italian name for a meteoric phenomenon nearly
allied to a mirage, witnessed in the Straits of Messina, and less
frequently elsewhere, and consisting in the appearance in the
air over the sea of the objects which are upon the neighboring
coasts. In the southwest of our own country, the mirage is very
common, of lakes which stretch before the tired traveller, and
the deception is so great that parties have sometimes beckoned
to other travellers, who seemed to be wading knee-deep, to come
over to them where dry land was.

Once, as they sat by their evening fire, there silently
    entered
Into the little camp an Indian woman, whose features
Wore deep traces of sorrow, and patience as great as
    her sorrow.
She was a Shawnee woman returning home to her
    people,
From the far-off hunting-grounds of the cruel Ca-
    manches,   1120
Where her Canadian husband, a coureur-des-bois,
    had been murdered.
Touched were their hearts at her story, and warmest
    and friendliest welcome
Gave they, with words of cheer, and she sat and
    feasted among them
On the buffalo-meat and the venison cooked on the
    embers.
But when their meal was done, and Basil and all his
    companions,   1125
Worn with the long day's march and the chase of the
    deer and the bison,
Stretched themselves on the ground, and slept where
    the quivering fire-light
Flashed on their swarthy cheeks, and their forms
    wrapped up in their blankets,
Then at the door of Evangeline's tent she sat and re-
    peated
Slowly, with soft, low voice, and the charm of her In-
    dian accent,   1130
All the tale of her love, with its pleasures, and pains,
    and reverses.
Much Evangeline wept at the tale, and to know that
    another
Hapless heart like her own had loved and had been
    disappointed.

Moved to the depths of her soul by pity and woman's
    compassion,
Yet in her sorrow pleased that one who had suffered
    was near her,   1135
She in turn related her love and all its disasters.
Mute with wonder the Shawnee sat, and when she had
    ended
Still was mute; but at length, as if a mysterious hor-
    ror
Passed through her brain, she spake, and repeated the
    tale of the Mowis;
Mowis, the bridegroom of snow, who won and wedded
    a maiden,   1140
But, when the morning came, arose and passed from
    the wigwam,
Fading and melting away and dissolving into the sun-
    shine,
Till she beheld him no more, though she followed far
    into the forest.
Then, in those sweet, low tones, that seemed like a
    weird incantation,
Told she the tale of the fair Lilinau, who was wooed
    by a phantom,   1145
That, through the pines o'er her father's lodge, in the
    hush of the twilight,
Breathed like the evening wind, and whispered love to
    the maiden,
Till she followed his green and waving plume through
    the forest,
And nevermore returned, nor was seen again by her
    people.

1145. The story of Lilinau and other Indian legends will be
found in H. R. Schoolcraft's *Algic Researches.*

Silent with wonder and strange surprise, Evangeline
   listened   1150
To the soft flow of her magical words, till the region
   around her
Seemed like enchanted ground, and her swarthy guest
   the enchantress.
Slowly over the tops of the Ozark Mountains the
   moon rose,
Lighting the little tent, and with a mysterious splen-
   dor
Touching the sombre leaves, and embracing and filling
   the woodland.   1155
With a delicious sound the brook rushed by, and the
   branches
Swayed and sighed overhead in scarcely audible whis-
   pers.
Filled with the thoughts of love was Evangeline's
   heart, but a secret,
Subtile sense crept in of pain and indefinite terror,
As the cold, poisonous snake creeps into the nest of
   the swallow.   1160
It was no earthly fear. A breath from the region of
   spirits
Seemed to float in the air of night; and she felt for a
   moment
That, like the Indian maid, she, too, was pursuing a
   phantom.
With this thought she slept, and the fear and the
   phantom had vanished.

   Early upon the morrow the march was resumed, and
   the Shawnee   1165
Said, as they journeyed along, — "On the western
   slope of these mountains

Dwells in his little village the Black Robe chief of
    the Mission.

Much he teaches the people, and tells them of Mary
    and Jesus ;

Loud laugh their hearts with joy, and weep with pain,
    as they hear him."

Then, with a sudden and secret emotion, Evangeline
    answered,   1170

" Let us go to the Mission, for there good tidings
    await us ! "

Thither they turned their steeds ; and behind a spur
    of the mountains,

Just as the sun went down, they heard a murmur of
    voices,

And in a meadow green and broad, by the bank of a
    river,

Saw the tents of the Christians, the tents of the Jesuit
    Mission.   1175

Under a towering oak, that stood in the midst of the
    village,

Knelt the Black Robe chief with his children. A
    crucifix fastened

High on the trunk of the tree, and overshadowed by
    grapevines,

Looked with its agonized face on the multitude kneel-
    ing beneath it.

This was their rural chapel. Aloft, through the intri-
    cate arches   1180

Of its aerial roof, arose the chant of their vespers,

Mingling its notes with the soft susurrus and sighs of
    the branches.

Silent, with heads uncovered, the travellers, nearer
    approaching,

Knelt on the swarded floor, and joined in the evening
    devotions.

But when the service was done, and the benediction
    had fallen   1185
Forth from the hands of the priest, like seed from the
    hands of the sower,
Slowly the reverend man advanced to the strangers,
    and bade them
Welcome; and when they replied, he smiled with be-
    nignant expression,
Hearing the homelike sounds of his mother-tongue in
    the forest,
And, with words of kindness, conducted them into his
    wigwam.   1190
There upon mats and skins they reposed, and on cakes
    of the maize-ear
Feasted, and slaked their thirst from the water-gourd
    of the teacher.
Soon was their story told; and the priest with solem-
    nity answered : —
" Not six suns have risen and set since Gabriel, seated
On this mat by my side, where now the maiden re-
    poses,   1195
Told me this same sad tale ; then arose and continued
    his journey ! "
Soft was the voice of the priest, and he spake with an
    accent of kindness ;
But on Evangeline's heart fell his words as in winter
    the snow-flakes
Fall into some lone nest from which the birds have
    departed.
" Far to the north he has gone," continued the priest ;
    " but in autumn,   1200
When the chase is done, will return again to the Mis-
    sion."
Then Evangeline said, and her voice was meek and
    submissive,

"Let me remain with thee, for my soul is sad and af-
flicted."
So seemed it wise and well unto all; and betimes on
the morrow,
Mounting his Mexican steed, with his Indian guides
and companions,   1205
Homeward Basil returned, and Evangeline stayed at
the Mission.

Slowly, slowly, slowly the days succeeded each
other, —
Days and weeks and months; and the fields of maize
that were springing
Green from the ground when a stranger she came,
now waving about her,
Lifted their slender shafts, with leaves interlacing,
and forming   1210
Cloisters for mendicant crows and granaries pillaged
by squirrels.
Then in the golden weather the maize was husked,
and the maidens
Blushed at each blood-red ear, for that betokened a
lover,
But at the crooked laughed, and called it a thief in
the corn-field.
Even the blood-red ear to Evangeline brought not her
lover.   1215
"Patience!" the priest would say; "have faith, and
thy prayer will be answered!
Look at this vigorous plant that lifts its head from
the meadow,
See how its leaves are turned to the north, as true as
the magnet;

It is the compass-flower, that the finger of God has
    planted
Here in the houseless wild, to direct the traveller's
    journey   1220
Over the sea-like, pathless, limitless waste of the
    desert.
Such in the soul of man is faith. The blossoms of
    passion,
Gay and luxuriant flowers, are brighter and fuller of
    fragrance,
But they beguile us, and lead us astray, and their
    odor is deadly.
Only this humble plant can guide us here, and here-
    after   1225
Crown us with asphodel flowers, that are wet with the
    dews of nepenthe."

So came the autumn, and passed, and the winter —
    yet Gabriel came not ;
Blossomed the opening spring, and the notes of the
    robin and bluebird
Sounded sweet upon wold and in wood, yet Gabriel
    came not.
But on the breath of the summer winds a rumor was
    wafted   1230

1219. *Silphium laciniatum* or compass-plant is found on the
prairies of Michigan and Wisconsin and to the south and west,
and is said to present the edges of the lower leaves due north
and south.

1226. In early Greek poetry the asphodel meadows were
haunted by the shades of heroes. See Homer's *Odyssey,* xxiv.
13, where Pope translates : —
           " In ever flowering meads of Asphodel."
The asphodel is of the lily family, and is known also by the
name king's spear.

Sweeter than song of bird, or hue or odor of blos-
som.

Far to the north and east, it said, in the Michigan
forests,

Gabriel had his lodge by the banks of the Saginaw
River.

And, with returning guides, that sought the lakes of
St. Lawrence,

Saying a sad farewell, Evangeline went from the Mis-
sion.   1235

When over weary ways, by long and perilous
marches,

She had attained at length the depths of the Michigan
forests,

Found she the hunter's lodge deserted and fallen to
ruin!

Thus did the long sad years glide on, and in sea-
sons and places

Divers and distant far was seen the wandering
maiden; —   1240

Now in the Tents of Grace of the meek Moravian
Missions,

Now in the noisy camps and the battle-fields of the
army,

Now in secluded hamlets, in towns and populous
cities.

Like a phantom she came, and passed away unremem-
bered.

Fair was she and young, when in hope began the long
journey;   1245

Faded was she and old, when in disappointment it
ended.

1241. A rendering of the Moravian Gnadenhütten.

Each succeeding year stole something away from her
    beauty,
Leaving behind it, broader and deeper, the gloom and
    the shadow.
Then there appeared and spread faint streaks of gray
    o'er her forehead,
Dawn of another life, that broke o'er her earthly hor-
    izon,   1250
As in the eastern sky the first faint streaks of the
    morning.

v.

In that delightful land which is washed by the Dela-
    ware's waters,
Guarding in sylvan shades the name of Penn the
    apostle,
Stands on the banks of its beautiful stream the city
    he founded.
There all the air is balm, and the peach is the emblem
    of beauty,   1255
And the streets still reëcho the names of the trees of
    the forest,
As if they fain would appease the Dryads whose
    haunts they molested.
There from the troubled sea had Evangeline landed,
    an exile,
Finding among the children of Penn a home and a
    country.
There old René Leblanc had died; and when he
    departed,   1260
Saw at his side only one of all his hundred descend-
    ants.

1256. The streets of Philadelphia, as is well known, are many
of them, especially those running east and west, named for trees,
as Chestnut, Walnut, Locust, Spruce, Pine, etc.

Something at least there was in the friendly streets of
    the city,
Something that spake to her heart, and made her no
    longer a stranger ;
And her ear was pleased with the Thee and Thou of
    the Quakers,
For it recalled the past, the old Acadian country, 1265
Where all men were equal, and all were brothers and
    sisters.
So, when the fruitless search, the disappointed en-
    deavor,
Ended, to recommence no more upon earth, uncom-
    plaining,
Thither, as leaves to the light, were turned her
    thoughts and her footsteps.
As from a mountain's top the rainy mists of the morn-
    ing 1270
Roll away, and afar we behold the landscape below us,
Sun-illumined, with shining rivers and cities and ham-
    lets,
So fell the mists from her mind, and she saw the
    world far below her,
Dark no longer, but all illumined with love; and the
    pathway
Which she had climbed so far, lying smooth and fair
    in the distance. 1275
Gabriel was not forgotten. Within her heart was his
    image,
Clothed in the beauty of love and youth, as last she
    beheld him,
Only more beautiful made by his deathlike silence and
    absence.
Into her thoughts of him time entered not, for it was
    not.

Over him years had no power; he was not changed,
    but transfigured; 1280
He had become to her heart as one who is dead, and
    not absent;
Patience and abnegation of self, and devotion to others,
This was the lesson a life of trial and sorrow had
    taught her.
So was her love diffused, but, like to some odorous
    spices,
Suffered no waste nor loss, though filling the air with
    aroma. 1285
Other hope had she none, nor wish in life, but to
Meekly follow, with reverent steps, the sacred feet of
    her Saviour.
Thus many years she lived as a Sister of Mercy; fre-
    quenting
Lonely and wretched roofs in the crowded lanes of
    the city,
Where distress and want concealed themselves from
    the sunlight, 1290
Where disease and sorrow in garrets languished neg-
    lected.
Night after night when the world was asleep, as the
    watchman repeated
Loud, through the dusty streets, that all was well in
    the city,
High at some lonely window he saw the light of her
    taper.
Day after day, in the gray of the dawn, as slow
    through the suburbs 1295
Plodded the German farmer, with flowers and fruits
    for the market,
Met he that meek, pale face, returning home from its
    watchings.

Then it came to pass that a pestilence fell on the
city,
Presaged by wondrous signs, and mostly by flocks of
wild pigeons,
Darkening the sun in their flight, with naught in their
craws but an acorn.   1300
And, as the tides of the sea arise in the month of Sep-
tember,
Flooding some silver stream, till it spreads to a lake
in the meadow,
So death flooded life, and, o'erflowing its natural mar-
gin,   .
Spread to a brackish lake the silver stream of ex-
istence.
Wealth had no power to bribe, nor beauty to charm,
the oppressor ;   1305
But all perished alike beneath the scourge of his
anger ; —
Only, alas ! the poor, who had neither friends nor at-
tendants,
Crept away to die in the almshouse, home of the
homeless.
Then in the suburbs it stood, in the midst of meadows
and woodlands ; —

1298.   The year 1793 was long remembered as the year when
yellow fever was a terrible pestilence in Philadelphia.   Charles
Brockden Brown made his novel of *Arthur Mervyn* turn largely
upon the incidents of the plague, which drove Brown away from
home for a time.
1308. Philadelphians have identified the old Friends' alms-
house on Walnut Street, now no longer standing, as that in which
Evangeline ministered to Gabriel, and so real was the story that
some even ventured to point out the graves of the two lovers.
See Westcott's *The Historic Mansions of Philadelphia*, pp. 101,
102.

Now the city surrounds it; but still, with its gateway
and wicket   1310
Meek, in the midst of splendor, its humble walls seem
to echo
Softly the words of the Lord: — " The poor ye al-
ways have with you."
Thither, by night and by day, came the Sister of
Mercy. The dying
Looked up into her face, and thought, indeed, to be-
hold there
Gleams of celestial light encircle her forehead with
splendor,   .   1315
Such as the artist paints o'er the brows of saints and
apostles,
Or such as hangs by night o'er a city seen at a distance.
Unto their eyes it seemed the lamps of the city celes-
tial,
Into whose shining gates erelong their spirits would
enter.

Thus, on a Sabbath morn, through the streets, de-
serted and silent,   1320
Wending her quiet way, she entered the door of the
almshouse.
Sweet on the summer air was the odor of flowers in
the garden,
And she paused on her way to gather the fairest
among them,   .
That the dying once more might rejoice in their fra-
grance and beauty.
Then, as she mounted the stairs to the corridors,
cooled by the east-wind,   1325
Distant and soft on her ear fell the chimes from the
belfry of Christ Church,

While, intermingled with these, across the meadows
    were wafted
Sounds of psalms, that were sung by the Swedes in
    their church at Wicaco.
Soft as descending wings fell the calm of the hour on
    her spirit ;
Something within her said, " At length thy trials are
    ended ; "   1330
And, with light in her looks, she entered the cham-
    bers of sickness.
Noiselessly moved about the assiduous, careful attend-
    ants,
Moistening the feverish lip, and the aching brow, and
    in silence
Closing the sightless eyes of the dead, and concealing
    their faces,
Where on their pallets they lay, like drifts of snow
    by the roadside.   1335
Many a languid head, upraised as Evangeline entered,
Turned on its pillow of pain to gaze while she passed,
    for her presence
Fell on their hearts like a ray of the sun on the walls
    of a prison.
And, as she looked around, she saw how Death, the
    consoler,
Laying his hand upon many a heart, had healed it
    forever.   1340

1328. The Swedes' church at Wicaco is still standing, the
oldest in the city of Philadelphia, having been begun in 1698.
Wicaco is within the city, on the banks of the Delaware River.
An interesting account of the old church and its historic associa-
tions will be found in Westcott's book just mentioned, pp. 56–67.
Wilson the ornithologist lies buried in the churchyard adjoining
the church.

Many familiar forms had disappeared in the night
    time ;
Vacant their places were, or filled already by strangers.

  Suddenly, as if arrested by fear or a feeling of
    wonder,
Still she stood, with her colorless lips apart, while a
    shudder
Ran through her frame, and, forgotten, the flowerets
    dropped from her fingers,   1345
And from her eyes and cheeks the light and bloom of
    the morning.
Then there escaped from her lips a cry of such terri-
    ble anguish,
That the dying heard it, and started up from their
    pillows.
On the pallet before her was stretched the form of an
    old man.
Long, and thin, and gray were the locks that shaded
    his temples ;   1350
But, as he lay in the morning light, his face for a
    moment
Seemed to assume once more the forms of its earlier
    manhood ;
So are wont to be changed the faces of those who are
    dying.
Hot and red on his lips still burned the flush of the
    fever,
As if life, like the Hebrew, with blood had besprinkled
    its portals,   1355
That the Angel of Death might see the sign, and pass
    over.
Motionless, senseless, dying, he lay, and his spirit
    exhausted

Seemed to be sinking down through infinite depths in
    the darkness,
Darkness of slumber and death, forever sinking and
    sinking.
Then through those realms of shade, in multiplied
    reverberations,   1360
Heard he that cry of pain, and through the hush that
    succeeded
Whispered a gentle voice, in accents tender and saint-
    like,
"Gabriel! O my beloved!" and died away into si-
    lence.
Then he beheld, in a dream, once more the home of
    his childhood;
Green Acadian meadows, with sylvan rivers among
    them,   1365
Village, and mountain, and woodlands; and, walking
    under their shadow,
As in the days of her youth, Evangeline rose in his
    vision.
Tears came into his eyes; and as slowly he lifted his
    eyelids,
Vanished the vision away, but Evangeline knelt by his
    bedside.
Vainly he strove to whisper her name, for the accents
    unuttered   1370
Died on his lips, and their motion revealed what his
    tongue would have spoken.
Vainly he strove to rise; and Evangeline, kneeling
    beside him,
Kissed his dying lips, and laid his head on her bosom.
Sweet was the light of his eyes; but it suddenly sank
    into darkness,
As when a lamp is blown out by a gust of wind at a
    casement.   1375

All was ended now, the hope, and the fear, and the
sorrow;
All the aching of heart, the restless, unsatisfied
longing,
All the dull, deep pain, and constant anguish of
patience!
And, as she pressed once more the lifeless head to her
bosom,
Meekly she bowed her own, and murmured, "Father,
I thank thee!" 1380

Still stands the forest primeval; but far away from
its shadow,
Side by side, in their nameless graves, the lovers are
sleeping.
Under the humble walls of the little Catholic church-
yard,
In the heart of the city, they lie, unknown and un-
noticed.
Daily the tides of life go ebbing and flowing beside
them, 1385
Thousands of throbbing hearts, where theirs are at
rest and forever,
Thousands of aching brains, where theirs no longer
are busy,
Thousands of toiling hands, where theirs have ceased
from their labors,
Thousands of weary feet, where theirs have completed
their journey!

Still stands the forest primeval; but under the
shade of its branches 1390
Dwells another race, with other customs and language.

Only along the shore of the mournful and misty
Atlantic
Linger a few Acadian peasants, whose fathers from
exile
Wandered back to their native land to die in its
bosom.
In the fisherman's cot the wheel and the loom are still
busy;   1395
Maidens still wear their Norman caps and their kirtles
of homespun,
And by the evening fire repeat Evangeline's story,
While from its rocky caverns the deep-voiced, neigh-
boring ocean
Speaks, and in accents disconsolate answers the wail
of the forest.

www.ingramcontent.com/pod-product-compliance
Lightning Source LLC
Chambersburg PA
CBHW032027120726
47901CB00004BA/1037